China & Japan: A New
Balance of Power

China & Japan: A New Balance of Power

Critical Choices for Americans

Volume XII

Edited by

Donald C. Hellmann

Lexington Books
D.C. Heath and Company
Lexington, Massachusetts
Toronto

Library of Congress Cataloging in Publication Data

Main entry under title:
  China & Japan.

  (Critical choices for Americans; v. 12)
  "Prepared for the Commission on Critical Choices for Americans."
  Includes index.
  1. United States—Foreign relations—China—Addresses, essays, lectures.
  2. China—Foreign relations—United States—Addresses, essays, lectures.
  3. United States—Foreign relations—Japan—Addresses, essays, lectures.
  4. Japan—Foreign relations—United States—Addresses, essays, lectures.
  I. Hellmann, Donald C., 1933-   II. Commission on Critical Choices for
  Americans. III. Series.
  E183.8.C5C46   327.73'051   75-44730
  ISBN 0-669-00426-x

Published simultaneously in Canada.

Printed in the United States of America.

International Standard Book Number: **0-669-00426-x**

Library of Congress Catalog Card Number: **75-44730**

Foreword

The Commission on Critical Choices for Americans, a nationally representative, bipartisan group of forty-two prominent Americans, was brought together on a voluntary basis by Nelson A. Rockefeller. After assuming the Vice Presidency of the United States, Mr. Rockefeller, the chairman of the Commission, became an ex officio member. The Commission's assignment was to develop information and insights which would bring about a better understanding of the problems confronting America. The Commission sought to identify the critical choices that must be made if these problems are to be met.

The Commission on Critical Choices grew out of a New York State study of the Role of a Modern State in a Changing World. This was initiated by Mr. Rockefeller, who was then Governor of New York, to review the major changes taking place in federal-state relationships. It became evident, however, that the problems confronting New York State went beyond state boundaries and had national and international implications.

In bringing the Commission on Critical Choices together, Mr. Rockefeller said:

As we approach the 200th Anniversary of the founding of our Nation, it has become clear that institutions and values which have accounted for our astounding progress during the past two centuries are straining to cope with the massive problems of the current era. The increase in the tempo of change and the vastness and complexity of the wholly new situations which are evolving with accelerated change, create a widespread sense that our political and social system has serious inadequacies.

We can no longer continue to operate on the basis of reacting to crises, counting on crash programs and the expenditure of huge sums of money to solve our problems. We have got to understand and project present trends, to take command of the forces that are emerging, to extend our freedom and wellbeing as citizens and the future of other nations and peoples in the world.

Because of the complexity and interdependence of issues facing America and the world today, the Commission has organized its work into six panels, which emphasize the interrelationships of critical choices rather than treating each one in isolation.

The six panels are:

Panel I: Energy and its Relationship to Ecology, Economics and World Stability;

Panel II: Food, Health, World Population and Quality of Life;

Panel III: Raw Materials, Industrial Development, Capital Formation, Employment and World Trade;

Panel IV: International Trade and Monetary Systems, Inflation and the Relationships Among Differing Economic Systems;

Panel V: Change, National Security and Peace;

Panel VI: Quality of Life of Individuals and Communities in the U.S.A.

The Commission assigned, in these areas, more than 100 authorities to prepare expert studies in their fields of special competence. The Commission's work has been financed by The Third Century Corporation, a New York not-for-profit organization. The corporation has received contributions from individuals and foundations to advance the Commission's activities.

The Commission is determined to make available to the public these background studies and the reports of those panels which have completed their deliberations. The background studies are the work of the authors and do not necessarily represent the views of the Commission or its members.

This volume is one of the series of volumes the Commission will publish in the belief that it will contribute to the basic thought and foresight America will need in the future.

WILLIAM J. RONAN
Acting Chairman
Commission on Critical Choices
for Americans

Members of the Commission

LEO CHERNE
Executive Director, Research Institute
of America, Inc.

JOHN S. FOSTER, JR.
Vice President for Energy Research
and Development, TRW, Inc.

LUTHER H. FOSTER
President, Tuskegee Institute

NANCY HANKS
Chairman, National Endowment for the Arts

BELTON KLEBERG JOHNSON
Texas Rancher and Businessman

CLARENCE B. JONES
Former Editor and Publisher,
The New York Amsterdam News

JOSEPH LANE KIRKLAND
Secretary—Treasurer, AFL-CIO

JOHN H. KNOWLES, M.D.
President, Rockefeller Foundation

DAVID S. LANDES
Leroy B. Williams Professor of History
and Political Science, Harvard University

MARY WELLS LAWRENCE
Chairman and Chief Executive Officer,
Wells, Rich, Greene, Inc.

SOL M. LINOWITZ
Senior Partner of Coudert Brothers

EDWARD J. LOGUE
Former President and Chief Executive Officer,
New York State Urban Development Corporation

CLARE BOOTHE LUCE
  Author; former Ambassador
  and Member of Congress

PAUL WINSTON McCRACKEN
  Professor of Business Administration,
  University of Michigan

DANIEL PATRICK MOYNIHAN
  Professor of Government
  Harvard University

BESS MYERSON
  Former Commissioner of Consumer Affairs,
  City of New York

WILLIAM S. PALEY
  Chairman of the Board
  Columbia Broadcasting System

RUSSELL W. PETERSON
  Chairman, Council on Environmental
  Quality

WILSON RILES
  Superintendent of Public Instruction,
  State of California

LAURANCE S. ROCKEFELLER
  Environmentalist and Businessman

OSCAR M. RUEBHAUSEN
  Partner, Debevoise, Plimpton, Lyons
  and Gates, New York

GEORGE P. SHULTZ
  President
  Bechtel Corporation

JOSEPH C. SWIDLER
  Partner, Leva, Hawes, Symington, Martin
  & Oppenheimer
  Former Chairman, Federal Power Commission

EDWARD TELLER
   Senior Research Fellow, Hoover Institution
   on War, Revolution and Peace,
   Stanford University

ARTHUR K. WATSON*
   Former Ambassador to France

MARINA VON NEUMANN WHITMAN
   Distinguished Public Service Professor
   of Economics, University of Pittsburgh

CARROLL L. WILSON
   Professor, Alfred P. Sloan
   School of Management,
   Massachusetts Institute of Technology

GEORGE D. WOODS
   Former President, World Bank

Members of the Commission served on the panels. In addition, others assisted
the panels.

BERNARD BERELSON
Senior Fellow
President Emeritus
The Population Council

C. FRED BERGSTEN
Senior Fellow
The Brookings Institution

ORVILLE G. BRIM, JR.
President
Foundation for Child Development

LESTER BROWN
President
Worldwatch Institute

LLOYD A. FREE
President
Institute for International Social Research

*Deceased

J. GEORGE HARRAR
Former President
Rockefeller Foundation

WALTER LEVY
Economic Consultant

PETER G. PETERSON
Chairman of the Board
Lehman Brothers

ELSPETH ROSTOW
Dean, Division of General and Comparative Studies
University of Texas

WALT W. ROSTOW
Professor of Economics and History
University of Texas

SYLVESTER L. WEAVER
Communications Consultant

JOHN G. WINGER
Vice President
Energy Economics Division
Chase Manhattan Bank

Preface

In the aftermath of the Second World War, China and Japan have experienced remarkable changes and have developed into global as well as regional powers. Both currently hold special but sharply contrasting relations with the United States. The challenge is not only to understand and to communicate more effectively with China and Japan, but to identify our own interests in Asia in ways that permit successful adjustment to the emerging differing interests of both these nations in the region.

China & Japan: A New Balance of Power is one of seven geographic studies prepared for the Commission on Critical Choices for Americans, under the coordination of Nancy Maginnes Kissinger. Companion volumes cover Western Europe, the Soviet Empire, the Middle East, Southern Asia, Africa, and Latin America. In myriad ways, America's goals, interests, and prosperity over the next decade will depend significantly on its relations with, and the shape of, the world around it. This world of nations has grown closer together and more interdependent as our own country and others find it impossible today to solve domestic problems in isolation of other countries' needs and priorities.

Donald C. Hellmann has brought together a group of specialists to prepare a study which brings to the reader the most knowledgeable and up-to-date information available today on China and Japan. Their work should be essential reading for policymakers, businessmen, and all of us who share in America's future.

—W.J.R.

Acknowledgments

Of the many people who contributed to this study, special acknowledgment must be made to those who were most directly involved in its successful completion. The contributors presented drafts of their essays to a meeting at the Commission offices in New York on February 7 and 8, 1975 and this spirited and stimulating interchange substantially shaped the overall direction of these two volumes. In addition to the paper writers, the participants included a number of distinguished scholars and government specialists on Asia who provided comprehensive and provocative commentaries; Professor Lucian Pye, Department of Political Science, Massachusetts Institute of Technology; Professor Edwin O. Reischauer, Harvard University; Dean Henry Rosovsky, Harvard University; Professor Paul R. Brass, Department of Political Science, University of Washington; Professor Klaus Mehnert, Professor Emeritus of the Institute of Technology, Aachen (West Germany); Winston Lord, Chairman, Policy Planning Staff, Department of State; Dr. Michael Armacost, Policy Planning Staff, Department of State; and W.R. Smyser, National Security Council Staff. The directors of the other area studies of the Commission, William E. Griffith (Soviet Union and Eastern Europe), Helen Kitchen (Africa), David Landes (Western Europe), and Avrom Udovitch (Middle East) and Nancy Maginnes Kissinger, the general coordinator of the Project, all took part in this meeting and offered valuable assistance in many other ways over the entire course of preparation. Charity Randall and Anne Boylan of the Commission staff provided exceptional help and counsel at all stages of the project. From my perspective, the critical ingredient was the forbearance, encouragement and felicitous editorial assistance of my wife, Margery.

Contents

                     Dwight H. Perkins   159

Chapter VI   Political and Strategic Aspects of Chinese
                     Foreign Policy   *Thomas W. Robinson*   197

Chapter VII   The United States and China
                     Michel Oksenberg   269

                   Index   297

                   About the Authors   307

List of Figures

List of Tables

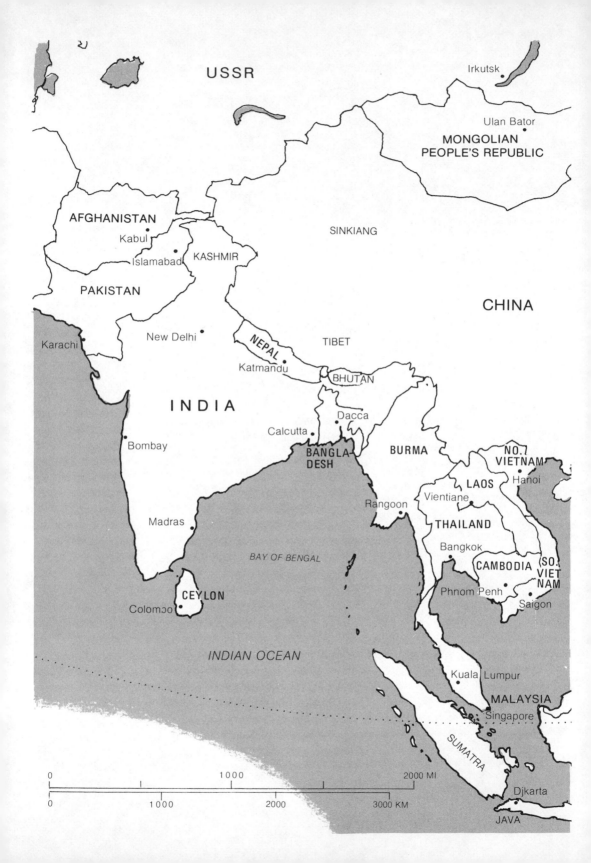

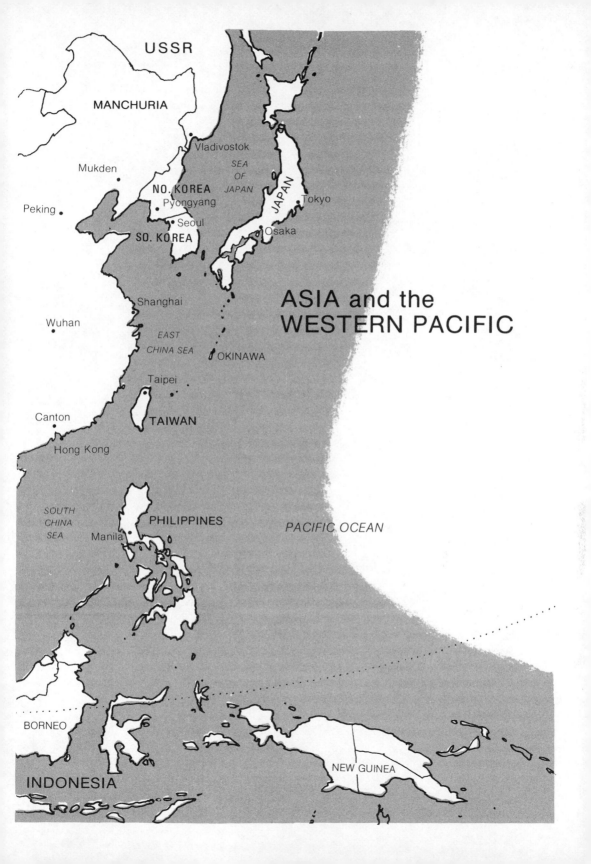

I Introduction: Toward a New Realism

Donald C. Hellmann

> The Walrus and the Carpenter
>   Were walking close at hand
> They wept like anything to see
>   Such quantities of sand
> 'If this were only cleared away'
>   They said, 'it would be grand!'
>
> If seven maids with seven mops
>   Swept it for half a year,
> Do you suppose the Walrus said,
>   'That they could get it clear?'
> 'I doubt it,' said the Carpenter
>   And shed a bitter tear

"The Walrus and the Carpenter"
Through the Looking Glass

For American foreign policy, most of Asia[a] has been a looking glass world of distorted and inverted images in which things have taken unexpected shapes and moved in unusual and unfamiliar ways. Even the successes, like Japan, somehow do not fit easily into the Western mold. It is a world that has repeatedly frustrated the most strenuous and prolonged efforts to change it (have it cleared

---

[a]In this study, Asia includes the countries of South Asia (India, Pakistan, Bangladesh and Sri Lanka), the mainland and island nations of Southeast Asia (Burma, Thailand, Vietnam, Cambodia, Laos, Malaysia, Singapore, Indonesia, and the Philippines), and Northeast Asia [China, Japan, Korea (North and South), and Taiwan].

away) and bitter tears and indifference now seem to many to be the most appropriate future prescriptions for much of the region. The past challenges to American policy have been on two levels: the moral, to the basic beliefs of our diplomatic and cultural traditions, and the political, to the successful conduct of diplomacy and strategy in keeping with our capabilities and short-term interests.

The challenges of the future will also be on both of these levels as Asia continues to be a testing ground for American diplomacy. This volume focuses on Japan and China, the dominant powers in the region and major actors in world affairs as well. The companion study, Volume XIII, *Southern Asia: The Politics of Poverty and Peace*, deals with South and Southeast Asia and the regionwide questions of defense and great power politics. Each of the individual studies provides interpretive analysis of recent and contemporary political and economic matters with an eye toward elaborating long-term U.S. policy options. These efforts at identifying true images in the looking glass would provide broad guidelines for a policy of "new realism" for Asia.

China and Japan: A New Asian Power Balance

American policy toward Asia revolves around relations with China and Japan. Both nations are global as well as regional powers, both societies have experienced fundamental and extraordinary political and economic changes in recent decades, and both currently hold special but sharply contrasting relations with the United States. Basic shifts in the political-strategic structures on the global and regional levels and in the world economic system insure that America's relations with the Chinese and the Japanese will continue to be in flux in the years ahead. In fashioning appropriate American policies, the challenge is not only to understand and communicate more effectively with these nations, but to identify our own interests in Asia in ways that permit successful adjustment to the differing and changing interests of China and Japan in the region—in short, to facilitate the creation of a new Asian power balance.

Northeast Asia: Policy Priorities and Dilemmas

From a variety of perspectives it is clear that within the region, Northeast Asia in general and China and Japan in particular are the most important areas for United States policy for at least the next decade. Because of Japan, this is overwhelmingly so in economic terms. Since 1972, East and Southeast Asia have taken a larger percentage of total American trade than the European Economic Community (EEC), and the gap is steadily widening. Of this figure, almost three-quarters goes to Northeast Asia with Japan as our largest overseas trading partner. For a variety of reasons, American investments in Europe (and other parts of the world) vastly exceed those in Northeast Asia, but the direct economic interests of the United States are truly substantial, and Japan must play a central role in any viable long-term international economic order.

The importance of this area in military-strategic terms is even clearer. China is central to virtually all of the critical choices the United States must make regarding future strategy: as a counterpoise to the Soviet Union; as a nuclear power; as a champion of the Third World; and as the dominant Asian military power. Moreover, since relations with Peking are the touchstone for Soviet policy in Asia, Peking-Washington ties have an added dimension for American policy. Japanese security concerns are centered in East Asia and integrally involve the United States and the two other powers. Not only do the interests of these four nations directly converge in Northeast Asia, but this area is the location of two of the most troublesome international problems in the region: the continued division of Korea and the status of Taiwan. Both situations, but especially Korea, have the long-term potential for armed conflict, neither is likely to be resolved in the immediate future, and both implicate all of the great powers—but especially the United States. Thus, the intensity and scope of our political-strategic interests require that America pay the kind of close, continuing attention to Northeast Asia that is accorded relations with Europe. At the same time, however, the inherent uncertainties and instability of the Asian situation and the unusual status of our alliances add a special dimension to the diplomatic tasks.

The Korean War led the United States to establish a ring of alliances in Asia to contain communism, and bilateral treaties with Japan, South Korea, and Taiwan (Republic of China) are still operative. The treaties were distinctive from their inception in terms of the total dependence of the three countries on the United States for their security. To be sure, the North Atlantic Treaty Organization (NATO) involved a similar one-sided security guarantee, but in western Europe local conventional forces were quickly incorporated into a regional defense coalition. Korea and Taiwan, parts of divided underdeveloped countries, literally owed their existence to the American military presence. Although provided with extensive military assistance, they were never incorporated into a regional force and in fact the mutual defense treaties had "restraining" clauses to inhibit them from unilateral military initiatives. The treaty with Japan, a country which faced no comparable direct security threat and which was then a demobilized, occupied society with a constitution barring the right to maintain arms, simply incorporated the nation into the regionwide cold war strategic arrangement of the United States. The Japanese-American alliance has subsequently grown into something much more significant as a result of vastly expanded political and economic ties, but Japan retains an extreme and anomalous security dependence on the United States. The defense treaty with Taiwan, which has been enormously attenuated and will be abrogated if the United States recognizes Peking, nevertheless will continue to complicate

American policy both in a strategic and "moral" sense no matter what happens in the short run. The treaty with Korea is a source of even greater perplexity because of the Hobson's choice it presents. If we were to abrogate the treaty (either in effect or formally) our credibility in Asia generally and in Tokyo in particular would be devastated. But if we continue our present commitment and troop deployment, there are risks of involvement in a land war in Asia on behalf of an ally whose disregard for democratic political rights is under increasingly severe attack in this country.[b] Thus, the prevailing alliance system further insures that the United States is ensnared in the web of international politics of Northeast Asia, in ways that complicate our diplomacy.

A further strategic dilemma for the United States has been created by the growing capacities of the two Koreas and Taiwan to operate with substantial independence from all of the great powers on a regional level. North Korea, a difficult ally for the Soviet Union since the early 1960s, has attained this relative independence through a belligerently extreme hard line on reunification and through the effective use of leverage with Peking and Moscow related to the Sino-Soviet split. Taiwan and South Korea are harbingers of a new species of nation which will make the management of conflict in Asia (and the world) much more difficult in the future. Both countries have acquired the aggregate wealth, technological capacity, and political will that will allow them to operate with substantial autonomy regarding the political-strategic issues that directly touch their well-being—including and especially on the nuclear level.

These once poor, "half countries" have prospered so well under the client relationship with the United States, that they clearly will have the capacity to raise the stakes dramatically in regional affairs in ways that will reach both the global strategic balance and the critical issue of nuclear proliferation. This new configuration of power has the effect of creating common interests for all the great powers in preventing conflict on the Korean peninsula and has driven the Chinese and the Soviets to support (implicit if not overt) a continuing American presence in Korea and Japan in order to add a restraining element to the situation. It also greatly complicates easy resolution of the Taiwan question and makes the future of Japanese defense policy peculiarly derivative from the actions of its smaller neighbors. What policies the United States may consider in these circumstances is a subject to which we will subsequently turn.

[b]There has been substantial pressure both within Congress and from prominent foreign policy specialists to measure our commitments to South Korea in terms of the way in which they fulfill democratic political ideals. This is in keeping with the moral cast of our past policies in Asia, despite the obvious fact that the prospects for "democracy" in Asia are, in aggregate, extremely low. The United States does not have to abandon its ideals nor withhold expressing displeasure over flagrantly repressive actions. However, in view of the precarious international situation, it is clear that if the boundaries between the moral bases of our policies and the demands of power politics are defined in public forums through political confrontation, the result will be heavy-handed diplomacy. Only through strong executive leadership and a consensus regarding policy goals that encompasses the impera- tives of international politics can this issue be met effectively.

China, Japan, and Visions of International Order

America's long-term policy options regarding China and Japan depend upon the fundamental nature of the global international system and how it is perceived by political leaders in Washington. As critical features of the bipolar cold war world have disappeared or been basically altered, a number of interpretive models of contemporary and future patterns of international reality have been set forth. In broadest terms, three visions have been particularly influential in American policy cirles: (1) a five-power world (the United States, the Soviet Union, China, Japan, and Western Europe) in which there continues to be a mix of traditional power politics (especially the Soviet-American strategic confrontation) and economic competition; (2) a "trilateral world" dominated by the non-Communist industrialized countries, featuring economic interdependence and a withering away of nation-centered power politics except at the periphery of the system (local conflicts in the Third World), and at the center, the United States–Soviet Union; and (3) a world afflicted with increasing scarcity of resources, pockets of overpopulation and environmental pollution necessitating a radical shift in policies away from matters of nation-state competition (security concerns) and toward an economic order oriented toward global welfare to prevent a planetary Armageddon.

Before considering Japan and China in terms of these visions, two features common to all should be noted. All stress a global perspective and emphasize (in varying degrees to be sure) the interdependence of the world. All take a "managerial" approach by assuming that the problems of international affairs are soluble under the leadership of the advanced nations, thereby down-playing the independent capacities for political-economic action by nations in the Third World.

The five-power world is a vision commonly ascribed to Secretary of State Kissinger and in several ways has been implicit in American foreign policy in the era of détente.[1] Its most distinctive features are the stress given to the persistence of strategy as a central feature of world politics and the likelihood that the Soviet Union will augment its capacities and efforts as an expansionist global power. Accordingly, the United States must create international conditions to facilitate communication with Moscow and at the same time cultivate relations with new centers of world power in order to operate effectively in an already existing political-economic multipolar world. China is seen as a radical nationalist power threatened by Moscow, but in turn a threatening and ultimately unmanageable thorn in the side of the Soviets. Japan, already a great economic power, is viewed as eventually becoming a major political-strategic actor in a fluid and pluralist world and therefore should be cultivated in accordance with a nation-centered concept of "realism." Politics, that is the political-strategic order, is seen as the foundation for world stability.

The appeal of this vision for understanding Asia lies in the continuity it presupposes, not only on matters of security policy, but also regarding the prospects for a nation-centered world in the future. With the notable exception of two of the chapters on Japan, all contributors to these volumes see the ensuing decades as an age of nationalism and nation-building in Asia. The prospects for the persistence of conflict in the region are also very high. Despite its congruity with basic international realities, there are nevertheless three shortcomings with this vision for China and Japan. First, its global orientation draws attention away from the fact that both countries are regional powers, with interests and capacities in East Asia that differ in important ways from those of the superpowers. In the years ahead, this regional dimension of foreign affairs will be critical in defining the limits of conflict and cooperation between the United States and these two countries.[c] Second, not only are Japan and China deeply enmeshed in regional affairs, but there are truly substantial discontinuities between European and Asian international relations. Any effort to incorporate Tokyo and Peking into a global American foreign policy will perforce have to display careful discrimination in taking these regional differences into account. Finally, there are doubts whether domestic conditions within China and Japan will allow them to be easily incorporated into a great power global balance.

Japan currently rejects power politics—*in principle*—in her foreign policy, and how manageable the Japanese will be in a world of *Realpolitik* depends on the circumstances that lead to their adoption of a dramatically more political and nationalist posture. To believe that China, still in the throes of the greatest revolution in modern history, will prove a "rational" actor in the global power game is to assume away the destabilizing political legacies of revolution as well as any serious domestic problems in a highly politicized, overpopulated, and underdeveloped society.

The vision of a world led by the industrialized non-Communist nations emerged in the early 1970s as a supplement to the "power-realist" approach to international affairs represented by the concept of a five-power world.[2] It was nurtured by a number of new international developments: the emergence of Europe and Japan as economic power centers rivaling the United States; the enormous growth of transnational, nongovernmental contacts, primarily through multinational corporations and especially among industrialized societies; a disenchantment with power politics induced by the Vietnam War; a general recognition that there were other problems for U.S. foreign policy beyond a strategy against the Communist world; and the common sense observation that an industrialized Japan really belonged in Europe.[d] Although the notion of a

[c]This point is drolly illustrated by calling attention to two "slogans" that have been used to indicate our interest in the region, "Asia for the Asiatics" and "a Pacific but not an Asian Power." However apt for our own position, it is mind boggling to imagine anyone in Tokyo or Peking applying them to their own policies.

[d]Indeed Secretary of State Kissinger announced with great solemnity in 1973 his hopes for "a new Atlantic Charter, plus Japan."

trilateral world grew out of concrete developments and a recognized need on the part of some elements of the elite, business, political, and intellectual circles to establish channels for international communication,[e] the idea also struck responsive chords in the American diplomatic tradition.

A rejection of power politics, and overwhelming emphasis on economic and commercial relations as the proper kind of relations among sovereign states are in keeping with the notions of progress and international affairs of eighteenth century economists and philosophers, many of whom strongly influenced the Founding Fathers. Although it is dressed in the clothes of "interdependence" and often cast in terms of specific policy criticism, the implicit premise is a belief in the promise of technology (industrialization) to solve the problems of mankind, including international political problems. Indeed, this vision of international affairs created a kind of bicentennial revival of the conflict between idealism and realism that troubled the first American statesmen. This excerpt from Washington's Farewell Address (in which "Asia" is substituted for Europe) strikingly illustrates this continuity.

The Great rule of conduct for us, in regard to foreign Nations is in extending our commercial relations to have with them as little *political* connection as possible . . .
  [Asia] has a set of primary interests, which to us have none, or a very remote relation. Hence she must be engaged in frequent controversies, the causes of which are essentially foreign to our concerns—Hence therefore it must be unwise in us to implicate ourselves, by artificial ties, in the ordinary vicissitudes of her politics, or the ordinary combinations and collisions of her friendships, or enmities.

The limitations of this vision regarding future international relations in Asia are apparent in a closer look both at Asian and global affairs and especially the international role of Japan.

While there still is a certain plausibility and attraction to this approach, it has been seriously challenged by the events. of the early 1970s, especially the effectiveness of the Organization of Petroleum Exporting Countries (OPEC), a retreat of the United States from dynamic global leadership, and the persistence of political (and ideological) conflicts in international affairs. It has become obvious that economic cooperation and interdependence can be nurtured only within the framework of a stable political-strategic order (e.g., *Pax* Americana), and in order to build such an order it is necessary to reach beyond the limits of industrialized non-Communist societies to the Third World nations. Regarding Japan, this vision is simply wrong in terms of elemental geopolitical facts and recent economic trends. It is true that Japanese foreign policy since 1945 has

---

[e]The Trilateral Commission, established in 1970, was a study group set up to promote communications among nongovernmental elites in the United States, Japan, and Western Europe, and in particular to work out common approaches to some of the more pressing international problems.

been primarily aimed at cultivating economic development and gaining political acceptance among Western industrialized societies, but geographically, culturally, racially, and historically, Japan is part of Asia. It cannot be towed to a position off the coast of France. Moreover, the directions of Japanese trade since 1970 suggest that economic ties with the advanced countries are not as strong as was inferred from the trends during the 1950s and 1960s. Since the late 1960s, Japan's trade with industrialized countries has dropped from slightly more than 50 percent of its total trade to approximately 35 percent and trade with the less developed world has risen from 35 to 48 percent—phenomena partly, but not wholly related to a rise in the price of oil. Even more striking, Tokyo now does 90 percent as much trade with South Korea, Taiwan, and Hong Kong (two small developing countries and a city colony in Asia) as with the European Economic Community—a market fifty to sixty times as large. Even from a narrow economic perspective, Japan must be seen as a regional as well as a global power and as increasingly tied to the politically volatile Third World in general and the countries of Asia in particular. These elemental incongruities between international realities and the trilateral vision make it at best of peripheral value in defining long-term policy options for the United States in Asia.

Finally, a world of extreme scarcity would have uneven and unpredictable effects on the international politics of East Asia. Japan, the most genuinely interdependent industrialized nation in terms of basic resource needs, would, given reasonable choice, accommodate to all schemes coping with scarcity— simply in order to assure national survival.[3] By the same token, a breakdown of such efforts in a world of true scarcity (a reasonably probable eventuality given the primitive state of political order in the Third World) would almost surely provoke a nationalist response from the Japanese. China, on the other hand, has (as demonstrated in recent decades) the political organization and basic resources to move in an autarchic fashion on behalf of preserving its national political integrity and, as a self-appointed leader of the Third World, can be expected to support efforts by poorer countries to create a "new economic order" even if this provokes severe disequilibrium in industrial societies. Furthermore, China remains an overpopulated poor nation *trying* to solve the problem of scarcity. Success is not assured. There are profound domestic political inhibitions to radically restructuring American policy toward the goals of global humanism to deal with world scarcity, but even if the change were made, unless these policies were to solve the problems of the human condition *in extremis*, there would be portentous international implications for China and Japan—and few real policy options open to the United States.

Japan: Close Ally with an Uncertain Future

The Japanese-American alliance remains the cornerstone of our policy in Asia and one of the most notable achievements of United States diplomacy since

1945. On the one hand, the United States maintained for more than two decades the international context, especially the *Pax* Americana in the western Pacific and the American dominated global international economic order, which underlay the "economic miracle" and political stability Japan has enjoyed. There also developed a web of bilateral ties, political and economic, formal and informal, that brought the two countries into a special and close relationship. If the future is essentially an extension of the past, there is indeed reason for optimism. Yet even a casual look beneath the surface into the basic but still inchoate changes in the international system and domestic political uncertainties in both countries raises doubts about the prospects for the future. Most importantly, the international framework in which Japan lives has been fundamentally altered since 1971 by a series of events: the American opening to China, the collapse of South Vietnam, the oil crisis, various monetary crises including the breakdown of the Bretton Woods system, and a realignment of Tokyo's relations with Asian nations. While this has eroded much of the old order, the shape of a new international order remains indefinite. There are differences among the contributors to this volume regarding both the problems that Japan faces and the appropriate solutions to them, but there is general agreement that the critical choices made in Washington will have a decisive impact upon the direction of Japanese foreign policy.

My own chapter focuses on two of the most critical issues regarding Japan in the years ahead: the impact of domestic politics on Japanese foreign and security policies. The approach is somewhat unorthodox and the conclusions lie outside much of the conventional wisdom about Japan, but, paradoxically, the implications for American policy do not deviate sharply from those of the other contributors, except in the emphasis on the salience of political, as distinct from economic, issues and considerably more skepticism regarding the long-term stability of the international and the Japanese political-economic systems.

The interpretation of the foreign-policy-making process can be easily summarized. Japanese diplomacy has succeeded primarily because the Japanese-American alliance and the scope of American commitments in East Asia have insulated the nation from the need to make major *political* decisions regarding foreign affairs, especially security matters. When the Japanese have had to confront policy choices, they have responded in a stumbling manner (e.g., 1960 revision of the U.S. Security Treaty) or procrastinated until external events compelled a decision (e.g., normalization of relations with China in 1972).

The reasons for this lie first in the structure and dynamics of domestic politics: bitter partisan divisions over foreign policy; fragmentation within the conservative party that has continuously ruled Japan since 1952; a culturally sanctioned style of decision-making that requires broad consensus and compromise; and a divided multiparty opposition that has remained permanently out of power. This has insured broker-type political leaders, an incrementalist approach to policy-making and a foreign policy noted for its passive and responsive character. Moreover, for the decade ahead the Liberal-Democratic party or a similar conservative dominated coalition is likely to continue to hold the reigns of power perpetuating this "immobilist" process of decision-making. This style of policy formulation proscribes a Gaullist posture of independence, but it also is manifestly unsuited for the fluid economic and strategic situation and the rapid changes of front required for successful operation in an indeterminate pluralist world. Furthermore, with economic growth no longer the bedrock of the policy consensus, relations between the government and business have become more strained and complex in ways that will directly affect foreign policy. In these circumstances, domestic political considerations will be projected even more deeply into the decision-making process, inhibiting the formation of "rational" choices and shaping the substance of foreign policy.

A number of lessons can be drawn from this situation for American policy. First, the limited capacities of the Japanese to formulate new policies together with continuing close bilateral ties combine to provide the United States with substantial opportunities to influence constructively Japan's policy—to practice "positive Machiavellianism." However, to practice "positive Machiavellianism" requires clear formulation of American aims in Asia, not the application of pressure to Tokyo without clear indications of our ultimate intentions—as was the case for a period in the early 1970s. More than any single group in Japan, the business community has a strong stake in preserving close ties with the United States and care should be taken to avoid eroding this support by applying pressure in response to American interest groups (e.g., the textile industry). Left simply to the changing tides of conservative factional politics or an uncertain "mass mood," the character of Japan's policy will ultimately be viscerally nationalist and progressively beyond the reach of American policy.

Japanese security policy is the most anomalous and controversial aspect of the nation's foreign affairs. Up to now it has been very simple: beyond the American alliance, there has effectively been no strategic policy regarding external threats or regional conflict and security has been defined in the narrow sense of preserving territorial integrity. This has allowed Japan "to separate politics and economics" and operate in highly successful fashion as a trading company as distinct from a nation-state. In addition, a mood of pacifism fostered by the "no-war" constitution severely inhibits any decision for an expanded security role. The argument here stresses that politics and economics are inseparable (especially in a world of scarcity); that Japan is so deeply involved economically in Asia and the world that a broadened security policy is likely unless peace breaks out; that the pressure for nuclear weapons in Tokyo will be generated by proliferation in other Asian countries; and that Japanese security can not be narrowly restricted to territorial defense but must include access to resources and markets.

Clearly it is in the interest of the United States to maintain a close but flexible bilateral security relationship with Japan. As is pointed out by Professor Scalapino,[4] our strategic credibility in Tokyo is integrally linked with our credibility in East Asia, and cannot be limited to Japan alone. Moreover, because of the fluidity of international politics in the region and our own somewhat diminished military role, American strategic credibility is now best established on an ad hoc basis and scrupulous efforts should be made to avoid pressing for policies which close options to the Japanese (e.g., seeking Japan's ratification of the Nuclear Non-Proliferation Treaty). If the Japanese ever enter a "five-power world," they should be given the widest possible latitude to determine the conditions and occasion for entry, for a rearmed and defensively nationalist Japan would have a profoundly unsettling impact on regional and global affairs.

Professor Chalmers Johnson's essay provides an exceptionally lucid *tour d'horizon* of the Japanese political economy and identifies the critical choices the Japanese must make in the decades ahead. The capacity of Japan to foster a remarkable rate of economic growth and to cope imaginatively with the multiple ills of a postindustrial society are examined and admired. Rapid growth is seen as the result of a calculated program of investment and management by government bureaucrats and business leaders—not a unique, culturally derivative phenomenon. The flexibility and effectiveness that the political-bureaucratic-business elites have displayed repeatedly in the past are seen as ultimately sufficient to meet the technical problems or barriers that Japan must surmount to continue to progress in the remarkable fashion of recent decades. Three of these problems, a polluted environment, a shrinking and more expensive work force, and the independent development of technology are essentially domestic and soluble by reestablishing domestic priorities and shifting expenditures from one sector to another. Two others, access to critical resources and to international markets for Japanese products, are international issues contingent for their solution upon the agreement of other nations and therefore involve political as well as economic considerations. The interdependence of nations will make these problems common to all states, but in order to establish a framework in which satisfactory solutions to these issues and to the additional question of defense are found, it will be necessary for the United States to take the lead internationally.

For Japan to continue to operate as a constructive, largely economic force in the world, to "go internationalist" not "go nuclear" it is essential that "the United States will have to continue to maintain the international balance of power." If the United States manages power in Asia and the world, then Japan will continue to function as a highly successful economic enterprise in a "trilateral plus OPEC" world. If not, and Professor Johnson suggests that the factors underlying the debacle in Vietnam point to severe weaknesses in the American will to play a constructive major global role, then Japan will be awash in a Hobbesian world of catastrophe and brutishness. In short, the future of Japan rests largely on the future foreign policies of the United States, and reasons are cited for cautious optimism.

The analysis and the prescriptions for American policy are convincingly presented, but two caveats are in order: one concerning the reach of American foreign policy; the other concerning the stability and effectiveness of Japanese domestic politics. As noted in my own chapter and elaborated in Professor Johnson's essay, the structure of the party system and the kind of leadership possible make uncertain the prospects for continued domestic political stability and a dynamic foreign policy. This is an increasingly serious issue, since the prospects for sustained high economic growth are diminished, while both internally and in regard to the electorate the Liberal-Democratic party is in the most serious trouble since its inception two decades ago. Whether this will eventuate in a defensively nationalist mood (which could distort and exaggerate response to the shifting international milieu or produce the kind of stalemated *immobilisme* of the Third Republic in France) is not clear. However, it cannot be simply assumed that there will be a basic continuity of politics (and therefore of policies) in Tokyo. Second, the prospects that the United States (or any power) can "balance power" in Asia in ways that allow the Japanese the same political-security aloofness that prevailed under *Pax* Americana are quite remote in a world of scarcity and polymorphous violence. Even under an alliance with the United States, Japan will find it increasingly difficult to pursue an exclusively economic diplomacy in Asia and a world in which politics and nationalism rival development as the basic forces in international affairs.

The essay of Professors Gary Saxonhouse and Hugh Patrick offers a careful and detailed review of economic relations between the United States and Japan. It does provide an inventory of critical choices for American economic policy toward Japan in the years ahead, but it does more. The history of American policy toward the Japanese economy in the 1950s and 1960s, from the special treatment provided toward a weak but important ally to the intense bilateral pressure of the early 1970s to bring Japan into line with the mature world economics, is a superbly succinct summary which sheds new light on economic factors underlying the so-called Nixon-shock of 1971. The authors see Japan growing at a 5 to 8 percent annual rate over the next ten to twenty-five years, which is smaller than that nation's previous growth rate but, more importantly, larger than the projected rate of growth for the United States. This differential may prove a source of increased tension, especially as the bilateral gap in direct economic power continues to narrow. Moreover, Japan's economy and technology are now highly developed and continued progress will place them in direct competition with the United States. Therefore, even if there is no disruptive intrusion of international politics, American-Japanese relations will be regularly tested.

How will bilateral relations be tested and what are the options open to the United States? The bulk of the essay addresses these issues with precision and detail: commercial policies (protectionism vs. interdependence); the new international financial system; foreign direct investments; resource nationalism, scarcity, and security (a global leadership role for the United States in energy policy); relations with developing countries (no commodity cartels but potential U.S.-Japan tensions); East-West trade. Although the policy options are cast in bilateral terms, the issues are placed in a global economic context. What emerges is a fairly comprehensive treatment of the major problems of the world economy seen from the perspective of Washington and Tokyo. The authors are relatively optimistic concerning the possibilities for preserving a liberal, if not American-run, system, which will be somewhat constrained by narrower conceptions of national economic self-interest—primarily due to domestic political pressures, regionalism, and cartelization (politically inspired). Japan is likely to become more important to and more interdependent (in absolute terms) with the United States, raising the danger of protectionist pressures from industries hard hit by imports. Conversely American agricultural exports are essential to Japan, and the United States can play a critical leadership role in solving energy issues in the future. The policy alternatives considered on these matters are provocative and apt.

As a specialist on politics, I would be remiss not to suggest that the arguments in the essay would have been more persuasive had the essay taken the political dimension more fully into account. It may be that economic issues have come to hold a more prominent place in international affairs generally and between the United States and Japan in particular. However, the primacy of economic concerns does not assure the imminent disappearance of politics. Indeed, it is the political use of economic resources (OPEC), the political pressures for protectionism, and the growing importance in the international economy of command (Communist) economies, that particularly sets off this era from the postwar American dominated international order. Finally, to ignore the persistence of conflict, the growth in armaments globally, and the inherent instabilities among poorer nations in an interdependent world, is to omit a major if not the basic dimension of the international system. In sum, political-strategic considerations are fundamental to all aspects of long-term relations between Japan and the United States.

China: The Continuing Enigma

China has for centuries been an object of fascination, bewilderment, and concern to the Western world. The Communist regime which came to power in 1949, following a century of political and social decay, imperialist exploitation, and protracted violence, continues to attract and bemuse statesmen, scholars, and Westerners in general. It is this aura, the universal perception that major historical forces are at work for all to see on one-fourth of humanity, and the astonishingly limited amount of elemental information available about the society, much less a sophisticated grasp or feeling for what is transpiring, that must be noted before any effort is made to set forth generalizations about the

directions of change in China. It is also worth noting that throughout the last
fifty years the Soviet Union, the United States, and Japan, the great powers
which have sought influence in China, have all made catastrophic miscalculations
and stumbled badly. Any effort to set forth trends in Chinese society over the
next 10-25 years in order to delimit the options for American policy is a task
which must be approached with modesty.

Past efforts by American specialists to understand the most basic political
features of the Communist government offer scant encouragement. During the
1950s there were virtually no dissenters from the view that China was an integral
part of a Soviet dominated monolithic Communist bloc. Following the Sino-
Soviet split, conventional (scholarly) wisdom saw Peking as a radical nationalist
regime with no serious domestic political instabilities now that the Great Leap
Forward program was ended. This judgment collapsed with the Cultural Revolution, an event that led to yet another interpretation, China beset by internal
problems was an unpredictable and potentially disruptive revolutionary force in
international affairs. Within four years, China was in the United Nations, had
been effectively accepted within the international political community, and had
welcomed the president of the United States to Peking. This ushered in the
development era, that is, a period in which the overwhelming majority of China
specialists saw the Chinese as concerned primarily with internal economic
growth and having a nonexpansionist foreign policy essentially directed against
the threat from the Soviet Union. Within three weeks after the death of Chou
En-lai, the pragmatists were under attack and, to the astonishment of almost all
observers, the new premier was a man (Hua Kuo-feng) about whom only the
scantiest information was available. In retrospect, what passed for scholarly
wisdom was more like a filmstrip chronicle of the passing scene which took on
the form of an intellectual *opera buffa*. The problem was partly a lack of
evidence, but more basically the failure lay in not asking the appropriate (i.e.,
critical) questions about Chinese society.

To delineate the dimensions of China's foreign policy in the last quarter of
the twentieth century, Professor Dwight Perkins avoids direct conjecture about
the goals or intentions of Chinese leaders ten or twenty-five years from now and,
instead, concentrates on the future state of the economy. Predictions regarding
the economy fall within a limited and largely known range of possibilities and
the level of economic performance does provide the material limits to future
foreign policy options. After a fine summary review of China's economic
programs and performance, several unsolved economic problems are discussed,
the most important of which is agriculture. Despite apparently successful efforts
to raise the productivity of the agricultural sector in the 1960s, farm output was
only brought back even with the population. But the population is still growing
and raising the grain output is proving an increasingly difficult task. Because of
the already high use of fertilizers and the limited relief that can be expected
from imports (partly because of the enormous aggregate needs of China), the

only way to meet the grain requirements is to raise productivity through a major technological breakthrough or the lowering of the birthrate of a population in which the natural trend is expected to rise. Moreover, China's industrial sector is not growing fast enough to absorb the population growth, so that the size of the rural population will still be rising by the year 2000 (more than fifty years after the revolution) creating an enormous problem of "education" to satisfy those sent down to a farm career. These circumstances raise substantial pressure on the government to accelerate growth in both the agricultural and industrial sectors— or face increasingly serious economic and political problems.

This raises a basic dilemma with major implications for foreign policy, because the leaders of China are divided over the question of whether development should be the primary goal of the government or whether equalitarian political and social goals should receive priority. These divisions are likely to persist and if there continues to be recurrent political turmoil the economic problems will worsen. To this I would add that the intense politization of the Chinese masses (in comparison, say, with India) raises the potential for truly disruptive repercussions if a breakdown rooted in overpopulation should occur.

If China grows at 5 to 7 percent per year over the next twenty-five years, it is still unlikely to be a major force in international trade, but will make significant progress in building a military force. China will be constrained for at least a decade or so by budgetary limitations, but the capacity to become a global strategic power and to establish the capacity to defend its territory alone is clearly within reach.

Professor Perkins reviews the patterns of economic growth (extraordinarily high with some exceptions) and political development (nationalism ascendent) of Asian nations on China's periphery, and Peking's capacity to influence them in the future. His conclusion, that China's capacities for either political or economic (or even military) influence are low, is provocative and controversial. A similar conclusion is reached regarding America's influence on the smaller states of Asia and, because of this, the United States is urged to work with China to decrease the competitive involvement of all major powers in this region. This plea for the suspension of international political rivalries in Asia (paralleling the recommendations of Alexander Woodside in the companion volume on Southern Asia[5]) gives short shrift to two basic realities of international affairs: (1) the linkages between the international politics of the region with global rivalries encompassing in particular the Soviet Union and (2) the ideological and power factors of international affairs—especially in a region engulfed in nationalism and an extended record of conflict.

China will remain a major participant in regional and global international politics, and a major challenge for American foreign policy is how to cope with the Chinese enigma in establishing our strategic priorities. A sophisticated and comprehensive assault on this problem is provided in Thomas Robinson's essay.

The critical variables are identified and analyzed in depth and then the analytical scheme is applied in two case studies of China's nuclear strategy (1965-1985) and of Peking's policy toward the Third World, and in a review of bilateral Sino-American relations since 1972. There is throughout the essay a careful elaboration of the linkages between domestic politics and the international system and between the regional and global affairs. The web of analysis is complex and not easily summarized, so it is appropriate here to move directly to the critical choices that are posed for American policy, comparing these views with the recommendations made in the final essay by Michel Oksenberg.

Both authors share a belief that American policy can be a decisive factor in shaping the future policy of Peking, but for differing reasons. Robinson views Sino-American relations as embedded in a number of independent processes (e.g., the international political system, Chinese politics, the developmental process within China, the global strategic system) and sees our influence as dependent on an orchestration of policy on as many levels as possible—which underscores the difficulties in identifying easily clear-cut long-term policy options. Nevertheless, he sees as highly probable the eventual emergence of a bureaucratic-pragmatic leadership in China, which would move toward limited détente with the Soviet Union while aggressively building up the accoutrements of economic and political power to compete with the Soviet Union and the United States both within Asia and globally.

The options for American policy are rather grim. On the one hand, the persistence of a radical-leftist regime in Peking will prolong the Sino-Soviet split and abet the development of a multipolar world, but presumptively it would also undermine the economic development of the country, with portentous long-term implications for internal political stability—and for foreign policy. On the other hand, if the United States works to encourage a pragmatic regime, this will lead eventually to a "limited détente" with the Soviet Union and at the very least maximize the global strategic capabilities of Moscow. Under these circumstances, the range of critical choices open to the United States necessarily involves continued high levels of military preparedness and cultivation of allies in Asia in the broad pattern of the cold war. The broad synthetic argument of this essay gives emphasis to the need for sophistication, modesty, and flexibility in American policy toward China during the next decades.

Professor Oksenberg casts his analysis more in bilateral terms and in the immediate future sees the United States and China as having a number of common interests (e.g., containment of the Soviet Union, the stabilization of the Korean peninsula). He urges that the United States move quickly to recognize Peking diplomatically and then to broaden substantially bilateral contacts to bring China more fully into world affairs. While acknowledging that there can not be truly close bilateral ties over the long run, because of the nature of the Chinese revolution and the culturally sanctioned Chinese concept of the purpose of the state, he believes that it is in our interest to keep China stable and independent from the Soviet Union—and that our policies can promote this development in important ways. This seems a benign and optimistic approach to China and to the critical choices the United States must make regarding Peking. The short-term prescriptions for improving relations with the People's Republic, handling the Taiwan question (leave its international legal status ambiguous and continue to sell arms),[6] and dealing with Japan and Korea are even-handed and represent the "pragmatic liberal" position. Whatever the merits of early recognition of Peking, over the longer run, a more skeptical view seems in order regarding the American capacity to influence the basic direction of China's foreign policy. The Chinese revolution is still unfolding and China remains in an unstable and volatile international setting.[f] This is not to retreat to a determinist position. The United States has only limited capacities to affect China's future, but by placing our short-term decisions in the context of the long-term problems, more realistic and effective policies than we have had in the past are within reach. The enigma of China may remain, but it surely can be made more intelligible.

Notes

1. For a summary and critique of this vision see Stanley Hoffmann, "Weighing the Balance of Power," *Foreign Affairs* 50, 4 (July 1972): 618-643.

2. For a general summary of the trilateral view see Zbigniew Brzezinski, "U.S. Foreign Policy: The Search for Focus," *Foreign Affairs* 51, 4 (July 1973): 708-727.

3. See for example Saburo Okita, "Natural Resource Dependency and Japanese Foreign Policy," *Foreign Affairs*, 52, 4 (July 1974): 714-724.

4. See Robert A. Scalapino, "Alternatives for the International Order in Asia," in Donald C. Hellmann, (ed.), *Southern Asia: The Politics of Poverty and Peace* (Lexington, Mass.: Lexington Books, D.C. Heath and Company, 1976).

5. Alexander Woodside, "Progress, Stability, and Peace in Mainland Southeast Asia," in Donald C. Hellmann (ed.), *Southern Asia: The Politics of Poverty and Peace* (Lexington, Mass.: Lexington Books, D.C. Heath and Company, 1976).

6. Compare this view of the Taiwan question with that expressed by Robert Scalapino, "Alternatives for the International Order in Asia."

fOver the past twenty-five years, Peking has been involved in wars either directly or indirectly with almost all countries on her periphery.

II Japan and America: New Myths, Old Realities

Donald C. Hellman

The Japanese alliance has been the outstanding achievement of American policy in Asia since 1945, and it will remain the cornerstone for future peace and stability in the region. To maintain the alliance even in a substantially modified form, however, will prove a demanding diplomatic task. Partly, this is because of America's altered and more limited role in international affairs in a pluralist world of scarcity. More importantly, however, it is due to the impact of the changed and changing international setting within which Japan must live and to basic alterations in the fabric of Japanese domestic politics. The success of Japanese foreign policy (and *pari passu* the alliance with the United States) has been built upon an extraordinary equilibrium of domestic political forces and the peculiar features of the *Pax* Americana and *Oeconomia* Americana that underlay the international order until the early 1970s. Japan was the beneficiary of a unique convergence of political forces, which have now begun to disperse.

What is most striking about Japanese foreign policy, is the degree to which it has avoided direct involvement in international politics beyond the American alliance. In a world twice convulsed by global wars and almost continuous conflict, the nonmilitary posture of Tokyo seems to many a model to be emulated by other industrial societies. For others, most notably Herman Kahn, the capacities of "Japan, Inc." to organize its own economy and to compete internationally with historically unprecedented results establish the nation as a model for success in the postindustrial age.

To be sure, the Japanese have demonstrated remarkable capabilities for excelling when insulated from the tensions and uncertainties of international

19

politics, and their domestic politics was stabilized by one-party rule. However, the critical questions regarding the future center on: (1) the prospects for creating an international order which continues to leave the world's third largest economic power effectively free from the major concerns of power politics; (2) the capacities for Japan to formulate policies appropriate to a nation-state rather than a trading company, in the event that this kind of millenial condition is not extended, and (3) the impact of political changes within the country on Japan's foreign policy, especially its security policy. Since the end of the hothouse conditions of *Pax* Americana in which Japan flourished for more than two decades, Tokyo has managed to cope with day-to-day diplomatic issues with some success. Nevertheless, it has also become clear just how dependent Japan is on stable international economic and political conditions, and how passive and reactive her diplomacy, perforce, will be. Whether Japan is a model for the more indeterminate and competitive world of the last quarter of this century ultimately depends upon the domestic and international political problems facing the country.

Japanese Domestic Politics and Foreign Policy

The remarkable success of Japan in gaining international wealth and status has led to the almost unanimous conclusion that Japanese foreign policies have been shrewdly calculated responses to the realities of world politics. Accordingly, virtually all commentaries by Japanese and American international relations specialists, especially strategic specialists, assume that Japan's decisionmakers have and will select the "appropriate" policy in terms of external realities and a given set of values.[1] Moreover, it continues to be an implicit premise of American policy, which presumes that various political and economic pressures will provoke an appropriate calculated response. However, it is especially important when considering long-term patterns of behavior to recognize that situational factors, both domestic and international, severely limit the options open to decisionmakers. Thus, a barefooted analysis of the policy debate (e.g., reasons pro and con on armament) stands as an incomplete and misleading guide to the basic influences shaping *any* nation's role in the world. This is particularly true in Japan, where the international conditions of the recent past severely limited the range of options open to policymakers and the institutions of decision-making produced reactive not active policies regarding major *political* issues in foreign affairs. The incapacity for bold leadership, the extremely politicized nature of the policy-making process, and the lack of partisan consensus assure that Japanese policies will be strongly shaped by the tangled web of domestic political forces in the foreseeable future.

The Party System

Basic to all other questions about decision-making in Japan are the prospects for electoral defeat for the pro-American Liberal-Democratic party (LDP) and the import of continuing parliamentary and extra-parliamentary confrontation by the essentially anti-American opposition parties. The electoral showings of the ruling conservatives have steadily weakened in recent years. While they are likely to retain power in the immediate future, it is quite possible that they will lose an absolute majority within the next decade. As problems relating to pollution, inflation, and inequities growing out of rapid economic growth have created genuine "bread and butter" issues, the four opposition parties have captured close to 50 percent of the popular vote and various left-wing coalitions have scored notable victories in local elections. In fact, Socialist or Communist mayors rule in every major urban center in the country. In the early 1970s this had a cumulative demoralizing impact on the conservatives, which reached the all-time low with the forced resignation of Prime Minister Kakuei Tanaka in late 1974. Tanaka was forced from office in a scandal over his personal financial dealings, widespread public and party criticism over the failure to halt inflation, and bitter intraparty objections to his heavy-handed tactics in the narrow conservative victory in the summer upper-house election. For the first time since the mid-1950s, the personal and political divisions among the Liberal-Democrats pushed the party close to a formal split. This was avoided only through a tentative compromise which made the prime minister (Takeo Miki) a man who at one point openly considered splitting from the Liberal-Democratic party and forming a coalition government. Needless to say, any fragmentation of the ruling party and the establishment of a coalition regime would have a profound and unsettling effect on future foreign policy.

Despite sporadic and dramatic challenges to their rule on specific issues (especially the alliance with the United States), the Liberal-Democrats were not, until very recently, seriously challenged for control of the government. There were five basic factors for the party's prolonged success: (1) the highly successful policies of economic growth which steadily raised the standard of living; (2) a broad consensus on the goal of growth among the public as well as the political, business, and bureaucratic elites; (3) an overwhelming advantage in access to money, talented candidates, and political organization; (4) a divided, highly ideological, and politically inept opposition; and (5) a national culture stressing deference to authority and group loyalties, which moderated the societal tensions—and the reformist political by-products—involved in the massive socioeconomic changes of the period.

All of these factors have weakened substantially during the last decade. Government policies shifted away from an unqualified emphasis on growth as a result of popular political pressure protesting pollution, a consumer movement, and finally a more general disenchantment with the government over inflation. In turn, the consensus within the elite, especially between the business world and the government, began to break down. A new political party, the *Kōmeitō*, appeared in the mid-sixties, drawing almost wholly from the uprooted on the fringes of the new mass, urban society. It is a political affiliate of the *Sōka Gakkai*, a large, aggressive Buddhist sect that has grown up since World War II, and the party has consistently polled 8 to 10 percent of the national vote. The four opposition parties (the others are the small non-Marxist Democratic-Socialists, the militant and Marxist Social Democrats, and the now pragmatic and growing Japanese Communist party) are sharply divided among themselves, but have greatly enhanced their overall impact through successful cooperation on local candidates, thereby breaking the near monopoly of the conservatives on political power and talent.

In these various ways, the foundations of the longest period of single-party dominance in any democratic society since 1945 have been seriously eroded. It is far from certain that the Liberal-Democrats will retain control of the government as in the past. Even if the conservatives cling to power, their capacities to act on foreign policy will be inhibited even more than in the past, first by a greatly intensified struggle within the party and with the other parties to build and lead a viable coalition, and second, by the absence of consensus on basic policy goals.

Although the recent rise in political strength of the opposition parties has been rooted in the exploitation of local issues, since 1950 the main source of conflict between them and the conservatives has been over foreign policy. Since Prime Minister Shigeru Yoshida negotiated the Peace Treaty of 1952, and the accompanying security agreement with the United States, the conservatives have steadfastly maintained a pro-American and anti-Communist posture. The Communists, the various socialist parties, and the *Kōmeitō* have consistently, and often militantly, opposed the government and voiced support for various forms of anti-American, pro-Asian neutralism. Unrelieved partisan conflict on all major international issues has deepened political divisions, precluded a constructive policy dialogue, and, by creating an atmosphere of confrontation, has inhibited policy initiatives by the government. Consequently, despite a considerably more benign attitude by the opposition parties toward the Japanese-American alliance since the collapse of South Vietnam, the prospects are extremely remote for a pragmatic, nonpartisan policy consensus overcoming the inertia of decision-making in a multiparty context.

Even if the opposition parties do not share power, they will continue to have considerable influence on foreign affairs. By virtue of their sizable popular support, the highly sympathetic mass media, and their direct access to foreign policy-making in the Diet, they occupy a strategic position from which to articulate and press their views. In the past, their influence has been used primarily for negative ends—to obstruct governmental action and turn the inevitably ambiguous results of all foreign policies to their own domestic political advantage through dramatic criticism of the government. Their effectiveness in these endeavors has been strengthened by the traditional Japanese notion of decision-making by consensus not majority vote, in which there must be at least a formal display of unanimity on all major decisions. In practice this makes dissent per se an effective means of opposition, because continuing open disagreement over any issue raises doubts about the legitimacy of the policy. This belief in consensus—that the government in power has a special obligation to respect and seek accommodation with the views of those out of power—has led the Socialists in particular to adopt rigid policy positions and gives special import to the huge gap between the conservatives and the opposition over the goals of international action. Not only has this gap obviated supra-partisan cooperation, it has forced the Liberal-Democrats (despite their majority in the Diet) to consider scrupulously the Socialist position on major issues or risk a serious political crisis that might, as in the 1960 Security Treaty incident, raise serious doubts about the stability of the entire political system.

The opposition affects Japan's international actions in another way. By stressing foreign policy matters to an extreme degree, a similar emphasis results in Diet debate, in electoral campaigns, and in the mass media. Tactics of extralegal direct action, disruptive public demonstrations (*demos*), and physical obstruction of Diet proceedings are often employed, and they receive extensive coverage in the media. Such incessant and open criticism exacerbates conflict over all international issues and correspondingly magnifies the importance of domestic political considerations in foreign policy decisions. It also assures that a vehemently anti-American position is continuously and conspicuously before the Japanese public. This capacity to shape both the intensity and the substance of the political debate will remain an important means of foreign policy influence for the opposition no matter what the party configuration may be in the future.

For the next decade or so, no viable and truly effective rival to the LDP will be fashioned out of the four opposition parties, even if their combined popular vote should exceed 50 percent and the number of Diet seats they hold should rise significantly. The long-standing rivalries in and among these parties, rooted in personal conflicts as well as profound differences in policy and ideology, make extraparliamentary collaboration all but impossible on anything but selected local candidates or specific major issues. Cooperation in parliamentary (rather than electoral) endeavors is much more likely (especially if the help of an "anti-mainstream" conservative group were to be forthcoming), and this would add another element of instability to the government decision-making process. Nevertheless, any challenge of this sort would ultimately force a reconstitution of the LDP coalition and this, in turn, would leave most of the opposition in its current divided minority status.

Opposition efforts to capitalize on the troubles of the LDP will be limited by the capacities of the conservative Liberal-Democrats to respond effectively to the substance of domestic and international problems and the demonstrated ability of the LDP to outmaneuver its opponents politically. The government has already indicated its intention to shift domestic priorities from economic growth to social welfare, and despite the enormity of these problems and the inevitable friction that such basic changes will entail, there is a good likelihood that these issues can be handled with only modest political costs.

International issues (for example, relations with China and the United States, and rearmament) are less tractable, but the LDP has left open all options and will be able to marshal national (and nationalist) sentiments behind whatever policies are adopted. Short of a major economic or political cataclysm (for example, a global trade war or a total breakdown of American security credibility), the Liberal-Democrats stand in as good a position as any group to cope with the visible ills confronting the nation.

Virtually insurmountable division among and within the opposition parties is another basic impediment to significant political gains. The Socialists are badly faction-ridden and as likely to split as the LDP conservative coalition. Although the Communists have steadily strengthened their electoral showing, it has been largely at the expense of the Socialists. Comprehensive cooperation between the Communists and the *Kōmeitō* is all but unthinkable, since their bitter confrontation of several years' standing. Cooperation between the Socialists and the Democratic Socialists is barred not only by deep political differences but by divisions in the Japanese labor movement that have definite political coloration.

To envision success in dealing with problems of common candidates, party organization, and platforms in the face of these underlying problems is an exercise in fantasy. A clear-cut party realignment directly affecting Japanese foreign policy is remote, but through the opposition's parliamentary and extraparliamentary tactics, the LDP's decision-making process will be made all the more difficult.

Conservative Decision-Making

In the immediate future the Liberal-Democratic party (LDP) or a similar, conservative-dominated coalition will hold the reins of power, perpetuating the essentials of the current pattern of policy formulation which is centered in the intraparty decision-making process of the LDP. All other components of the political system—the opposition, pressure groups, public opinion, and the bureacracy—reach the major foreign-policy decisions primarily through access to this process. Formally, the prime minister (the president of the majority party in the lower house of the Diet) is vested with the responsibility for policy leadership. In practice, however, his powers have been limited, primarily by the fragmented composition of the party and the close relationship between the formulation of policy on critical international issues and intraparty politics. Thus the masterkeys to conservative foreign policy-making are the structure and dynamics of conservative politics.

Despite repeated efforts to create a unified party, the LDP remains a coalition of factions (*habatsu*). The factions, built around a single personality, are in a basic sense autonomous parties, having their own independent sources of finance, running their own candidates under the Liberal-Democratic party label, and regularly caucusing for discussion of political strategy and, occasionally, of policy matters. There are many causes for the existence of factions—traditional social mores, the electoral system, the financing of political careers—but they have taken on a quasi-institutional form since the late 1950s and are likely to persist short of a major upheaval in the *modus operandi* of the political system. Leadership within the party is recruited from those members of the Diet who can best operate in the complex and constricting world of the *habatsu*. In such circumstances it is inappropriate to see the personalities of future Japanese prime ministers as shaping in any new and basic way the fundamental direction of Japanese diplomacy. There is no real possibility of an individual-centered, personalized style of leadership emerging in the LDP (or a conservative-dominated coalition) as a substitute for the faction-dominated, collectivist decision-making that now prevails—barring a major political and economic breakdown of catastrophic proportions.

In addition to assuring the recruitment of broker-type leaders, the commingling of factional politics with foreign policy-making imposes serious restraints on the prime minister's capacity for leadership. As head of a coalition, he must seek at least the agreement of the other faction leaders concerning not only the merits of policy but the current balance of power within the party. Beyond the usual constraints any coalition leader must face, the Japanese case is further complicated by a style of traditional authority that requires at least tacit consensus among all the responsible parties involved in policy-making, in this case the party faction leaders. Limits are placed on the kinds of policies that are undertaken. Initiative tends to be confined to issues with minimum risk and controversy, and having relatively calculable costs—which excludes all important international political matters. Moreover, by confounding domestic and international considerations, the policy debate gives undue emphasis to the specific and short-term effects of each decision. Only in the special "incubator" conditions in which Japan was able to operate through the early 1970s can salutary results be produced by this style of policy formulation. Japanese foreign policy has been successful in the past because it was restricted to issues free from the imperatives of long-term strategic planning and decisive action required of a nation fully engaged in international politics.

A review of all the major foreign policy decisions taken by Japan since the end of the occupation (the peace agreement with the Soviet Union, renewal of the Japanese-American security treaty in 1960, normalization of relations with

Korea and, more recently, with China), illustrate the inhibitions that this process of decision-making has imposed on positive leadership in foreign policy. The decision to recognize Peking in 1972, provides a superb illustration.

To a degree exceeded only by relations with the United States, the China problem has been central to the foreign policy debate within Japan, and extraordinary emotional and symbolic importance surround this matter for all politically articulate groups. While formally adhering to the American position, during the 1960s the Japanese developed a de facto "two Chinas" policy involving more extensive regular contact with Peking than any other country, and the government repeatedly asserted its special role in bringing China into international relations. Yet the Japanese remained on the sidelines until China was admitted into the United Nations, almost all other major powers had recognized Peking, and the president of the United States had made a formal visit to the country. Moreover, the subsequent decision to recognize Peking was deeply colored by intraparty factional considerations. Kakuei Tanaka, a neutral on the China issue, was chosen prime minister in mid-1972 by putting together a factional coalition including three pro-Peking rivals (Takeo Miki, Masayoshi Ohira, and Yasuhiro Nakasone), all of whom made normalization one of the critical conditions for their support. There is little to suggest that the dynamics of decision-making will break out of its immobilist cast. Rather, Japan will continue to remain a passive and reactive actor on the international scene.

Despite the vision of intimate business-government collaboration conjured up in the image of "Japan, Inc.," the role of business in decision-making regarding foreign affairs is ambiguous and varies widely from issue to issue. Business leaders are closely tied to the conservative party through their overt and covert financial support, through a sharing of basic political values, and through continuous and intimate personal contacts. Ties between business and the Ministry of International Trade and Industry (MITI) and the other government agencies that exercise careful control over the day-to-day conduct of Japan's international economic activities are similarly close—inevitably so given the overwhelmingly economic character of postwar foreign policy. Despite these connections, and despite the establishment by the national business organizations of committees to deal with specific foreign affairs issues and continuing questions such as rearmament, there is no clear mutual understanding regarding the procedures through which business opinion should be brought into the policy-making process. Nor is there automatic agreement on the goals of the nation's foreign policy. The complexity and diversity of the Japanese business world is mirrored in the viewpoints of the various individuals and groups who speak out on international affairs. Consequently, as political and security considerations become involved with policies previously geared toward maximizing economic benefits, it is as probable that the businessmen will become further divided among themselves as it is that they will simply rally round the flag.

The impact of organized business and individual businessmen on major

Japanese foreign policy decisions has varied. Regarding diplomatic normalization with the Soviet Union in 1956 and the extension of the Mutual Security Treaty in 1960 (both issues involving essentially political questions), business was not able to reach the policy process in a decisive way. It played a somewhat more important part in the normalization of relations with South Korea and with China, but not regarding the critical political decisions involved. As the links between politics and economics grow (as a direct result of Japan's commercial stake in East Asia and the world) and Japan moves toward full participation in power politics, the relationship between the business world and the Liberal-Democratic party will take on added importance *and* at the same time be placed under increasing strains—especially regarding security policy.

The structure and dynamics of Japanese foreign policy-making will not change much in the future, but the inadequacies of this process for providing suitable responses to the new international milieu will become increasingly evident. The groups comprising the policy-making elite for the last two decades (the LDP conservative-coalition politicians, the bureaucrats, and the business-men) will continue to interact through the same diffuse and essentially immobilist process of compromise and consensus that has characterized all past major *political* decisions regarding foreign affairs.[a] This pattern of decision-making, which virtually prohibits bold leadership, is manifestly unsuited for the current fluid economic and strategic international situation and for the frequent and rapid changes of front required for successful operation in an indeterminate multipolar world. Purely reactive policies can hardly be expected to serve as well in the future as they did in the immediate past when Japan was on the periphery of a far more predictable international system. Moreover, the efforts required to cope with recurrent external crisis will "feed back" into domestic politics, aggravating relations among members of the conservative elite and inevitably affecting the increasingly precarious electoral dominance of the Liberal-Democratic party. Thus, the links between internal politics and external events will have reciprocally negative influences, both on domestic political stability and on the development of a positive international role for Japan.

Postwar Japanese foreign policy has succeeded primarily because the Japanese-American alliance and the scope of American commitments in East Asia have insulated the nation from the need to make major foreign policy decisions (especially regarding security). When the Japanese have had to confront policy choices, they have responded in a stumbling manner. There is little promise that this pattern of policy formulation will be adequate to cope with the fundamental decisions Japan will inevitably face as a great power in an uncertain

[a]This largely negative appraisal of Japan's capacity to function as a political actor on the international scene is quite compatible with the highly positive appraisal of the Japanese abilities to operate in the world economy discussed in both other essays on Japan in this volume. The significant differences center on: (1) a more skeptical judgment of the long-term flexibility and stability of the business-party-bureaucracy coalition and (2) considerably more skepticism about the stability of the international political-economic system.

multipolar global system or in an East Asia with a dramatically reduced American military presence. Japan is unlikely to be a skilled diplomatist, and even less likely to be an effective practitioner of *Realpolitik*.

Two trends in domestic politics will have particular importance for Japan's performance in foreign policy during the next decade: (1) a fluidity within the LDP and in parliamentary relations among the parties, but also extending to the government-business relations, which will make the formulation and effectuation of new policies more difficult; and (2) a mood of uncertainty pervading the entire political scene that is best categorized as defensively nationalist and which could distort and exaggerate response to the shifting international milieu. These changes make it certain that domestic political considerations will be projected even more deeply into the decision-making process, inhibiting the formulation of "rational" choices and ensuring that the style of policy-making will affect the substance of foreign policy to a degree matched in few other nations. If confusion and frustration mount in the fact of ineffective leadership, the response will be policies cast more and more in terms of narrow national interests. The critical point in the political process will be the attitudes of the political elite, and the mood generated by its actions will eventually touch the entire society. Indeed, participation in a competitive and uncertain international order (especially in East Asia) cannot but continue to add fuel to the already glowing embers of Japanese nationalism.

Postwar Goals and the Domestic Political Debate

The broad themes of Japanese foreign policy since independence are modest in character and limited in number. Regarding the global system, they have centered on cultivating the alliance with the United States to provide for Japan's security and to fuel national economic development, achieving a respected status in the world international order, and developing economic relations with all nations while gaining acceptance within the club of advanced industrial powers. Additionally, unique emphasis has been placed on relations with the countries of East Asia. Although these themes are most obviously manifested in the pronouncements of political leaders, the details of the picture are filled in by the aims implicit in the actions that have been taken. In the same style employed by the conservative factions in intraparty politics, the nation has moved expediently in foreign affairs, without ideological or even policy commitments beyond vague slogans praising peace and propitiating the status quo, while allowing maximum room for maneuver on specific issues. A straightforward acceptance of the articulated goals of the government provides only a partial representation of the direction of Japanese foreign policy. This can be properly grasped only through a broad examination of the actual pattern of Japan's international behavior and how it is perceived through the prism of domestic politics.

"Status" and "peace" have been the keystones to this policy. Reflecting the peculiar importance which is accorded to status within Japanese culture and paralleling the successful diplomatic campaign during the Meiji period, which brought initial acceptance in the Western international system, a self-conscious effort has been conducted since the end of the Occupation, in order, as former Prime Minister Sato put it, "to occupy an honored place in international society." Negatively, it has involved an attempt to eradicate the stigma connected with the outbreak and conduct of the Great East Asian War. Positively, it has taken on concrete meaning through participation in various international organizations, especially the United Nations and the Organization for Economic Cooperation and Development (OECD), in sponsoring international extravaganzas such as the 1964 Olympics and "Expo '70," and in cautious efforts at aid and cooperation legitimatized in terms of international brotherhood and humanitarian ideals.

Japan, a "great power" throughout the first half of the twentieth century, has taken as her postwar reference group the industrialized Western nations. International respectability has been successfully pursued by achieving economic well-being while gaining full and unqualified political acceptance among the global elite. Policies toward the poor and newly independent nations have been accorded lower priority. Despite the moral tone of Japan's diplomacy, no real effort has been made to identify with the Third World or the causes that these countries have championed. Modest gestures in extending aid have been clothed in the accepted shibboleths of "development," but in reality they have served primarily to cultivate markets and resources directly beneficial to Japan and not to promote the broader international goals commonly associated with the North-South problem. In a manner befitting to a rising member of the Victorian middle class, Japan has prudently sought status within her economic means and with minimal political costs and commitments.

Above all, Japan in this quest has specifically eschewed military competition and chosen the banner of peace. Indeed, throughout the history of modern international politics no nation of comparable size and importance has effectively implemented an overtly pacifist position for such an extended period. This in itself constitutes a formidable barrier to any abrupt change of course toward an autonomous military role. In the immediate future, a *volte face* from the pacifist tune that has been trumpeted for more than two decades, would involve political risks prohibitively high for any government. Similarly, the timing and scope of any move toward a more independent security posture would necessarily be tempered by the web of political and economic interdependence with the global international community and the world economy. This is not to imply, however, that the future will simply be an extension of the past, devoid of change. There are strong incentives for Japan to participate fully in international politics, especially in the Asian region.

Japan is geographically, culturally, racially, and historically part of Asia. This truism needs restatement because short shrift is given to the special importance of Asia to Japan in many discussions of the contemporary scene which emphasize the "modernizing" effects of prosperity and the strong ties which have concomitantly grown between Tokyo and the distant but advanced nations in Europe and North America. The burden of history alone tilts Japan's international perspective sharply in the direction of the neighboring region. From the war with China in 1894-95 until defeat in 1945, Japan was continuously engaged in far-reaching military, political, and economic activities in Northeast Asia. Her position as a great power and her relations with the other great powers were defined in terms of her policies and capacities in this area. That is, Japan's status in the global system was a function of her position in the region, not the reverse. Since Japan emerged as a modern nation state, the country's diplomatic ideals have been most fully defined in terms of relations with the region, especially in the vague and romatic concept of Pan-Asianism. In view of the muted and inchoate aims pursued since 1945, this Asian-oriented nationalism constitutes the only fully developed international mission in modern Japanese history.

Both the reality and vision of this diplomacy were shattered by defeat and the elaborate effort during the American Occupation to discredit completely the ideals on which it was based. It is common to view 1945 as a watershed in Japanese history, one marking political, social, and psychological discontinuities in the society. In some ways, this is true and certainly the radical changes that touched all aspects of the political socialization process make it necessary to distinguish between prewar and postwar generations. However, it is easy to exaggerate the break with the past, especially for the elite that has made foreign policy since 1952. These men were all nurtured in the highly developed nationalist tradition of the earlier era, which neither the agony of defeat nor the new circumstances of the post-1945 scene totally eradicated. Furthermore, because age is strongly correlated with leadership, during the next decade or two the government will continue to be controlled by the prewar generation. In the critical years immediately ahead when the problem of a new, more independent international strategy in Asia will be confronted, the destiny of the nation will be guided by men who straddle two contrasting diplomatic traditions.

With the end of the postwar era there has been a general recognition within Japan of the need for a new "independent" foreign policy, but there is no consensus on what the content of the policy should be. Part of the confusion grows out of uncertainty regarding the future shape of the international order, but the *Alice in Wonderland* quality of the internal policy debate will continue to impede the easy formulation of a new strategic posture. Foreign policy discussions among the conservatives have transpired mainly in private and in response to external (international) pressures, and have been colored by intraparty factional considerations.

Since 1950, the opposition left and the media have been deeply absorbed in international affairs, but they have either rigidly clung to abstract moral positions (e.g., anti-Americanism and an undifferentiated moral commitment to peace) or used specific issues to further their own political purposes. One consequence has been to give a curiously involuted focus to the foreign policy debate. The Japanese have moved from one concrete issue to another absorbed in short-term international goals and internal political tactics, avoiding to an extreme degree matters of *Realpolitik* beyond the American alliance. Consequently, the foreign policy debate within Japan and actual developments in international politics have progressed on largely parallel planes. Creating a realistic debate regarding the strategic alternatives confronting Japan, far less creating consensus on a new set of policy goals, will profoundly test the stability of the domestic political system. Indeed, what Japan will confront in the next few years is not just the choice of more appropriate new policies, but a challenge to the quasi-isolationist and pacifist assumptions underlying the policies of the last two decades—an ironic mirror image of the kind of challenge that the United States now faces.

American Policy and Japanese Politics

The new uncertainties about the direction of Japanese politics require that the United States modify the means employed to influence Japanese foreign policy in constructive ways. Past efforts have aimed broadly at "the people" on the one hand and focused narrowly on those holding power on the other. The fluidity of the contemporary (and future) Japanese scene requires that American policy show much more discriminating regard for the shifting political currents among the elite groups which permanently stand on the fringes of power.

There is considerable latitude for the United States to shape the fundamental direction of Japanese policy in the short run. The close ties of the past, the broad, basic compatibility of Japanese and American interests, the uncertainty of the Japanese regarding new policy goals, and their limited capacities for formulating new policies combine to provide the United States with substantial opportunities to exercise "positive Machiavellianism." However, the successful implementation of "positive Machiavellianism" requires clear formulation of American strategic aims in Asia and communication of these aims to all of the appropriate groups in Japanese politics. In an indeterminate international situation, a policy of applying pressure to Tokyo without clear indications of our ultimate intention—the approach taken in the early 1970s—may yield short-term diplomatic benefits but will be disastrous in its final effect on the foundations of Japan's foreign policy. Two factors, the incapacities of the Japanese for making major decisions and the deep internal division over the question of defense, virtually insure that any effort to force Japan to become a great power in an uncertain multipolar world will exacerbate political instability within the country and reduce our capacity for influence.

In view of the massive and comprehensive bilateral economic ties, the
Japanese business community has a greater stake in preserving close relations
with the United States and participating positively in restructuring global
international stability than any other group in the society. The business world is
the bedrock of internationalism in Japan and if the nation's foreign policy is left
simply to the changing tides of conservative factional politics or an uncertain
"mass mood," its character will ultimately be viscerally nationalist and progressively beyond the reach of American policy. To erode the pro-U.S. orientation
of Japanese business by applying strong pressure on Tokyo in response to
appeals from American domestic interest groups (as was done, for example in
the late 1960s and early 1970s as a result of political leverage in Washington of
the textile industry) is particularly inappropriate. This is especially true at a time
when the foundation of the alliance and the basic security posture of Japan are
open questions. For the United States as well as Japan, the inseparability of
politics and economics must be recognized as an essential feature of successful
diplomacy.

Security and Foreign Policy: New Myths, Old Realities[b]

Security has been the pivotal issue in postwar Japanese foreign policy. During
the Occupation, a concern for the past and future role of Japan in world affairs
underlay the sweeping American sponsored constitutional and political reforms
and established the conditions on which independence ultimately was granted.
During the ensuing cold war years, the alliance with the United States served
both as the foundation for the integration of Japan into the international
economic and political order and as the focal point of conflict between the
conservative and opposition parties within the country. The emergence of a
more pluralist, multipolar era has underscored the linkage between political-
security affairs and international economic relations, thereby posing fresh
dilemmas for Japan's strategic policy at a moment when the now multiparty
domestic political system is under its most serious strain since 1952. In Japan,
security policy has been the critical point at which domestic and international
politics has converged most fully and dramatically. Consequently, proper
consideration of this issue must necessarily look beyond the modest military
forces and defense plans of the government and evaluate the past crises and
current strategic problems from a broad political and historical perspective.

In a basic sense, Japan's strategic policy can be seen simply as one dimension
of Japanese-American relations. Since 1945, Japan either has been occupied by

---

[b]In this section and in the following one, I have drawn heavily on the ideas elaborated in my
own writings on Japanese security, especially: *Japan and East Asia: The New International
Order* (Praeger, 1972) and the chapter "Japanese Security and Postwar Japanese Foreign
Policy" in a volume on postwar Japanese foreign policy edited by Robert A. Scalapino and
to be published in 1976 by the University of California Press.

American troops or been a defense satellite under a hegemonial alliance arrangement within which Japanese security interests are seen ultimately as identical with those of the United States. These explicit ties on defense matters have been reinforced both by the cultivation of close and extensive bilateral economic and political relations and by the shrill anti-American campaigns of the Japanese left, which have narrowed the focus of the foreign policy debate to an obsessive concern about relations with the United States. With the unfolding of the so-called Nixon Doctrine and in the face of the monetary, trade, and resource crises that have devastated the international economic system in the last few years, this one-sided defense relationship has undergone significant changes, in fact as well as perception. Still, the United States continues to hold the key to Japan's security policy and when and how the nation will move to an expanded defense posture will be shaped as much as by what is done in Washington as in Tokyo.

Analysis of the current defense problems is possible only after identifying and elaborating the critical variables that have shaped Japanese security policy in the past. There are three. First, special consideration must be given to the basic principles which underlay the individual policies taken and which delimit the substantive consensus within which most of the domestic debate has occurred. In short, the assumptions underlying the postwar Japanese diplomatic tradition must be made clear. Secondly, perhaps the single greatest influence on Japanese policy since 1945, has been the nature of the external environment. Of particular importance in understanding the past passive and derivative role of Japan in foreign affairs is the structure of the international system, notably the peculiar features of the bipolar world and the emergence of political and economic multipolarity. The key to Japan's security policy in the contemporary more pluralist and indeterminate world of scarcity lies in the links between the low politics of international economic relations and the high politics of strategy. Finally, specific attention must be accorded to the place of security policy in the domestic political process and the limits it imposes on the adoption of certain substantive policies (e.g., nuclear armament) and on flexible leadership responsive to international crises. Despite the analytical utility in distinguishing and dealing separately with each of these variables, it should be stressed that in fact there is an integral and dynamic relationship among them. Indeed, it is by delineating some of those linkages that security policy can be properly placed in the context of Japanese foreign policy.

New Diplomatic Tradition

To a degree extraordinary for a country of its size and importance, Japan has conducted international relations without a foreign policy in the usual sense of the word. Ensconced behind the American alliance, the Japanese have avoided questions of security and power politics while aggressively concentrating on aims appropriate to an expanding international trading company, i.e., enlarging overseas contacts for the purpose of maximizing economic well-being. Not only have Japanese actions abroad resembled those of a trading company rather than a nation, but the policy debate within the conservatives and among many left-wing critics has been implicitly based upon assumptions appropriate to this perspective. To be sure, this debate has concentrated on the day-to-day problems of diplomacy and has been cast in the issues and the lexicon of contemporary global and regional politics, but until very recently there has been a consensus that defined Japan's international role in narrowly economic terms within the framework of a nation-state system.

If there are prophets for this policy, they are not Marxists or any contemporary figure; but the nineteenth century English liberals. The prescriptions of men like Bentham and Cobden for Victorian England correspond closely with Japan's postwar priorities. Their abomination of war and armaments and derision of military intervention and the balance of power concept in international affairs strike responsive and recurring chords in contemporary Japan. Cobden's faith that free trade could serve as a sufficient cause for international harmony is only slightly beyond the main thrust of Japanese policy and the equation of national welfare with increased productivity captures the essence of the postwar mood. By simply substituting "Japan" for "England" and "Asia" for "Europe," Cobden's century-old policy prescription reads like any number of position papers published by the Foreign Office during the past two decades.

Japan, by calmly directing her undivided energies to the purifying of her own internal institutions, to the emancipation [and increase] of her commerce . . . would aid more effectively the cause of political progression all over the continent, that she could possibly do by plunging herself into the strife of Asian wars.

More important than the coincidental similarity between the views of a Victorian liberal and contemporary Japanese foreign policy is the identity this gives to the latter in the Anglo-American diplomatic tradition. This tradition stresses the application of moral concepts in determining the goals of foreign policy, reluctantly accepts the existence of international power politics, and extends the belief in "progress" rooted in democratization and economic development from intrastate to interstate politics. As Arnold Wolfers has convincingly argued, these predispositions in large part grow out of political experiences of the United States and Great Britain, especially the freedom from direct attack or invasion enjoyed by both countries prior to the shattering political and technological impact of World War II. Japan, similarly insulated from the pressures of *Realpolitik* following catastrophic defeat in 1945, has understandably slid into a comparable approach to foreign affairs, one which her American "tutor" did much to promote.

This constitutes a radical break with the premises and actions of prewar Japanese diplomacy. From the latter part of the nineteenth century, Japan was deeply caught up in imperialist power politics in East Asia in a manner more keeping with the continental European tradition, with its emphasis on compelling and impersonal forces that shape relations between states, the pervasive and continuous presence of conflict, and the necessity for substantial military capacities to carry out successful diplomacy. In the 1920s and 1930s, Anglo-American efforts to promote international peace through disarmament were categorically rejected by Japan as "too idealistic" for Asia. Thus, Japan is now living with a fractured diplomatic tradition. This is of special significance since today the formulas of disarmament and the "outlawry of war" are even more utopian for the establishment of peace in Asia than in the earlier era.

For Japan, this presents a particularly agonizing and difficult problem, for as the anomalous isolation from East Asian and world politics have dissolved with the bipolar order, not just the policies, but the fundamental assumptions underlying the policies, of the past two decades are challenged. For Japan to move from a largely apolitical position of noninvolvement toward a political and interventionist one is likely to precipitate deep internal political cleavages—such as the United States experienced first in the 1940s, in the move from isolationism to internationalism and more recently, in the continuing, more bitter turmoil touched off by the indecisive and "immoral" war in Vietnam. Consequently, in considering the specific policies that make up present and future Japanese diplomacy it should constantly be borne in mind that their full meaning must include their cumulative effect on the basic premises underlying the country's general posture toward the international system. It is very much an open question whether Richard Cobden alone can for long continue as the prophet for Japan's foreign affairs.

Japanese Domestic Politics and Security Policy

In considering the development of Japan's security policies, the domestic political influences and the external environment must be scrupulously distinguished and separately evaluated. Normally, a nation's strategic policy reflects a dynamic balance between internal and international considerations, but in Japan this relationship has been disrupted. Prolonged withdrawal from all power politics and the peculiar features of the new diplomatic tradition have led to a perspective that is to an extraordinary extent derived from politics and ideals unique to conditions *within* the country. It is essential, therefore, to consider the evolution of the security policy with an eye to ascertaining: (1) the substantive features of this policy; (2) the way in which this issue is caught up in the dynamics of domestic politics and (3) the degree to which the nation has the capacity to formulate a pragmatic security policy appropriate to a fluid and uncertain pluralist world.

Japan's approach to defense has been remarkably unvarying and subdued and is built around full and unqualified United States security guarantees. Beyond the American alliance, there has effectively been no strategic policy regarding external threats or regional conflict. Security has been defined in the narrow sense of preserving national territorial integrity. Government defense measures have been aimed, firstly, at maintaining internal order and, secondly, at supplementing American forces to cope with a conventional invasion—a contingency that has been singularly implausible since the early 1950s. Every Japanese government has supported this narrow definition of security as defense of the home islands, within which there is not likely to be a clear or present military danger from any country that could not be met by their own modest conventional forces.

The development of the Japanese Self-Defense forces, despite the fact that they are structured around five-year plans, display two characteristics of Japanese foreign policy generally—a lack of clear, long-term goals involving more independent actions by the nation and an emphasis on domestic over external considerations. The very comprehensiveness of dependence on the United States has allowed the defense plans to develop in a kind of international vacuum, in which the direction and tempo of expansion have been treated more as a budget than a strategic issue and in essence stands as a kind of weapons procurement review. The extraordinarily modest level of military expenditures—a record completely out of line with comparable expenditures of other industrial powers—has many causes, including the political opposition to rearmament and the demands of rapid economic growth. However, the basic causes lie in the dynamics of decision-making and in the low priority (indeed, almost inadvertent attention) that has been accorded to the question of external defense. Without any independent strategic goals beyond holding operations for the United States, and with no immediate political incentives for establishing any, even the limited appropriations requests of the Defense Agency have been grist in the mill of the Finance Ministry and more powerful elements of the bureaucracy and reduced to proportions in line with other ministries' demands.

Within the ruling conservative party, there has been a consensus on the need for the Mutual Security Treaty, the principle of collective defense, the need to gradually strengthen the Self-Defense Forces, the importance of educating the public to a greater awareness of national defense requirements, and (with some dissent) on the need to preserve the constitution. Two things have been notable about the posture of conservative politicians on defense; a reluctance to speak out on the issue of security because of the potential domestic political repercussions and a desire to keep all policy options open—including the nuclear one.

The previously noted process of foreign policy-making that prevents bold leadership on all major questions in which political rather than economic matters are involved is particularly relevant to the issue of security. Because the security issue is such a highly politicized and controversial question within the Liberal-Democratic party (as well as among all the parties) it will inevitably be caught up in factional politics if and when a shift to a new strategic posture is undertaken. Furthermore, the vehement and unqualified opposition of the Japanese Left to any move toward a more activist position beyond a disarmed neutralism will discourage government initiatives by increasing the domestic political risks that are involved. Barring the sudden emergence of a strong nationalist consensus, the internal political situation will proscribe a Gaullist-style move to develop a more autonomous political and military role in the world and insure that any basic shift in security policy is closely tied to changes in the international milieu, not independently initiated by policymakers in Tokyo.

Questions of defense have been of central concern to all the opposition parties and this has given broad definition to mass opinion as well as structure to the debate in the mass media and intellectual journals regarding the security question. Despite many differences within and among these parties regarding details, the two most significant effects of their actions have been to fuel anti-American feelings and to enhance and give political identity to pacifism. The Left has made Article IX the most dramatic symbol of the new constitution so that, other than weak and abortive challenges from several leaders in the 1950s, the basic principle of the peace clause has not been directly and effectively challenged.

In consequence, the government has operated in a pacifist milieu and has been continuously on the defensive in all efforts to develop a security policy. With the very legality of the military forces vehemently questioned by the Left, it is not surprising that it has proved difficult for the government to articulate clear and positive national strategic objectives. Above all, the idealism embodied in this article has given all matters of defense a peculiarly moral cast and drawn the question of security deeply into the issue of constitutional revision and into the basic attitudes held by individuals regarding the very foundations of the postwar political order—that is, the bases of citizenship. The emotional and political legacies of Article IX, nurtured by the opposition, stand as major imponderables for the future direction of Japanese defense policy.

All of the opposition parties have different reasons for opposing the current military alliance with the United States, but the substantive differences among their positions is less important than the overall political effect, to feed proto-nationalist and anti-American sentiments. Much of the public partisan clamor against the Security Treaty has been provoked primarily by periodic campaigns to exploit the issue. In a world featuring détente with Communist powers and intensified economic competition among all states, the conservatives will be increasingly vulnerable to attacks on their cold war style dependence on the United States and the implicit nationalist appeal of such attacks.

Even a cursory examination of the nature of foreign policy-making in Japan and the substance of the security debate raise profound doubts about the capacity of Japan to devise a security policy suitable for a world of fluidity, uncertainty, and conflict. The immobilist decision-making process at best insures that Japan will proceed incrementally from one issue to another without a strategic calculus. Beyond the American alliance, there has been no real consideration of strategic options and the debate over defense policy has come to be defined in highly moral and emotional terms. Therefore, any attempt to devise a new policy will raise issues challenging the assumptions of the new diplomatic tradition and the stability of the domestic political system. The main result of this situation is to assure a passive role for Japan in foreign affairs, at a time when change and uncertainty have come to characterize both the political and economic dimensions of the international system.

The External Environment

When and how Japan's security policy will change is essentially a function of international developments in global and East Asian international politics. The special features of the bipolar, cold war international order which allowed Japan to remain aloof from power politics have become radically transformed in recent years. Not only has the global political-strategic situation become more complex (pluralist) and indeterminate, but the international economic order has undergone a basic upheaval in the wake of the collapse of the monetary system, the massive transfer of capital from the developed states to the oil producing nations, and a global scarcity in basic resources which has in the short run aggravated worldwide inflation. As a resource-poor nation heavily dependent on a free and expanding flow of trade, and as a kind of American defense satellite, Japan is, *prima facie*, extremely vulnerable to any disruption of the international economic order. While the tempo is uncertain, there are sure to be increasing pressures on Tokyo to develop an expanded and more autonomous defense capability. The changed nature of threats likely to face the Japanese and the new directions in which this strategic policy may move can be more fully understood by examining the major external forces impinging on Japan.

The American Alliance

During the last quarter century, the single most important determinant of Japan's security role was American strategic policy toward East Asia. Immediately after World War II, the United States still saw Japan as the main threat to peace in Asia. However, with the onset of the cold war, the triumph of the Communists in China, and the outbreak of the Korean War, the Japanese came to be seen as major and essential allies. Japan thus returned to international politics in 1952 in a comprehensive political and economic alliance in which the

United States was the predominant partner. Moreover, the attendant security arrangements were not cast simply in bilateral terms, but with regard "to the maintenance of international peace and security in the Far East" and thereby brought into accord with the broad cold war aims of the United States in the region.

Major changes in international realities in Asia during th⌣ 1960s, most particularly China's development of nuclear weapons and the escalation of the Vietnam War, led to slight modifications in this policy. The United States then tried to move Japan into a leadership role in Asia in economic and, to a lesser extent, political affairs under a one-sided military partnership featuring an American nuclear umbrella. This policy assumed that the United States would continue to remain deeply engaged militarily in the region, both on nuclear and conventional levels, that there was and would continue to be a basic identity of Japanese and American security interests, and that the economic and political dimensions of policy could be effectively separated from security matters. The war in Vietnam ultimately challenged all these assumptions, demonstrated that the United States lacked the capacity to control conflict effectively in the region, and shattered the bipartisan, internationalist domestic consensus on which postwar American policy had been built. This led to the first fundamental reordering of American foreign policy priorities since the start of the cold war, expressed initially in the so-called Nixon Doctrine.

This "doctrine" never achieved the status of a fully developed policy position but rather consisted of a set of responses to new international conditions and the shift in the mood within the United States away from internationalism and anti-communism. Despite the vagueness of the vision and the impact of the unique Nixon-Kissinger diplomatic style, the basic points of departure from previous policy have endured as permanent features of American policy toward Asia and are likely to persist in the future. First of all, existing commitments notwithstanding, it is most improbable that the United States will intervene massively by military means to "contain communism" as in the past quarter century. Despite the affirmation that existing alliances would be honored, the president also made clear that "we are not involved in the world because we have commitments; we have commitments because we are involved. Out interest must shape our commitments, rather than the other way around."

Thus, the certitude of the containment era has been replaced by a more pragmatic and unpredictable posture by the United States in response to a more fluid and indeterminate situation in Asia. Second, there has been a notable shift, more implicit than explicit, from the globalist ideals of previous policy to an emphasis on more narrowly defined national security interests. This clearly underlies the assumption that East Asian nations can and will assume fuller responsibility for their own defense. Third, there is a commitment to create a stable new international order in Asia ("a generation of peace") through diplomatic maneuver with other great powers (now including China as well as

Japan) rather than a string of alliances and the direct American military intervention that characterized the recently ended "era of confrontation." Finally, priority is given our relations with Japan and China, which along with the Soviet Union are seen as critical to the conduct of diplomacy in an unsettled and volatile region.

This fundamental shift in the goals of American policy cannot but test the basis of the Japanese-American alliance in the long run. Were this change simply a controlled and calculated move to more appropriate aims, the prospects for eventual adjustment of bilateral relations would be good, however difficult this might prove in the short run. But this change in American policy is much more. Most importantly, the shift in policy aims rests not simply on choice, but on the reduced capacities and will of the United States to maintain global peace and to manage conflict in Asia. Even if future American statesmen are able to surmount the persistent internal political divisions to reassert foreign policy leadership, the task of maintaining a credible nuclear and strategic umbrella regarding the defense of Japan will be challenging. The existing security arrangements may prove adequate to assure defense of Japanese territory, but Tokyo will find this narrow definition of defense increasingly untenable because of Japan's place in the radically altered international landscape.

Two features of this landscape are particularly important: (1) the massive and growing involvement of Japan in regional and global international affairs (especially with the politically volatile Third World) and (2) the long-term impact of the world economic and resource crises on the fundamental stability and *modus operandi* of the global international system. It will become increasingly difficult to keep in proper balance the economic and strategic aspects of Japanese-American relations and, even more importantly, the direction of Japan's security policy cannot but be shaped more and more by factors other than American policy. Rather than conjecture about whether or when Japan may move from almost full strategic dependence on the United States to a more autonomous and activist security policy, it is more instructive to explore the general kind of diplomatic challenges the Japanese will face in the more pluralist and competitive international conditions now unfolding and the implications this holds for the use of military power by Tokyo as an instrument of diplomacy.

Japanese Foreign Policy in a Pluralist World of Scarcity

Japanese Defense Policy

Are any future international conflicts involving war likely to impinge upon Japan? An answer to this question is elusive not only because of the peculiar domestic political situation within Japan and the unusual and successful security policies of Tokyo in the postwar era, but because the place of war in international affairs is itself now a matter of dispute. What is clear is the confluence of destabilizing factors of staggering proportions on the contemporary international scene: an acute shortage of basic resources (most notably a malthusian situation in some poor countries), an incredibly massive and rapid shift of wealth to oil exporting countries, a general weakening of the international economic and political institutions previously devised to mediate and moderate conflict, a persistence of profound national and ideological differences, the erosion of traditional values and cynicism regarding political institutions in most democratic societies, and nuclear proliferation.

As in most periods of extreme uncertainty in world affairs, views regarding the place of war tend to cluster around two poles. Some see an end to the war as a calculated instrument of policy except for the very strong (the superpowers) or the very weak (the chronically poor on the periphery of world society) and therefore not germane to the ordinary conduct of international affairs. Others perceive an inexorable drift toward war as part of a more deeply rooted malaise leading to the Armageddon of civilization as it is now known.[2] From either perspective, there is little need for Japan to maintain a security policy in the traditional sense of the word. Indeed, from the first viewpoint, more important because it moves beyond an almost wholly determinist position, the current nonmilitary posture of Japan can be seen not as a transient aberration, but "as a model of what all nations might become in an interdependent world."[3] Three basic arguments, *inter alia*, are offered to support the obsolescence of a substantial security role for Japan: (1) the unlikelihood of military conflict in terms of the Communist-non-Communist lines of the cold war (viz, the détente syndrome); (2) a growing degree of economic "interdependence" with a wide range of countries which makes conventional diplomacy involving national security policies obsolete and counterproductive; and (3) the obvious impracticality and irrationality of war itself in a nuclear and post-Vietnam era. However, a more careful look at each of these arguments in terms of Japan's specific international situation raises serious doubts that the Japanese can in fact proceed without major concern for an expanded security policy.

At first glance, détente seems to provide a formidable reason against change from the present strategic policy. The relaxation of tensions between the United States and the Communist world (most notably the Soviet Union and China), the concomitant efforts to expand diplomatic and economic contacts with these countries, and modest progress in strategic arms limitation agreements with the Russians may have contributed to the short-term prospects for peace. Most certainly they have altered the hegemonial cold war alliance systems and the global strategies of the superpowers. However, to alter the strategies related to the cold war is not to suspend the use of force from a central place in international affairs. To assume that the Soviet Union and China will effectively renounce the use of force as a central component of their foreign policies as a result of détente is on the face of it an untenable, utopian denial of the continuity of international politics. Moreover, as the Korean and Vietnamese wars illustrate in exaggerated ways, the situation in Asia is complicated further by the fact that several smaller Communist and non-Communist states have both the military and political capacities to initiate violent conflict at times and under circumstances that the great powers can neither fully control nor totally ignore. Moreover, in the post-Vietnam era, these capacities will substantially expand. Conflicts will persist in Asia, détente notwithstanding, and in view of the preeminent economic and mounting political commitments of Japan in the region, complete aloofness for the indefinite future will prove increasingly difficult. Military conflict will not be banished to the periphery of international politics in Asia in the decades ahead and thereby remove the need for a Japanese security policy. On the contrary, because of the implicit nationalist (as distinct from globalist) orientation of the current trend in international affairs in this part of the world, pressures will continue to mount on Japan to look to itself more fully in defining national interests and adopting policies appropriate to those interests.

The immediate problems of the current international political situation that may push Japan into an expanded security policy center around the credibility of the United States in Tokyo and the gap between the realities of the contemporary scene and the existing alliance arrangements. Even a cursory inspection of the Asian political landscape shows that the profound political and ideological differences generated during the last three decades between the Communist states and movements on the one hand, and the non-Communist states and groups on the other, remain as critical features and a potential cause of conflict in the region. Moreover, the web of political and economic ties binding Japan to the non-Communist states in the region are very substantial. At the same time, the indeterminacy of the contemporary pluralist world and the more nationalist orientation of American and Soviet policy has made the Sino-Soviet Treaty of Friendship and Alliance drolly obsolete and the Japanese-American Mutual Security Treaty a serviceable but strategically anachronistic alliance. In the immediate future, the credibility of the United States' commitment to Tokyo will, in particular, be tested by two continuing problems: the disposition of Taiwan and the political division of Korea. Resolution of the Taiwan question, a controversial issue within Japan, remains basically in the hands of Washington and Peking in the short run, but the prospects for major war in the latter situation can be substantially determined by local conditions. If major military action takes place, particularly if it leads to an extension of Communist control, the inevitably limited nature of the American response would raise doubts about the general security role of the United States in East Asia. In short, anything short of an outbreak of peace in the region will force Japan to reconsider its own policies and interests and at the very least to place the bilateral security treaty on a new and more appropriate footing.

Nuclear Arms

The basic dilemmas of Japanese security policy during the coming decade can be illustrated by considering the question of nuclear armament. From one perspective, even the possibility of Japan "going nuclear" is both unlikely and unwise. First of all, there are truly formidable internal political and legal barriers to such a development. Article IX of the Constitution proscribes rearmament; the Atomic Energy Act bars the use of nuclear power for "non-peaceful" purposes; there is no broad consensus among the public or the elite[c] regarding rearmament, far less nuclearization; and the only sectors of the political world to push overtly for keeping the nuclear option open are the right-wing of the conservative party and the Japanese Communist party. Moreover, the recent ratification of the Nuclear Non-Proliferation Treaty by Japan has created another formidable obstacle to the development of nuclear weapons. It can safely be said that no Japanese political leader could or would choose to move in the fashion of De Gaulle or Indira Gandhi. Yet it is one thing to note these unique and truly formidable obstacles and quite another to say that they will serve as a permanent bar to this policy option. Most basically, when and how Japan may "go nuclear" is essentially a function of external, not simply internal, events and would be in the form of acquiescence to the operating mores of the international system, not by means of a Gaullist strategic flourish.

What conceivable international circumstances could create a context in which the development of nuclear arms would be considered? In providing answers to this question it is essential to transcend a barefooted approach from the orthodox perspective of strategic analysis that is commonly used. It is absurd to suggest that an island nation with population and industrial centers compressed onto coastal plains can devise an appropriate defense or nuclear counterforce strategy to assure national security. To protect Japanese territory in a narrow military sense is not likely to be the raison d'être for nuclearization. Moreover, it is extremely improbable that a Japanese decision to develop nuclear arms will lead *ipso facto* to a race for weapons parity with the United States and the Soviet Union, as many are wont to suggest. The spread of nuclear weapons has been geared not as much to superpower ambitions but to coping with national and regional security issues and to the international leverage that has come to members of the nuclear club. These are also the potential incentives for Japan.

There are three political-strategic conditions which individually or together could lead Japan onto the nuclear road. First, a general withdrawal of the United

---

[c]The antinuclear feeling has been quite strong among almost all Japanese prime ministers, a fact that the Nobel Peace Prize Committee found so astonishing and praiseworthy that it gave a Peace Prize to the Japanese prime minister (Eisaku Sato) who was in office during the years (1966-72) when pressures for Japan to join the nuclear club were seen as substantial.

States from the power politics of East Asia with the abrogation or severe modification of the Japanese-American Security Treaty would force on Japan a series of choices that could easily end in the nuclear option. Second, the spread of nuclear weapons among the smaller Asian powers (South Korea and Taiwan are the most likely immediate prospects) would place great pressures on Japan to follow suit. Third, the general proliferation of nuclear weapons in an interdependent world of conflict and scarcity could well lead Japan (and other nations) to the acquisition of nuclear arms as a means for functioning fully and effectively in international affairs *by other nonnuclear means*.

Thus, the critical choices for Japan regarding nuclear armament will be made not so much by politicians in Tokyo as by the drift of world events which are beyond their capacity to control. It is singularly unrealistic to fail to consider such a contingency or to write it off as a political Armageddon for Japan. Any realistic critical choices regarding future American policy toward Japan must confront this prospect, especially in light of the limited hope for blocking proliferation and the distinguished record of failure by the Soviet Union as well as the United States in controlling conflict in East Asia.

Security and Scarcity

The future security policy of Japan will, of necessity, focus on access to vital raw materials and markets to assure the survival and health of the national economy. No matter how successful the government may be in the short run in solving the problems of cost and availability of resources and energy, Japan will remain perhaps the most vulnerable of the advanced industrial societies to any breakdowns in the international economic system and to the political machinations of Third World countries involving critical raw materials. While there is little dispute over these assertions, there are substantial differences regarding their implications for Japanese policy. Again, there is a polarization of views. Economists and political analysts beguiled by the "interdependence" of the world economy, see the present highly restricted security policy of Japan as both appropriate and continuing. In their most extreme form, these arguments take on an extraordinary ahistorical cast: "multiple dependence on other countries . . . and the effects of affluence" will keep Japan from "exerting traditional forms of power around the world";[4] the extension and permanent dependence of Japan on imports of raw materials, energy, and food has rendered obsolete power politics as a guideline to policy.[5] Others, starting from the same premise of interdependence, reach the sharply contrasting conclusion that the oil crisis and the attendant monetary problems have pushed the world to the brink of a situation "comparable in its potential for economic and political disaster to the Great Depression of the 1930's"[6] (and by implication future resourced crises could do the same) and that this can be avoided only through creative acts of diplomacy and cooperation unprecedented in modern history. In such a world of chaos, force would inevitably become the medium for the resolution of conflict.

If there is a total collapse of world order, or conversely, a withering away of international politics because of economic interdependence, the question of Japanese security will be wholly determined by factors beyond the reach of Tokyo. However, short of the millenium or an apocalyptic collapse, Japan is destined to live in a pluralist world of scarcity in which an expanded and more autonomous security policy is adopted in the course of establishing viable international economic and political relationships.

In ways the United States is not, Japan is truly interdependent with resource-exporting nations (as well as the largely industrialized capital goods importing nations) which tend to be underdeveloped, chronically unstable countries and have more and more come to use their economic assets for political purposes. Real interdependence of this sort leads the nations involved either to create institutions to regulate their interlocked affairs or to a drive for dominance by one (or more) of the partners.[7] Efforts such as those devised to coordinate the energy policies of the industrialized, oil-importing nations, will have to be successfully devised time and time again to cope with recurring crises in a resource scarce world, and it is quixotic to postulate undeviating success. Under conditions of shortage, the possibility for international cooperation becomes more remote, the pressures for competition in terms of narrow national interests increase, and political power becomes deeply and inextricably linked with economic policy. Under these circumstances, interdependence leads not away from security policy, but rather is the likely catalyst for Japanese participation in *Realpolitik*.

There are, of course, limitless possible scenarios regarding when and under what circumstances Japan might be led to military intervention or a more active security policy, but the issues and problems are perhaps most clearly seen in the East Asian region where extensive economic interests are bolstered by special and long-standing political interests. Japan is not economically dependent on any country in Asia in the sense that there is dependence on the Middle-East for oil. However, with Indonesia, for example, there is a highly significant level of imports of several critical materials (e.g., oil, bauxite, timber), and with South Korea there is a high level of trade and investment, the loss of which would be costly in a precariously balanced economic situation—and which would carry political and psychological costs as well. The cumulative commercial (trade and investment) and aid entanglements of Japan with these countries do not add up to a short-term economic *necessity* for Japanese military involvement. Incentives for any such drastic action will also be political, both *external*, pressures from nations fully participating in a world of *Realpolitik* and *internal*, the political imperatives associated with maintaining a popularly accepted level of prosperity. These can not but be intensified by the inherent propensity toward aggressive national actions in terms of narrow self-interest in a world of scarcity.

This is not to suggest that conflict (and Japan's military involvement in that conflict) will proceed from a kind of anarchy in Asia, for there will certainly be a web of collective and cooperative endeavors in a number of fields, especially security. However, a basic and often forgotten condition of international politics is that in *all* international situations involving cooperative action (interdependence), one can not always rely on others even when all agree on the goal and have an equal interest· in the project. The inherent difficulties in cooperative endeavor suggested in the parable of the stag by Rousseau, in his writings on the state of nature, is brilliantly and aptly applied to international politics by Kenneth Waltz.

Assume that five men (nations) who have acquired a rudimentary ability to speak and to understand each other happen to come together at a time when all of them suffer from hunger. The hunger of each will be satisfied by the fifth part of a stag, so they agree to cooperate in a project to trap one. But also the hunger of any one of them will be satisfied by a hare, so as a hare comes within reach, one of them grabs it. The defector obtains the means of satisfying his hunger but in doing so permits the stag to escape. His immediate interest prevails over consideration for his fellows.[8]

It is important to recognize that the rabbit-snatcher was rational and predictable from *his* point of view and capricious only in regard to the others. The implied lesson seems to have been learned by the United States, which currently is taking the lead in a cooperative venture of sharing with the oil importing nations (the stag) and at the same time pressing hard on a project for energy self-sufficiency (the hare).

For Japan, the implications of the parable are profound. Not only will domestic politics make it difficult for Tokyo to participate in cooperative ventures regarding security-economics, but the limited amounts of resources under Japanese political control make success in such cooperative ventures the only option open—other than a massive, autonomous expansion of security policy. In a world of scarcity in which the mores regulating relations among states take on the more traditional political-economy cast, the prospects for conflict and some sort of expanded security policy for Japan are very high indeed.

If war is to be a peripheral feature of international politics,[9] then the minimal security option currently followed by Japan is indeed the best. The development of nuclear arsenals by the United States and the Soviet Union in the 1950s, and the doomsday character of the destructive force involved, led many to conclude that the technological threshold had been crossed that made war obsolete because of the costs involved for all parties. Furthermore, both the prolonged strategic stalemate between the superpowers and the modest progress toward arms control seem to demonstrate that the unacceptability of all-out war was recognized by those with the capacity to act. However, efforts to prevent the spread of nuclear weapons have not worked and, more importantly, the political conflicts that underlie the use of force in international affairs have persisted— and led to widespread violence with conventional arms. As Aron and Kissinger[10] early recognized and as the history of the last quarter of a century has shown, the issue was never total peace or complete annihilation, but really the meaning of the nuclear dimension in the conduct of strategic policy by the major powers. For Japan, as for other nations, the nuclear era does not mean an end to strategy, but simply a more complicated strategic calculus.

In the wake of the Vietnam War and the other costly military excursions of the United States since the end of World War II, doubts have been raised regarding the utility (and even the legitimacy) of any sort of large-scale military intervention abroad by any great power. The notion is, on the face of it, questionable in a world of scarcity, of economic interdependence, and poly-morphous violence. To be sure, in certain areas of the world, most notably Western Europe, the possibility of war among the nations of the region in the manner of the past has been greatly reduced, because of superpower strategic confrontation and prolonged and institutionalized economic cooperation. How-ever, in the Middle East, in Asia, and in other economically poor or politically precarious areas, there has been recurrent violent conflict. It is utterly quixotic to postulate the end of conventional or internationalized insurgency warfare in the Third World and it is only slightly less so to suggest that Japan (or other industrialized nations) can remain completely aloof from such conflicts indef-initely. Alteration in the nature of warfare has not destroyed the need of a security policy by Tokyo.

Security for Japan in a pluralist world of scarcity can no longer be conducted under the liberal diplomatic principles sustained by the anomalous bipolar cold war world. Politics and economics are no longer separable, and Japan's extensive overseas economic involvement, especially in Asia, will force the development of a foreign policy in which strategic considerations have a greatly expanded role.

Conclusions

Certainly, the most critical immediate challenge for American policy is to place security relations between the two countries on a footing appropriate to the new circumstances rather than waiting for events to force the adjustment. Because the current bilateral security treaty explicitly ties Japan's security to "the Far East," a general revision of United States commitments in the region would have to proceed hand in hand. In the wake of the collapse of Indo-China and the continuing fluidity of the international environment in Asia, the commitment of the United States to stay involved in the region must be tempered by realism regarding its capacities to influence events. This is especially true regarding Japan, a nation which more than any other Asian society shares common security, economic and political interests with the United States. However stable the current alliance may appear in the short run, it is essential to cast our long-term objectives in terms of the fundamental political and economic forces on which the current arrangement rests. From this perspective, it is essential to recognize the basic changes which are taking place both within Japan and internationally. In the strategic area American credibility is probably best achieved on a case-by-case basis within a flexible alliance arrangement, rather than through undifferentiating commitments rooted in the globalist premises of the cold war (e.g., the Nuclear Non-Proliferation Treaty). Most importantly, special efforts must be made to devise and institutionalize cooperative efforts on a wide range of political and economic endeavors. Despite a special and close relationship since 1945, the Japanese-American alliance does not rest upon the deep-seated cultural and political ties that link America to Europe and, for that reason, continues to be susceptible in crisis situations. Moreover, while Japan has joined the first ranks of the industrialized societies, she is an Asian nation and the context of its security problems is not Europe, but the far more indeterminate and intractable world of Asia. The issues involved in Japanese-American relations over the next decades touch upon the most vital and basic issues of international politics. The successes of the recent past, provide few assurances regarding the future and American policy depends, above all, on perceiving just what are the critical choices involved.

Notes

1. See, for example, Robert E. Osgood, *The Weary and the Wary: U.S. and Japanese Security Policies in Transition* (Baltimore: The Johns Hopkins University Press, 1972) and Martin E. Weinstein, *Japan's Postwar Defense Policy* (New York: Columbia University Press, 1971).

2. The former view is implicitly and explicitly part of the huge literature treating "supranationalism" and economic independence as the critical variables in international affairs (e.g., Miriam Camps, *The Management of Interdependence* [New York: Council on Foreign Relations, 1974]) while the latter runs through the equally profuse publications focused on the dire international consequences of the problems of population, ecology, resource scarcity, and especially the politics of oil.

3. William P. Bundy, "International Security Today," *Foreign Affairs* 53, 1 (October 1974): 33.

4. Ibid., p. 32.

5. Saburo Okita, "Natural Resource Dependency and Japanese Foreign Policy," *Foreign Affairs* 52, 4 (July 1974): 714-24.

6. Walter J. Levy, "World Oil Cooperation or International Chaos," *Foreign Affairs* 52, 4 (July 1972): 7.

7. For elaboration on this point see Kenneth N. Waltz, "Conflict in World Politics," in S. Spiegel and K. Waltz (eds.), *Conflict in World Politics*, (Cambridge, Mass.: Winthrop Publishers, Inc., 1971), p. 461.

8. Waltz, *Man, The State and War*, pp. 167-168.

9. See Louis J. Halle, "Does War Have a Future," *Foreign Affairs* 52, 1 (October 1973): 20-34, for an illustrative example of the "no-war" argument.

10. See Raymond Aron, *On War* (Garden City, New York: Doubleday, 1958) and Henry A. Kissinger, *Nuclear Weapons and Foreign Policy* (New York: Harper, 1957), *passim*.

III The Japanese Problem

Chalmers Johnson

Fifty years ago, following the First World War, all persons sensitive to politics knew what was meant when someone referred to "the German question" or "the German problem." It was a shorthand way of bringing to mind a group of interrelated issues: what was Germany's rightful place in the world? Had the war been caused by the Allies' refusal to acknowledge Germany's rightful place? Was Germany making any progress toward evolving a social structure that would sustain and nurture liberal democracy? Would Germany rearm? As A.J.P. Taylor has written, "The history of Europe between the wars revolved round 'the German problem.' If this were settled, everything would be settled; if it remained unsolved, Europe would not know peace."[1]

I do not wish for a moment to suggest that during the last quarter of this century the world faces a comparable "Japanese problem" or that the Japanese problem we do face is likely to be resolved as was the earlier one in Germany. But I do believe that it is useful to think of the issue of Japan in contemporary international politics in these terms—that is, as a group of interrelated questions which only achieve genuine significance when considered together and in light of their interrelationships. Will Japan's economy continue to grow? Will Japan rearm? What is Japan's rightful place in the world? How stable is Japanese democracy? It is possible to answer each of these questions individually, and several recent attempts have been made to answer one or another of them.[2] Unfortunately, the results, while academically interesting, often strike the policymaker as narrow or beside the point. As particular issues, these questions concerning Japan have not attracted widespread interest among American policymakers, nor certainly among the broad American public, except perhaps for the most contingent question of them all, "Will Japan rearm?" But taken together, it seems that the world, the United States, and indeed the Japanese do have a "Japanese problem," one not totally dissimilar in terms of its scope from the old German question. The Japanese problem thus refers to a series of contingencies, each impinging on the other and influencing how the overall situation is likely to be resolved. The most obvious evidence that there is a Japanese problem is the fact that no one, including the Japanese, is confident that any one of these questions can be answered independently of the others.

A different way to make this point is to borrow two concepts from economic theory. In partial equilibrium analysis, the controlling concept is *ceteris paribus*, other things being equal. It allows the analyst to study a single market, or firm, or transaction in depth. So, for example, in reply to the question "Will Japan rearm?" the partial equilibrium answer clearly is, "No, *ceteris paribus*." In general equilibrium analysis, the controlling concept is *mutatis mutandis*, the necessary changes having been made. Here the "other things" have altered. In fact, all items in a general equilibrium determine each other, and to change one is to change all the others. Thus, in reply to the question "Will Japan rearm?" the general equilibrium answer clearly is, "Yes, *mutatis mutandis*." Both concepts are necessary for economic analysis, the first being perhaps more important than the second if any kind of concrete research short of studying everything is to be accomplished. But it is necessary to be reminded of the second and to recall how infrequently the other things do remain unchanged in the real world. Our idea of a "Japanese problem" belongs to the realm of general equilibrium analysis, where the resolution of the broad questions concerning Japan's role in the world is contingent upon and itself affects a myriad of other, identifiable variables.[3]

Japan's gross national product (GNP) in 1960 was about US$43 billion. By 1970, it had grown to about US$200 billion, a fivefold increase in a single decade. By 1973, it had again doubled. The ratio of Japan's GNP to that of the United States was 1:12 in 1960, 1:5 in 1970, 1:3 in 1973, and will probably be 1:2 before 1980.[4] If Japan were to maintain this rate of growth and if global exports of raw materials continued at 1973 levels, Japan by 1980 would be buying up half of all the natural resources exported by the other countries of the world.[5] Clearly, that is not going to happen. But these figures give some idea of the weight of Japan in the world—over a hundred million people, half the population of the United States, living in four resource-poor, overcrowded, highly industrialized islands. Japan is also allied with the United States, is China's leading trading partner, is the major supplier of developmental assistance to the non-Communist nations of East and Southeast Asia, is the world's largest importer of petroleum, and is located within sight of the Soviet Union.

Politically, Japan maintains what it likes to call a "low profile." International political crises involving Japan do occur with fair frequency, but they seem to resolve themselves in much more favorable ways than crises elsewhere. Consider a few Japanese crises from the recent past. In 1960, massive demonstrations against the renewal of the Japanese-American Security Treaty appeared to threaten Japan's most important alliance. But after the prime minister was replaced, the treaty continued in force throughout the sixties and down to the present time. Under its arrangements the United States extends the nuclear umbrella over Japan, guarantees freedom of the seas in Northeast Asia, and maintains the balance of power in Korea, thereby enabling Japan to devote less than 1 percent of its GNP to armaments, the smallest expenditure for security of any industrialized nation.

Again, in 1964 and 1967, when Japan began lifting its protectionist barriers against the importation of foreign goods and capital, the local press likened these developments to "the second coming of the black ships," meaning that Japan was to be opened up to American economic power in the same way that Commodore Perry's squadron of black ships opened Japan in 1853. As it turned out, a resident of Tokyo can now buy a McDonald's hamburger, a tub of Kentucky fried chicken, or a Coca-Cola, but Japan remains the most domestically-owned economy of any advanced industrial country.

Then came the "Nixon shocks" of July and August 1971: the unilateral change in American relations with China and the defense-of-the-dollar policies. The latter resulted in an upward revaluation of the yen, but Japan's reserves still climbed to around $20 billion before the oil crisis of 1973. As for the Nixon-Kissinger China policy, in its wake Japan recognized Peking, doubled its trade with the mainland, and also doubled its trade with Taiwan. Although the Japanese (and some Americans) used to talk about Japan being a bridge between the United States and China, it had long been apparent that a much more likely scenario would see the United States serving as a bridge between China and Japan. This is, of course, precisely what happened.

These "crises" were not unimportant, as we shall see, but their more-or-less favorable resolution signals the need to proceed cautiously and remain alert to the dangers of exaggeration in this age of mass societies and mass media of communications (the subject of the impact of the media on world politics awaits its Marx or Freud). At the same time this recitation of past crises should remind us of Walter Laquer's warning, "The occupational disease of the historian is to consider essentially new situations in the light of previous experience, to ignore what is novel and unique in them."[6]

During 1973 and 1974 Japan underwent yet another "crisis"—the *sekiyu shokku*, or oil shock—and once again the cries of alarm were deafening. *Business International* headlined in its January 11, 1974 issue the "End of the 'Japanese Miracle.'" Japanese housewives battled in the supermarkets to buy up supplies of toilet paper, soap powder, and anything else the press had identified as likely to be in short supply; and the *New York Times Magazine* of March 3, 1974 featured "The Short Happy Life of Japan as a Superpower." Had it really happened at last? Had the Japanese experienced a genuine crisis, one that would halt the advance of the world's fastest growing industrial economy? Did Herman Kahn, author of *The Emerging Japanese Superstate*, spend his time at the Hudson Institute removing egg from his face? Would the international economist who, when asked at a seminar by a Colombian official what he would recommend for the development of Colombia, replied "Deport all Colombians and import Japanese" be forced to eat his words? The answer to all of these questions is a qualified no, but the qualifications are more interesting and tell us more about Japan than the answer itself.

In attempting to elucidate these qualifications and to relate them to the future of the Japanese-American alliance, we propose to proceed in the following manner: first a *tour d'horizon* of the current Japanese political economy; second, a more detailed examination of Japan's critical problems for the future, how Japan has typically dealt with such problems in the past, and how it proposes to deal with some of them over the coming decade; and last, what these problems mean for the United States, how United States policy can help to resolve them in ways advantageous to both parties, and what might happen if either Japan or the United States chooses to attempt to resolve these problems independently of or at the expense of the other.

The Japanese Political Economy

Japan is a "follower nation," economically and politically. This does not mean that Japan is without policies or that it is invariably weak-kneed or unreliable. What it does mean is that Japan's processes of policy formation begin with concrete problems, often created by other actors in the international system, and then go forward to generalized principles and grand strategy, not vice-versa. Until quite recently Japanese external policy, both political and economic, has been much more concerned with what we might call operative variables than with parameters and parameter-maintenance. By parameters we mean the structural characteristics of international life, including commercial life, during a particular period; by operative variables we mean a country's policies for maximizing its own gains within a given parametrical structure. Given this characteristic of Japanese policy, it is best to begin with a concrete case in order to illustrate some of the typical patterns of Japanese operations and then move on to more abstract and generalized statements. The oil crisis is a good example and also one of the more important.

The Oil Crisis

Japan is dependent on petroleum for over 70 percent of its total energy consumption, and virtually 100 percent of that petroleum is imported. In 1972, the Middle Eastern area supplied 80.7 percent (the two leading sources being Iran at 37.3 percent and Saudi Arabia at 16.7 percent), and the Southeast Asian area 16.4 percent (Indonesia alone contributed 13.7 percent). Japan's petrochemical industry is the enterprise most obviously dependent on foreign oil sources, but it should be noted that as of January 1974, approximately 80 percent of Japan's electric power was produced through thermal generation and of that, 94 percent of the electric companies' boilers were fired by oil (the remaining 6 percent used coal). In terms of international comparisons, the share of petroleum in energy consumption is high for Japan and Italy, at over 70 percent, and low for the United States and the United Kingdom, at about 45 percent. The United States' import dependency is also extremely low by international standards. In terms of the structure of domestic oil consumption, the United States consumes more than 50 percent in the transportation sector while Japan consumes more than 50 percent in the industrial sector. Therefore, when on October 17, 1973 the Organization of Arab Petroleum Exporting Countries declared an embargo-by-stages against all countries supporting Israel, Japan clearly had a problem.

After consulting with Secretary of State Henry Kissinger and discovering that he had no oil, nor as yet an oil policy, Japan on November 16 ended its neutrality in the Middle Eastern disputes and adopted a verbal pro-Arab, anti-Israeli policy. This had the desired result of causing the Arabs to designate Japan a "friendly nation" and to restore the flow of oil. Japan's ruling conservative party was careful to phrase its new policy in terms of United Nations resolutions and to rule out breaking relations with Israel, as its left-wing opposition (particularly the Japanese Communist party) advocated doing. However, the Japanese also set out to improve their image with the Arabs. Between December 10 and 28, 1973, then-deputy prime minister Takeo Miki visited Abu Dhabi, Saudi Arabia, Egypt, Kuwait, Qatar, Syria, Iran, and Iraq. Between January 15 and 30, 1974, former foreign minister Zentaro Kosaka visited Morocco, Algeria, Tunisia, Libya, Lebanon, and Jordan. Between January 7 and 17, former minister of International Trade and Industry Yasuhiro Nakasone visited Iraq, Iran, and Britain (the last in order to offer Japan's assistance in the development of North Sea oil).

All of these men sought to convince Middle Eastern leaders of Japan's firm commitment to the Arab side, and they received in return shopping lists of investments that the particular states would be willing to accept as earnests of Japan's good faith. Nakasone was clearly startled in Iran when, after agreeing to put up $1 billion for a local refinery, the Iranians asked for another billion for a petrochemical complex. In addition, the Japanese foreign ministry planned to open embassies in Abu Dhabi and Jordan (Japan had embassies in only eleven of the eighteen Middle Eastern countries, reflecting her previous indifference to the area), and a large number of Middle Eastern heads of state were invited to visit Tokyo. Japan also increased its aid to the Palestinian refugees by some five times over her previous level. The total tab for all of these gestures stood in mid-February of 1974 at somewhere between $3 and $3.5 billion.

Meanwhile, of course, the energy problem confronting Japan had totally changed. At the end of January 1974 a senior official of Keidanren, the leading federation of Japanese industrialists, said that "The oil crisis—in terms of volume—is over. But in terms of price and cost . . ." he just shook his head. In retrospect, it seems clear that the Arab exporters used the Arab-Israeli War as a pretext to jack up oil prices, as well as to force a change in American policy toward the Middle East. Japan was not without clues that the oil crisis involved more than the Arab-Israeli War: Iran, Japan's leading supplier, did not join the embargo but still quadrupled oil prices along with all other Third World producers.

As is typical of Japanese foreign policy at the opening stages of an unfolding international problem, Japan was on every side of the various responses to the petroleum price increases, offering no particular solution of its own. Japanese leaders publicly deplored beggar-thy-neighbor policies of competitive devaluations in order to protect reserves, but Japan engaged in some of this (although much less blatantly than France). In July 1973, the yen stood at around US$1=¥260; after the oil shock, the Bank of Japan allowed the yen to fall to c. US$1=¥300 before intervening to sell dollars, although this greater strength of the dollar was also caused by the United States' comparative invulnerability to the oil cartel. Japan in fact devalued the yen by about 11 percent before the French float and by about another 3.3 percent afterward. In contrast to this go-it-alone policy, Japan also agreed to attend the Washington conference of oil-consuming nations in February 1974. The Japanese press asserted that the decision to attend was made only after all the European nations (except France) had accepted invitations. Japan was being careful to avoid advocating a consortium of consuming nations, in order to preserve the commitments already made by the Arabs; but after such a consortium materialized, Japan wanted to be and became a part of it.

Japan was aware of the dangers to its entire trading position had the oil producers' policies caused a wave of economic nationalism throughout the world. At the same time, Japan did little to support a multilateral search for solutions and engaged in a modest policy of economic nationalism of its own. Japan did not anticipate much help from the United States in meeting its energy needs, and the British appeared to be cool to Japanese proposals to participate in the North Sea petroleum development project. Japan could not be counted as a strong advocate of international cooperative efforts to solve the petroleum price problem—until such efforts showed signs of succeeding.

At a press conference on January 3, 1974, Secretary of State Kissinger remarked, "I can only say that an attempt by Japan to deal with its problem on a purely national basis will bring it up against almost insoluble problems, either of price rises or of competition with other countries. . . . We are not trying to contain Japan. We are trying to enable Japan to meet its requirements within the only framework in which it is possible to meet them, and I am confident that the Japanese see it in the same way." These comments were widely reported in Japan, and on January 7, 1974 Takeo Miki left for the United States in order to "mend the rift" with the United States following the oil shock. Actually, there was not nearly as big a rift between the two allies as the Japanese had feared there might be. Expecting boycotts and denunciations in the United States, Japan in fact received a good deal of sympathy as a nation obviously singled out by the Arabs for the full pressures of their resource nationalism, because it was both the most dependent on Middle Eastern oil of all industrialized nations and the most closely allied with the United States. Miki talked with Jewish leaders in New York about Japan's tilt toward the Arabs, but it hardly seemed necessary since little of the reaction that Japan feared actually materialized.

Japan has long taken as its basic principle in foreign policy the attempt to remain aloof from the major disputes of the world—superpower rivalries in the Middle East, the Sino-Soviet dispute, the Sino-Taiwanese dispute, and so forth—and to trade with all sides. A corollary has been its refusal to take political initiatives, instead waiting to see the way the wind blows and then reacting (in China policy, for example). This policy is, of course, dictated by Japan's absolute need to trade because of its unusual dearth of raw materials, despite the declining percentage of foreign trade as a component of the overall Japanese GNP. Thus far the Japanese have pursued the separation of politics from economics with great success; however, they have won for themselves in the process the reputation of being "economic animals" with few or no principles. With the achievement of great economic power the policy has become increasingly hard to follow, as they discovered in the wake of their initial response to the oil crisis.

Whether the role of "economic animal" is actually unprincipled is a matter of debate; it is in any case a role that ought to be more highly valued in the contemporary world. In its overseas enterprises and joint ventures in the Arab and other parts of the Third World, Japan is at least not a source of political agitation nor is it a major arms supplier, as are Britain, France, the USSR, and the United States. Through its trade Japan contributes to the economic growth of all East Asian countries, including China, and to the level of living enjoyed in its own country, the United States, and its other trading partners. Alternatives to the role of "economic animal" for Japan, including the possibility of its rearmament, are neither easy to find nor conducive to peace.

The shift of focus of the oil shock from an Arab embargo to a quadrupling of global oil prices may prove to be a blessing, since it has moved the various energy problems to a plane on which Japan and the other industrialized nations—perhaps Japan better than the others—can resolve them. With over 70 percent of its energy needs being met by imported petroleum, Japan was obviously vulnerable and overdependent on this single source. It could not do anything about it before the oil crisis, however, because it was uneconomic to develop alternative sources of energy and energy-economizing machines and processes so long as oil prices hovered at around $3.50 a barrel. One could argue that the short-term costs in inflation and crisis management during 1973 and 1974 more than equalled what a little precrisis diversification away from oil would have cost, but this is hindsight and also ignores the great advantages Japan has obtained in the past from cheap Middle Eastern oil. Before the oil shock, Japan, the economic animal, was not compelled to buy expensive or inferior domestic materials but could and did buy from the cheapest source in the world.

Japan's precrisis situation should be contrasted with that of the United States or Australia, which have domestic oil reserves but ones which were substantially more expensive than imported oil. In both the United States and Australia, the governments, for a variety of reasons including "national security" and the political influence of indigenous oil producers, compelled their economies to buy the more expensive domestic oil, contributing to their economic disadvantage so long as the cheaper oil was being used by competitors like Japan. It is also hindsight, but true, to observe that the United States would have been wiser to have hoarded its domestic reserves and imported its own current requirements.

Now that it is no longer uneconomic—to say the least—to invest in alternative sources of energy and in alternative means of using energy, the opportunities for an ingenious, imaginative, savings-oriented population with a desire to make money are unlimited. Japan is well-endowed with such a population; it is, in fact, its most important, virtually its only, "natural resource." One leading American investment house has already advised its clients interested in investing in Japan that "many new product opportunities are likely to present themselves in the form of replacements for current high-energy-consuming machines of modern society." These considerations do not portend the "end of the Japanese economic miracle"; they suggest instead a renewal of precisely the game that Japan has thus far played so successfully.

The Foundations of Rapid Economic Growth

Why has Japan's economy grown as fast as it has since Japan regained its independence in 1952? Western analysts have advanced many answers, but most of them cluster around the cultural determinism favored by Herman Kahn: Japanese save more, invest more, work harder, and strike less than other people simply because they are Japanese. This view, of course, begs all of the questions. We reject it for two reasons: first, it is really no explanation at all; and second, we do not need it in order to understand the Japanese achievement. Japanese do save more and invest more than other peoples, but to explain their behavior in terms of national character is merely to substitute an unprovable hypothesis for serious research. As one of Europe's leading sociologists has written, "Prehistoric national characters have a status somewhat similar to that of instinct theories:

they repeat an observable state of affairs in terms that are removed from the control of intersubjective experience, and thus manage to add nothing to the original observations except a mystical air of obscurity."[7] Unfortunately, some Japanese have themselves promoted such theories, because in this case they are nationally flattering and because on some occasions it has been advantageous to particular Japanese interests to escape international comparisons by pleading that Japan is incomparable.

Japanese leaders, notably the officials of Japan's Ministry of International Trade and Industry (MITI), do not explain Japan's advance from the shattered hulk of 1945 to the status of the world's third most productive economy in terms of cultural characteristics or inevitabilities. They would prefer that Japan's rapid economic growth be understood as a particular form of economic development. In postwar Japan, the government consciously led a massive, popular, difficult campaign to develop a capital-intensive, technology-intensive industrial structure in the face of the theory of comparative costs, which would have recommended labor-intensive types of industries for a country with a large population, few resources, and little accumulated capital. The enormous funds required to bring about this capital-intensive structure came, during the first period of the campaign, from Japan's low wages (and, of course, from other factors such as low social investment and low defense expenditures) and later from the high rate of personal savings of the Japanese people. This high savings rate was itself caused more by Japan's inadequate social security system, a wage system that includes high semiannual bonuses, an underdeveloped state of consumer credit, and the forced savings caused by the low welfare orientation of official policies than it was by any special value placed on frugality in Japanese culture. This is not to say that culture was of no importance; only that its contribution was residual rather than primary.

The main advantage to the people as a whole in the capital-intensive structure is its greater growth rate of productivity. If Japan had pursued a comparative-costs, light-industry economic policy in the postwar world—more or less like that envisaged by the Allied occupation authorities—it is extremely unlikely that it could have raised per capita income above that prevailing in comparably organized economies (e.g., several in Latin America).

A former administrative vice-minister of MITI (the highest nonpolitical career post in the ministry) explains the Japanese government's economic policy as follows: "The Ministry of International Trade and Industry decided to establish in Japan industries which require intensive employment of capital and technology, industries that in consideration of comparative costs of production should be most inappropriate for Japan, industries such as steel, oil refining, petrochemicals, automobiles, aircraft, industrial machinery of all sorts, and electronics, including electronic computers."[8] Another MITI spokesman adds, "Continuous investment based on [the] high savings rate, appropriate guidance, and protection have so far comprised the mechanism of industrial development in Japan."[9] And a Western economist observes

Ultimately the biggest source of growth has been a continuous and deliberate structural change of the economy. In other words, factors of production were induced, and assisted in various ways, to move out of unprofitable and unpromising industries into industries that promised greater returns. This last factor is so important that it cannot be overstressed. Indeed, in part, the extraordinary high rate of Japanese economic growth is explainable by the simple fact that Japan had a very large inefficient sector of the economy (agriculture, small-firm manufacturing, and distribution) to start with, from which it has been rapidly shifting the factors of production into the advanced modern sector.[10]

But who in Japan, one might ask, actually "induced and assisted in various ways" Japanese capitalists and industrialists to go into one line of activity and not another? Most Japanese citizens and any Japanese businessman can answer that: five ministries and one agency of the Japanese government, headed by the Ministry of Finance and the Ministry of International Trade and Industry, which are known collectively as the "economic bureaucracy." This governmental structure, particularly the relatively small, low-budget (1 percent of the national budget), but all-powerful Ministry of International Trade and Industry, has no exact counterpart in any other country, Communist or non-Communist. Interestingly enough, Herbert Stein, former chairman of the President's Council of Economic Advisers, told the 1973 convention of the American Economic Association that the United States may "need an economic planning agency like the Japanese or French," and "pointed to the . . . Japanese Ministry of International Trade and Industry for a model for the United States."[11]

The Japanese government has played a key role in Japan's economic growth, not primarily through subsidies, but more often by means of tax advantages, protectionism, government-guaranteed loans, government-sanctioned cartels, government-sponsored research, and direct orders to businesses known euphemistically as "administrative guidance." As Ohkawa and Rosovsky observe, "Since the 1950s, Japan has been not only a businessman's economic paradise— it has been an economic *and* political paradise."[12]

But structural reform under bureaucratic auspices is not the whole picture. One of Japan's leading economists has analyzed the various causes of Japanese economic growth as follows: (1) rehabilitation factors (industries severely disorganized by the war had a high potential for rapid recovery through the introduction of advanced technology); (2) low defense expenditures (a consequence of the United States' commitment to defend Japan); (3) abundant labor until the 1970s; (4) the high quality of labor, due to the extensive educational system, and the comparatively high level of entrepreneurial ability; (5) aggressive credit creation through government guarantees of so-called overloans by the commercial banks, leading to the world's highest investment ratio; (6) the high savings ratio; (7) the very rapid introduction of foreign technology; (8) the maintenance of an undervalued exchange rate and vigorous export promotion; (9) a combination of export-led and investment-led growth patterns; (10) a high capacity to transform the industrial structure; and (11) a combination of government intervention to foster infant industries and of strong, sometimes "excessive," domestic interfirm competition.[13]

Of this list, we must dwell briefly on one factor that is mentioned and on two additional ones that are not. Number (7), the very rapid introduction of foreign technology into an extremely receptive economic environment, is often singled out by economic analysts as the critical variable. Ohkawa and Rosovsky conclude that "autonomous investment based on borrowed technology is the major driving force of Japanese economic growth." They also note the startling fact that "Japan's economic modernization ... has been a history virtually devoid of core inventions."[14] Some 60 percent of Japan's imports of technology have come from the United States, followed by West Germany (11 percent), Great Britain, and Switzerland. Japan's payments of royalties and license fees rose from $10 million in 1952 to $314 million in 1967. To take merely two examples, during the 1960s, some fifty-three Japanese manufacturers were importing electronic technology under license from the Radio Corporation of America, and some seventeen Japanese companies were paying patent fees to the Peabody Company for permission to use the Sanforizing process.

This issue of technology is important in assessing Japan's future because technology is much harder to import today than it was even a decade ago. Owners of industrial property rights now seek higher fees or, more commonly, wish to develop and sell the products derived from the technology themselves. Japan is, however, aware of this trend. Whereas in 1968 Japanese governmental expenditure on science and technology was $535 million, much lower than the United States' $17 billion, the rate of increase of Japan's research and development (R&D) spending has been consistently above the rate of growth of national income. During 1973, Japan was third in the world, after the United States and the USSR, in R&D expenditures. Equally important, some 75 percent of Japan's R&D payments are private rather than governmental. Available evidence indicates that the income-creating effect of private R&D is greater than that of the defense-related type. It is to be expected that Japan will increasingly become a technology exporter to the developing countries of East Asia, thereby contributing indispensably to these nations' effective industrialization.

One factor not mentioned above but related to Japan's imports of technology is the role played by the United States in Japan's economic growth. It is a story that remains to be told in its full detail, but we might mention here only three aspects of it: first, the United States did sell a good deal of technology to Japan at reasonable rates when Japan needed it most; second, the United States made itself available as Japan's leading foreign market after Japan's traditional markets in East Asia were greatly diminished by the war and subsequent revolutions (needless to say, the Japanese themselves made the necessary analyses and developed the products that they sold in the American market); and third, during the last years of the occupation and throughout the 1950s, the United

States contributed to Japan's growth in many smaller but cumulatively important ways. For example, the United States encouraged and financed the establishment of the Japan Productivity Center, created in 1955 and modeled after those that existed in Europe under the Marshall Plan, which by 1958 had sent its two thousandth visitor-student to the United States in order to compare Japanese and American management and production methods. Although somewhat exaggerated, the Japanese director of the center once commented, "It was just like centuries ago, when so many envoys were sent to China so that Japan could absorb its continental culture."[15]

This aspect of Japanese-American relations, often overlooked on the American side in the arguments between the two nations during the late 1960s and early 1970s, is mentioned here not to praise the United States for its generosity; many American-supported policies and schemes, such as the trust-busting Japanese Fair Trade Commission, have become quite controversial in Japan. It is rather to point out that during the period of Japan's most rapid growth, Japan enjoyed an unusually propitious international environment, beginning with the Korean War, which was in fact the equivalent of the Marshall Plan for Japan.

This environmental factor is related to our earlier distinction between parameters and operative variables. Japanese economic analysts readily point out that Japan's economic growth could not have occurred if such structural givens as the International Monetary Fund (IMF) and General Agreement on Tariffs and Trade (GATT) systems had not existed.[16] In order to expand exports, there must be some form of relatively stable system whereby goods that one nation wishes to buy may be purchased freely and goods that one nation wishes to sell may be sold freely. This is not a question of prices. It is rather a matter of ending discriminatory exchange rates, preventing dumping, lowering tariff and nontariff barriers to trade, and avoiding the creation of economic blocs such as those that existed in the 1930s and that contributed directly to the war. The GATT and IMF systems provided this open, nondiscriminatory structure within which Japan operated with exceptional ability.

Unfortunately, by 1971 the dollar-centered IMF system was in disarray, and disturbing signs of protectionism were appearing in the United States and in the European Community. Much of the blame has to be placed on United States' fiscal and foreign policies, but Japan itself, which had not been involved in the creation of this structure, also received considerable international criticism for its insensitivity to parameter-maintenance and for merely trying to get as much out of the system as it could. For example, rapidly developing nations normally meet the foreign exchange bills necessary for their developmental programs either through export promotion or through import substitution; Japan did both, which was good for Japan but hard on the system. It is fair to say that over the past five years, Japan has moved rapidly from a relatively protectionist position to a relatively free-trade position. Nonetheless, the parameters of a new trading system comparable to that of the 1950s and 1960s still remain to be formulated. Japan alone cannot create a new structure. This must be a first priority for the United States, in collaboration with Japan and other open societies.

It is no exaggeration to say that the growth of international commerce among the nations of North America, Western Europe, and Japan was probably the most truly revolutionary and transforming development of the postwar era. Total world trade expanded some 6.8 times between 1949 and 1972, exceeding the rate of growth of the world's total production. The continuation of this commercial relationship lies at the heart of the "Japanese problem."

Let us attempt to summarize our discussion of Japan's economic situation to this point. The pace of economic growth is determined fundamentally by a people's desire to improve their future well-being, their willingness to save, and their innovative capabilities. As a result of the oil crisis, Japan experienced an inflation rate of 29 percent in 1973, one of the highest in the world, and inflation continued during 1974 with a further rise of from 10 to 15 percent. Although by the end of the 1960s Japan seemed to have outdistanced its chronic balance of payments difficulties, these reappeared following the oil crisis.

Japan's wages have also risen by some 50 percent in only two years, seriously affecting its international competitive ability. There is no likelihood of change, however, in Japan's will to improve its quality of life or in the savings commitment of its people (the rate of personal savings against personal disposable income continues to be around 16 percent, the highest of any society). In addition, the Japanese have learned to live with extremely rapid economic changes and are among the world's most experienced and successful implementers of structural reforms of the economy. Today the Japanese are retooling their apparatus of government-business cooperation in order to diversify the economy's energy requirements away from a reliance on oil. Thus, we do not differ with the Organization for Economic Cooperation and Development's (OECD) mid-1974 assessment: "If past performance is a good guide for the future, it can be expected that the resilience of the Japanese economy and the efficiency of the administration will face up successfully to the new challenges."

Political Leadership

The real crisis in Japan today, and the real qualification to the statement that the economic miracle has a healthy future, is political. After more than twenty years of rule by conservative, pro-business, growth-oriented political parties, the voters are looking for alternatives. This would probably be desirable if Japan had developed a true two-party system, or some other effective means for holding the political leadership responsible to the citizenry, but the truth of the matter is that loss of its majority by the dominant Liberal Democratic party (LDP) would lead at best to a highly unstable coalition government. At worst, it could produce a social revolution.

The Liberal Democrats are opposed by four parties—the Socialists, Communists, Democratic Socialists, and Buddhists—none of which commands anything approaching majority support in the country, but which collectively ended the Conservative party's majority in the 1974 elections for the upper house of the Japanese Diet, or parliament. The LDP now holds 126 seats, exactly half of the 252 seats in the upper house, and is dependent on three independent legislators who normally vote with the conservatives, in order to pass legislation on which the LDP is itself able to produce total party unity.

Opposition to the LDP has been building for a long time, primarily as a result of irritation with the lags and imbalances imposed on the society by high-speed industrial growth. The public is angry over pollution, inadequate housing, high-rise buildings that block sunlight, noise, inflation, and, in general, the policy of putting gross national product ahead of net national welfare. The average Japanese also clearly no longer believes that the conservative leadership will do something to alleviate these conditions, although a decade ago he warmly supported the conservatives because of their popular policies for economic growth. A Watergate-like ennui has become endemic.

Still, until 1974, it did not seem likely that the electorate would turn out the conservatives, largely because the alternatives were so unpalatable. But the opposition parties have begun to try to appeal to the voters, rather than merely offering them ideologies, and every major metropolitan area in Japan is today ruled by Socialist or Communist mayors. The Communists, in particular, have finally diagnosed and remedied their single greatest political liability: the voters' belief that they were subservient to either Moscow or Peking or both. The Japanese Communist party is today independent and nationalistic; it was the only Japanese political party that criticized the recognition of Communist China. In the last general election (1972) the Communist party increased its strength in the lower house of the Diet from fourteen to thirty-eight seats, the largest parliamentary representation it has ever enjoyed. More than five million Japanese voted Communist in this last election. The vote was clearly a form of protest—an attempt to "send them a message"—and may not hold up if it means bringing a left-wing coalition to power; at the same time, the public's extensive experience with leftist local governments may have made it more amenable to a national leftist front.

Twenty years ago the conservatives built their party on a rural constituency and then, through their policies of rapid urbanization and industrialization, proceeded to undermine that constituency. Today there is not much left of the rural population, although the electoral system, which greatly favors the rural voter, helps to keep the LDP in office. In the cities, the consequences of the oil shock have made it hard for the conservatives to gain a hearing. Also, the public has been reading daily about police raids on the offices of major trading firms that have been charged with withholding products from the market and creating artificial shortages. Big business has been the main backer of the conservative party, and for it to be involved in exploiting the public under camouflage of the oil crisis may be the last straw for the Japanese voter.

Another problem haunting the conservatives is labor. Japan's economic growth has been relatively free of labor strife, for various reasons that have usually been misinterpreted abroad as fixed features of Japanese society. In recent years Japanese management has not waited for wage demands to be presented but has raised wages regularly, usually at a level just under the gains of productivity. This was easy and wise so long as GNP was going up at around 10 percent a year and economic slowdowns were temporary. Another way of maintaining labor peace has been to guarantee lifetime employment to the unionized work force. This contributed to Japan's capacity for structural reform of the economy because innovative or automated techniques could be introduced into enterprises without creating union opposition: under lifetime employment, the employer assumes an absolute obligation to retrain the existing work force for the new technology. Continuous changes of job definitions also tended to inhibit the development of horizontal, craft-oriented unions.

The resultant made-in-heaven labor relations were usually portrayed to foreigners as something peculiarly Japanese. However, continuous increases in wages require continuous growth of the economy, as does lifetime employment, under which labor becomes a fixed cost. With raw material costs going up and growth going down, at least for the short-term conversion period, labor is becoming militant (and confusing the sociologists). Unless the political leadership is able to inspire the workers to endure a few years of wage restraint in order to restructure the economy toward energy conservation—and also convince them that the hardships are being equitably distributed—labor demands could build a rigidity into the Japanese economy that it has thus far avoided. The rigidities of uncooperative labor have been major obstacles to structural reform of other economies, such as those of Great Britain and our own. Throughout 1974, the Japanese economic press harped on the dangers of Japan's contracting the dread "English disease," understood as cost-push inflation based on persistent wage demands and lowered labor productivity.

Inflation and labor militancy have become critical issues in Japanese politics. During 1974's "spring labor offensive" (or annual bargaining session at the beginning of the fiscal year), the four main labor federations for the first time cooperated with each other in an organization they called the Spring Labor Offensive Joint Struggle Committee. It was composed of the General Council of Trade Unions of Japan (Sohyo), the largest—circa 4.5 million members—and the most militant of the federations, which provides the main backing for the Socialist party; the Japanese Confederation of Labor (Domei), more conservative and with only about two million members, which provides the main electoral support for the Democratic Socialist party; the Federation of Independent

Unions (Churitsuroren), with 1.2 million members and politically neutral; and the National Federation of Industrial Organizations (Shinsambetsu)—circa 70,000 members—which is a relatively conservative splinter from the original Sohyo federation.

The numerical strength of these organizations is deceptive (all of them are made up of independent unions and none commands the firm loyalty of its rank-and-file members), but the Joint Struggle Committee nominally spoke for 8.3 million workers out of approximately 10 million union members throughout the country. The demands put forward included a very substantial wage increase plus fringe benefits linked to price rises, and recognition of the right to strike by unions in the public sector. The last demand is a recurring favorite of Sohyo's, since its main affiliates are the All-Japan Government and Public Workers Union, the National Railway Workers Union, and the Japan Teachers Union, which are all paid from the national treasury. Strikes by public employees are illegal, but they occur with considerable frequency nonetheless, since their unions are also the most militant. As a result of three short "semi-general" strikes in March and April 1974, the Joint Struggle Committee did win wage increases averaging 30 percent or better and caused negotiations to begin concerning its other demands.

In the July 1974 election for the upper house of the Diet, inflation was virtually the only issue, despite efforts by the conservatives to develop new issues, such as leftist control of the teachers' union, the government's proposal to make one of Tokyo's Shinto shrines into a war memorial (prohibited by the American-inspired Constitution of 1947), and other "silent majority" type issues. This preoccupation with domestic problems was in marked contrast with the upper house election of 1971 and almost all previous national elections since 1952 when foreign and defense policies dominated the campaigns.

Inflation is, of course, an issue in all advanced, open societies, and as in other countries, it has been accompanied in Japan by serious weakness in the leadership of the ruling Liberal Democratic party. The LDP has long been split internally into non-issue-based factions formed around individual political leaders, who provide campaign financing for their supporters in the Diet. These factions bargain with each other and trade off support within the party in order to promote the political careers of each faction's members. The cabinet normally reflects factional strength at any given time. The prime minister is, of course, the leader of his own faction, but he requires the support of other factions in order to obtain and hold his position. He must reward the leaders of rival factions with cabinet posts and promises of future support in order to obtain their aid.

The existence of these factions is testimony to the overwhelming dominance of the LDP in Japanese politics in the postwar era: because the huge conservative party has never really been threatened by the opposition parties, it could afford the luxury of internal disunity. In an important sense, the most significant Japanese political activity has taken place within the LDP rather than between parties. However, the toleration of the electorate for factional politics among the conservatives, particularly for *kinken-seiji* (power-of-money politics) that factions engender, is today very weak. Precedents are quite influential in Japanese culture, and the precedents of Watergate in the United States and of the Brandt resignation in Germany clearly conditioned the forced resignation of Prime Minister Kakuei Tanaka in November 1974 after the press had charged that he was corrupt.[17]

The LDP still has its factions, but it is also showing signs of splitting further along a new, cross-factional dimension—namely, age. Young conservative Diet members in their thirties and forties, educated after the war and representing urban constituencies, have become extremely critical of the LDP's senior leadership, charging it with opportunism, the loss of public confidence, ineptness, and a lack of farsighted policies. This attitude reflects the growing nationalism of younger Japanese—a desire for national self-respect, not a return to prewar militarism—as well as a fear among young party members that bungling by the leadership might cause the LDP to lose its hitherto unassailable majority in the Diet.

An important new inner-party group in the LDP is the Seirankai, perhaps best translated as the "Young Storm Association." It *is* an ideological group, distinguished by its advocacy of a "two Chinas" policy instead of the government's pro-Peking policy. The emergence of the Seirankai has also elicited the formation of a counter group of "doves." (Young LDP members refer to themselves as "hawks" and "doves," not as leftists and rightists, which are terms they dislike. They particularly avoid "rightist" or "right winger" because these phrases evoke connotations of prewar fascism and militarism, which they disavow.) Dissatisfaction with the LDP as it is today thus appears to be breeding new, younger, more nationalistic, urban-based conservatives, who may well find greater support with the voters than the aging former-bureaucrats who dominate the party.

If relative continuity of political policies is maintained in Tokyo, then it seems reasonable to expect that Japan will be among the leaders of nations attempting to build post-petroleum industrial societies—and continuing to grow in the process. In that case, the oil "crisis" of 1973-74 will join Japan's other recent crises as an event that ultimately did it more good than harm. If not, it is likely to be remembered—by the rest of the world and by Japan itself—as something more than just a crisis.

Critical Problems and Japanese Solutions

In his speech before the twenty-ninth session of the UN General Assembly (September 23, 1974), Secretary of State Kissinger made the following point:

The economic history of the postwar period has been one of sustained growth—for developing as well as developed nations. The universal expectation of our peoples, the foundation of our political institutions, and the assumption underlying the evolving structure of peace are all based on the belief that this growth will continue.

But will it? The increasingly open and cooperative global economic system that we have come to take for granted is now under unprecedented attack. The world is poised on the brink of a return to the unrestrained economic nationalism which accompanied the collapse of economic order in the thirties. And should that occur, all would suffer—poor as well as rich, producer as well as consumer.[18]

The verb "poised," it seems to me, is the operative word in this passage. The catastrophe the secretary warned against—a return to economic nationalism, not necessarily the slowing or ending of growth in at least some advanced economies—has not occurred, and there is no analytic reason why it should occur. That is to say, the knowledge required to avoid it is available; what is needed is the international cooperation and political leadership necessary to translate such knowledge into organized activity. With regard to the Japanese dimension of this overarching world problem, we must stress, together with Secretary Kissinger, that since it is a global problem, the Japanese cannot solve it by themselves, although if they fail to deal with it domestically they could certainly exacerbate it.

It has become something of a cliché to speak of global "interdependence"; therefore perhaps we should stress less the aspect of interdependence and more that of synergism—the simultaneous action of separate agencies which, together, have a greater total effect than the sum of their individual effects. An example is the effect on the human organism of barbiturates and alcohol taken simultaneously. Powerful synergisms are at work in the world. Domestic attempts to solve environmental pollution problems, for example, have soaked up the capital needed to develop new energy technologies or to expand productive capacity for fertilizers, required to solve global food problems. At the same time, overseas investments intended to secure stable sources of raw materials, or to meet the demands of developing nations for the creation of jobs in exchange for extraction rights, often have the effect of exporting pollution, with its consequent local and potentially global health hazards. We shall return to this problem below; it is mentioned here because any list of the particular critical problems faced by Japan, or by other comparable nations, runs the risk of obscuring the interdependence among the items on the list, and of ignoring the synergistic implications of proposed solutions to any one particular problem. As one scholar has put it,

There is a tendency to launch attractive crash programs designed to deal with a single ill or take advantage of a single boon. . . . Social development programs should not be judged by criteria of immediate advantage or benefit. Instead, they should be self-consciously geared to the kind of integrated human and national development thinking that shows awareness of the dangers and possibilities of the longer-range multifold trend.[19]

The concrete, technical problems facing Japan can be reduced to five in number, often spoken of by the Japanese as "barriers" or "walls" that must be surmounted. These are: the environmental barrier, the work force barrier, the resources barrier, the technology barrier, and the market barrier. Let us begin by examining briefly the nature and implications of each of these barriers. Various lessons, both positive and negative, for other nations may be derived from this exercise.

The Environment

One economist has estimated that the capacity of nature to absorb the refuse of the population and to purify the environment of Japan is limited to approximately a $100 billion level of annual gross national product based on a heavy industrial economic structure.[20] That level was reached and exceeded during the mid-1960s, and subsequently serious environmental pollution problems have developed. These problems are not simply ones of public nuisances or a decline in social amenities; they include disastrous poisonings of the population through the discharge of heavy metals such as cadmium and mercury into the water supplies of various localities, and the generation of levels of air pollution that necessitate the wearing of gas masks by traffic policemen in some sections of the major cities. It has been suggested that if the Japanese are unable to solve this problem, by 1985 the gas mask may become as normal a part of their daily appurtenances as the umbrella is today.

The long-range suggested solution to this problem—changing the industrial structure to emphasize tertiary industries (to be discussed later)—carries with it several synergistic consequences, including the export of pollution by relocating secondary industries abroad and the raising of Japan's level of import dependency. Meanwhile, immediate crash programs to control pollution are having an important effect on the Japanese growth rate, particularly when they are combined with the effects of international monetary instability and the oil crisis. In recent years pollution-control projects have absorbed a large share of available investment capital, reducing the amounts that could be used for the expansion of production. This is undoubtedly one of the causes of "stagflation" in Japan and of "slumpflation" in other countries such as Italy and England.

In the Japanese auto industry, for example, fully 25 percent of total plant and equipment investment has gone for projects to develop clean engines, while much of the remainder has been allocated to labor-saving projects—in order to deal with another critical problem, the shortage and consequent rise in the price of labor. Relatively little has been invested in expanded productive capacity, which thereby reduces supply and contributes to inflation. Similarly, Dr. Addeke Boerma, director general of the Food and Agricultural Organization, declared in August 1974 that the worldwide shortage of pesticides, which was threatening food production, was caused primarily by environmental restrictions in the developed countries (including Japan) which complicate and discourage investment in the pesticide industry.

Some direct solutions to the pollution problem, in contrast to the long-range approach of changing the industrial structure, appear to be more readily available in Japan than in other countries. These direct solutions—e.g., promotion of industrial relocation, public investment in antipollution devices, and antipollution R&D—characteristically require statutory acts by the government, combined with effective and coordinated administration by the bureaucracy. Japan's renowned economic bureaucracy has moved easily into this field, implementing new programs and, above all, establishing benchmarks and monitoring services which allow the bureaucracy to make adjustments in ineffective programs before they create new problems.

The major long-range problem remains, however. The most important *direct* solution to current pollution problems is the development of equivalent, pollution-free technologies—such things as nonpolluting engines of all kinds, laser communications technologies, and new forms of high-speed transport. But these projects require such enormous amounts of R&D investment and entail such high risks that no unit of society other than government is able to contemplate undertaking them. These decisive, large-scale investments have not been made, and the demands on general treasury resources are rising at a time when the shortage of private capital is becoming more acute.

It may be, however, that measures to conserve and to diversify the sources of energy in response to another critical problem, that of limited natural resources, may also help solve the basic environmental pollution problems. The Japanese government has already begun to implement the following resource conservation measures, all of which have implications for controlling pollution: (1) the setting of goals for the reduced industrial use of oil and electric power, with large users required to submit regular reports to the government; (2) governmental guidelines for energy conservation, including standards and information on means for conserving indoor lighting, temperature, and machine operations (including business machines); (3) government-led improvements in heat-management facilities and heat-management technology; (4) technological research in government laboratories on the development of equipment and instruments of a resource and energy saving type, on the recycling of wastes into resources, and on the utilization of unused resources; (5) governmental attempts to improve after-sale services in order to prolong the effective life of products of all kinds; and (6) a governmental campaign to reduce excessive packaging and model changes. The Japanese government is able to do these things because of the high prestige of the bureaucracy, the public's trust in it, and the long record of public-private interaction and cooperation.

The Work Force

The second critical problem, or barrier, Japan faces is its work force. Since World War II, Japan's birthrate has fallen some 50 percent, a result of both long-term demographic trends and deliberate population control policies. Speaking to the United Nations World Population Conference held in Bucharest in August 1974, Japanese Health and Welfare Minister Kunikichi Saito said that Japan was heading soon toward a period of "stationary population." This development is having major economic consequences, however, since the Japanese do not contemplate a "stationary economy" and one of the factors that made possible Japan's spectacular postwar growth—an abundant supply of high-quality, inexpensive labor—is running out.

This developing labor shortage is complicated further by a fundamental change in the composition of the population. Japan's labor force is aging, thereby becoming more expensive to employ in Japan's heavily age-graded society and requiring ever greater payments in the form of retirement benefits and pensions. In 1964, for example, the number of young men turning eighteen years of age was 1,234,000, whereas the figure for 1974 was 770,000. Incidentally, this demographic shift is relevant to any proposal for Japan's conventional rearmament, since to use a part of the manpower pool for an expanded armed force would have direct and serious consequences for the supply of labor to the economy. It would also raise the costs of both military and civilian labor.

The work force barrier has a qualitative as well as a demographic dimension. The forty-hour week is just beginning to come into full implementation in Japan, but the Industrial Structure Council of the Ministry of International Trade and Industry predicts that it will decline to thirty-four hours per week by 1985. The population is also insisting on more "meaningful"—usually translating as more white-collar—work, which combined with the shorter work week will undoubtedly raise the demand for and supply of educational services and leisure activity industries.

The solutions to this problem are manifold. First of all, government must become more responsive to the blue-collar sector of the society if it is to prevent rising wage demands from eroding Japan's international competitive ability. The Japanese worker is exceptionally responsible and public-spirited, but in the face of major distributive inequities in the society, he is going to ask for and obtain his share, through strikes if by no other means. Although Western sociologists have tended to see Japanese workers as culturally-conditioned paragons who would never behave "selfishly," these same specialists have also tended to ignore the degree to which these workers were exploited during the 1950s and early 1960s, when they had comparatively little collective power.

It is sometimes taken as a rule of thumb that no democratic government can survive a 20 percent inflation rate; Japan exceeded that rate in 1973 and is today susceptible to a serious case of the "English disease." The longer-range solutions to this problem include a basic change of industrial structure in favor of tertiary industries and Japanese overseas investment, subjects we shall discuss later since they concern all of Japan's critical problems.

In general, the work force barrier makes a decline in the Japanese growth rate inevitable—from circa 10 percent during the late 1960s and early 1970s, to circa 6 percent from 1975 to 1980, and to circa 6.5 percent between 1980 and 1985. Obviously enough, however, such a decline does not necessarily mean economic stagnation. The Japanese should not have much difficulty in adjusting to this reduction in their previous super high-speed growth, and the lower growth rate will have a beneficial, if mixed, impact on the pollution problem. On the one hand, the rate of growth of domestic heavy industry will decline; on the other hand, as the population becomes richer and has more free time, the rate of private automobile ownership will increase—from about twenty-three million units in 1972 to an estimated thirty-seven million in 1985. (Domestic demand for cars in 1985 is expected to total approximately 5.8 million vehicles, compared with 4.4 million in 1972. Automobile exports, however, are expected to rise from 1.7 million cars in 1972 to 5.5 million in 1985, thus making automobile production an equally important export industry.)

Japan has probably been fortunate, because of the legacy of World War II and of Japanese colonialism, in not being able to attempt a European-type solution to the work force barrier. It is simply unthinkable in Korea, China, or Southeast Asia that Japan should import labor from these countries in light of Japanese exploitation of their populations both before and during the war. (Only the reversion of Okinawa to Japan has provided a marginal increment to the labor force.) Even if large groups of other nationals were willing to work in Japan, the Japanese home population is incapable of tolerating rates of immigration comparable to the almost half-million southern Europeans and North Africans who emigrated to Germany during 1972, or the over one hundred thousand to France, or the almost three hundred thousand to Switzerland.

However, precluded by history and national attitudes from employing overseas labor at home, the Japanese have also escaped the ethnic divisions, racial strife, and proletarianization that plague the most important economies of western Europe.[21] This gives Japan a major comparative advantage in terms of organizational ability and of unity on national goals for its home population, which is of course larger than that of any single western European nation, although not as large as that of the European Economic Community (EEC) as a whole. Japan today enjoys the largest homogeneous population of any advanced, industrial economy.

Resources

Prior to the oil shock, Japanese economists believed that the Japanese economy would be restrained first by the work force barrier; after the shock they revised this estimate, concluding that Japan had actually collided with the resources barrier and that the latter posed the greatest challenge of all the barriers to Japan's continued prosperity. We doubt this. Japan was actually running into the pollution and market barriers prior to that of resources, and the resources problem may not prove to be as formidable as the Japanese fear. Obviously enough, Japan has a resources problem. Japan's rate of self-sufficiency in major resources is virtually nil, except for lead (33.3 percent) and copper (16.4 percent). Japan must import the raw materials and fuels used in its industries, and in order to pay for these imports, Japan must export, which of course ties the resources barrier in with the market barrier discussed below. In an age of rising commodity nationalism among primary producers, the Japanese are naturally worried.

The resources problem is, however, faced by all industrialized nations—which both makes a multilateral solution more probable and relieves Japan of the need to search for a purely national answer (which, in fact, does not exist). The immediate danger is that producers will withhold supplies in order to make a political point or to punish particular importing nations (as they did during the Arab-Israeli war of 1973), in addition to attempting to create monopolistic price conditions. The two broad countermeasures of the importers are, firstly, to diversify their energy sources and supplier countries, and secondly, to develop new energy sources. Since the second approach cannot be expected to pay off before about 1985, a third approach must also be included: to change the industrial structure to an energy-saving type. The Japanese are attempting to do all three.

By far the most important concrete step taken by the Japanese in order to guarantee supplies and to diversify sources is a campaign of direct overseas investment. Licensing by the Japanese government of overseas investment projects jumped extraordinarily during the 1972 fiscal year. The amounts licensed in recent years are FY 1969, $665 million; FY 1970, $904 million; FY 1971, $858 million; FY 1972, $2,338 million. The figure for the first three quarters of FY 1973 was $2,794 million. The total gross amount licensed as of the end of December 1973 was $9,567 million in some one hundred countries, of which some 72.0 percent was licensed during the preceding four years.

Investments by manufacturing industries led all others with a ratio of 30.7 percent, but mining investments, at 28.0 percent, were close behind. Classified by areas, Japanese investment was highest in North America (24.1 percent), followed by Asia (23.2 percent), Europe (20.1 percent), and Central and South

America (16.9 percent), the last being the fastest growing area of Japanese penetration. (Prime Minister Tanaka's trip to Mexico and Brazil during September 1974 might be noted in this connection.) Japan's overseas direct investments in developing countries accounted for 50.8 percent of its total investment as of the end of December 1973, which is a greater proportion than that of any other advanced country. The Japanese Ministry of International Trade and Industry is unmistakable in terms of its interest in this activity: Japan's "vigorous overseas direct investment activities are now under way in order to cope with the rapid growth of domestic demand for resources."[22]

Without undertaking a comprehensive analysis of Japan's overseas investments, we may say that no activity seems more open to misunderstanding abroad and more demanding of political attention and action for the coming decade than competition among the advanced nations for resources. Japan's activities have already begun to produce friction with the United States. Although American direct foreign investments outstanding in 1972 amounted to $128.4 billion, while foreign investment in the United States was only $17.4 billion (of which less than $1 billion was Japanese), Americans were already wildly criticizing Japanese investments in Hawaii (invariably the criticism is directed to the buyer and not the seller). In October 1974, the Mitsui Mining Company decided to abandon efforts to import strip-mined coal from Montana because of the public criticism its preliminary activities had aroused.[23] No doubt part of the problem in these cases is not economic but cultural: Americans are unaware of the size of the United States' investments abroad, and the Japanese tend to move too fast and to reserve the facilities acquired by direct investment for exclusive use by Japanese nationals, an affront to Americans as well as a violation of American laws. In January 1974, Prime Minister Tanaka heard heated criticism of Japan in Bangkok and Jakarta on the same score.

If the advanced industrial powers are unable to coordinate their activities and to cooperate with each other, overseas direct investment appears likely to become, during the last quarter of the twentieth century, the functional equivalent of nineteenth century imperialism and colonialism. Like the other democratic nations, but in a more acute form, the Japanese face several dilemmas in this area. Firstly, the Japanese government does not possess total control over the overseas activities of independent Japanese firms (although it may have more control than the U.S. government does over American multinationals). Secondly, if the Japanese refrain from direct investment they face the danger of being preempted in desirable areas by competitors in North America or the EEC. Thirdly, the Japanese cannot decide whether to reduce their strong holdings in places such as Taiwan and the Republic of Korea in order to try to gain a foothold in larger but politically dubious markets such as mainland China or the Soviet Union, or to hold on to what they have until the true dimensions of the threat of economic nationalism become clearer. Fourthly and finally, the

Japanese want to participate in multilateral agreements for allocation of resources and orderly commerce, but they do not fully trust their allies in the United States and western Europe to take into account Japan's needs, nor do they fully trust their own diplomatic abilities in order to overcome this potential danger. A kind of "Gaullist" thinking, if not Gaullist policies, is just under the surface in Japan.

Overseas direct investment is not and need not be entirely a source of nationalistic competition and friction. It is of direct advantage to the under-developed nations, probably of greater value than grant aid. "One point to note," writes Japan's Ministry of International Trade and Industry, "with respect to resource development is the rising demand of resource-holding countries for local processing industries. For this reason, resource development investments of Japanese enterprises will probably shift from the mere purchase of ores through loan extension and the single-unit acquisition of mining rights to a systematic resource development investment form which incorporates all activities from digging to processing."[24] At the same time, unchecked competition among the industrialized nations for overseas resources is probably the surest way to elicit the full-blown economic nationalism that Secretary of State Kissinger warned against in his 1974 UN General Assembly speech. It should also be noted that the American people, who are not particularly attuned to international commerce and who operate one of the major resource exporting economies of the world, are as susceptible to economic nationalism as any Third World nation. Education and political leadership can contain this tendency, but the only long-range solution to this problem, vitally necessary for the transition period to new energy and energy-conserving industrial structures, is international consultative and regulatory institutions comparable to the IMF and the GATT.

Technology

The role of imported technology in Japan's economic growth has already been discussed. What the Japanese mean when they refer to a technology barrier is that they are too dependent on imported technology, that the access to foreign technology is becoming more difficult, and that the price is rising. In the long run, Japan must develop a self-sustaining R&D capacity and become a technology exporter. Current figures reveal both the progress that Japan has made and the distance it has yet to go. During FY 1972, Japanese technology exports increased by 55 percent over the previous year, although imports remained almost four times as valuable while growing by only 29 percent. During 1972 the United States and Great Britain exported more technology than they imported, while West Germany and France were in the red on this account, although much less so than Japan. Of Japan's technology exports, 48 percent were to Southeast Asia, 24 percent to Western Europe, and 14 percent to North America. Chemical technologies represented a preponderant 39 percent, followed by electrical machinery (13 percent) and iron- and steel-making processes (10 percent).

Japan is moving ahead rapidly in this field, but the demand for technological innovation is probably increasing more rapidly. Japan's governmental and industrial spending for technological research and development rose 17 percent during FY 1972, to ¥1,800,000 million, while the number of researchers increased by 13 percent, to 280,000. However, the outlay per researcher of ¥8,370,000 was markedly less than Great Britain's ¥21,400,000, or France's ¥18,500,000, or the United States' ¥17,400,000.[25]

The Market Barrier

The market barrier is the most political of the five critical problem areas, but requires the least explanation. It refers to the international commercial environment and specifically to the degree of access Japan can obtain for its products in the various markets of the world. Japan's big market in Southeast Asia remains relatively secure despite anti-Japanese demonstrations in the area during 1974 and the collapse of resistance to communism in Indochina during 1975. In addition, three other markets require some discussion—those of the United States, the EEC, and the Communist countries.

Japan's difficulties in its major market, the United States, appear to have lessened since the highly political textile dispute of the early 1970s.[26] The situation is not, however, tranquil. So-called "voluntary" import control agreements demanded by the United States from Japan still irritate the Japanese, and, more importantly, they aggravate another aspect of Japanese economic practice that bothers the Americans—namely, the seemingly excessive Japanese governmental intervention in economic affairs. This is because import agreements imply export cartels in the exporting country, since some agency has to allocate the export shares among manufacturers up to the agreed level of exports to the American market. It is the Ministry of International Trade and Industry that performs this task in Japan. Rather than restricting imports directly, the United States requires that the Japanese government restrict exports, which preserves the reputation of the United States as a free trader while worsening that of Japan.

During 1973 and 1974, Japan corrected its previously unbalanced trade with the United States more than any other American ally, largely through direct investment in the United States. This had the effect of draining down Japan's enormous dollar reserves of a few years ago, as demanded by the American government, but it also provoked a different kind of American protest, as we saw earlier in the case of Hawaii. Nevertheless, it does appear as though the dangers of utilizing these disputes for domestic political advantage in either country have been recognized and heeded.

Japan's attempts to diversify its markets away from the United States have not been as successful. European countries, particularly France and Italy, continue to discriminate against products from Asia, including those of Japan, and there seems no doubt that the European restraints on Japanese imports have been one of the major causes of the strong Japanese emphasis on market development in the United States. Another major problem affecting trade between all the advanced industrial democracies is nontariff barriers. These include discrimination in governmental purchases, export subsidies and unfair government aids to domestic firms, tax devices which favor exports and limit imports, unusual taxes and fees on the administration of international commerce, standards and specifications favorable to domestic producers' products, state trading, import quotas, and discriminatory business "cultures" in the areas of ownership, licensing, distribution, and so forth. All the major trading powers utilize some of these barriers, but the Japanese have gotten the reputation for being the most serious offenders, and this reputation is used as an excuse in Western Europe to retaliate against Japanese products. There is ample need for continuing multilateral negotiations among the leading trading nations of the world in order to establish rules concerning these barriers, as much as to lower tariffs.

Japan has also given attention to diversification of its markets in favor of the Communist world. A major part of the domestic political support in Japan for Tanaka's recognition of the Chinese People's Republic on September 29, 1972 came from the business community, particularly from the so-called Kansai *zaikai* (i.e., the trade and industrial interests of the Osaka and Kobe areas). They believed that the China market was about to open up decisively and wanted to be in the forefront of nations gaining access to it. However, even though trade with the mainland doubled following diplomatic recognition, trade with Taiwan (with which Japan had to break relations) also doubled and is more valuable in absolute terms than trade with Communist China. The Japanese have made themselves very unpopular in Taiwan, and, because of an insulting remark by the Japanese foreign minister about Taiwan, Japan Air Lines was prohibited from landing in Taipei from mid-1974 to mid-1975, cutting off the airline's single most lucrative route.

Japanese-mainland trade has not expanded as much as the Japanese government and press led the public to believe that it would at the time of recognition, and the government has become politically vulnerable on the issue of China policy. Since Japan's China trade is unlikely to become *very* large until China begins to have more foreign exchange available to spend (probably through oil exports) and until China decides that it wants to engage more fully in international commerce, Japan's enthusiasm for China is likely to wane. It can therefore be expected that Japan will attempt to improve its relations with Taiwan, one of the fastest growing economies in the world, since it has a proven and reliable market there. This is a particular consideration in Japan in light of the current international economic uncertainty. Japan's dreams of rapid expansion into eastern Siberia have also become more sober, due to the easily predictable but nevertheless ignored difficulties of negotiating fair and trustworthy agreements with the Soviet Union. The Chinese and Soviet markets remain attractively large, but their actual development depends on unpredictable factors which the Japanese are unable to control.

One thing the Japanese are able to control is their own economy, and there, in addition to the piecemeal solutions to the particular problems already mentioned, the Japanese are also undertaking a comprehensive solution to all of their current problems through a fundamental, structural change of the economy. A word of preface is necessary before examining this ambitious plan. As we saw earlier in our discussion of Japan's postwar economic growth, Japan has probably had more experience than any other advanced industrial society with deliberate structural change of the economy. The combination of a very high-prestige bureaucracy, a homogeneous population, and a tradition of close government-civilian cooperation has given Japan a unique capability for economic planning and direction within the context of an open, market economy.

The key institution for this economic leadership is a blue-ribbon civilian consultative body—one of some 236 such legally established organs for public-private consultation and cooperation within the Japanese government—that advises the Minister of International Trade and Industry. Entitled the Industrial Structure Council (Sangyo Kozo Shingikai) and composed of the absolute top leadership of Japanese industry and finance, it studies and passes on the schemes for long-range economic planning and development that are prepared within the Industrial Structure Section of the Ministry of International Trade and Industry. It is in the work of the Industrial Structure Council and of the official bureaucratic department associated with it that one sees the strongest features of the Japanese approach to public problem solving; the magazine *Nikkei bijinesu* recently wrote that if there is such a thing as "Japan, Inc.," as some foreigners have charged, then the Industrial Structure Council is its epitome.[27]

Beginning in 1971, the Industrial Structure Council recognized that the Japanese economy could not simply continue along the lines that it had followed during the 1960s. Pollution was already a serious problem in the country, and the public was becoming increasingly disillusioned with super-fast growth of industry while other pressing needs were ignored. Therefore, in addition to numerous shorter range plans and studies, it commissioned a 173-page "1980 Vision Plan," prepared by some fifty officials of the Ministry of International Trade and Industry, which the Council adopted on May 25, 1971. This plan called for the conversion of the Japanese economic structure within a decade from one emphasizing secondary industries to one emphasizing tertiary industries. These tertiary industries were subsequently defined by the Council as "knowledge-intensive industries," of which four types appropriate for Japan were identified. These are: (1) a research-and-development type (e.g., electronic

computers, synthetic chemistry, new metals, special ceramics); (2) a sophisti-
cated-assembly type (e.g., telecommunications equipment, business machines,
industrially-made housing); (3) a fashion type (e.g., high-quality clothing and
furniture, expensive sundries); and (4) a knowledge-supplying type (e.g., data
gathering and processing services).

During the initial years of this plan little attention was given to what the
Japanese economy would actually look like in 1980. Instead, major efforts were
made to insure that Japan would possess a domestic manufacturing capability in
such fields as computers and transport aircraft, even though Japan faced severe
competition in these areas. However, as the monetary and energy crises overtook
Japan and as the Industrial Structure Section of the ministry sought to turn the
plan into policy, the "1980 Vision Plan" was transformed into a series of goals
for totally restructuring the economy by 1985. (Although the 1971 plan has
been altered almost annually since it was published, it is worth underscoring that
the Japanese adopted it before the "Nixon shocks" of 1971, before the
monetary crises of 1972, and before the oil crisis of 1973, which is a better
record of early warning about the problems of the 1970s than most other open
societies can claim.)

As of the summer of 1974, the Council makes the following assumptions for
its plan (now subject to annual reformulation): (1) the real economic growth
rate will be kept through governmental measures and guidance at 6 percent per
annum until 1980 and at 6.5 percent from 1980 to 1985; (2) the annual increase
in wholesale prices will average 7.6 percent until 1980 and 2.2 percent between
1980 and 1985; (3) consumer prices will rise by 8.5 percent annually until 1980
and 3.9 percent between 1980 and 1985; and (4) wage increases will be kept to
16 percent in 1976, 12 percent in 1977, and 10-11 percent from 1978 to 1985.

If these assumptions are fulfilled, the Japanese government in 1985 intends to
have some 53 percent of the work force engaged in tertiary industries; overseas
capital investments will have grown tenfold; the ratio of the rate of increase of
energy consumption to growth of GNP (currently 1.16) will be reduced to 0.95
by the end of 1979 and to 0.9 by 1985; the rate of increase of Japan's exports
to the growth of world exports will have fallen from the 2.2 of the 1960s to
slightly over one; and the growth rate of the nation's imports relative to the
increase of GNP will be down from the 1.32 of the 1960s to about 1.05 in 1985.
By that year a great part of Japan's heavy industry will have been relocated
overseas, and the number of employees in primary industries will have dropped
from the current 9.0 million to 5.8 million.[28]

It is not necessary to go further in detailing this plan in order to observe that
it is an ambitious, serious effort to change the very nature of the Japanese
economy. The only major criticism that the plan has aroused thus far in Japan is
that it does not contain measures to guarantee the food supply, which of course
merely reflects the appearance of the latest of the 1970s' political/economic
"crises," the global food problem. Food has now joined the pollution, energy,

and raw materials problems as a new element that the Council and its sponsoring ministry will have to build into their new plan.

If this plan is successful—and the Japanese have already once in the postwar era changed their industrial structure—it will pose certain problems for the world economy. While greatly contributing to the growth of the underdeveloped countries and improving the quality of life in Japan proper, it will increase Japan's dependence on the world economy. Interdependence in 1985 will be not just a slogan but an absolute reality, and a Japan with 50 percent of its work force in tertiary industries will be a highly internationalized country. These are goals of peace and prosperity and are much to be desired; but they emphasize the need to build during this same decade an institutional structure that will sustain the coming international interdependence.

The United States and Japan

Following Nobutaka Ike, we may conceive of Japanese foreign policy, including Japanese international economic policy, as located on and moving between the poles of a continuum that ranges from a fully internationalist position (e.g., Hong Kong, Holland) to a highly nationalist, inward-looking position (e.g., China during the 1960s).[29] Given Japan's need to trade, it is surprising that Japan for so long has been so far away from the internationalist pole. One might expect that Japan would always have been a staunch defender of free trade, minimal tariff and nontariff barriers to trade, easy access to its own market in return for Japanese access to foreign markets, and internationalist in terms of its domestic economic culture. This has not been the case, for more substantive reasons than are commonly supposed abroad, but the significant fact for the future is that Japan is in the process of decisively altering its previous stance. "One should not be surprised," write Ohkawa and Rosovsky, "if, in the coming decade, Japan assumes a most unaccustomed role as champion of free trade, while other advanced countries turn more to defensive tariffs, quotas, and other restraints."[30] This new Japanese orientation is much to be welcomed and needs to be encouraged, while the opposite trends in other advanced countries must be discouraged.

Japan, in the past, put its protectionism to a good use. Through very hard work behind governmental protectionist barriers, the Japanese developed their own country, raised their per capita GNP to one of the highest levels in the world, and created the foundations upon which they could both take care of themselves and contribute in major ways to the prosperity of other advanced and developing nations. Today Japan is entering a period in which it can make good on its potential contributions to the rest of the world; it is therefore important that Japan not be driven back into a defensive, protectionist stance by the misguided policies of its most important political and economic partners.

Japan is not "going nuclear" but rather "going internationalist" in what may prove to be one of the most important and beneficial examples in modern history of an advanced industrial nation exercising great economic power but little military power. The trend toward internationalism has been underway in Japan since at least 1967, the year in which Japan began to liberalize capital movements, and the crises of the 1970s have merely confirmed the necessity of the trend and made it irreversible, unless global tragedy intervenes. In attempting to harvest the payoffs for the rest of the world from this Japanese experiment, the United States will play a role as crucial as the one it played during the first two postwar decades in helping Japan to get to a position where it could make a contribution.

Security Relations

Let us begin by examining that aspect of Japan's future course in which its economic power is not translated into military power, the facet of Japanese policy in which the stance of the United States is most directly relevant. Japan's much heralded postwar pacifism was easier to believe during the 1950s than during the 1960s and early 1970s. During the 1950s, the commitment of the United States to maintain the global balance of power was unquestioned, and security threats to Japan other than from the Soviet Union were nonexistent. Beginning with the formal rupture of 1960 between China and the Soviet Union, however, security problems started to develop for Japan. As a result of the Sino-Soviet split, China took the decision to develop its own, independent nuclear strike capability as a means of defending itself from the Soviet Union or any other nation possessing an advanced weapons capability (including the United States) and as a means of exercising greater influence over the course of international events. After 1960, China also vastly increased its conventional munitions manufacturing capability, becoming a leading supplier of arms and ammunition to the Communist forces in the Vietnam War, whereas during the Korean War it had had itself to rely on the Soviet Union.

Although the official Japanese reaction to the Chinese nuclear weapons program was slow and guarded, the Japanese press and public began to take China much more seriously than they had in the past. China came to be seen as a potential threat—not in terms of a direct invasion but of a possible nuclear strike or nuclear blackmail. The Chinese atmospheric tests, some fifteen in number by 1974, and the resultant fallout over Japan kept the issue before the public. At no time did the Japanese government seriously consider a decision to "go nuclear" in response—for which Prime Minister Sato won the 1974 Nobel Peace Prize—but the Japanese did begin to discuss the pros and cons of an independent nuclear capability. The Japanese, for example, signed the Nuclear NonProliferation Treaty but did not ratify it. Between approximately 1969 and 1972 the

Chinese themselves reacted violently against this Japanese thinking-out-loud on defense questions, and they mounted a major propaganda campaign to denounce what they called "revived Japanese militarism." Even some American observers (although not those knowledgeable about Japan) speculated on when Japan would "go nuclear."

By 1974, it was clear that Japan had come to as firm a conclusion as is possible concerning so contingent a matter that it would continue to pursue its policy of not possessing offensive weapons of any kind. In a sense Japan has no other choice. The political barriers to rearmament are formidable: every Japanese government and political party has opposed it; no domestic consensus in favor of it exists; and the Constitution of 1947 prohibits it. (It should be noted that the Japanese do not amend their constitutions readily, neither the prewar nor postwar constitutions having ever been amended.) The Japanese know that even the appearance of rearmament, particularly given Japan's enormous industrial power, would threaten the peaceful relations that it has with its trading partners and on which Japan's current prosperity is based. Equally to the point, the Japanese can count, and they have costed out the options open to them. They understand that they cannot *guarantee* their security through military means—for example, by building a huge navy and using it to try to protect their far-flung merchant fleet and shipping lanes. They have concluded that it would be cheaper to build replacements for any losses Japan might suffer due to a lack of military might than it would be to build and maintain a navy.

This case for continued Japanese pacifism rests on political considerations, and an independent observer might object that the political environment could change very rapidly. However, even if one assumed that all of these factors had been reversed—that is, that the people and government had become united behind rearmament, that the constitution had been revised, and that considerations of international goodwill and financial cost had become secondary (none of which, let us repeat, is a realistic assumption)—then serious problems would still remain. They include: (1) Japan has no domestic source of fissionable material; (2) Japan has no test site; (3) Japan has no industrial site free from the dangers of earthquake or typhoon; and (4) Japan has no large group of militarily-oriented scientific personnel.

Even if these obstacles were overcome, Japan would still face enormous difficulties in producing a credible, minimum deterrent, second-strike nuclear capability against either China or the Soviet Union. Given both the extreme vulnerability of the main islands of Japan (28 percent of the population is concentrated in the Kanto plain around Tokyo) and the fact that Japan would need to possess a strategic rocket force capable of hitting Moscow, Leningrad, and Kiev some 6,000 miles away, Japan would have to build a satellite-borne guidance and defensive warning system and deploy at sea a ballistic-missile submarine fleet of the most advanced specifications. If Japan merely tested a nuclear device without also building the means to deliver it, Japan would only worsen its security problems. Yet that delivery system, requiring forms of advanced technology in which Japan is not proficient, would have to be second to none in the world today. Japan is a rich country, but not that rich.

The direction in which the Japanese are taking their economy will only enhance these obstacles to nuclear rearmament. By 1985, the islands of Japan will still possess roughly the same size secondary industrial base that they have today, but most of the future growth in that sector will be located abroad. Moreover, the technology required to defend an industrial nation through independent nuclear strike forces is becoming ever more complex and expensive, as the appearance of MIRVs (multiple, independently-targeted, reentry vehicles) testifies. Thus, by undertaking the structural reform of its economy in order to deal with the five barriers discussed earlier, Japan is throwing in its lot with international interdependence—which is where its desires tend, its comparative advantages lie, and, very likely, its only chances of success in maintaining its independence exist. This internationalist policy also offers the world the opportunity to utilize Japanese talents for development and prosperity rather than seeing them go into the arms race. (Japan does, of course, maintain conventional, defensive armed forces, but their main mission is to defeat a domestic insurrection fomented from abroad and to serve as a temporary blocking force in case of international attack.)

As should be obvious by now, the United States will have to continue to maintain the international balance of power if this Japanese trend toward internationalism is to continue. This means, among other things, that the United States must avoid acts and policies that deceive the rest of the world about its true strength and that create destabilizing uncertainties about its willingness to fulfill its unavoidable commitments. It will have to avoid, for example, talking about "renting the nuclear umbrella" (an idea some Americans have proposed in the past), both because the size of the American strategic forces is ultimately dictated by the requirements of the defense of the United States (a decision by the United States not to defend Japan against nuclear attack would not reduce the U.S. defense budget by one dollar) and because the renting of nuclear defense would be to share control over its use, which is unacceptable to the United States.

It goes without saying that the United States should expect from the Japanese people and press, as well as from the Japanese government, some recognition of these global realities, and that the United States cannot play its role all by itself (the idea of role, it might be noted, is a social concept; no nation occupies a status or plays a role all by itself). Conventional defensive commitments to territories such as Korea and Taiwan are subject to change and to negotiation in light of changing circumstances. But if the United States decides to "go-it-alone," or if it performs its role in the strategic balance in such a way that ambiguity rather than certainty is the norm, then it is futile to imagine that Japan, or any other comparably placed nation, is not going at least to attempt to bring order out of the resultant chaos through military deterrence. Japan's path for the rest of the century depends, *ceteris paribus*, on the other things remaining more or less equal, and it is up to the United States, tired or disillusioned with international politics though some of its people and most of its mass media commentators may be, to see that they do. It is, after all, the path that the United States outlined for Japan ever since the victory of 1945, and it is the only path that serves the interests of the United States.

Commercial-Economic Relations

A logic similar to that in the military field prevails in most other areas of Japanese-American interchange. Japanese-American commercial, technological, and resource allocation interests are compatible and, to say the least, mutually profitable; the relations on which they rest must be protected if their breakdown is not to result in major costs to both societies, including potential military costs. This is one way of saying that Japan *is* an "economic animal" and that it is a good thing that Japan is one since all the other kinds of animals Japan might become are considerably less appealing. By economic animal, we do not mean that Japan should lack for self-respect or pride, or that Japan is not making an extremely important contribution to the creative and fine arts and to the humanistic concerns of all peoples. But it is to urge that the role of economic animal is the right and challenging one for Japan, as distinct from the possibilities of it turning into a military animal, an ideological animal, a revolutionary animal, a starving animal, or a racist animal, each of which is all too frequently encountered in the world today. It is to Japan's everlasting credit that it has used its energies to build a powerful and expansive civilian economy, and it is to be hoped that Japan will be allowed to continue to develop in the more open, internationalist direction that its leaders have chosen.

Some of the problems associated with the Japanese economy in the past will subside over the coming decade. As Japan's ratios of the growth of exports and imports to the rate of growth of global exports and imports equalize, Japan will be able to maintain equilibrium in its international accounts without resorting to feverish export promotion campaigns. At the same time, the level of living of those nations that trade with Japan should rise steadily, and their domestic economies will not be subject to the dangerous political side effects that can accompany trade with closed societies, such as mainland China or the Soviet Union. Japan and the United States already occupy very strategic positions in each other's standards of living—Americans like Japanese electronics, automobiles, and other products, while Japan is the world's largest purchaser of United States' agricultural produce.

Policy Recommendations

What do these considerations mean for United States policy? They draw attention to the dangers of the United States' continuing to flirt with the possibilities of autarky and isolationism while Japan and other nations take the road to international interdependence. The United States must come to see itself as part of an international division of labor, as part of a system in which the maintenance of Japan's or any other ally's place is as important as its own because all are dependent upon each other.

Concretely, this means the fostering of a much greater degree of international economic consciousness in the United States than currently exists—a consciousness perhaps equivalent to the international political consciousness that prevailed during the 1940s and 1950s. Americans need to become aware of the size of the United States investment in other parts of the world; they might then become less hostile when America's trading partners invest in the United States. Americans need to become aware that whereas American investment has created millions of jobs in other countries, foreign investment in the United States creates jobs here, as well as creating purchasing power abroad with which to buy American products. Americans need to become aware of the demands of international marketing—with the fact, for example, that Japanese have lived for years with brand names such as Panasonic and National because these very un-Japanese names made their products more salable in the United States. Americans need to become aware, in short, that the alternative to developing an international economic consciousness is to develop a "fortress America" consciousness, and that such a fortress, even if it could survive, is going to create a much more pinched existence than Americans have become accustomed to or than is available.

Many specific goals and policies are required of the United States if it is to fulfill its part in maintaining and bringing to full realization the potentialities of the Japanese-American relationship. The following is a partial list of those that seem most clearly indicated.

1. Fundamental to any discussion of the future of Japanese-American relations is the assumption that the United States economy will remain strong. Nothing would be more salutary for the economic health of the rest of the world than a determination by the American people and government to live within balanced budgets, to restore faith in work (as contrasted with pressure group activities in order to win benefits from the bureaucracy) as the basis of value, and to guarantee equity through genuine tax reform. Inflation, it hardly needs saying, must be controlled.

2. Technological innovation is the only certain means of overcoming the resources problem (including that of oil), as well as relieving many other problems such as pollution. This technological development will require enor-

mous investments, which can only come from government, perhaps on an international scale. With luck and cooperation the world can live with the oil cartel until 1985, which should be the target date to begin to bring new energy technologies on line. However, the investments are needed now, and the United States must take the lead in supplying them. Japan will cooperate, by reducing its own energy requirements and investing in domestic technological research, but it will be unable alone to produce the energy saving and new energy technologies that must come into use before the end of the century.

3. Many of the disputes that have arisen in Japanese-American relations, as well as in relations between the United States and its other allies, have a basis in inadequate information, misinformation, or biased information. Today the United States needs to develop an investigatory and analytic monitoring system on the politics and economics of the advanced industrial democracies that is at least comparable to the system it deployed during the cold war for studying Russian and Chinese societies. It is simply intolerable that American policy toward Japan, in the absence of a cadre of genuine authorities on the country and on the types of problems it faces today, should be influenced either by special interests using Japan as a scapegoat for their own failures or by "friends" of Japan who are unable to make the informed criticisms of specific Japanese activities that are occasionally required. Americans are not well-informed about Japan or about the problems of societies like Japan; in order to change this situation a lead must be taken by government, academic institutions, and foundations to bring American research up to par. Too many educated Americans sensitive to international politics know more about the Communist parties of Russia and China than they do about the economic bureaucracies or legal systems of countries such as Japan or France. A reorientation of American international social science research toward the advanced industrial democracies rather than toward the totalitarian or developing nations would also, perhaps, help correct the inescapable impulse of the mass media toward sensationalism and crisis mongering.

4. The kinds of measures that will be implemented over the coming generation to deal with the five barriers discussed in this chapter and to manage the emerging system of international interdependence will unquestionably give rise to more official bureaucracy. It would be wise to recognize this fact at the outset and to face directly the general and the specifically national characteristics of official bureaucracies—such things as the tendencies of bureaucracies to proliferate, to maintain themselves after their function has ended, to form mutually beneficial alliances with politicians, to compete with each other, and to lose sight at any particular time of both what they ought to be doing and what they actually are doing. Japan, as well as most other American allies, already relies on bureaucracy more than the United States does—or, in any case, is more explicit about its reliance. There are things that the United States could learn from Japan, such as the strengths and weaknesses of its highly developed system

of civilian consultative bodies like the Industrial Structure Council, which both work with and check the official bureaucracy. Monitoring and comparative study of the open industrial societies should have benefits for the United States in drawing attention in advance to the unintended political and administrative consequences of substantive American policies for the new era.

America and Japan After the Collapse of Indochina

Long-range forecasting is notoriously easier than short-range forecasting. Our analysis of the critical choices facing Japan and the United States has stressed in the main a longer-range perspective—i.e., the problems of 1985 and beyond. But the comparatively optimistic vision of the 1980s presented here could be aborted by short-range developments. The most important of these, demanding discussion even though it risks being overtaken by events, are the effects of the Communist victories in Vietnam, Cambodia, and Laos.

In an important sense the Communist conquest of Indochina is meaningless: it will become meaningful only as the United States, its allies, and the Communist nations give it precise meanings. Some analysts believe that the Vietnam War may prove, by its impact on the United States and the world, to have been the decisive war of the century. Certainly if it results in the Americans acquiescing in their own strategic surrender to the Soviet Union, it will deserve to be so regarded.[31] A fundamental alteration in the role played by the United States in the global balance of power will affect Japan as profoundly as any other nation or region in the world. Our analysis of the Japanese problem and its most advantageous resolution for all parties depends upon the Vietnam War having only a minimal and passing effect on international politics. We are unable to predict how significant Vietnam will appear from the vantage point of the year 1985, but we are able to draw up a balance sheet of short- and long-range, positive and negative, contingencies that the Vietnam debacle generated during the year 1975.

The Short-Term Prospects

On the positive side, the ending of the Vietnamese war for the United States offered certain desirable "liquidation effects." There can be no question but that the American public was confused and discouraged by a situation in which the country had spent over $125 billion and had sent an expeditionary force of over half a million men and yet could not obtain a favorable result. The liquidation of the Vietnamese involvement freed the United States from an expensive, highly divisive, operation and thereby initiated a general rationalization of American international commitments. Americans do not feel that they can be fairly charged with "abandoning" Vietnam. Instead, they tried in the most obvious and costly ways to save Vietnam. When it became obvious that they did not know how to do so, it was only sensible to cut their losses and to liquidate the venture.

These short-run liquidation effects may cause Americans—and Japanese—to ask some vital questions. Why did the United States fail, given the size of its commitment? What was wrong with the military strategy? Did American political leadership blunt the effectiveness of military actions? Why were allies of the United States, such as Japan, so reluctant publicly to support American actions in Vietnam—particularly when some of them, such as Japan, were the only nations to profit from the war? Did the American domestic antiwar movement encourage North Vietnam to fight on rather than negotiate? These questions must be asked and answered if the United States, and the nations dependent for their security on the United States, are to avoid repeating the mistakes of Vietnam.

In a basic sense, the collapse in Vietnam has had the desirable effect of stimulating nations allied with the United States to do more to help themselves. One lesson of the Vietnam War was that when the United States actually gets involved in the fighting in order to preserve the independence of an allied nation, the allied nation may let down its own efforts. Although both North and South Vietnam were supplied with military equipment, from China and Russia on the one hand and from the United States on the other, the North Vietnamese did their own fighting. Partly this was because North Vietnam was on the offensive, whereas the other side always feared that an invasion of North Vietnam might provoke Chinese or Russian intervention. However, in light of the Vietnam precedent, many threatened nations, including Japan, are looking to their own preparedness—in the general context of United States assistance—in case a security threat should arise. This is a highly desirable outcome, because there seemed to have developed among the people of South Vietnam, as also appears true of Japan and Western Europe, a feeling that they could safely leave their defense to the United States.

Another positive factor is the "demonstration effect" of the fall of Indochina. A good deal of learning is taking place around the world from the events of the spring of 1975 in Indochina, and much of the propaganda and commentary about the Vietnam War is being put to the test. Critics of the allied war effort, for example, have argued for years that the common man in South Vietnam would welcome a Communist victory because the Communists were actually "nationalists." Yet in the final days of the defense of the south, the world witnessed one of the greatest refugee flows, in per capita terms, of modern history—and one that was entirely away from Communist-held territories. It has been said that these refugees were merely fleeing the war, despite the fact that all of the major cities of South Vietnam fell with hardly a shot being fired, but in any case, none of the refugees moved into Communist-controlled areas, even if they were trying to avoid the fighting that did exist. This movement of refugees has yet to be satisfactorily explained.

Similarly, the fall and subsequent forcible depopulation of the city of Phnom Penh raised major doubts about the accuracy of the picture of the Khmer Rouge given to the citizens of the United States and Japan by their governments (including congressmen and Diet members) and by the mass media. Again, the overwhelming presence of North Vietnamese troops and political leaders in Saigon after its fall suggests the possibility that the Provisional Revolutionary government—the so-called Viet Cong of the south—was primarily a front organization of Hanoi's and that the indigenous basis for revolt in the south was seriously exaggerated.[32] These questions have more than mere historical significance.

The fall of Vietnam ought to subject much of the cant in America and Japan to the test of accuracy, and in a democracy it is always desirable to expose error or hypocrisy wherever it may exist in public life—in government, in the universities, or in the press. The issue of the kind of society that the allies ought to defend, for example, may well be debated during the later half of the 1970s. During the Vietnam War, it was commonly urged that the former government of Nguyen Van Thieu was repressive and lacked popular support. It was said that South Vietnam was a corrupt, divided, open society, unable to organize itself for defense against the committed northerners. Yet no one doubts that an opposition to President Thieu existed in South Vietnam throughout his period of rule, which was not true of the north. Moreover, in the former South Vietnam a person could practice the religion he or she wanted to (Buddhist, Catholic, Hoa Hao, and so forth), could read more or less what he wanted to, had around half-a-dozen newspapers to choose from, could attend a university of his choice, and could obtain a passport and go abroad. None of this is true in any of the Communist-dominated countries.

"Openness" of a society, like democracy, is a matter of degree and of political culture. Nations such as South Vietnam, the Republic of Korea, the Philippines, and others are not as open as the United States or Japan, but they are infinitely more open than their Communist opponents. The fall of South Vietnam "demonstrated" these truths again; if this demonstration should reawaken allied interest in the moral basis of democratic foreign policy, the fall of Vietnam will have had one positive effect.

On the negative side of the balance sheet, there are both short- and long-term effects, although so far in both instances the effects have taken the form of serious possibilities rather than actualities. Whether these possibilities will become reality depends on how Americans, allies, and Communists define the meaning of the fall of Indochina and the actions that they take in light of such definitions.

The short-term negative effects can be grouped into three broad categories: the problem of overseas bases, challenges to American credibility by Communist nations, and doubts among allied nations about American willingness to meet its treaty commitments. The basing problems are obvious. With the collapse of South Vietnam and the subsequent initiatives by Thailand and the Philippines to move closer to the Chinese People's Republic, the United States has been presented with a series of new difficulties in meeting its remaining treaty commitments to Korea and Taiwan and in projecting an American naval presence into the Indian Ocean and Persian Gulf areas. Under the terms of the Japan-U.S. Security Treaty, the United States is not permitted to use its mainland Japanese or Okinawan bases for general area or global security purposes. If the Philippine bases are closed or become politically unusable, the maintenance of an American presence in the Western Pacific region will become technically and economically much more difficult.

So far the most significant Communist test of American credibility since the defeat of South Vietnam has been the visit of North Korean leader Kim Il-sung to Peking. It was clearly no accident that this visit, Kim's first to China in almost fifteen years, occurred just at the time of the celebrations of the Communist victories in Indochina. Following Kim's visit, a worried Japan launched a major debate over defense policy and sent its foreign minister and prime minister to Washington to consult with American leaders on the Korean situation. In Korea itself, both sides accused the other of preparing to violate the truce. There seems no doubt that discussions took place in Communist capitals about the possibility that the period following America's humiliation in Vietnam offered the most propitious circumstances since the cease-fire of 1953 for reopening the Communist campaign to unify Korea.

A third short-term effect of the Indochina collapse was the open questioning by other nations of the willingness of the United States to meet its treaty commitments. This questioning came about because the United States did not simply decide that it had had enough in Indochina and withdraw; the United States also negotiated an agreement with North Vietnam—the Paris Agreements of January 1973—which it then allowed the North Vietnamese to violate flagrantly and with impunity. If the United States was willing to allow this agreement to be turned into a sham, would it live up to its other agreements and treaties? The revelations that former President Nixon assured President Thieu of American aid if the agreements were violated only worsened this situation. The whole area of treaty commitments was further confused by the existence of the War Powers Act of 1973, which puts a time limit on the American president's powers to act unless he obtains the consent of Congress. Some allied leaders said privately that the American president's word was good only for sixty days. Although the president and the secretary of state sought to reassure allied nations of American readiness to meet all treaty commitments, the situation cannot be resolved until a test actually occurs.

Long-Term Implications

The longer term negative possibilities are much more important than these immediate effects. They revolve, above all, around the question of why the United States allowed the Communists to win in Indochina. Was it solely because the Americans decided to liquidate a costly and seemingly futile venture? Or was it perhaps because of some deeper malaise? At the time of the collapse in Vietnam, Secretary of Defense James Schlesinger observed that the Indochinese peninsula was only of marginal importance strategically to the security of the United States or of its main allies. By contrast, the decision during the early 1960s of Fidel Castro to ally Cuba with the Soviet Union was of much greater *strategic* importance to the United States than the fall of Indochina to communism. However, the differences between the two situations point to the very real long-range danger posed by the way the Vietnamese War ended.

Cuba, although a threat to the United States, was never regarded as having an impact on the world balance of power; its movement into the Soviet orbit had no effect at all on American preparedness or on the credibility of American alliances. Vietnam, by contrast, although of much less strategic importance than Cuba, perhaps ought to be understood as one *symptom* of a more general deterioration in the United States. Seen as an isolated event, Vietnam is only an American mistake; seen in the context of many other problems of American society, Vietnam may be a portent of things to come.

Elements of the contextual background include: (1) the failure of the United States for a full eighteen months after the Organization of Petroleum Exporting Countries (OPEC) oil embargo to formulate and implement an energy conservation policy for itself and its allies; (2) deep divisions in American society over Watergate, combined with the most serious inflation and depression since the 1930s, and widespread distrust of government; (3) the fact that many basic American systems—such as the criminal justice system, the public education system, and the municipal government system—appear to be crumbling and that public discussion of these issues is primarily partisan rather than diagnostic; (4) the tendency of the United States to perform its role as one of the two superpowers in the world balance of power in a highly confusing and untrustworthy manner (e.g., internal attacks on the United States' foreign intelligence services, the establishment of an expensive and untested volunteer army, unemployment among basic scientific manpower, etc.); and (5) finally, the trends toward ethnic lobbying in the area of foreign policy (Jews for Israel, Greeks against Turkey) and the emergence of neo-isolationism among sectors of the population.

In this perspective, Vietnam is not necessarily to be regarded as a serious setback for the open societies but rather as one more sign of a gradual decline into impotence of the leader of the non-Communist world. It is precisely in this sense that Soviet negotiators often speak of what they call the "correlation of forces"—by which they mean the sum total of all productive and operational systems in the Communist and non-Communist countries—and in this sense that they conclude that the Soviet Union and its satellites are slowly emerging as the dominant forces on the globe.

We are unlikely to know whether this idea of Vietnam-as-symptom is valid until it is too late. Should it prove to have some validity, however, we might then construct a possible "worst case" scenario for the future, one decidedly different from the optimistic vision presented earlier. It would run something like this.

First, nuclear proliferation would run rampant, with atomic weapons being acquired by nations such as Japan, Algeria, Argentina, Brazil, Cuba, Israel, North Korea, Saudi Arabia, Uganda, and North Vietnam, none of whom, except for Japan, are signatories of the Nuclear Non-Proliferation Treaty.

Secondly, the decline of the United States as a superpower might lead to a Sino-Soviet war or, more likely, to some kind of a Sino-Soviet *modus vivendi.* China's main reason, in 1971, for changing its policy toward the United States was to promote the role of the United States as a counterweight to the Soviet Union. To the extent that the United States is unable or unwilling to perform this role, China may be forced to accommodate itself to Soviet power. The ending of the Sino-Soviet dispute would release almost fifty Soviet divisions, one-third of the Soviet army, now stationed along the Chinese border for redeployment.

Thirdly, the clear emergence of the Soviet Union as the predominant power in the globe would result in the so-called "Finlandization" of Western Europe, by which is meant the subordination of these nations to Soviet leadership in all foreign policy matters. Such a development would probably be the final shock that would awaken the American people to their peril. At such time the Americans would most likely call for a strong government to rearm and to prepare the United States in order to try to reverse the trends running in favor of the Soviet Union. It is precisely at such a time that the danger of global thermonuclear war would be most acute. The Soviet Union would see itself as clearly superior but with its situation deteriorating every day that it allowed the United States to proceed with its remobilization. It might conclude that a preemptive strike would be less risky than the war that it would conclude the United States was preparing to fight.

It should be repeated that this is a "most worst" case; the very fact that it can be identified is good evidence that it is unlikely to occur. Nonetheless, this line of reasoning or a variation on it was being discussed in cabinets and ministries of defense and foreign affairs around the world during the months following the surrender of Saigon. If it is not to be realized as anything more than "most worst" speculation, there must take place a higher level of debate on foreign policy in the United States than existed during the late 1960s and early 1970s, and there must emerge from that debate a new, widely supported, and firmly implemented United States foreign policy. This conclusion draws attention to the postulate with which we began this essay: the contingent nature of the "Japanese problem." Like the German problem of fifty years ago, although in a reverse sense, solutions to the Japanese problem are contingent upon decisions taken in foreign countries.

Notes

1. A.J.P. Taylor, *The Origins of the Second World War* (Harmondsworth, England: Penguin Books, 1964), p. 66.

2. Compare Kazushi Ohkawa and Henry Rosovsky, *Japanese Economic Growth* (Stanford, Calif.: Stanford University Press, 1973); John K. Emmerson and Leonard A. Humphreys, *Will Japan Rearm?* (Washington, D.C.: American Enterprise Institute, 1973); John K. Emmerson, *Arms, Yen, and Power: The Japanese Dilemma* (New York: Dunellen, 1971); Nobutaka Ike, *Japanese Politics: Patron-Client Democracy* (New York: Knopf, second edition, 1972); Nobutaka Ike, *Japan, The New Superstate* (San Francisco: W.H. Freeman and Co., 1973); Donald C. Hellmann, *Japan and East Asia, The New International Order* (New York: Praeger, 1972); and Chalmers Johnson, *Conspiracy at Matsukawa* (Berkeley: University of California Press, 1972).

3. For a discussion of these two economic concepts, see Charles P. Kindleberger, *American Business Abroad* (New Haven: Yale University Press, 1969), pp. 51, 94.

4. See Saburo Okita, chairman of the Japan Economic Research Center, "Japan's Economic Influence," *Japan Times*, December 19, 1973.

5. See Professor Haruo Naniwada, Waseda University, "Growth to Catastrophe," *Japan Times*, November 17, 1973.

6. Walter Laquer, in *Commentary* 56, 6 (December 1973): 47.

7. Ralf Dahrendorf, *Society and Democracy in Germany* (Garden City, N.Y.: Doubleday, 1967), p. 25.

8. Former vice-minister Yoshihisa Ojimi, in Organization for Economic Cooperation and Development, *The Industrial Policy of Japan* (Paris: OECD, 1972), p. 15.

9. Naohiro Amaya, director general, International Economic Affairs Department, International Trade Policy Bureau, Japanese Ministry of International Trade and Industry, "On Japan's Trade and Industrial Policies" (Tokyo: MITI Report JR-1 (73-2), February 1974), p. 13.

10. K. Bieda, *The Structure and Operation of the Japanese Economy* (Sydney, Australia: Wiley, 1970), p. 17.

11. *New York Times*, December 30, 1973, p. 1.

12. Kazushi Ohkawa and Henry Rosovsky, *Japanese Economic Growth*, p. 245.

13. Miyohei Shinohara, "Causes and Patterns in the Postwar Growth," *The Developing Economies* 8, 4 (December 1970): 351.

14. *Japanese Economic Growth*, pp. 39-40, 226.

15. Nobuo Noda, *How Japan Absorbed American Management Methods* (Manila: Asian Productivity Organization, 1970), p. 27.

16. Naohiro Amaya of the Ministry of International Trade and Industry, "On Japan's Trade," pp. 14-15.

17. See Chalmers Johnson, "Japan: The Year of 'Money-Power' Politics," *Asian Survey* 15, 1 (January 1975): 25-34.

18. Bureau of Public Affairs, Office of Media Services, U.S. Department of State, *News Release*, September 23, 1974, p. 5.

19. Ernst B. Haas, *Tangle of Hopes, American Commitments and World Order* (Englewood Cliffs, N.J.: Prentice-Hall, 1969), p. 285.

20. Toshio Sanuki, Waseda University, in *Japan Economic Journal*, June 25, 1974.

21. See Jonathan Power, "The New Proletariat," *Encounter*, September 1974, pp. 8-22.

22. Ministry of International Trade and Industry, *Japan's Overseas Investments* (Tokyo: MITI, September 1974), pp. 3-4.

23. "Japanese Halt Stripped-Coal Bargaining," *New York Times*, October 6, 1974, p. 1.

24. MITI, *Japan's Overseas Investments*, p. 8.

25. "Japan Lags in Technology Export," *Japan Times*, June 2, 1974.

26. See Chalmers Johnson, "The Alliance that Hangs by a Thread, or the Japanese-American Textile Dispute," *Interplay, The Magazine of International Affairs* 3, 11 (August 1970) 11-15.

27. *Nikkei bijinesu*, July 26, 1971, pp. 68-70.

28. See Japanese Ministry of International Trade and Industry, *Direction for Japan's Industrial Structure* (Tokyo: MITI Report NR-36 (74-51), October 8, 1974), plus statistical appendix; *Mainichi Daily News*, June 30, 1974; *Mainichi shimbun*, editorial, July 2, 1974; *Japan Times*, July 11, 1974 and September 14, 1974.

29. Ike, *Japan, The New Superstate*, pp. 100-103.

30. Ohkawa and Rosovsky, *Japanese Economic Growth*, p. 249.

31. Cf. Sir Robert Thompson, *Peace Is Not at Hand* (London: Chatto and Windus, 1974); and the commentary of Alexander Solzhenitsyn in the *New York Times*, June 22, 1975, p. E15.

32. On Communist strategy in Vietnam, see Chalmers Johnson, *Autopsy on People's War* (Berkeley and Los Angeles: University of California, 1973).

IV

Japan and the United States: Bilateral Tensions and Multilateral Issues in the Economic Relationship

Gary Saxonhouse and **Hugh Patrick**

Introduction

Viewed in broad historical perspective, the growth of the Japanese economy to its present large size must be considered one of the most remarkable and fundamentally significant economic transformations of the postwar era. In the twenty-five years since the onset of the Korean War, Japanese per capita income has increased from $150, a sum characteristic of many Third World countries to Western European levels. It is already some years since anyone needed to be reminded that Japan is the non-Communist's world second largest economy although, of course, it is still far behind the United States. While international comparisons are now more precarious than before because of the recent, distortions created by relative price changes, inflation and recession, Table IV-1 does provide helpful albeit crude indicators.

As a consequence of its growth, it is now widely recognized that Japan can no longer enjoy the freedoms of nor be subjected to the constraints imposed on a relatively small economy. Nations which possess small economies have little influence on the determination and operation of the international economic system; they must, instead, formulate policies which enable them to work within that system. At the same time, a smaller nation has more freedom than a larger one; it can adopt trade policies without fear of reaction from the major participants in the international economic system, unless it is a major supplier of a needed commodity. While Japan may have appeared economically insignificant to the United States, even in the 1960s, its present size makes it an important

Table IV-1
Growth Performance of Major Industrial Nations

Country	Growth Rates[c] Real GNP[d] (computed in 1963 prices)	GNP/Capita[d]	1974 Levels ($) GNP (Bill $)[d] (1974 Prices)	GNP/Capita[d] (1974 Prices)	1974 Population (Mill. Persons)
Japan (1952-74)	8.65	7.51	437.6	3989	109.7
W. Germany[a] (1950-74)	6.63	5.74	412.5	6653	62.0
France[a] (1950-74)	5.66	4.70	298.1	5680	52.5
Italy[a] (1951-73)	5.43	4.73	133.2	2426	54.9
Canada (1950-74)	5.21	3.14	142.1	6315	22.5
Belgium[a] (1953-74)	4.24	3.89	57.3	5847	9.8
USA (1950-74)	3.43	2.06	1397.4	6595	211.9
UK[b]	2.86	2.45	169.3	3029	55.9

[a]CP1 deflator used.

[b]GDP deflator used.

[c]Growth rates are substantially reduced (by almost one percentage point for Japan) by the fact that 1974 was a year of major recession and underutilized capacity.

[d]GNP (current prices, Exchange Rates, and Population):
   IMF, *International Financial Statistics, 1972 Supplement*
   IMF, *International Financial Statistics, 1965-6 Supplement*
   IMF, *International Financial Statistics*, January 1976.

Sources: GNP Deflators: OECD, *Main Economic Indicators, Historical Series 1955-71*, and *Historical Series 1955-71, Main Economic Indicators*, May 1975. Trends were extrapolated backwards for early year deflators. Deflators for 1974 calculated by conversion from 1970 price base.

factor in shaping the world economic environment. Accordingly, Japan has become a major factor in the formulation of the United States' international economic policy. While Japan has and will always have to take into account American interests in its approach to multilateral issues, the United States has had and will increasingly have to continue to consider Japanese interests when it seeks to solve any global or multilateral economic issue. There will be many opportunities for mutually beneficial cooperation, but, at times different perceptions of and interests in multilateral problems will directly or indirectly serve as a source of friction between the two countries. Whether the United States and Japan agree or disagree, their policies will have very important direct economic impact upon each other. These basic truths hold despite the topsy-turvey events of the past five years.

The Bilateral American-Japanese Economic Relationship

Ironically, just as the dawn of the Japanese Century was being proclaimed, and just as detailed thirty-year projections of the Japanese domestic and external economic accounts, fraught with ominous portents for the bilateral relationship between the United States and Japan and for the organization of the world economy, were coming into fashion, the October 1973 Yom Kippur War broke out and a new locus of world economic power arose in the Middle East. Seemingly, the Japanese Century died aborning. The oil embargo and the subsequent quadrupling of the price of oil demonstrated a new Japan's vulnerability. Had the price and the availability of oil remained as they were before October 1973, in January 1975 Japan's gross national product would have been 10 percent higher, wholesale prices and consumer prices would have been 20 percent lower, and foreign exchange reserves would have increased by $7 billion. Whatever bilateral economic issues may have seemed important now appear swamped by the more fundamental concerns of developing new institutions to cope with the new economic power of the Organization of Petroleum Exporting Countries (OPEC) and, to a lesser extent, the "Group of 77," the organization which represents more than one hundred developing countries.

Economic wisdom, at least since the eighteenth century, has stressed that international commercial and financial relations are best viewed in a multilateral context. It is thus easy to applaud the submerging of bilateral American-Japanese economic issues. Nonetheless, the history of pre-1973 international economic relations should not be neglected. A large number of Japanese-American economic difficulties during the latter 1960s and early 1970s were attributable to conditions which were systemic, i.e., inherent in the nature of the international economic system. However, the close structural economic intimacy of the American and Japanese economies tended to result in viewing these systemic problems politically and in terms of bilateral relations. It will be argued in this essay that in the absence of major and highly unlikely systemic changes, the intimacy and structural interrelations which spawned this bilateral perspective are unlikely to be altered during the last quarter of this century. Consequently, it is probable that there will be periods of renewed political friction reflecting the problems of the economic relations between the two countries. The vital interests of the American polity and economy require a sensitive appreciation of the potentiality for tension as well as an awareness of the benefits to be derived from bilateral economic activities.

The remainder of the chapter is divided into three sections. First, a postwar history is provided, primarily in terms of the evolving American perceptions of its economic interests vis-à-vis those of Japan. In the second section, the prospects of Japanese growth in the coming decade becoming a basis of continuing bilateral tension is discussed. The final, and major section, analyzes the future contours of the American-Japanese relationship in a global context, and emphasizes the critical choices that Americans confront in their economic policy towards Japan.

The Evolving Perception of American Interests Vis-à-vis the Japanese Economy

Special Treatment for Japan: End of War-Early 1960s

Because the transformation of the Japanese economy has been so profound in the postwar period, Japanese-American economic relations have, of necessity, undergone a process of continuous and fundamental alteration. From the late 1940s until the early 1960s, American interests vis-à-vis the Japanese were defined largely by the cold war and America's policy of containment. The early American goals of the Occupation, the reform and democratization of the Japanese economic system, had by 1949 been replaced by policies aimed at simply reconstructing and strengthening Japan's economy. A fully recovered Japan was seen as one of the vital building blocks in the newly envisioned American East Asian security system. To this end, American policymakers were prepared to accord Japan special treatment in the American-sponsored postwar economic system. Japan was allowed to restrict severely imports in order to improve its balance-of-payments position and, at the same time, to retain the American market.

During the 1950s strenuous efforts were made to encourage Western Europe to accept commercial and financial policies consistent with a liberal international system. No comparable pressure was exerted on Japan at that time, partially because it was recognized that Japan was relatively less developed. Thus, Japan was allowed to be laggard in assuming the responsibilities of participation in the economic system, while receiving many of the benefits which accrued to fully responsible participants. At the same time that the Japanese government was using the economic controls inherited from the Pacific war and the subsequent American occupation to screen out all but essential, noncompetitive imports and virtually all foreign investment, Japanese businessmen were allowed virtually free access to the enormous American market, with the important exception of cotton textiles.

There should be no misunderstanding that the primacy of political goals in America's foreign policy was such that Japan was given total freedom from economic responsibilities. During the 1950s and into the 1960s, the Japanese economy was neither large enough nor sufficiently technologically sophisticated to be of interest to American policymakers and businessmen, since it was not a large market for American goods and did not seriously threaten the viability of large sectors of American industry.

The attitude of European policymakers towards the Japanese economy was very different. The European economy was much less strong than that of the United States; its major industries had suffered directly from Japanese competition in the 1930s; its technological superiority over Japan was less; its resource endowment was rather similar to Japan's; and its foreign policy interests in Japan were minimal. Rather than according Japan special privileges because of its semi-developed status and strategic position in East Asia, European policymakers were reluctant to allow unrestrained Japanese participation in the international economic system—especially in view of Japan's continued reluctance to enter such a system on the same basis as the United States and Europe. Thus it was not until 1955 that, under American sponsorship, Japan was allowed to enter the General Agreement on Tariffs and Trade (GATT). Japan's entry caused Europe and other nations (comprising a third of world trade) to invoke Article 35 under which special restrictions on imports from Japan could be maintained. As late as 1960 when trade among the nations of Western Europe and the United States had been substantially liberalized, Japanese goods remained subject to considerable discrimination. For example, of the 1,097 products classified by the standard Brussels Tariff Nomenclature, France had quotas on 357 products of Japanese origin, Italy on 228, and West Germany on 34.

Transition to the Responsibilities of Economic Power: Early
1960s-1972

By the late 1950s and early 1960s, the Japanese economy was clearly well out of the reconstruction and recovery phase. In 1958, Japan recorded its first postwar commodity trade surplus. At first, such surpluses were purely cyclical phenomena, but from 1965 they became a structural feature of Japan's external economic relations. Shortly thereafter, Japan's increasing competitiveness came to be reflected in substantial, and soon overwhelming, balance of payments surpluses.

Japan's gradual improvement in its global balance of payments was reflected also in its bilateral economic relationship. Until 1965 the United States had a persistent, though diminishing, trade surplus with Japan. Thereafter the pattern was reversed, and Japan's trade and current account surpluses with the United States became a structural feature of the Japanese balance of payments (see Table IV-2).

The increasing strength of the Japanese economy provoked a gradual, but sharp shift in official American attitudes: they changed from benign tolerance of

Table IV-2
United States-Japan Bilateral Trade, Trade and Current Account Balances 1953-74, and 1975 First Two Quarters
($US million)

Year	Japanese Commodity Exports to U.S.			Japanese Commodity Imports from U.S.			U.S.-Japan Trade Balance*	U.S.-Japan Current Account Balance
	Amount (1)	% of Japan Total Exports (2)	% of U.S. Total Imports (3)	Amount (4)	% of Japan Total Imports (5)	% of U.S. Total Exports (6)	(7)	(8)
1953	261.5	18.3	2.4	686.4	31.5		−424.9	330
4	279.0	17.3	2.7	692.7	35.3	4.6	−413.7	76
5	431.9	22.7	3.8	682.5	31.3	4.4	−250.6	264
6	557.9	22.0	4.5	997.8	33.0	5.3	−439.9	132
7	600.5	21.1	4.6	1319.3	37.9	6.4	−718.8	−209
8	666.5	24.0	5.2	986.9	34.8	5.6	−320.4	178
9	1028.7	30.3	6.9	1079.5	31.0	6.2	−50.8	383
60	1148.8	27.2	7.8	1447.2	34.6	7.1	−298.4	50
1	1054.8	25.2	7.3	1837.3	36.1	8.9	−782.5	−480
2	1358.0	28.5	8.4	1573.8	32.1	7.4	−215.8	8
3	1497.8	27.6	8.8	1843.6	30.8	8.0	−345.8	−346
4	1768.1	27.6	9.5	2009.3	29.4	7.7	−241.2	−211
5	2413.8	29.3	11.3	2080.1	29.0	7.7	333.7	365
6	2962.8	30.4	11.7	2363.5	27.9	7.9	599.3	710
7	2998.7	28.8	11.2	2695.0	27.5	8.7	303.7	280
8	4054.4	31.5	12.3	2954.3	27.1	8.7	1100.1	829
9	4888.2	31.0	13.6	3989.7	27.2	9.3	1398.5	1270
70	5875.3	30.7	14.8	4652.0	29.4	10.9	1223.3	857

1	7258.8	31.2	15.9	4054.8	25.3	9.3	3204.0	2750
2	9064.3	30.9	16.4	4941.2	24.9	10.1	4123.1	4782
3	9644.8	25.6	14.0	8311.8	24.2	11.8	1333.0	1631
4	12799.4	23.0	12.8	12682.2	20.4	13.0	117.2	1050
75:1	2626.0	19.9	10.5	3132.2	21.7	11.2	−506.2	230
:2	2552.0	18.6	11.6	2969.0	20.8	11.6	−417.0	—

*Negative figure indicates Japan in deficit. Columns 1, 3, 4, 6, 7 and 8 based on U.S. government figures; columns 2, 5 based on Japanese government figures.

Sources: U.S. Department of Commerce, Bureau of Economic Analysis, *Survey of Current Business* (1971-75 figures), various issues; *Business Statistics 1971* (1953-70 figures); Bank of Japan, Statistics Department, *Economic Statistic Annual 1975*; *Economic Statistics Monthly*, Sept. 1975.

Japan's special position in the postwar international economic system to an effort at encouraging and, in the early 1970s, virtually forcing Japan to align its external relations to the GATT, IMF, and OECD guidelines for advanced industrialized countries, and also to assume some responsibility for adjustment in its balance of payments. The motivation for this change in policy sprang partially from America's interest in preserving the legitimacy of the painfully constructed postwar international economic system. If a liberal international commercial and financial order was to be preserved, Japan had to accept fully the obligations incumbent upon a major economically advanced nation.

Perhaps more important even than these systemic concerns was the increasingly widespread belief in the United States that the continuation of special treatment for Japan within the world economic system directly threatened the health of American multinational corporations. American concern was not limited to the direct loss of sales suffered by American industry as a result of the protectionist commercial and investment policies pursued by Japan. An intimate connection was seen between the inaccessibility of the Japanese domestic market and the highly strenuous Japanese competition in the American home market.

Actually, the spectre of intense Japanese export competition in American markets had been raised a decade earlier (and even in the 1930s) in cotton textiles—from gray goods to "dollar blouses." The political power of the American textile industry was mobilized in Washington to force upon Japan "voluntary export quotas" in lieu of higher American tariffs or outright import quotas. This formula (originally worked out in the 1930s) was to haunt Japan thereafter, since "voluntary export quotas" were expanded to include a wider range of textiles, table flatware, and eventually steel, among other product categories. These, however, were not macro problems, but problems of specific American industries which were losing their comparative advantage at a time when effective competition from the Japanese was expanded rapidly. In the 1960s, consumer electronics: first radios; then monochrome television sets; and eventually even color television—were hard hit by Japanese competition. As long as both American and Japanese global balance of payments were in equilibrium, these specific industry problems were properly regarded as the inevitable consequence of evolving comparative advantage. While there were certainly problems of adjustment in declining American industries as well as associated social costs; nonetheless, the issues were seen in rather precise and narrow terms.

As Japan's bilateral trade surplus with the United States grew rapidly in the late 1960s and the early 1970s, Japanese competition was increasingly seen by many as forcing both the pace and degree of structural adjustment in a number of American industries well beyond that considered socially desirable. Labor and capital were being forced out of older, established American manufacturing industries by newly competitive Japanese industries. It was widely argued that the smooth adjustment of these resources in line with America's working comparative advantage was seriously hampered by the lack of reciprocal trade and investment opportunities for American industry in Japan. American managerial resources could not move from industries declining at home into comparable but expanding industries in Japan through foreign direct investment. Moreover, certain American industries, such as automobiles, could not protect themselves from aggressive Japanese marketing in the United States, by threatening to retaliate through investment and production in or export to the Japanese home market.

As great as was the American concern about Japan's investment and import controls, it was still greater about Japan's overall balance of payments policies. While the panoply of high tariffs, quotas, subsidies, licenses, and other regulations found in Japan's foreign sectors in the early 1950s masked a weak economy and a greatly overvalued exchange rate, the growing Japanese trade surplus, after 1965, produced large surpluses in the overall balance of payments by the late 1960s; by 1970, many realized that the yen's dollar value had to be increased. The yen's overvaluation exaggerated and was exaggerated by the Japanese government's commercial policies. There was fear that however socially desirable the pace of structural adjustment being imposed on the American economy by Japanese competition might be, the magnitude of this adjustment was beyond that dictated by comparative advantage. What was worse, however, was that the continuing overvaluation of the yen and the refusal of the Japanese government through August 1971 to alter the dollar-yen parity was seen as threatening the by-then precarious Bretton Woods international monetary system.

The American dollar was the primary financial instrument of the Bretton Woods system. As is true of the post-Bretton Woods world, transactions among central banks were cleared in dollars and the international reserves of their central banks were maintained in dollars. The special feature of the Bretton Woods system was the fixed exchange rate between the dollar and other national currencies and, as a corollary, between the dollar and gold. Given the interwar experience of national attempts to export unemployment through competitive devaluation, the rules of the Bretton Woods system were intended to limit exchange rate adjustment to times when a country had a fundamental disequilibrium in its balance of payments, i.e., when it continually bought (sold) more goods, services, and financial assets from foreigners than it sold (bought). While other nations in these circumstances were expected to change the value of their currency, the system was organized around the stability of the American dollar.

At the onset of the postwar period, the relative strength of the American economy endowed the dollar with all the requisite attributes of an international unit of account, store of value, and medium of exchange. So great was the confidence in the American economy that continuing deficits in the American balance of payments were seen, in the late 1940s and the 1950s, as a highly desirable means of adding desperately needed liquidity to the world economy.

By the 1960s, American balance of payments deficits were no longer viewed so positively by the European participants in the Bretton Woods system, although the Japanese remained sanguine, even appreciative. The deterioration of the American balance of payments position was the result of declining competitiveness in trade and strong capital outflows as well as an increasing European reluctance to finance U.S. deficits forever (especially at the time of the Vietnam War).

To some degree this undermining of the system was inherent in the efforts to encourage the economic growth of Europe, Japan, and the lesser developed countries (LDCs); while the economic power of the United States increased absolutely, it could only decline in relative terms. In part, it was also the result of the asymmetries in the operations of the Bretton Woods system which forced devaluations by countries suffering from balance of payment deficits but did not necessitate analogous appreciation by surplus countries. The system made the overvaluation of the dollar almost inevitable. From the mid-1960s, the world was increasingly awash in dollars, so much so that the dollar's traditional acceptability in international transactions was threatened. The reversal of the surplus which the United States had long enjoyed with Japan was seen by 1970 as a major element in the American deficit.

The fundamental pressures upon the Bretton Woods system, with the United States at its core, resulted in President Nixon's unilateral New Economic Program on August 15, 1971. It ended the fixed exchange rate between the dollar and other currencies, severed the dollar's formal peg to gold, and temporarily imposed a 10 percent surcharge on imports. American policy was aimed particularly at the Japanese, whose foreign economic policies and practices seemed to be the source of the difficulties. Exploring the inherent asymmetry in economic power relations between the two countries, the United States forced Japan, by the end of 1971, to appreciate the value of its currency in terms of dollars by almost 17 percent and to restrain its exports of synthetic as well as natural fiber textiles to the American market. In addition, the Japanese government was compelled to agree to liberalize restrictions on imports and foreign investment for the benefit of American industry.

Domestic Issues and Multilateral Issues Viewed Bilaterally

The perspective afforded by the passage of time since bilateral Japanese-American economic relations moved off center stage allows new insight into the nature of the difficulties during the early 1970s. Problems which were seen as deep-rooted and even cultural in origin in 1971 had largely vanished by mid-1973, even before the oil embargo had begun. The bilateral trade balance, which had earlier approached an annual rate of some $4 billion in Japan's favor, had been reduced to a surplus in annual terms of no more than $300 million by the fourth quarter of 1973. In the first quarter of 1974, this surplus became a deficit of almost $500 million.

The change in the bilateral balance was a part of the massive reversals of both the American and Japanese balance of payments. In 1971, the American basic balance was in deficit by $9.5 billion. By 1973, this deficit was approximately $1 billion. In Japan, during the same period, the basic balance shifted dramatically from a $4.6 billion surplus to a $9.9 billion deficit. As these massive shifts in trade and payment flows occurred, American protectionist sentiment weakened substantially. The highly protectionist Burke-Hartke Bill, which hovered like the Sword of Damocles over bilateral discussions in 1971 and 1972, never passed Congress. The comprehensive trade bill enacted in 1974 in preparation for the new multilateral trade negotiations, despite its potentially restrictive escape clauses, cannot be characterized as a protectionist document.

The waning of protectionist sentiment and the improvement of bilateral Japanese-American economic relations were based on more than the belief that changes in Japan's commercial and financial policies had led to the successful adjustment of trade and payments flows between the nations. Rather the broader concern about the fundamental viability and competitiveness of the American economy has diminished substantially. In 1971 and 1972, it was fashionable for union presidents and leaders of declining industries to present to the press and to congressional hearings tables with two columns purporting to show the correlation between import increases and domestic job losses. Such types of evidence, with accompanying hyperbole, were used to buttress testimony stressing the need for new legislation protecting such presumably injured domestic industries.

The upturn of the American economy, which accelerated after mid-1972 and continued throughout 1973, proved that the protectionist fears were groundless. The same, essentially domestic, forces which pulled down the aggregate unemployment rate from over 6 percent in 1971 to 4½ percent in mid-1973 also had considerable influence on those American industries which were purportedly threatened by import competition. For example, notwithstanding the continued rapid growth of imports in 1972 and 1973, employment in the United States electronic product industries reached 511,000 workers in December 1972 and, by October 1973, had hit a peak of 600,000 workers. This was fully 30 percent above the trough in 1971, when the industry had sought help from Congress. Thus, while Japanese foreign commercial and financial policies have had a small negative influence on American employment, virtually all American localities and industries, which complained about import competition in the early 1970s, were incomparably more negatively affected, insofar as profits and employment were concerned, by the anti-inflation policies of the Federal Reserve System.

Similarly, the failure of the Japanese to revalue the yen-dollar parity early enough in 1971 and in 1972 may now be viewed as a quite legitimate unwillingness on the part of the Japanese government to bear a disproportionate

share of the domestic political costs of maintaining the inherently flawed
Bretton Woods' financial system. This unwillingness was surely buoyed by the
perception that the Bretton Woods system persisted largely because the advanced industrial nations could not agree on the allocation of the benefits and
costs of creating and maintaining new international financial arrangements.

In spring 1971, the Sato government had announced that it preferred to bring
Japan's balance of payments into equilibrium through an eight-point program,
under the terms of which: import quotas and tariffs would be liberalized; a
variety of subsidies for exports would be eliminated; substantial direct and
portfolio investment would be encouraged by Japanese enterprise abroad; and
the reflation of the domestic economy would be accomplished by government
expenditures in the neglected areas of social welfare and social infrastructure.
When this program was announced in June 1971, it was greeted with considerable skepticism by American governmental officials and businessmen. They
considered the plan to be unequal to the tasks of offsetting quickly the
burgeoning Japanese current account surplus, excessive competitiveness in
American markets, rising foreign exchange reserves, and the attendant speculative pressure on the dollar.

In retrospect a case might be made that the massive monetary and demand
expansion of the Japanese economy in late 1971 and throughout 1972 (in part
an overreaction to fears of the adverse effects, including the prolongation of
recession, of any yen revaluation) and the government-encouraged massive
outflow of long-term capital from Japan alone would have eliminated Japan's
untenable balance of payments surplus. None of the recent studies of the early
impact of the 1971 and early 1973 yen revaluations suggests that the direct
effects were sufficient to cause anything like the swing from the surpluses of
1971 and 1972 to the $9.9 billion deficit in the balance of payments recorded in
1973.

In light of this, it might be argued that an unnecessary policy with potentially
serious and unwanted domestic consequences was foisted upon Japan, because
American policymakers overestimated the benefits flowing from a patched up
Bretton Woods system. While it was widely recognized that the Bretton Woods
system, built upon the primacy of the dollar and fixed exchange rates, had
resulted in an overvalued dollar which encouraged the outflow of American
long-term capital and, thereby, damaged American domestic industry, the
imperative need for fundamental reform of the system got lost in a flurry of
debate which ranged, at one extreme, from whether the American economy was
flabby and Americans should work as hard as Japanese, to the other extreme
that the world as a whole needed special protection from "Japan, Inc."

This brief review of economic relations between Japan and the United States
can hardly leave one sanguine about the future course of these relations. This
lack of optimism need not spring primarily from a sense that there still remain
unresolved major, substantive, bilateral economic issues, but rather from the

simple observation that in both Japan and the United States it is not uncommon for what are essentially domestic issues, at one extreme, or multilateral issues, at the other extreme, to take on an almost exclusively bilateral character.

Future Japanese Growth: A Source of Continued
Bilateral Tension

In the early 1970s, what were essentially multilateral problems were too often perceived as bilateral difficulties, but this was not characteristic of the public discussion of American foreign economic policy in 1974 and 1975. Major efforts have been devoted to seeking cooperation among advanced industrial nations for coping with a world in which raw materials (or at least oil) suddenly appear scarce, where national interests controlling such raw materials seem prepared to use that power to maximize their economic and political advantage; and where major international commercial and financial institutions appear unable to cope with the problems. Japanese-American relations are seen in a predominantly multilateral context in relationship to these great new difficulties. There has not been much discussion or recognition of the continuing potential for tension that exists and will continue to exist, both in the immediate and long-term future, in bilateral economic relations between the United States and Japan. Indeed, throughout 1974 and 1975 American and Japanese policymakers noted with great satisfaction the lack of outstanding and significant bilateral economic issues.

The assessment that considerable potential for tension in the bilateral economic relations between Japan and the United States will continue in the foreseeable future rests, in large measure, on the premise that Japan will continue to grow and evolve structurally more rapidly than its major trading partner, the United States. The next section presents an analysis of the future growth of the Japanese economy. In the following section, a discussion of the critical choices facing Americans in international commercial, financial, technological and natural resource policy will proceed from the perspective of the tensions as well as the opportunities inherent in American-Japanese economic relations.

Dangers of Extrapolating Past Growth Trends

The extraordinarily rapid leap of the Japanese economy from semi-development to advanced industrial status in the postwar period was achieved in many respects in a remarkably stable fashion. Between 1953 and 1973, yearly growth was almost always rapid. The growth rates in real gross national product (GNP) for the 1950s averaged 7.5 percent annually. In the 1960s, they averaged some

50 percent higher. The variance (actually the coefficient of variation) of the annual growth rates within each of these decades is lower than that of the United States. Growth was straining the full potential of the Japanese economy most of the time. Periodic slowdowns at a rate of 4-6 percent were mild and brief; rapid growth soon resumed. Quite unremarkably, this pattern of very rapid, relatively surprise free and smooth growth became part of the expectations of virtually all participants in Japan's economic life, including those whose profession it was to analyze and project Japan's performance.

Most analyses of the future performance of the Japanese economy are set in a comparative statics framework; almost exclusive attention is given to those supply factors such as capital, labor, raw materials and technology which define the growth potential of the Japanese economy. It has been common practice to examine each of these factors and to determine if, over the relevant time period, its growth and influence is likely to change. On the basis of such assessments, the projected growth rate is adjusted upward or downward (usually downward) from an initial presumption of stable growth at, say, an annual ten percent rate.

Such an approach may have been (but probably was not) adequate at one time. However, in light of Japan's economic performance in 1974 and 1975, the sole use of this approach now may well yield quite misleading conclusions. If one is making a five, ten, or twenty-five year projection of the growth rate of an economy which has expanded continuously and steadily at 10 percent a year, it may make sense to use this figure as a benchmark from which to adjust, based on a special analysis of one or another of the widely accepted determinants of that steady growth. Unhappily, in 1974, the Japanese economy did not grow at all; rather, GNP declined by 1.8 percent. And recovery in 1975 was very slow and characterized by only limited increases in output. Any projection of the long-term future growth rate of the Japanese economy must include the consequences of this enormous departure from what had come to be thought of as Japan's normal growth path. An analysis is needed which explicitly considers the actual situation of the economy at the beginning of the projection period and its interaction with the economy's changing growth potential in order to predict future economic performance.

The Japanese economic present will impinge on the Japanese economic future in a variety of ways. The Japanese economy has not completed its macroeconomic adjustment to the great international and domestic turmoil of the last three years. Japan has had the most serious recession of all the major industrial nations in terms of declining production and the development of excess capacity; output was approximately 20 percent below full capacity levels. Among the industrial countries, Japan had one of the most serious rates of inflation; the consumer price index rose 24 percent in 1974. And Japan's foreign terms of trade declined more seriously than any other major economy, except Italy. (Both Japan and Italy are more heavily dependent than others on imported oil as their primary energy source.) Only in measured rates of open unemployment did Japan do better than other countries in recession. This was the result of the special labor-management practices which generally prevailed, despite the tremendous pressure to which they were subjected.

It should be understood that Japan's poor economic performance in 1974 was the result of a policy of tight monetary and fiscal control, designed to cope with both the inflationary overhang of 1973 (the partial result of the yen reevaluation overreaction) and the new inflationary pressure and balance of trade and payments problems generated by the oil crisis. Since prices were already rising at annual rates of 20 percent in mid-1973, the governmental efforts to curb excessive aggregate demand preceded the oil crisis. These efforts did accelerate markedly, however, as aggregate supply capacity unexpectedly began to slip away during and after the Yom Kippur War.

During 1975, inflationary pressures abated markedly in Japan, and the Japanese balance of payments once more neared equilibrium. Nonetheless, until September 1975, the Japanese government persistently resisted pressure to reflate the economy fairly rapidly. The government's continuing reluctance throughout fall 1975 seemed grounded in the very real fear that the inflation, the initial causes of which were clearly excessive demand, joined with the special but overwhelmingly important problem of OPEC oil, might well resume as a result of new rounds of cost-push inflation. Perhaps because Japan's inflationary spiral was more serious, perhaps because of that nation's relatively greater need to increase exports on a sustained basis in order to compensate for the deterioration in the terms of trade, the Japanese government has maintained a more restrictive stance than the other industrialized nations. Without far greater expansionary policies than those that Prime Minister Miki is presently committed to (as of October 1975), it is unlikely that there will be more than a slow cyclical recovery from the current recession before late 1976.

The consequences of current efforts by the government to stabilize the Japanese economy will affect substantially the aggregate growth performance through 1980 and possibly through 1985; it simply will take time to restore the operation of the economy to full capacity, much less to expand capacity. One suspects that a far more important long-run influence will be the sheer difficulty of returning to a high and stable rate of growth, given the present magnitude of the departure from the pattern of the past. While it is well known to economists, specializing in an analysis of economic growth by mathematical methods, that one large departure from a stable path of growth may be enough to prevent an economy from regaining its momentum, this same conclusion may be reached on a more intuitive level and applied to the Japanese economy.

It must be understood that no small measure of the explanation of rapid Japanese economic growth is the rapid economic growth itself. Indeed, among the many conjectures about the growth of the postwar Japanese economy, self-reinforcement is empirically the most well founded one. Econometric studies on the causes of rapid growth: the Japanese propensity to save, the demand for manufacturing investment, the demand for technology imports, and the celebrated Japanese practice of permanent employment, all suggest that in the recent past the rates of economic growth are in themselves the main determinants, whether directly or through the formation of expectations. Equally, when a large component of the high rate of savings seems to have been the result of a lagging adjustment to ever higher rate of increase of real income, where the decision to invest and/or to license a foreign technology and/or extend a commitment of permanent employment is based on expectations about future profitability formed largely on the experience and performance of the very recent past, a large and fairly long-lasting departure from the previous pattern of high growth certainly creates the presumption that it will be some time before the resources and confidence for anything like a secular real growth rate of 10 percent will prevail.

The kind and degree of widespread optimism and confidence in the future so characteristic of just a few years back will take time to nurture. Moreover, it is not likely to be encouraged by the forecasts now generated by the Japanese planning process. Rather, the economic environment is likely to be clouded by governmental emphasis on the continuing possibility of limitations on Japanese access to raw materials together with a recognition that downward price flexibility, once so characteristic of the products of the Japanese economy, now seems diminished in both foreign and domestic markets. Neither business nor government in 1975 and 1976 and perhaps beyond are likely to be nearly as optimistic about Japan's future economic prospects as they were in the past.

The Growth of Japanese Supply Potential

Regardless of the overhang of the unsettled and uncertain present on the future, Japan's economic performance will, hereafter, ultimately be bounded by the growth in the nation's supply potential, namely, the growth and qualitative change of capital, labor, technology, entrepreneurship and managerial skills, and natural resources. It is difficult to estimate the future growth potential of the Japanese economy because, in spite of considerable research, the reasons for the rapid growth of the past are not really well understood. Most studies of supply potential, after carefully considering changes in the level and composition of labor and capital inputs, conclude that between 30 and 60 percent of Japanese postwar growth *cannot* be attributed to these conventional factors. Suggestions that the remaining, unexplained growth can be attributed to increases in knowledge, economies of scale, and other such elements are little more than presumptions, without strong empirical support.

In light of the state of the art, it is hardly surprising that careful examination of any given factor or group of factors leads to the conclusion that growth will be only slightly affected if their hitherto benign influence is impaired. For example, in the late 1960s and early 1970s many commentators were concerned by what they interpreted to be the economic implications of the slowing of the growth of Japanese labor force, from the 1 1/2 percent figure of the 1960s to no more than one-half that rate in the early 1970s and to less than one-third that rate in the late 1970s. This concern diminished under an avalanche of studies suggesting that only slightly over 1 percentage point of the average annual 10 percent growth in productive potential during the 1960s was attributable to the labor force's growth!

Similarly, the changing composition of future increments to Japanese capital stocks has been singled out by many observers as a potentially strategic element in assessing future growth prospects. Between 1963 and 1973, over one-half of gross domestic fixed capital formation was from the corporate sector. It is now widely expected that, during the coming five to ten years and throughout the rest of this century, the share of housing and social overhead capital, coupled with investment in pollution abatement equipment and energy-related investment expenditure will rise to almost 60 percent of gross domestic fixed capital formation. Such a change in composition, together with whatever other marginally diminishing effects the piling up of ever more plant and equipment per worker will have on productivity, will surely have some perceptable influence on the future contribution to growth of the capital stock. Yet, not much more than 2 1/2 percentage points of average annual growth in the 1960s have been attributed to capital stock growth. To hang the heavy burden of the decline in the Japanese growth rate on this factor alone would seem unwise indeed.

Since the more tangible determinants of Japanese economic growth cannot be fully specified, attention has turned to the pace with which Japan has borrowed and assimilated foreign technology. It certainly seems that this process, namely, the growing capacity of Japanese companies to borrow and absorb foreign technology, combined with continual creation of new technology abroad, is at the heart of the remarkable postwar transformation of the Japanese economy. Yet, what is known about this process is again surprisingly little. The comprehensive collection of materials which the Japanese maintain only serve to underline how limited our understanding is. For example, in relation to the very high rate of growth achieved during the 1960s by an already large Japanese economy based on foreign-developed technology, the payment of royalties to foreigners for this technology seems almost ridiculously modest. During 1961, $100 million was paid. No more than $500 million was paid during 1971.

If technology imports have anything like the influence normally ascribed to them, the foreign owners of this technology are certainly not reaping much of the benefits. Even allowing for the fact that producers of knowledge cannot easily appropriate the full benefits of their efforts, the divergence is simply too great to be credible. The nature of the technology adopted by the Japanese during the 1960s was too complex and the negotiating power of the Japanese purchasers in combination with MITI was not so great that a surplus of the size implied here could have been extracted from foreign producers and owners of technology. There is probably too great an emphasis placed on the technology gap, "catching up with the West," and the inevitable petering out of this process. More emphasis should be put on the domestic sources of Japanese technological improvement.

Excluding military research and development, Japanese research and development expenditures, as a proportion of GNP, are almost equal to the rates in Western Europe and the United States. This has been true since the early 1960s. The distinctive characteristic of the Japanese research and development effort is its direct commercial orientation. An unusually high percentage of R&D expenditures in Japan is financed through private sources. The emphasis is unmistakably on applied rather than pure research, that is, on derivative research aimed at commercial feasibility. It can be argued that the very substantial Japanese R&D base has been engaged not so much in helping Japan close the technological gap between itself and other industrialized nations as it has in utilizing imported innovations already more or less at the technological frontier.

In this view, the spurt of the Japanese economy during the 1960s may be thought of not so much as the last great surge out of semi-developed to advanced modern status, but rather as the first part of a new growth phase. In this phase, technological progress rested upon domestic research and developmental activities which exploited the fruits of more fundamental research done abroad. Naturally the increasing size of the Japanese economy in relation to worldwide research and developmental activities, both pure and applied, requires (to the extent that one is prepared to attribute such vital importance to these activities) a certain amount of growth in the proportion of GNP devoted to research and development and some shift toward more basic research. Given the sizable research base now available this may not be so difficult as is sometimes alleged. Whether Japan is fully capable of growing at high single or low double digit rates may be unclear, but the relationship between the economy and the sources of technological advance will not change markedly in the next decade. Japan will not enter a new era in which, unlike the past, it will be unable to rely on foreign borrowing as the wellspring of progress.

The immediately preceeding discussion suggests that, insofar as the contribution of technology and domestic inputs to the process of economic growth are understood, there is comparatively little to suggest that the growth of supply potential in Japan will slow to rates that are characteristic of the rest of the world's advanced industrialized economies. If the Japanese GNP were currently growing at 10 percent, an analysis of supply potential would conclude that the average annual growth over the next ten years would range from 7 to 9 percent. Such an evaluation would be consistent with, although not really derivative from, the work of a wide range of Japanese authorities, such as the very comprehensive but essentially *ad hoc* projections of Hisao Kanamori and his associates at the Japan Economic Research Center and the long-term simulations of the more recent Economic Planning Agency Long Term Macro Forecasting Model. However, these projections ignore the state of the economy at present and in the recent past. It is possible to simulate the future course of the Japanese economy by taking as initial conditions the state of the economy in the second quarter of calendar year 1974 but otherwise accepting the policy variables used in the Economic Planning Agency's earlier simulations. Since the conditions of 1974 were so unlike the sample period used in the forecasting model (that is to say, so unlike previous experience) the simulation which used 1974 as its starting point is no more than an interesting failure: the economy exhibits negative growth in many of the forty-plus quarterly forecast periods and never achieves more than 5 percent positive growth GNP in any one period. This simulation does serve to underline the point made earlier: regardless of the growth in an economy's supply potential, sharp divergence from previously normal growth can have a profound influence on the future growth path.

These cautionary remarks notwithstanding, it is essential to have some concrete projection of Japan's longer run growth prospects since it vitally affects the critical choices for American foreign economic policy vis-à-vis Japan. In our judgment, Japan will be capable of economic growth at some 5-8 percent annually over the next ten to twenty-five years. This rate will be more rapid than that of the United States, although it is below Japan's performance between 1960 and 1975. At the same time, it is appropriate to emphasize that there will be transitional difficulties in returning to even these lower rates of increase in aggregate productive capacity.

Future Contours of the American-Japanese Economic Relationship in a Global Context—Critical Choices for Americans

The slower rate of growth for Japan is unlikely to change the basic nature of bilateral American-Japanese economic relations. The material, if not the institutional conditions which created so much tension in the past, will persist: the Japanese economy in 1975 is so much greater in absolute terms than in 1965 and the reduced rate of Japan's growth will still exceed the projected rate of growth for the American economy. In the future it will be the quantity, not just the rate, of Japanese growth that counts. The increase in Japan's real GNP in the period 1975-85 will almost certainly be at least one-half of that of the United States; between 1962 and 1972, the increase in Japan's GNP was, despite a faster growth rate, about half the amount of America's and, in the decade 1952-62, only about one-quarter. The narrowing of the gap appears graphically in Figure IV-1; it is based on the conservative assumptions that the United States will grow rather rapidly (4 percent annually) and Japan rather slowly (6 percent annually).

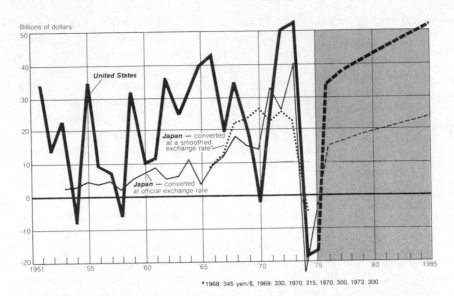

*1968: 345 yen/$, 1969: 330, 1970: 315, 1970: 300, 1973: 300

Note: Growth for 1975-1985 is assumed at a 4 percent annual rate (in real terms) for the United States, and 6 percent for Japan. A greater differential between the growth rates would mean more rapid convergence between the two lines.

Sources:
    United States: 1950-72, Calculated from U.S. Department of Commerce, *Business Statistics 1973 Biennial Edition*, pp. 1, 203; 1973-74, Ibid., *Survey of Current Business*, Feb. 1975, pp. 4, 7; 1975- , Calculated as 2 percent compounded decrease from 1974.
    Japan: 1952-67, Japan, Economic Planning Agency, *Revised Report on National Income Statistics*, pp. 82-83; 1968-72, Calculated from Bank of Japan, *Economic Statistics Annual*, various years; 1973-74, Calculated from Ibid., *Economic Statistics Monthly*, pp. 167-68; 1975- , Calculated as 1.5 percent compounded increase over 1974.

Figure IV-1. Changes in U.S. and Japan GNP (in 1965 Constant $, billion)

Thus, in the 1970s-1980s, despite somewhat slower growth rates, Japanese industries, because of their comparative increase in size, will have the same arithmetic possibilities they did in the 1960s to obtain a proportion of this growth in overseas markets and to cause disruptions. This is equally true of markets to which Japan exports manufactured goods and those from which Japan will import both raw materials and manufactures. Similarly Japan's larger size and continued growth will ensure that Japanese domestic and international financial policies will have the potential to create significant bilateral tensions in the future.

Japan's capacity for rapidly obtaining larger market shares of a major American product line or for dramatically affecting the market price of an American agricultural export will surely remain undiminished; indeed, it will probably increase during the next decade and quarter century. Although there are now and will be in the future more rapidly growing manufacturing nations in East Asia and elsewhere exporting to the United States, Japan will remain a source of conflict for the United States in the international trade of goods. Countries such as Taiwan, South Korea, Mexico, and Brazil will export manufactures that American producers have long since learned to cope with as a result of their exposure to Japanese competition. Imports from these nations may well replace those of Japanese origin rather than directly competing with American products. At the same time, technologically more sophisticated American product lines will, for the first time, find themselves exposed to newly arising Japanese competition. And once again Japan will bear the brunt of tensions emanating from American labor and capital in newly declining industries.

What is true of the international markets for goods and services will be equally valid for Japan's position in international financial markets and for its role as an overseas direct investor. Larger size and continued growth will ensure that Japanese domestic and international monetary policies will have the capability of creating as significant bilateral and multilateral tensions in the future as during 1971-1973. Moreover, the combination of Japan's size and growth and the level of technological accomplishment these factors imply, will provide significant new potential for overseas direct investment. As will be discussed, however, it does not follow that giant Japanese corporations of the present and future can act as the great American manufacturing and resource development corporations did in the postwar period. Both Japan's potential for overseas direct investment and what must be Japan's increasingly important position as the largest single actor in the international market for many primary commodities will ensure that Japan's international economic policies will do much to shape an international economic system in which the United States will remain the leading, but no longer the dominant, member.

Size, growth, and industrial structure will be the bases of possible Japanese and American foreign economic policy dilemmas in the future. The character of these dilemmas, however, and the critical choices which will confront American policymakers will be shaped by Japan's relative material circumstances within the global framework, which is being formed by epochal changes in international economic institutions and policies. Successive subsections take up issues of commercial policy for manufactures and agriculture, the international monetary system, direct foreign investment, energy relationships with the developing countries, and East-West trade. While each issue is treated separately, it is clear they are all intimately linked. This overview considers evolving American and Japanese perceptions of these potential problem areas, looking beyond the immediate recession and inflation. The objective in each subsection is to identify the issues and critical choices for American foreign economic policy for the coming decade and beyond, particularly in terms of the economic relationship between the United States and Japan. The main purpose is to raise issues rather than to provide answers.

Commercial Policies

Growing Strains from Changing American Policy. Even though the special constellation of forces which raised Burke-Hartke protectionism to a major political force in the early 1970s may have dissipated, 1971 was truly a watershed in American foreign economic policy. Secretary of the Treasury Connolly and Secretary of Commerce Stans, moving in tandem with the Nixon-Kissinger conception of American self-interest in a multipolar world, publicly crystallized what had been a new and slowly evolving American commercial policy, directed towards Japan and all economically advanced nations. This policy has involved two major shifts in strategy: a change in emphasis which stresses economic rather than political objectives and a narrower interpretation of America's economic self-interest.

This hitherto unusual posture of aggressively asserting a narrowly defined view of American interests in international trade relations was most dramatically displayed in Japanese-American economic relations of three to six years ago; however, since that time, the public display of this posture has sharply subsided. Nonetheless, it can be argued that American commercial policy, in contrast to American public opinion and Congressional sentiment, has not deviated substantially from the stance articulated at that time. A variety of actions indicate that the United States has not changed its position. For example, the number of investigations of foreign products by the United States Treasury Department and the United States Tariff Commission (and its successor body), under the provisions of old and new injury from imports and anti-dumping statutes, have increased sharply over the past three years: the specialty steel finding against Japan, announced in January 1976, will have a substantial impact. Japanese officials have been informally expressing real concern over this apparent trend in the United States. While the unilateral American export embargo of soybeans in summer 1973 has been widely admitted by policymakers to have been a mistake, talk of using American food exports as an overt instrument of foreign policy raises anxiety in Japan as elsewhere.

The American Trade Act of 1974 contains, for the first time, highly protectionist as well as more liberal provisions. The United States does not appear to have very high hopes for or plans to take much initiative in the Tokyo Round of negotiations now underway in Geneva for the reduction of tariff and nontariff barriers to trade, except in the area of liberalization of European and Japanese impediments to the importation of agricultural commodities. It is not surprising that the Japanese and others perceive American commercial policy as harboring much greater protectionist tendencies than in the past.

Japan in a New Era of International Commercial Policy. The 1970s has also witnessed a major change in Japanese commercial policy. It derived in substantial part from enormous diplomatic pressure from the United States. But, at the same time, there was growing appreciation in Japan of the benefits to be gained from full participation in a liberal, multi-lateral trading system as well as of the need for positive action to protect and enhance that system; there was also recognition that the removal of most restrictions on manufactured imports, would have a very small negative domestic impact, given Japan's stage of development. Not only were active steps taken to remove the remaining legal and administrative bars hampering the importation of manufactured products, but also positive action was taken to encourage American imports.

American pressure has also had some influence on the direction of Japanese exports. Members of the European Community were encouraged to reduce their remaining, not inconsiderable, formal barriers to the import of Japanese manufactured products. This was among the important elements which were responsible for the substantial increase in the share of exports that Japan directed to Western Europe in 1972-73. Since that time, the American share of Japanese exports has declined further, because Japan has taken advantage of the new Organization of Petroleum Exporting Countries (OPEC) markets. The critical ending of legal Japanese restrictions against competitive manufactured imports and improved Japanese access to Western Europe, together with the possibilities for East-West trade implicit in political détente with the Soviet Union and China, are important steps toward achieving the early postwar ideal of truly universal liberal, multilateral trade. The Japanese urging of a Tokyo Round of new negotiations on trade liberalization is perhaps the capstone of this dramatic shift in Japanese commercial policy.

Evolving comparative advantage and rapid Japanese growth have important bilateral as well as multilateral implications for the United States and Japan. Fundamentally, the two economies are highly complementary, as seen in the contrast between Japan's meagre and America's abundant natural resource endowment in energy, industrial raw materials, and agricultural, pasture, and timber land. However, in aggregate, Japanese labor skills, capital per worker, and technological capabilities will become closer to American levels (without raising the issue of which will be ahead in X number of years).

This suggests greater Japanese competitiveness vis-à-vis the United States in producing many manufactures; it may result in some reallocation of capital and labor among American industries. In practice it is highly unlikely that major American industries will disappear: the domestic market is too great; American firms are well established in various product lines; brand names, transport costs, information flows, consumer preferences, and the like confer advantages to domestic firms; and American business will continue to innovate and respond positively to competition whether it be foreign or domestic. Thus, viewed in macro terms, only relatively marginal reallocations will be involved. Food and mineral production will rise because of America's abundance of resources. Within manufacturing there will be somewhat greater specialization, not only on relatively skilled-labor-intensive and technology-intensive industries but also within them. The United States will probably remain commercially very strong in such industries as large commercial aircraft, nuclear power equipment (though this is less clear), and sophisticated military hardware.

One of the features of postwar international trade in manufactures has been the growth in trade in machinery *among* industrial nations. Japan is likely to share increasingly in this trade since its comparative advantage in this area will become increasingly evident. At the micro level, comparative advantage is apparently shaped significantly by such factors as the specifics of entrepreneurial and innovative talent, R&D activity, and just plain luck. Once an advantage is achieved in high-technologies industries, it may be maintained for substantial periods of time. This makes it difficult to predict in precisely which narrowly defined product lines Japan's exports will boom.

These evolving patterns of comparative advantage will put pressure on an increasing number of Japanese industries in their own home markets. Whereas LDC manufactured exports will mainly supplant the exports of others in the American domestic market, in Japan they will compete with Japanese producers. Protectionist sentiment in Japan will shift its focus from fear of the United States' superior competitive power to concern over the cheap labor products of the LDCs. It is unclear whether, in practice, Japan will succeed in reallocating resources rapidly. The Japanese will probably, and correctly, feel caught between the burgeoning competition from LDCs and their inability to produce competitively in all the high-technology industries they consider strategic. It seems reasonable to think that the Japanese government will continue an infant-industry policy of protection (by one means or another) for a select few high-technology industries which they perceive as essential to their long-run economic security. Candidates for such protection include various components of the energy sector (petroleum refining, nuclear power plants) and ocean resource development (if major technological breakthroughs should occur elsewhere).

The direction of American commercial policy has made the Japanese pause in their thrust toward full trade liberalization. This has been nowhere more evident than in Japan's trade policies towards agricultural products. While the economics of Japanese agricultural production imply that the country would be much better off using its land, labor, and capital for nonagricultural purposes and importing almost all of its food, national security interests demand some foregoing of these benefits in order to assure supplies of food. Any action which suggests that food importation will not be possible makes the security issue all the more relevant. It is in this context that the American soybean embargo—essentially an attempt to deal with a domestic problem (inflation) at the expense of trading partners—should be viewed.

This action, affecting a major source of protein in the Japanese diet, became symbolic of a whole range of food supply problems in 1973 and 1974. It very likely resulted in tipping the resolution of forces in Japan surrounding international agricultural trade policy in favor of increasing protection. It was a very serious setback for the prospects of liberalizing international agricultural trade, in which the United States has important long-term international economic interests. In 1972 and early 1973, Japanese government planners and private research organizations were forecasting a continued and even accelerating decline of the role of agriculture in the Japanese industrial structure as a result of government programs of rationalization and liberalization. However, in early 1975, ten-year projections assumed that strenuous government efforts will be made to raise Japan's self-sufficiency in food. The share of agriculture, forestry and fisheries in GNP is now, according to these projections, expected to be almost twice as large as previously estimated. In Japan as elsewhere, the soybean embargo greatly strengthened the position of the ever-tenacious protectionist farmers' organizations as well as the bureaucrats in the Ministry of Agriculture and Forestry. These projections are probably optimistic; Japan will have to rely increasingly on direct and indirect food imports. But if trade reliance cannot be reduced, at least it can be diversified in order to reduce the risk of unilateral action by a simple source of supply. As by far the most important supplier of Japan's agricultural imports, the United States stands to lose.

The "New" International Commercial Policy: Critical Choices for the United States. At its most fundamental level the critical choice for American foreign commercial policy, and indeed for all components of foreign economic policy, is: in which direction, and to what degree, is it in American national interest to move—toward greater insulation from the rest of the world or toward greater interdependence with it? Are the benefits of still further economic integration with the world economy commensurate with the further loss of comprehensive sovereignty over domestic matters? Are the international political benefits commensurate with this loss? In the event that the potential diplomatic benefits greatly exceed the economic benefits derived from a substantial loss in sovereignty, how is American foreign policy to respond? The new "primacy of economics" would demand full economic reciprocity from any projected trade liberalization. Is this wise?

The relevant choices are not between extremes, but in future step-by-step liberalization of an already liberal system, or maintaining the status quo, or in small-scale moves toward insulation, or in rather more substantial efforts at insulation. There are costs and benefits to movements in either direction along the complex spectrum between insulation and interdependence, and they accrue to different groups of Americans. Greater interdependence—the fundamental assumption and consequence of the ideal of a system of free multilateral trade and payments—clearly produces great economic benefits to American consumers. A wider range of commodities are available and their prices are lower than under a system of trade restrictions; overall economic productivity and output is higher because capital and labor are allocated to their most efficient uses. On the other hand, labor and capital in industries facing severe import competition suffer, and there are real private and social costs in transferring these resources to more productive sectors. This is all the more true in a country as geographically large as the United States. At the same time, labor and capital in industries competing effectively in export markets benefit from a more liberal trade system.

Concretely, a number of the commercial policy issues are closely related to the future of American agriculture exports. For example, in the future choices must be made about the extent to which negotiations concerning American liberalization of trade in manufactured goods should be tied to European Common Market and Japanese liberalization of agricultural imports. A related choice must be made about the use of food as an instrument of foreign policy. To what extent, and under what circumstances, should the United States tie the guaranteed export of foodstuffs to economic or political concessions by importing countries?

Agriculture is also a prime example of a future bilateral issue between the United States and Japan. Choices must be made regarding the conditions under which the United States would guarantee Japan access to food imports. How might Japan be persuaded to rely on food imports and on those imports emanating from the United States? Or is it desirable to encourage such reliance? To what degree should the United States government intervene in private market transactions in food trade? Much depends, of course, on an assessment of whether world food supplies will be adequate or not. What incentives can Japan build into American food production and stockpiling to ensure adequate supplies? How should the United States balance, if any period of food shortage should occur, exports on commercial terms to Japan against food aid grants to poverty-stricken, food-deficit nations? Clearly, these issues involve important choices for American commercial policy vis-à-vis Japan, requiring substantial negotiation and cooperation if the needs of both countries are to be satisfied.

Japan's position on the cutting edge of foreign competition with maturing American industries ensures that the insulation-interdependence debate about America's international commercial policy will have strong bilateral Japanese-American overtones. Maturing American industries will argue that the foreign-induced structural evolution in the American economy has gone far enough and that no purpose is served by the destruction of traditional American industries. Others will not deny the theory of comparative advantage but will argue once again that the social costs and economic costs of structural adjustment might outweigh the longer-term advantage of a very liberal commercial policy. While a buoyant, growing full-employment economy provides opportunities for easier adjustment, but if a liberal trade policy persists Americans will still be asked to deal with injury resulting from this policy. One choice will be whether to respond only to injury suffered as a result of importation or to all sources of injury domestic or foreign. Should foreign injury be met by adjustment assistance or by insulation (protection)? What type of adjustment assistance might be used? Does it really help to redeploy capital and labor effectively, or is it merely protection in another guise? How long should the adjustment process take? If insulation is used, over what time period should it be reduced?

Finally, it is important how the United States decides to use its commercial policy vis-à-vis Japan. Should the United States take a hard line, defining national interest in narrow commercial terms? To what extent should the United States be prepared to accept compromises in the commercial arena in order to achieve other economic goals vis-à-vis Japan? How hard, or soft, should be the economic line vis-à-vis political and other noneconomic objectives?

The New International Financial System

From the perspective of developments in 1973 and 1974, the end of the Bretton Woods system in late 1971 with the severing of the dollar's link to gold and the realignment of exchange rates among major currencies was fortuitous. The adjustable peg (fixed) exchange rate system, which facilitated massive riskless speculation even as it discouraged serious public discussion of international financial problems, could hardly have survived anyway. If it had come to an end any later, it might have seriously exacerbated the extraordinary pressures placed on the international financial system by the energy crisis, worldwide inflation and worldwide recession.

At the same time it is truly remarkable how well the series of *ad hoc* arrangements which have evolved since 1971, and particularly since 1973, have negotiated this treacherous terrain. In 1944, the Bretton Woods conferees constructed formal institutions to guard against depression-induced competitive devaluation. Thirty years later, the Bretton Woods-less international economy faced worldwide depression and its constituent members resolutely avoided beggar-thy-neighbor policies. In 1944, cooperation on flexible exchange rate policy in times of high unemployment was seen as having the attributes of a zero-sum game; therefore, it was decided cyclical flexibility should be ruled out from the start. Rather, in the first blush of Keynesian enthusiasm there was widespread agreement that international cooperation among governments committed to full-employment monetary and fiscal policies could alone make the system work. In 1974, a similar sense of cooperative spirit prevailed among the large industrialized market economies, but this time exchange rate flexibility was viewed, within a more sophisticated post-Keynesian conceptual framework, as an added instrument with which to cope with a complex crisis.

This cooperative spirit appears to be the hallmark of the post-Bretton Woods international financial system. Indeed, a well-functioning system built largely on informal understanding necessarily relies on working together. Whether such cooperation can persist remains open to question. As has been discussed, when the Bretton Woods system was breaking up almost the only subject on which there was common agreement, was the treatment of the dollar; it was generally held that the dollar should be more symmetrically aligned with other major national currencies in any new system. Other industrialized nations hoped that the United States would lose its unconstrained privilege to print international money which gave it the right to economically unconstrained international political and economic activities. For its part, the United States wanted the freedom to influence directly the external value of its currency.

Since the collapse of the Bretton Woods system, international financial arrangements have evolved through a series of phases. First, the link between gold and the dollar was broken and exchange rates among the currencies of the market economies were realigned. The Smithsonian agreement of December 1971, which ratified this realignment, envisioned the new exchange rates in equilibrium relationships. A system of fully floating exchange rates was at that time deemed neither necessary nor acceptable. With the dollar still weak and subject to massive speculative attacks, in early 1973, the Smithsonian arrangements also collapsed and a de facto floating exchange rate system began.

The massive but uneven impact of worldwide inflation and the energy crisis led to wide swings in the relative values of the major currencies in the following two years. By late 1975, with the largest balance of trade surplus in American history in the offing and the dollar taking on the renewed glow of a strong currency, the international financial system seemed to be returning to more familiar operational norms. Currency floating, which, since 1973, was always controlled by central bank intervention, now appears more circumscribed than it was. With the exception of the United States, virtually all major trading nations apparently desire to return to some regime of relatively fixed exchange rates. The Jamaica meeting of the Interim Committee of the IMF in January 1976 put this agreement and disagreement on record.

In the years since the demise of the Bretton Woods system, the general assessment of the dollar's future as international money has experienced substantial ups and downs. In the early 1970s, with the dollar weak and its link to gold severed, the Deutschemark, the Swiss franc, and to a much lesser extent the Dutch guilder and the Japanese yen all became key currencies to some degree, replacing the dollar as a unit of account, medium of exchange, and store of value. It was also during this period that Special Drawing Rights (SDRs) became attractive as a potential alternative to the dollar as a reserve asset and, more significantly, as a unit of account.

The growing strength of the dollar has once again slowed this change. Indeed, there seems to be a growing consensus that in the absence of a special initiative in which the United States would probably have to take the lead, the dollar's role as international money in the foreseeable future is likely to remain what it has been throughout the postwar period. No other medium of exchange reserve asset possesses the advantage the dollar derives from the sheer economic mass of the United States, the comparative absence of controls over American trade and foreign exchange, and the depth and breadth of American capital markets. As a corollary, this line of reasoning must also attribute the bulk of the relative decline in the dollar's role as international money in the early 1970s to the weakness of the American balance of payments and to a secular improvement in the financial facilities, size, and international importance of the West German economy, which, probably, is not likely to improve at the same relative rate in the future as it did in the past.

Thus, the dollar's new strength seems to spark a return towards a system resembling Bretton Woods in substance if not in form. Only the United States Treasury seems concerned that the experiences of the late 1960s and early 1970s might be forgotten—or at least it draws different lessons from that experience. At the same time this divergent American view, together with divisions on detail among the other major international financial actors, seem to be preventing any effort at negotiating new rules of behavior for the international financial system. This procrastination on the development of a new international financial system must be considered discouraging. The attempt by some to put a good face on this impasse by bravely talking about a "common law" or "case law" path to new rules of behavior seems to overlook the dangers which spring from a lack of formal agreement. The English Common Law to which analogy is optimistically made developed over hundreds of years. As the important English philosophers of the seventeenth century observed, the informal character of law's development led to chaos in the absence of an ultimate sovereign power able and willing to supervise the law's application. Notwithstanding the differences between the mass of medieval cottagers and the small fraternity of twentieth century's central bankers, it is not hard to imagine how the absence of legitimate final authority in the international financial system might lead to similar difficulties.

This same absence of final authority has made the negotiation of a new system of international financial rules most difficult. American financial and political preponderance made the negotiation of the framework of the Bretton Woods system possible. The absence of such preponderance, however, need not make negotiations fruitless. If English Common Law and the Mosaic Code were imposed by force, Americans should rightly remember that the Federal Constitution was the result of the deliberations of thirteen coequal states facing a common crisis. What is remarkable in the current context is that the common international financial crisis of the early 1970s has not yielded sufficient resolve among the industrialized trading nations to make the construction of new and explicit rules of behavior possible.

On the basis of the renewed strength of the dollar, the international financial system is slowly but surely returning to a system which is more similar to the previous adjustable peg arrangements than to floating or gliding and in which the dollar, no longer tied to gold, remains the prime medium of exchange and store of value. Should this return to the old system be informally accomplished, the risk of the dollar once again becoming overvalued would be real. Whether the severing of the dollar's link to gold will leave the United States free to reduce the external value of its currency remains to be seen. The dollar "overhang," the potential competition from the mark, yen, and other currencies, and the unwillingness of other major industrialized countries to accept such changes might force the United States into policies reminiscent of just a few years ago. In other words, the absence of the political will to negotiate a new adjustment mechanism and a symmetrical means of liquidity creation might lead the trading nations back into a crisis not unlike that so recently experienced.

Japanese Interest in the International Financial Negotiations. The Japanese perception that its wealth still does not permit its diplomats to play a truly major role in the discussions of a successor international financial system has retarded the formulation of a real consensus of the Japanese stake in these negotiations. Japanese policymakers still apparently view their main role as responding to proposals put forth by the United States and the European Community, and their positive contribution to be as a mediator between the two. Of course, Japan together with other major actors in the world economy states its broad needs; it wants an international financial system which contributes to worldwide economic efficiency and political harmony. Yet a coherent, articulate Japanese position on a number of specific issues is lacking—on the degree and means of exchange rate flexibility in the future, on the respective responsibilities of surplus and deficit nations, on the means by which new international liquidity will be created, on the future role of Special Drawing Rights, the dollar, gold, and other key currencies in official international financial transactions; and on the degree of restriction if any, appropriate for private international short-term and long-term capital transactions.

This failure to reach a consensus is related in some measure to fundamental disagreements within Japan regarding the very nature of the Japanese economy. Japan stands almost alone in the world as a very large economy with a rather small trade sector, which, nonetheless, is vital to its well-being. Many but by no means all analysts believe that the Japanese economy finally has greater balance of payments independence than ever before. The experience with the revaluations in late 1971 and early 1973 and the pegged float since then reinforces the view that the specific exchange rate of the yen is not of overwhelming importance; thus, costly domestic programs the primary purpose of which is to defend the yen at any particular value are unwise. Such an analysis leads inevitably to support for international monetary regimes which provide considerable scope for market determination of exchange rates between national currencies without substantial central bank intervention, i.e., substantial exchange rate flexibility.

By contrast, there is a considerable segment of opinion within Japan—particularly within the Japanese government—which, rather than viewing ongoing flexibility in exchange rates as a means of insulating the domestic economy from foreign developments, fears the results of possible arbitrary, speculative movements in the external value of the yen. Given Japanese dependence on imported raw materials and food, such movements could set off an unhappy spiral of cost-push inflation. The sharp decline of the yen in late 1973 is seen, rightly or wrongly, by this group as having seriously exaggerated the inflationary spiral which ensued. In addition, particularly within the Japanese Ministry of Finance, there is great concern that the usefulness of a balance of payments excuse for constraining government expenditure and balancing the budget will be undercut under a more flexible exchange rate. A Ministry of Finance thoroughly lacking in liberal traditions does not view its replacement by the market mechanism as mediator between the domestic Japanese economy and external financial transactions benignly.

Finally, the Japanese government's concern with a formal system of flexible exchange rates is not unrelated to international political considerations. A fully articulated flexible exchange rate system inevitably promotes the development of a yen bloc. Trade patterns indicate that many, if not all, of the non-Communist nations in East Asia and particularly Southeast Asia would tie their currencies to the yen. Both the real problems and the symbolism of such a yen bloc are viewed by Japanese officials as further complicating serious Japanese political difficulties in the area. Even more important, there is considerable concern within the Japanese government that the emergence of various currency blocs, not only in Asia but elsewhere, would be a major step down the road to restrictive regionalism with extremely undesirable consequences for Japan.

Quite apart from the direct consequences that alternative international adjustment mechanisms might have on the Japanese domestic economy or on Japanese relations with East Asia, Southeast Asia, and Oceania, the consequences for Japanese relations with the major industrialized nations must also be considered. In designing a new international monetary system it is important to remember not only the usually dynamic character of the Japanese economy, which highlights the need for a flexible system, but also Japanese distinctiveness. In the late 1960s and early 1970s Japan became the first among a succession of new major actors in the international economic system whose cultural traditions and backgrounds are outside Western civilization. Despite a long history of misunderstanding and suspicion, despite a major change in relative economic positions—a change requiring new modes of behavior—economic intimacy is growing between the West and such nations and groups of nations as Japan and OPEC. Given the cultural differences, one cannot hope for ready popular understanding and charity when reviewing the problems arising out of this intimacy. More is clearly necessary than the pious hope that there will be more and better popular international communication in the future.

Successful operation of the Bretton Woods System necessitated a reliance on the subtlest modes of international cooperation, since the rules for exchange rate adjustment were hardly operational and since national public discussion of the need for adjustment was virtually impossible. The dominance of a highly homogeneous international elite made such cooperation more or less feasible. The emergence of Japan and OPEC as major international economic powers may well make any future system relying heavily on subtle understandings a dubious proposition. The current international financial arrangements seem to place even heavier reliance on such understandings than did the Bretton Woods system. In their dealings with one another, the Japanese prefer informal understandings to contractual obligations. Whether Japanese policymakers now are sufficiently well assimilated and received in the elite of the international financial community to avoid the grave misunderstandings of the recent past surely remains in some doubt.

Petrodollars and the International Financial System. The addition of OPEC as the second major non-Western actor in the international financial system has raised many of the same issues which were aired when the first large Japanese balance of payments surpluses appeared. The great change in terms of trade in favor of oil producing nations and their inability, initially at least, to spend all their new petrodollars has raised a whole host of new problems. At the global level, when OPEC runs trade and current account surpluses, the rest of the world must run deficits of equal magnitude. How are those deficits to be divided among individual nations? Would each have sufficient foreign exchange reserves to cover oil deficits? Would competitive depreciation among industrialized countries emerge as a threat once again?

As OPEC nations build up surpluses they must hold them in foreign assets—ranging from foreign exchange, short-term deposits, longer-term portfolio investment, or real assets. Will their holdings be used in a politically disruptive fashion? Thus far, the OPEC nations tend to hold their foreign assets mainly in relatively few industrialized nations. These have not been, necessarily, the nations with the largest oil-induced balance of payments deficits. Would their petrodollar holdings be recycled adequately to other countries in balance of payments deficits?

In the year since the petrodollar issue was first raised, much of the initial concern has dissipated. In late 1974 and early 1975, there were many proposals afoot to provide OPEC with assets in which they could invest their surplus petroleum earnings. The assets would be designed to deprive the OPEC nations of the economic and political power which might normally be associated with such massive investment. Despite the number of such plans proposed at that time, today such talk is rarely heard. OPEC earnings of the scale originally contemplated just have not occurred. OPEC imports have grown more rapidly than anticipated, the industrialized nations as a group have succeeded in increasing exports sufficiently to maintain current account balance, and the worldwide recession has resulted in the reduction of the magnitude and certainly the growth rate of petroleum imports by industrialized nations. Unhappily, the burden of the OPEC-related balance of payments adjustment that has been required since 1975 has fallen almost entirely on the developing countries.

Whether the return of the world economy to full employment coupled with rapidly increasing world trade in crude oil will raise anew concerns about petrodollars remains to be seen. Renewed anxiety about petrodollars might very well be associated with long-range concern about the possibility of Japan in pursuing balance of payments objectives which would be inconsistent with American and European objectives. Since, in addition to its standard import needs, Japan now and in the future must have foreign exchange earnings for two new purposes: to pay for high-priced oil and to finance a potential massive expansion in Japanese overseas direct investment. Provided Japan obtains a proportional share of petrodollars (through exports to OPEC, direct or indirect borrowing from OPEC) these objectives might prove no special problem. If Japan, however, is unable to finance these objectives by petrodollars or other long-term borrowing but rather, must do so by running a current account surplus achieved through strenuous competition with manufacturing industries in the major industrialized countries, international tension might be considerable. Governmental projections regarding Japan's changing net foreign asset position over the next ten years suggest that such problems might well develop. In the subsequent section on international investment the reasonableness of these projections is considered.

The United States and the Future International Financial System from the Perspective of U.S.-Japanese Relations—A Summary. The historic shift in official American thinking about the international financial system is having surprisingly much less long-term impact than might have been expected. American commitment to a managed, market-determined exchange rate and to a more symmetric treatment of dollar is having much less influence on the forms of the new international financial system than might have been expected. The United States must decide whether it can really accept an exchange rate adjustment mechanism which relies primarily on informal cooperation with other countries, when almost all of which the United States is in fundamental disagreement regarding the appropriate use of exchange rate adjustment, to equilibrate international currency markets. Similarly, the United States must once again examine the relationship between the use of the dollar as international money and American domestic and international economic and political interests. How far is the United States prepared to go to achieve a symmetry of rights and obligations within the international monetary system? How is the United States to view the development of supplementary key currencies? Should the United States give new impetus to negotiated efforts to transfer the dollar's function as the world's main monetary base to SDRs?

Underlying these issues is a fundamental decision about how much participation in (or insulation from) the international economy the United States really wants and how much it can really have on any terms. An enhanced ability to influence the external value of the dollar and a diminished international role for the dollar serve to provide some protection to the increasingly large export- and import-competing sectors of the American economy from the vagaries of the financial policies chosen by America's leading industrial competitors. This insulation can be purchased only through some reduction in the American capacity to exert international economic and political leadership (or hegemony).

These multilateral issues have direct bilateral implications for the United States-Japan relationship, as already implied. An informal, consultative system for exchange rate adjustment (or any policy coordination) may work well when the United States and Japan are in substantial agreement. When serious disagreements arise, such a system may generate considerably more friction than would a more formal system of rules. Much depends on the working relationships that policymakers in both countries develop with each other. It is surprising to many that Japanese Ministry of Finance officials apparently prefer a less flexible system—given the future potential of a Japanese-instigated disruption of the system—and this stance differs substantially from the enunciated American position. It remains to be seen whether different national objectives, and different perceptions of problems, will result in renewed bilateral tension in the financial sphere.

Foreign Direct Investment Issues

At one point Japan and the United States were far apart in their policies concerning both foreign direct investment in their own country and investment abroad by their own home-based companies. The United States was the champion of completely free investment anywhere by anyone. Japan was extremely fearful of foreign domination and restricted foreign investment at home; for balance of payments reasons it also restricted direct investment abroad by Japanese firms. In the last few years the United States has retreated slightly from its position, while Japan has liberalized its stance very substantially. In particular, a previously latent xenophobia in the United States has been manifested. Hawaiians and Californians resented the influx of Japanese capital which preempted for Japanese tourists some of the best hotels, golf courses, land, and the like. But perhaps more important has been the fear of Arab petrodollar investment. The fear is not simply one of economic competition but of the possible misuse of economic power in foreign hands; namely, that economic power might be used for purposes not in the interests of American citizens.

Changing View of the American-Based Transnational Corporation. These changes have been occurring in a world environment in which the desire for more careful regulation of the activities of transnational (also frequently termed multinational or international) corporations has been on the rise—not just in the developing countries, but in Canada, Western Europe, and even the United States. In part, this is the result of a new awareness of the lack of identity of interests among the triangle of home country, host country, and transnational corporation. Host countries increasingly express concern about the actions and presence of international corporations, concerns reflected in Japanese policy in the 1960s. Not surprisingly the anxiety of host nations focuses mainly on American-based corporations, the major actors in the international investment scene. They worry about foreign nationals preempting the limited opportunities available in the host country for gaining relevant experience, about loss of sovereignty over monetary policy, erosion of the tax base, intrusion of American foreign policy into the activities of the domestic subsidiaries of American-based transnational corporations, unfair distribution of the benefits of such foreign participation in the economy, and the like.

Host countries have not been adverse to taking actions to deal with these problems. Quantitative and qualitative job quotas for domestic nationals in foreign-owned manufacturing activities have become a common regulation. For some time many countries have required that no export restriction or regional restrictions be placed on the local subsidiaries of foreign corporations; local opportunities for worldwide growth must not be stifled by an oligopolistic strategy of market segmentation. Closely following earlier Japanese practice, many host countries have been seeking majority control or at least 50 percent ownership of local subsidiaries. Local control, it is thought, will better ensure subsidiary activities consistent with the economic and political objectives of the host government.

The long-term success of these policies remains to be evaluated, but it is clear that their impact is being felt in all sectors in which transnational corporations operate, not just in natural resources. The United States government is increasingly concerned lest the distribution of benefits flowing from the activities of American-controlled transnational corporations move sharply away from the United States. While it was once believed that American interests so coincided with those of the trans-national corporations that the firms could be relied upon to preserve these benefits for the American polity and economy, this view no longer prevails. Recently various measures of control and restriction have been considered by the American government. The most extreme proposal has been the investment provisions of the Burke-Hartke bill, which would have severely restricted American direct investment abroad. There is an increasing propensity for the American government, through legislation and other means, to insert itself into the negotiations between American-based corporations and foreign governments in order to protect American national interests—in issues of taxation, corruption, cartelization, and the like.

Japanese International Investment Policy as Host Country. While the trend in the developed and developing world has been moving somewhat toward the earlier pattern of Japanese economic nationalism in the treatment of and policies towards foreign direct investment, Japanese policies themselves have become more liberal. This has been the result of various forces: intense foreign pressure, increased self-confidence in the competitive strength of Japanese industry, the changing character, pattern, and terms for obtaining of the technological information Japan needs from abroad; and an increasing recognition that Japanese policies towards foreign direct investors would surely have considerable impact on the way in which the rapidly expanding foreign investment activity of Japanese-based corporations would be treated. In principle, Japan now allows or will allow by late 1976 the automatic approval of fully-owned subsidiaries of foreign corporations in virtually all Japanese industries except for agriculture, mining, oil refining, leather manufacture, banking, public utilities, and armaments.

This new attitude towards foreign direct investment in Japan represents a remarkable change from long-held policies which heavily restricted even minority ownership in many joint ventures as recently as 1971, but it is consistent with the liberalization of international commercial policy by the Japanese. Nonetheless, Japan is a considerable distance from a fully free policy on direct foreign investment. While the establishment of wholly-owned subsidiaries is, in principle, allowed automatically in almost all industries, foreign-owned corporation cannot readily purchase an existing Japanese firm; such an act requires governmental approval, which is by no means automatic and indeed remains quite difficult to obtain. Even for newly established ventures implicit and even explicit barriers remain; again, automatic governmental approval is not necessarily automatic and remains quite difficult to obtain.

The very lengthy and as yet unresolved issue of Dow Chemical's planned venture in the lucrative caustic soda industry in Japan is a well-known example. That case has made clear that MITI had not taken into account, in its process of liberalization, the possibility that a foreign firm in an important, well-established industry in Japan might develop a new, superior technology and refuse to share it with Japanese firms, demanding instead to use it in production in Japan. One interpretation of the lengthy, choreographic process of negotiations with Dow Chemical is that MITI both wanted to buy adjustment time for the Japanese industry and to establish the precedent that it can intervene when new circumstances arise, in order to participate in the shaping of terms under which a foreign firm with superior technology enters Japan.

In view, however, of the international context of the technology market in which Japanese firms must operate, it can be expected that further capital liberalization will occur. It is increasingly difficult to purchase by license arrangements that technology and information which Japan does not now have and probably will not in the future produce. In the few areas where Japan remains technologically backward, the sophistication is such and the producers of such technology so few that Japan's bargaining position will be too weak to force an unpackaging of information and expertise from foreign direct equity and managerial participation in production. Indicative both of Japan's rising technological prowess and still relatively weak bargaining position is that Japanese firms are increasingly required to share their technological information in return for such information from American firms. This in itself is an epochal change. In contrast to Japan's large purchases of foreign technology, sales of its own technology are still meager. This is in the process of change, however; Japan's technology exports may be expected to expand substantially in the future.

Future Japanese Overseas Investment. The past few years have witnessed a remarkable upsurge of Japanese direct investment abroad. Though much has gone into natural resource projects, manufacturing and commerce-finance are of equal importance. The general expectation is that Japanese investment abroad will continue to rise significantly over the coming decade; a substantial number of Japanese firms will have significant overseas operations and Japan will have a major new position in the international sphere. The economics of labor-intensive production and of production in energy-using, high polluting industries encourage investment abroad rather than at home. Both Japanese firms and the government desire to increase involvement in natural resource projects in order to enhance prospects for stable supplies as well as any rents they may obtain. And commerce, finance, and related services will increase hand in hand with Japan's growing international commercial and investment presence. MITI in its ten-year "vision" published in fall 1974 projected Japanese direct investment outstanding in 1985 to be $98.5 billion, up almost ten times from 1974. The MITI fall 1975 "vision" was somewhat less optimistic, projecting an $80 billion level for 1985.

Given the changing world environment of the 1970s, in contrast to the 1950s and early 1960s, it seems doubtful that Japan will achieve the foreign asset ownership levels of even the MITI 1975 projection. Japan has neither the monopoly on technology, managerial expertise, nor capital which the United States enjoyed when the great expansions of American overseas investment activities were accomplished. As already noted, host countries are driving harder bargains, as recent evidence on terms of Japanese transnational companies indicates. The great majority of American overseas manufacturing activities are wholly-owned subsidiaries—the heritage of the one-time American hegemony. By contrast, a large majority of Japanese manufacturing ventures, many of which were started in the last three years, are joint ventures between Japanese and host country firms. In many cases Japan has only minority ownership. Japan's recent experience has been rather different from other advanced economies; it suggests that projecting future Japanese foreign direct investment on the basis of the experience of other advanced nations in earlier periods leads to considerable overestimation.

Foreign Direct Investment Policy: Issues for the United States. Japanese policy on American direct investment in Japan remains rather different from present American policy on Japanese investment in the United States. Moreover, the interests of American consumers and American producers are not identical. American consumers have benefited substantially from the development of Japan's large industrial base: they are able to buy imported goods of quality at lower prices than would be the case if Japan had not grown; and Japanese large-scale entry into world markets has increased the number of competitors internationally, reducing the ability of American and European firms to exercise oligopolistic market power by charging higher prices.

One choice for American policy revolves around how to respond to a possible future situation where Japanese firms desire to purchase a major American corporation, given the Japanese policy to control analogous American purchases of Japanese firms. Should the United States continue to maintain its relatively free stance, despite Japanese policy; should it adopt the Japanese policy as a general policy; or should it use such a policy directly as a bilateral bargaining tool with Japan?

How should the United States respond to any renewed ability of MITI to intervene in the "automatic" approval of the decision by an American firm to establish production facilities in Japan? How tough should the United States be? Contrarily, should the United States plan to establish controls and limits on Japanese investment in the United States, for either strategic or tactical purposes?

What should American policy be regarding international price-fixing, which involves American and Japanese firms, either through explicit cartels or more informal collusion? In practice American policy has been ambiguous, while talking an antitrust, anticartel, antiprice fixing, antimarket restraint game, the United States has forced Japan to establish export cartels for so-called voluntary export controls to the American market. It forced the Japanese steel industry to join the United States and European steel club, raising prices and restricting shipments. The measured loss in consumer economic welfare has been very large; but capital and labor in American steel and similarly affected industries have gained. Under what circumstances are such arrangements in the American national interest?

Various multilateral issues have implications also for the American relationship with Japan. Should the United States press for an international agreement defining codes of conduct for private foreign investors and host countries? On what terms? Where will American and Japanese views converge? Diverge? Should tax treatment of foreign profits be changed? Under present arrangements American-based transnational corporations and host governments can deprive the United States of potential tax revenues. What sorts of arrangements can be made for sharing tax revenues between host and home governments?

As Japan invests more abroad, Japanese-based transnational firms will confront their American counterparts more frequently and in more ways. Moreover, Japanese involvement in a number of countries and regions of high American involvement (Latin America, Australia, the developing countries of East and Southeast Asia) will increase substantially. Mutual involvements in third countries will increase the complexity of political and economic relationships beyond what has been true of the essentially bilateral relationship. It is not clear what the policy issues and choices for the United States vis-à vis Japan will be in this context, but they may well be a source both of tension and of cooperation toward mutual objectives.

*Changing Opportunities for Oil and Other Natural Resource
Development: Resource Nationalism, Scarcity and Security*

As in other areas, the very success of the international economic system in spurring the growth of the advanced market economies has ultimately undermined salient features of the markets for the many renewable and nonrenewable natural resources which had done so much to facilitate this growth. From the Korean War peak until 1960, world prices for food, nonfood agricultural raw materials, oil and mineral raw materials fell sharply both relative to the prices of manufactured products and also in absolute dollar terms. After 1960, the rate of relative price decline of primary commodities slowed and, in dollars actually began to increase. This accelerated sharply in 1973 and 1974 as prices of basic commodities rose so much, both absolutely and in relation to manufactured products, that the terms of trade returned to their 1950 Korean War peak relationship.

While the recent general trends of raw material prices are clearly explained by the unusually rapid world economic growth followed by widespread and deep recession, relative scarcity alone does not dictate the particular outcomes observed. A more precise explanation requires consideration of market power, nationalism, and of important miscalculations, real and monetary, all of which are complicated by the lengthy periods it takes to increase supply capacities of raw materials.

One of the great unforeseen factors which served to increase primary commodity prices in the 1960s was Japan itself. Between 1960 and 1970 Japan alone imported 30 percent of the world's increases in wheat exports; 55 percent of the increases in iron ore exports; 22 percent of increases in crude oil exports;

25 percent of increases in soybean exports; and 50 percent of all increases in the export of wood. Japan's explosive growth during the 1960s was certainly unanticipated by virtually everyone, including the Japanese themselves. Indeed the Japanese government and Japanese business groups, in a position to make some assessment of Japanese conomic growth prospects and its implications for food and raw material imports and profitably use such information to increase worldwide capacities, only partially did so. Trading companies relied substantially on spot purchases, in part to earn for short-run speculative gains. On the other hand, Japanese purchasers did secure long-term access to certain raw material supplies—notably coal and iron ore from Australia—through the innovative development of long-term contractual arrangements which did not require much equity investment. The buoyancy of Japanese, and world, demand for basic commodities during the 1960s and early 1970s, with eventual sharp rises in prices, suggests that Japanese and other calculations on increasing supplies were nonetheless deficient.

Another miscalculation of a different sort (already described) occurred during the early 1970s and again greatly affected commodity prices. While Japanese macroeconomic policymakers probably erred to the greatest degree, the misunderstanding of what Nixon Administration macroeconomic policy intentions would be in the year of the 1972 election was worldwide, and cumulatively resulted in a new tidal wave of world liquidity in 1972 and 1973. When joined with American government disinterest in the worldwide and domestic consequences of billion-dollar wheat sales to the Soviet Union, this led inevitably to the observed price explosion, given short-run inelasticities of supply of primary commodities.

The Rise of Producer Market Power. With demand straining supply, nations selling primary commodities began to take advantage of the possibilities of organizing cartels. Governments of primary producing developing nations have long been unhappy about the terms of trade between manufactured goods and their primary commodities and about the role of foreign-dominated corporations in the development of what was often the country's major economic asset. Fortified by increasingly easy access to the technology, capital, managerial expertise, and knowledge necessary for such development and marketing, primary producing nations have, from the early 1970s, tried increasingly to extract all possible rents from foreign-owned companies developing natural resources within their jurisdiction while, at the same time, joining with other primary product producing nations in attempts to gain market power, which could then be used to improve the terms of trade by raising the price of their resource exports.

The best known and by far most effective of these efforts, the Organization of Petroleum Exporting Countries, has been remarkably successful since the Teheran Conference, and particularly since the oil embargo in late 1973, in increasing the price of crude oil and altering markedly the distribution of world purchasing power. The petroleum case is exceptional, however. While resource nationalism and OPEC-like cartels can hardly be ignored in understanding the recent movement of other basic commodity prices, attention to these factors must not obscure the more important monetary and cyclical determinants already discussed. This perspective is necessary to assess the position that natural resources will play in the evolving international economic environment as well as their implications for Japanese and American foreign economic policy.

The Future Terms of Natural Resource Availability. If the world economy grows as rapidly in the next ten years as it did between 1960 and 1970, it is unlikely that the relative price of primary commodities will decline. However, sharp increases in basic commodity prices of the kind recently witnessed will result only from a conjunction of the same causal forces. Thus, it is not expected that long-term scarcity will act to increase basic commodity prices over the next decade and probably for considerably longer. It is now well understood that known reserves of virtually all minerals and fuels remain at their ample historical levels. Similarly, rapid expansion in the production of foodstuffs and other agricultural raw materials should, over the next few years, return agricultural prices to relative levels more characteristic of the 1960s.

The importance of cyclical and monetary phenomena in generating the commodity boom of the early 1970s is underscored by the sharp declines in most basic commodity prices since late 1974, with the notable exception of oil. As the earlier cyclical upswing sharply buoyed prices of basic commodities whose supplies are relatively inelastic in the short run, so the recent downturn has worked to depress their prices sharply. With the important exception of crude oil, virtually every important commodity entering international trade has fallen in price from peak levels by at least 20 percent. In most cases, the price declines are far sharper. Indeed, if the prices in future markets are any indication, further declines may be expected. These cyclical swings will probably continue in the future; they should not be confused with the more important secular changes in relative prices.

OPEC and Japanese Foreign Economic Policy. The global economy is not likely to face a condition of "natural" scarcity (in the sense either of outright exhaustion or highly inelastic long-run supply schedules) during the immediate years ahead. However, contrived scarcity, the result of organized attempts by primary producers to exert market power, is and will remain an important issue. Can and will OPEC continue to be an effective cartel? Will the relative price of oil be raised still higher in the future? Will OPEC serve as a model for other producers of primary products? The case of oil is considered here as one important part of the wider problem of natural resources and relations with the developing nations discussed in the next subsection.

The continuing existence of OPEC as an effective cartel depends most fundamentally on the continuing willingness of Saudi Arabia, and to a lesser extent Kuwait, to accept large declines in their production and hence in their oil revenues. Both Kuwait and Saudi Arabia are major low-cost producers with enormous oil reserves. Given their relatively small populations, and, therefore, their relatively modest import needs and their already large foreign exchange holdings, only these two among the OPEC members are in a position to absorb disproportionately major production cutbacks in order to obviate the need to assign rigid production quotas to OPEC members. In light of the number, diversity, and fiscal needs of the other OPEC members, it is doubtful that the cartel could continue to operate effectively in the presence of gaps between overall production and overall capacity of the present magnitude, if anything like equi-proportionate cutbacks among all members were required.

The willingness of the Saudis and the Kuwaitis to underwrite the present price of crude oil, so many times above production costs, as well as possible future price increases depends on the subtle interplay among many political as well as economic variables: expectations about the nature of supply and demand relationships for crude oil in the future; the desirability of substantially aiding an increase in the relative economic (and military) political power of Iran, Iraq, and Algeria by allowing them to produce crude oil near capacity at high prices at the same time as relatively weakening the United States, Western Europe, and Japan; and the political capability of the Saudis and the Kuwaitis to withstand pressure from Iran, Iraq, and Algeria. Any projection of the outcome of this process is hazardous. It is clear, however, that in this important area of natural resources, the structure of the international economic system has been changed beyond recognition. While the increased price of oil by itself will have only a modest direct long-run effect on the rate of economic growth in advanced nations, the concentration of economic power in OPEC national government hands, which could have enormously disruptive consequences through renewed embargo or through politically calculated use of large foreign exchange holdings, is entirely unprecedented in the postwar period and the very antithesis of the early liberal vision.

Energy Policy Cooperation Among Industrialized Areas. The coming into existence of this vast power in the energy market has led directly to the establishment of countervailing institutions. While it was once expected that the (mostly American-dominated) international oil companies would of necessity protect the interests of the consumer countries, it is now clear that there is no such identity of interests. New institutions are necessary if the market power of the oil producing nations is to be curbed. These new institutions will be effective to the extent that: they can develop alternative sources of energy supply at competitive prices; that they are able to encourage and coordinate conservation steps among the consumer nations; that the construction of new oil purchasing procedures succeed in exploiting potential weaknesses and mistrust among cartel members; and that crude oil stockpiles are developed of sufficient magnitude to blunt the cartel's ultimate weapon of embargo. The prime international institution which has been created to deal with OPEC market power in international energy transactions is the International Energy Agency. Though it is premature to judge, in terms of its potential importance directly and as a model for handling such relationships systemically, the IEA may prove comparable in significance to the IMF.

Consumer country cooperation in the energy market can certainly be beneficial. However, the difficulties of arranging significant cooperative steps among purchasing nations on each of the four dimensions of energy policy—new supplies, conservation, purchasing, and stockpiles—are great. This is seen most clearly in the context of Japan's position within the international energy market and an examination of the Japanese interest in various modes of international cooperation.

Japan and the Development of New Energy Supply Sources. Japan can hardly fail to benefit from the development of alternative sources of energy, but the precise Japanese role in such development remains unclear. Under any conceivable technology likely to be practicable in the next few decades, Japan cannot have its own Project Independence. Other than some exploration on the Northeast Asia continental shelf, there is little Japan can do in territory under its own jurisdiction to add to known world energy reserves. Unlike corporations and public institutions in the United States and Western Europe, Japan has participated only modestly in overseas exploration for and development of crude oil bearing structures. In view of the very large share of oil in Japan's total imports, there is considerable interest within the Japanese government in vastly increasing Japanese participation in exploration and exploitation. This would take place within the context of a restructuring of purchasing, refining, and distributing of oil within Japan.

Whether a continued rapid increase (a large increase from a very small base has already taken place) in such overseas Japanese efforts is in the interest both of other consumer nations and Japan depends critically on the nature of exploration opportunities, and the opportunity cost of the Japanese resources which might be devoted to exploration efforts, particularly in relation to those costs in the United States and Europe. One can construct examples either way: Japanese activity would be beneficial to all consumer nations by widening the pool of exploration opportunities examined, or such activity would result in redundant competition and uneconomical use of resources.

Given the insignificance of Japan's past activity and the cost involved in developing expertise in overseas exploration and production, what benefits particular to Japan might flow from such a program? Aside from the (unlikely) possibility that this might be an especially profitable, if risky, area of investment the benefits are presumably those of future access to scarce supplies. This reflects a not surprising shift in Japanese behavior. In an era when prices were falling and Japan was not an overwhelming influence on world markets, flexibility was the hallmark of Japanese procurement of raw materials. Now, in a different era, Japan is doing everything possible to develop and maintain long-term supply relationships through exploration, managerial, and capital participation.

Yet, in a new era of natural resource nationalism, the reality of special benefits for Japan either through long-term price protection or security of supply seems doubtful. As long as the OPEC-contrived artificial scarcity persists, virtually all rents associated with the exploration and production of crude oil will be extracted for the benefit of the national government which is host to Japanese (as well as any other foreign) activity. Whether or not some other countries were to interrupt their supplies, the host to Japan is unlikely to hold back from passing on any general price increases to the fullest possible extent. What Japanese policymakers apparently believe is that a combined investment-purchasing arrangement will give Japan preferential access to supply at times of temporary or artificially-induced supply shortages. This, however, will depend both on the more comprehensive state of the bilateral relationship and the actual international situation at a time of crisis.

It is unlikely that the United States or other industrial nations, much less Japan, will return to gunboat diplomacy: recent history has well demonstrated it no longer works. Yet ironically if gunboat diplomacy were to be used again and successfully, the benefits accruing to any users, including Japan, would flow from the enhanced legitimacy they presumably have in protecting previous investments in natural resources in the host countries.

The Guaranteed Price Floor for Oil in Consumer Countries. If Japan will not be investing in overseas petroleum exploration and production on anything even remotely approaching the American scale and if the development of domestic resources is geologically out of the question, how is Japan to view American proposals to establish a guaranteed price floor for oil in consumer countries? With the American government contemplating encouraging large private capital investment (potentially at an annual rate of some $100 billion) in order to increase energy reserves available for world consumption in order to break OPEC's market power, the United States has developed an interest in keeping energy prices sufficiently high to make such investment privately economic. Even though these new sources may be located in the United States or owned by American-based corporations, their beneficial impact will accrue to all consumer nations; it is not surprising that the United States should wish to recoup this investment. Unless such investment can be recouped, financing from private sources will not be forthcoming.

To this end, under the auspices of the IEA, the United States has sought agreement with other industrialized consuming countries to prevent oil from being sold in their respective domestic markets below an agreed common price. Agreement in principle has been reached and in December 1975, a common floor price of $7/barrel was agreed upon. Each country will presumably use its own methods to determine how to implement the agreement, though it is anticipated that if world prices fall below $7 compensatory, import duties will be levied to raise the domestic price to that level. More important, in the long run it is not clear how to assure that countries purchasing oil at a lower price, when it is available, will impose the floor price on its domestic users.

Given the great Japanese interest in increased energy sources, it can be anticipated that Japan will adhere to the floor price at least in the intermediate run. What Japan and other energy-poor industrialized nations will do once this newly-developed energy becomes available, however, remains in some doubt. If the Japanese government believes that for national security reasons it is wise to continue to try to limit dependence on imported Arab oil even after OPEC's market power is broken, then of course its considerable enforcement machinery will be used to maintain the agreed price domestically.

Japan might decide, however, that in a world of more abundant energy, such security issues no longer apply and that continued discrimination against their energy-using industries is not in the long-run interests of the Japanese economy. The floor price might well be breached. It would be argued that Japanese consumers should not have to bear the burden, through excessively high prices, of guaranteeing profitable returns to investors in American- or other foreign-based investors in energy development. Accordingly, why not allow competitively-determined world market prices for oil prevail once again? From the American perspective, this might well be interpreted as Japanese cheating on an international agreement directly affecting American interests.

How should the United States respond? Should it once again accept a two-tier world price system for oil such as prevailed in the 1960s? Japan's weight in the world economy is now and will be in the future of such magnitude that the United States might find it necessary to swallow the capital loss dealt it by Japan rather than attempt to force Japanese compliance through economic counter-measures. However speculative such conjecture might be, geography dictates that the possibility of numerous conflicts of this character be considered.

The International Conservation Issue. While the result of increased petroleum exploration and the development of alternative energy sources might alone be sufficient to diminish OPEC's market power significantly, the great expense and uncertainty of new exploration and development have dictated that major stress be placed, particularly in international contexts, on energy conservation programs by the large consumer nations. In fact, over the longer run much conservation will occur as the inevitable market result of the higher prices of oil and other energy sources. These higher prices will ensure, by themselves, that the historical relationship between economic growth and energy use will differ in the future from the past. Some of this conservation will rely on newly profitable but already known technologies, but much will be the result of new energy-saving innovations. To the extent that the potential producers of such innovations perceive the possibility of making substantial profits (many energy-saving innovations may not be of this character at all), substantial individual and national efforts fully comparable to efforts at increasing supply may be expected within the range of activities normal to the marketplace.

The long time horizon associated with market-led conservation activity (and, for that matter market-led exploration activity) has led to a variety of attempts to impose, by international agreement, short-run, government-managed conservation goals for the consumer nations. The precise manner in which the burdens of such conservation will be shared among these nations is a problem closely analogous to the problem of distributing production cutbacks among crude oil producers in order to sustain higher prices.

The International Energy Agency initially proposed as a near-term goal conservation sufficient to provide a 10 percent cutback in petroleum imports by all member nations. Many in the Japanese policy-making elites reacted by stressing the inequitable character of such a goal. They have argued that 10 percent conservation of imports is 10 percent conservation of crude oil consumption for Japan and less than 4 percent conservation of crude oil for the United States, given the latter's large domestic oil production. Moreover 75 percent of Japanese energy is derived from crude oil; compared to 43 percent in the United States. In Japan it is also suggested, quite apart from dependence on imported crude oil, that Japan simply has much less room for energy conservation than in the United States and most Western European countries. Energy for so-called comfort uses (household and transportation) consumes only 36 percent of total usage in Japan as compared with 58 percent in the United States.

The initial goal of the IEA has not been without its defenders; in particular, there has been some criticism of the Japanese complaints in the United States. It is argued that because Japan has become so heavily dependent on oil, there is presumptively considerable opportunity for taking some of the easier reconversion steps to coal. Moreover, the presumption that opportunities for conservation in the household and transportation sectors are greater or such conservation socially more appropriate or easier reflects ignorance or perhaps bias. In fact, considerable evidence suggests that the reasonable opportunities for conservation are perhaps three times as great in the industrial and electricity-generation sectors as they are in the "comfort" sectors. For example, there is thought to be considerably more opportunity (perhaps twice as much) for energy conservation by more efficient production processes in paper, steel, aluminum, plastics, and cement manufacture, and in electricity generation than by fuel economy in the proverbially energy-inefficient American automobile. In this connection it is often noted that in international perspective, Japanese industries are relatively

energy intensive in their production structure, both in the energy-using composition of industry and the energy-using processes in each industry. The recent
finding of the IEA that Japan has done better on conservation than the United
States reflects more the differential impact of recession than the success of
respective governmental conservation policies.

Oil Purchasing Agencies. In assessing the reasons for the present success of
OPEC within the context of present day supply-demand relationships, great
attention has been focused on the manner in which crude oil is purchased from
producers. In the American context it has been argued that the fully integrated
American-based international oil companies, which produce crude oil, refine it
into a variety of petroleum products, and then distribute these products, serve
the interests of the producer nations at the expense of the United States or other
purchasing nations. With direct access to the consumer market, the international
oil companies are in a position to attempt to pass along to the consumer the
monopoly prices set by the producer nations. It is suggested that were
purchasing centralized in a national agency, perhaps in connection with an
auctioning arrangement, the probability that the OPEC cartel might be undermined would be significantly increased. For example, a single institution
controlling access to the large American market for imported crude oil could do
much to stimulate competition among the many oil producing nations of the
world. The proposal that access to the American market ought to be limited by a
strict import quota and rights to a share in this quota be auctioned off via sealed
bids to the highest bidder has much to commend itself. Since successful bidders
might resell their import licenses there is considerable scope for hiding the true
identity of the actual bidder and should make producer nation cheating on
OPEC commitments easier.

Foreign-based, vertically integrated, international oil companies no longer
completely dominate the Japanese petroleum industry as a result of concerted
MITI action to stimulate competition at the refining and distribution stage. Yet
this policy has also made it difficult for Japan to use its potentially strategic
position as the probable single market for crude oil to stimulate competition at
the very important pre-refinery stage. This structural failing is now widely
recognized both within and without the Japanese government. In the same way
that MITI has encouraged the consolidation of many Japanese industries,
previous policies are in the process of being reversed. It is planned that the
comparatively large number of distributors and refiners will be consolidated into
two or three groups which will then be explicitly tied to Japanese exploration
and overseas production ventures.

MITI's planned mode of consolidation is not without its critics. It is argued
that there has been too much emphasis in MITI on establishing a vertically
integrated, Japanese-controlled oil company which would be heavily involved in
overseas exploration and production, and that not enough attention has been

given to developing a crude oil purchasing institution, like that described for the United States, which would control access to the Japanese petroleum market. As suggested in the earlier discussion on petroleum exploration, there is the danger that the seeming effort to create a Japanese "oil major" is an outmoded response for securing access to oil at reasonable price for an era that no longer exists.

It would appear that American as well as Japanese consumers of oil would benefit from a policy designed to centralize Japanese purchasing of crude oil. The largest single national purchaser, or even second largest, of internationally traded crude oil has the potential to exert considerable influence on prices from the buyers' side of the market. While it might appear that such a policy would remove some of the advantages now possessed by the considerable American-owned interests in refining and distribution in Japan, in fact, centralized purchasing alone might do these interests far less harm than the further agressive development of Japanese oil majors.

National and International Stockpiles of Crude Oil. Analysts have suggested various alternative strategies for coping with contrived energy scarcity. If energy prices will not decline substantially, the public benefit of massive new investment in exploration and conservation will be to prevent future large increases in energy prices and to place Arab oil producers in the position of residual supplier to the large industrial nations, thus severely limiting their capacity for politically motivated embargoes and other means of oil-related financial disruption. Some analysts have suggested less expensive means of coping with both high prices and the threat of embargo posed by OPEC market power; namely, new purchasing arrangements, the more readily available modes of conservation, and increasingly large stockpiles of oil in consumer nations.

There is at least widespread agreement in Japan, Western Europe, and the United States that large petroleum stockpiles are an important component of any new energy policy. Stockpiles should be large enough to allow maintenance of close to normal economic activity until replacement for disrupted supplies can be found. The time between the beginning of a supply disruption and production from alternative sources will vary exponentially with the size of the supply disrupted. The larger the role of supplies from insecure sources the geometrically larger the necessity of stockpiles. And the larger the aggregate national stockpiles the more expensive they are to maintain.

While the precise point at which stockpiling of the sort described here will become more expensive than reliance on new technology, or high cost new sources, or increased conservation, remains the nub of the debate raging throughout the industrialized world; the observed behavior of most nations indicates that they feel such a point has not been reached. All nations are adding to their stockpiles. In Japan, stockpiles, while low by international standards, have increased by almost 50 percent since late 1973; and continued increase is scheduled. Advocates of large stockpiles in Japan have been bolstered by recent government studies showing, that providing there is slow buildup, the economic cost of maintaining 120-day stockpiles against all oil imports (and thus perhaps double that against supplies from insecure areas) is, in aggregate terms, relatively small—about 7 percent of the price of oil.

For all the Japanese desire to increase stockpiles, the interests of the relatively energy-rich industrialized nation and the energy-poor industrialized nations are not entirely congruent, notably in the extent to which stockpiling is substituted for developing new energy sources. While the maintenance of large national petroleum stockpiles does diminish the possibility that supply interruptions will be initiated, energy-rich nations will be able to maintain a larger presence in the international oil market than otherwise, to the potential detriment of Japan and similarly situated nations. Also, it is not altogether clear just what access to alternative sources Japan might have as it draws down its reserves during an embargo. Unlike energy-rich industrialized nations, Japan does not have the option of delaying the use of domestic energy resources, it is doubtful that Japan can easily delay the development of foreign Japan-associated secure sources with this security end in view.

A Leadership Role for the United States—A Critical Choice. In many respects the discussions regarding alternative strategies designed to free the large energy-consuming nations from exclusive dependence on the pricing and production decisions of the OPEC nations point up the problems which make cooperation among the major consumer nations, some of which are also producers nations, so very difficult. For this reason, in the same way that success or failure of OPEC depends not so much on widespread producer cooperation as on the policies of Saudi Arabia and Kuwait, so the success or failure of IEA programs for conservation, purchasing, and stockpiling depend ultimately on the leadership of one or two countries. Most elements of these programs have significant external effects and therefore cannot rely on decentralized initiative.

Despite some projections that, in the future, Japan will import from the Middle East as much crude petroleum as Western Europe and the United States combined, it is expected that the United States will again bear the responsibility of leadership. Among the major buyers in the international oil market, only the United States can ever hope to reduce imported oil to a strategically unimportant part of its overall energy supply. Only the United States has proposed a Project Independence. Given the high value the United States has traditionally placed on strategic autonomy, its other international relations goals, its relatively rich natural resource position which makes the political costs of high profile leadership bearable, this remains one area of future international economic relations in which the United States can be expected to assume its accustomed postwar role. How America chooses to define this leadership role will doubtless critically affect the future character of the international economic system and United States-Japan economic relations.

A further bilateral issue, though not of immediate importance, may arise within a decade. Suppose the efforts to conserve oil, to develop non-OPEC energy sources, and to reduce OPEC's price-setting power are eventually successful, and an oil glut in world markets emerges. If the floor price of oil is adjusted upwards over the period to reflect general world increases in prices and costs, the floor price might well be breached. From the Japanese perspective, circumstances may well be judged to be sufficiently changed that new policies are called for. As discussed earlier, the Japanese might opt for a policy of allowing a relatively low, competitively-determined world market price for oil to prevail once again. This would be contrary to the American policy to provide adequate returns to investors in newly developed, relatively high-cost oil. One alternative would be to accept once again a two-tier world price system. Another policy option would be to encourage Japanese direct investment participation in American and other such new energy projects, thereby locking Japanese interests also into maintaining relatively high prices for oil. How significant an issue this becomes depends upon the success of other energy policies, the extent of Japanese involvement in fairly high-cost energy sources, and the degree to which a real floor price system is relied upon.

Relations with the Developing Countries and
Use of Market Power

Since the rise of OPEC the relations of the industrialized world, especially the United States, with the developing nations have become more complicated and difficult, with some spillover of potential tension spots into the bilateral relationship with Japan. The developing countries, spurred on by OPEC's success, increasingly stridently have enunciated demands of the industrialized world—demands ranging all the way from specific concessions to, at their most comprehensive, a substantial say in the shaping of the new world economic order.

Developing countries have organized in various ways to push their presumed common goals—through the United Nations Conference on Trade and Development (UNCTAD), the Group of Seventy-Seven (embodying now more than a hundred nations), the Group of Twenty-Four, and various regional groupings. Objectives are not just economic. The developing countries share debilitating legacies of colonialism, dependency, and a sense of impotence; their new nationalist feelings quite naturally are reflected in goals of independence, autonomy, even a tweaking of the powerful First World nations. Thus non-oil producing developing countries have supported OPEC despite the great burdens high prices of oil have brought on their own economies; OPEC offers a hope, symbolic as well as real, that they too may unite to wrest gains from the rich and powerful West.

The developing country confrontation with the developed is nonetheless carried on primarily in economic spheres. This is the main source of whatever power the developing countries may have, and the real needs of the developing countries are seen very much in economic terms. Put simply, the economic need of developing countries is to obtain from abroad increases in their total resources—physical, human, and technological—flowing more stably over time, and on better terms. These resources can be obtained in three ways. They can be earned through exports; they can be borrowed through loans and foreign direct investment; and they can be received as grants or other concessionary aid.

The specifics of ongoing policy issues between the developing and the developed can be viewed in terms of each, and frequently of combinations, of these ways of obtaining more resources. Developing countries seek commodity agreements both to stabilize the flow of export earnings and to increase those earnings (relative to import prices) by higher-than-competitive-market terms of trade. They seek open, indeed preferred, access to the import markets of the developed nations. They seek capital, but as much as possible on concessionary (aid) terms; they desire foreign investment and its associated technologies, but not at prices which enable rents (excess profits) to accrue to foreign owners. They demand aid, much of which now in fact is in the form of concessionary loans rather than grants, from the richer nations—bilaterally, through multilateral consortia, and through regional and global international institutions (the World Bank, International Development Agency (IDA), the IMF, Inter-American Development Bank, Asian Development Bank and the like). They lay claim to all the gains from the IMF creation of international liquidity through SDRs, as well as the gains from any international demonitization of gold by IMF sales. They also want to obtain the rents accruing from ocean and ocean-bed development.

Examination of the sources of economic power of developing countries suggest that it is not so large, with the exception of the OPEC nations. Most of their power is negative; denial of the developed countries to the LDC markets, investment opportunities, contiguous ocean resources, and supplies of natural resources. But denial will hurt the developing countries themselves far more than the developed countries. The main power of the developing countries is to withhold supplies of those relatively few natural resources and in which they constitute a major source, as indicated in Table IV-3. For commodities other than oil, embargo is a possibility but it is a most unlikely one—especially given the large stockpiles held in the United States. One can think of a variety of tropical food crops—such as sugar, coffee, tea, cocoa, and bananas—the supply of which LDCs might attempt to control. More likely than export embargoes are LDC attempts to raise price through OPEC-type producer cartels, in other words contrived scarcity if not natural scarcity. Indeed, such attempts have already been made in bauxite and copper.

However, are oil and OPEC a good model? Probably not really, simply because of oil's overwhelming importance. No other agricultural or mineral raw

Table IV-3
Japan and United States Dependency on Imports and Share of Total World Imports of Major Basic Commodities
(in percentage)

	Degree of Dependency on Imports		Share of Total World Imports		Sources of World Exports		
	Japan	U.S.	Japan	U.S.	Developed Nations	Developing Nations	Communist Nations
Beef	14.1%	5.4%	2.8%	26.7%	65.1	31.4	3.5
Wheat	95.1	0.0	9.4	0.0	88.1	3.6	8.3
Maize	99.5	0.0	16.3	0.1	85.0	14.6	0.4
Wool	100.0	26.9	30.6	2.7	88.0	10.1	1.9
Cotton	100.0	0.0	20.7	0.4	22.7	7.9	5.4
Lumber	50.0	0.2	31.2	12.6	49.1	48.0	1.6
Iron Ore	98.9	34.1	41.1	13.4	55.3	42.7	2.0
Copper (ore and base metal)	89.0	16.0	22.0	9.9	45.4	54.0	0.6
Lead (ore and base metal)	72.0	28.0	8.0	18.4	51.5	47.7	0.8
Zinc (ore and base metal)	63.0	46.0	14.7	25.8	84.2	15.6	0.3
Tin (ore and base metal)	97.8	10.0	18.1	32.3	4.3	95.4	0.3
Nickel (ore and base metal)	100.0	90.0	12.4	29.9	76.3	23.3	0.4
Bauxite	100.0	87.9	12.9	28.7	9.6	88.9	1.5
Manganese	97.6	97.7	31.9	16.4	7.6	87.0	5.3
Chromium	99.1	100.0	28.6	24.0	13.3	86.7 }	
Tungsten	68.3	39.9	9.0	15.6	0.0	100.0 }	
Phosphoric ore	100.0	0.0	15.0	0.5	n.a.	n.a.	n.a.
Coal	63.6	0.0	25.8	0.0	81.8	0.3	17.9
Crude oil	99.7	19.2	13.7	13.4	4.8	83.0	12.2
Natural gas	34.9	4.0	1.9	37.9	75.6	22.5	1.9

Note: Dependency is the ratio net imports (imports-exports) to domestic use, while shares of world imports are gross (without deducting exports). Data are in most cases for 1972, but 1971 for lumber, and 1973 for dependency ratios for copper, lead, zinc, tin and nickel. "World imports" refer to OECD nation imports for iron ore, copper, lead, bauxite, tin, nickel, manganese, chromium, tungsten, phosphoric ore and beef.

Sources: Japan, MITI, *White Paper on International Trade 1975* (Japan External Trade Organization, 1975), pp. 24-25, 41-42; UN, *Yearbook of International Trade Statistics 1974*; OECD, *Trade by Commodities: Market Summaries: Exports 1972*, Vol. I and Imports 1972, Vol. I.

material moving in international trade, including wheat, plays a strategic role in economic life comparable to oil; indeed the sum total of international trade in all mineral and agricultural commodities is only equal in value to that of crude oil. Even if producer cartels were to be successful, they are unlikely to be sufficiently important to warrant major attention from economic policymakers.

But such cartels are not likely even to be successful. Of the many primary commodities which figure importantly in international trade, only comparatively few do not have readily available substitutes either directly or in the production of goods in which they are used. Even within the restricted category of commodities without close substitutes, their location and production is widely distributed geographically, since they are produced in many countries in fairly substantial amounts. Without very large producers able, much less willing, to play the Saudi and Kuwaiti roles it seems unlikely that cartels, organized under such conditions, can long be effective in manipulating prices and quantities. Moreover, in many commodities the dominant sources of supply are developed countries, notably, the United States itself, Canada, and Australia; these nations are unlikely to join (LDC) producer cartels, or to form their own. The Communist bloc, notably Russia, is an important supplier of chromite, manganese, and palladum-platinum, but the United States' stockpiles amount to two to three years consumption.

The winnowing of likely candidates for new LDC-based cartels leaves but a handful of primary commodities of any significance: bauxite, phosphate rock, uranium, possibly timber, copper, and tin are usually mentioned. Of these, only bauxite producers through the actions of the Jamaican government have had any measure of success in raising prices through the exercise of market power. However, the bauxite cost component of refined aluminum is very low. Copper, in contrast to bauxite, is to date a clear case of failure to maintain high prices. Since 1967 a copper producers association, Inter-governmental Council of Copper Exporting Countries (CIPEC), modeled on OPEC has been in existence. Despite continuing vigorous efforts and a remarkable run-up in copper prices for a brief period in 1974, CIPEC has failed in every attempt to determine prices in the market. The amount of copper involved in international transactions is sufficiently small so that it is within the resources of individual firms or groups of firms to acquire substantial market positions.

For example, in late 1974, Japan became a major exporter of copper as trading firms began to unload their speculative positions. That helped break the back of CIPEC's attempt at market stabilization. This underlines what has often been lost sight of in discussions of Japan's position as a raw material poor, large industrialized economy. Vulnerability has been stressed; underplayed is the fact that Japan is in a major position to influence world market price as a buyer! Japan is already a significant factor in world markets for virtually every basic commodity, as indicated in Table IV-3. Given the absence of natural scarcity in most commodities and the small number of Japanese firms accounting for nearly all Japanese raw material imports, it is surprising that, except in Southeast Asia, there is not more discussion of the Japanese exerting market power to keep raw materials prices artificially low! If past experience is any guide, for example, Japanese trading firms' role in the pre-World War II raw cotton market, action quietly directed to this end is as likely as attempts from the seller's side of the market.

Implications for United States–Japanese Relations. Clearly the demands of the developing countries affect the international economic system—and the national interests of both the United States and Japan—in all of the policy areas already discussed: commercial policy for manufactures and agriculture; the international monetary and financial system; oil and other natural resources; and foreign direct investment and capital flows. It is in the long-run interests of both the United States and Japan that the developing countries achieve sustained, relatively rapid real economic growth per capita. The benefits, even measured in narrowly economic terms, to the United States and Japan are likely to be substantially greater than the costs of domestic reallocation of resources and of the amounts of resources transferred on concessionary terms to the developing countries.

The process by which the developing countries are brought into participation in the shaping of the new rules for the international economic system, as well as finding the solution to specific issues, will be complex and difficult. Success will not be easy to achieve. The twenty-seven nation Conference on International Economic Cooperation (CIEC) initiated in December 1975 with twenty members from the developing world bodies to be a useful institution for North-South dialogue. Even so, confrontation is likely to dominate the negotiating mode for some time—perhaps more than a decade. There are many specific issues, each complicated; the developing countries will be emotionally intransigent and probably unrealistic not only in their demands but also in their expectations. The total package of resource provision to the developing countries is likely to be far less than they want. Eventually confrontation will probably be reduced. The leading developing countries will be increasingly coopted into the decision-making apparatus, and the lack of basic unity of interests among various developing countries and their limited ability to influence fundamental economic forces will be gradually perceived by developing country leaders. It will be an uneasy period nonetheless.

How does First World confrontation with the Third and Fourth Worlds affect the Japanese-American economic relationship? To date, the major LDC focus of attention has been the United States, as the richest nation, the home for most transnational firms, and the world leader. This probably will continue. The LDCs as a global group—in distinction to the developing countries of East and Southeast Asia—have paid relatively little attention to Japan. It is ideologically easier for the LDCs to unite against the United States than Japan. At the same time, Japan's very importance in major natural resource markets makes it both vulnerable and strong. A developing country for which Japan is the major buyer must feel constrained in how much pressure it can put on Japan; typically Japan is far more diversified in its sources of supply than the developing country is in its markets.

Japan potentially has more to lose in confrontation with the developing countries than the United States because of its far greater reliance on natural resource imports and also on developing country markets for exports. In particular, it fears commodity arrangements which result in higher relative prices for natural resource imports. It is not surprising that the Japanese support the Lomé Convention approach of ensuring stability of the export earnings of developing countries, rather than agreements which directly fix prices of natural resources. In practice Japanese policymakers have been very pragmatic and rather tough in their negotiations generally with developing countries and certainly in their dealings in commodity markets.

Because the United States has less to lose than Japan, and perhaps more to gain, from conciliatory compromises with the developing countries, it is likely to grant more and larger concessions to them. Japan will be under pressure—from the United States as well as the developing countries—to go along. On some issues, especially those involving trade in natural resources, Japan may find the price very high. This is likely to generate bilateral tensions between Japan and the United States.

Thus one choice for the United States is whether to seek, or at least acquiesce to, commodity stabilization agreements urged by LDCs (or possibly others). There are political and diplomatic reasons for doing so, although economic benefits are less clear. A more sophisticated choice is whether to seek agreements that really work, or to maintain a choreography of friendly negotiation but to build in such loopholes and structural difficulties that agreements are not really operative. Is success defined as stabilization of export earnings around some presumably market-determined price, or as raising the price above market-determined levels?

Certainly American and Japanese interests concerning trade arrangements in natural resources will differ, both in intensity and at times even in direction. As indicated in Table IV-3, imports of natural resources are much more important for Japan than the United States; moreover the Japanese structure of GNP requires relatively more natural resource inputs than the United States. On the other hand, as already noted, no other commodity anywhere approaches the importance of oil; the amounts are far smaller, the possibilities of substitute commodities or sources of supply far greater, the opportunities for producer exercise of market power far less.

While consumers in Japan and the United States have an identical interest in obtaining stable supplies of basic commodities at relatively low and stable prices, producer interests diverge in those cases in which, unlike Japan, the United

States has large domestic production and even exports. Where Japanese and American interests differ, how should they be reconciled, or perhaps more relevant, what should be the trade-offs among American national interests regarding American consumers, American producers, LDCs, and Japan?

Like Japan, the United States is a major purchaser of certain basic commodities (see Table IV-3, and, unlike Japan, a major seller of certain others. The United States faces a host of choices revolving around the issue as to whether, and under what circumstances, it should exercise this potential market power. To do so would go against the entire liberal trade framework, based on setting of prices through competition among private firms in competitive world markets. But if the United States were to act as a monopsonistic buyer, is it to its advantage to do so in collusion with Japan? Probably more relevant, how should the United States respond if "Japan, Inc." were to emerge in natural resource markets, that is, if the Japanese government were to allow, encourage, or force major Japanese trading companies to collude as monopsonistic buyers in world commodity markets? Such action would be much against American interests, in the differential in import prices facing the United States and Japan and in American relations with countries exporting to Japan.

It is possible that issues of aid and resource transfers will be sources of tension between the United States and Japan. Although both are low providers of aid at present (official development assistance only about 0.25 percent of GNP, far below the commitments through Development Assistance Committee (DAC) of 0.7 percent), suppose each country decides on substantially different aid level targets? The country with the higher target is likely to put considerable pressure on the other to accept the higher level.

The United States and Japan are likely to have overlapping involvements in multilateral aid agencies and in bilateral aid programs to the same countries. To what extent, and under what circumstances will the two nations cooperate or compete with each other? Will the United States come to support fully a Japanese-dominated Asian Development Bank? Will Japan continue to support U.S.-dominated organizations such as the World Bank and IDA? American and Japanese aid programs in developing countries have somewhat different goals, philosophies, and means of implementation. Japanese aid is much more specific project oriented, related to Japanese private investment activities, and involved in generating raw material exports to Japan. Will conflicts arise in third countries—in aid, as in investment and trade—which impinge directly on the U.S.-Japanese relationship? It is clear that increasing Japanese direct involvement in developing countries through investment and aid will enhance possibilities of tension between the United States and Japan, and will certainly make the bilateral relationship more complex than in the past.

Japanese and American Interests in East-West Trade

One of the best illustrations of the fact that the postwar international economic system's very success has undermined parts of its foundation lies in the changing attitudes among American policymakers towards trade between Communist and non-Communist nations. When initial postwar American enthusiasm for universalism gave way to a strong defense against the expansion of communism, institutions such as the IMF and the General Agreement on Tariffs and Trade (GATT) came to be viewed as structures shoring up the weaker economies of the anti-Communist alliance, as an integral part of the defense of Western Europe. The success of the international economic system in promoting economic recovery and economic growth have given existing political institutions sufficient legitimacy and have created sufficient defense potential in Western Europe so that strident anti-communism is unnecessary and, indeed, potentially dysfunctional. Communist nations are now being considered for membership in the GATT and the IMF. Already Poland, Romania, and Hungary have become full members of GATT.

While American interest in East-West trade is relatively recent, such trade has been growing quite rapidly for some time, albeit from a very small base. As a share of world trade, East-West trade was 1.3 percent in 1953. By 1967 it accounted for 2.8 percent, and by 1973 had expanded to over 4 percent of total world trade. In the wake of contrived energy shortages in the non-Communist industrialized economies and an increasingly well-recognized technological lag in the Communist world, the positive advantages of some increase in economic interdependence are apparent to policymakers in both camps.

Unlike the views of the Soviet Union, China and Eastern Europe, the United States does not see the benefits of increased economic interdependence as primarily direct or economic. Rather, over a shorter time horizon, there appears to be the belief among American policymakers that other American diplomatic interests can be served in exchange for helping to promote the economic advancement of the Communist bloc. Over a longer horizon there is the hope, prompted by the same kind of considerations which led to early postwar liberal universalism, that increased economic interdependence will create powerful interests which will prevent that particular kind of tension which resolves itself in international violence.

For all the newly found American enthusiasm for trade between Communist and non-Communist countries, there are sufficient obstacles to an acceleration of such commercial interactions as to make it highly unlikely that this facet of the international economic system will differ greatly in the future than it has been during the last decade. For example, prices in the nonmarket Communist countries bear little relation to opportunity costs and are seldom changed. In international trade, Communist traders must sell their products at world market prices. This severely constrains Communist exporters of manufactured products, since their areas of real competitive advantage in international trade are not necessarily reflected in their domestic cost and price structures. At the same time, any attempt by Communist nations to cut export prices below world market prices would almost certainly bring charges of dumping. Given the Communist pricing system and disequilibrium in exchange rates, such charges would be most difficult to refute.

Through the postwar period the fastest growing major component of international trade has been the exchange of manufactured goods among the industrialized nations; this comprises more than 40 percent of all world trade. In the absence of a full commitment to market socialism, it is doubtful that Communist countries will be anything more than residual participants in this area of international economic interaction. Natural resources and agricultural products however may be another matter.

Communist Trade in Natural Resources and Agricultural Products. Given the interest in non-Communist industrialized nations in diversifying sources of supplies for mineral and agricultural raw materials, the institutional problems cited above are relatively unimportant. American potential trade patterns are by no means homogeneous among the Communist bloc nations. Trade with the Soviet Union is potentially the largest. The main flows, and issues, involve American wheat and feedgrain exports, oil, and other mineral resource imports. Trade with China is likely to be far less, though wheat may at times be of some export importance.

Trade prospects are far greater for Japanese trade with the Soviet Union and China, importing natural resources from both (plus possibly soybeans from China) and exporting manufactures, especially machinery. Japanese interest in Soviet and Chinese raw materials will ensure the continued rapid growth of imports from Communist areas, provided relative Japanese dependence on the two areas can be kept in some balance and overall dependency be relatively low. The latter factor will probably not operate as much of a constraint since the base (in terms of Japan's share of imports) from which continued growth will come remains very low in relation to Japan's large resource needs.

The problem for Japan of balance between China and Russia is more serious. The complexity of project negotiations and the long lead times involved in almost every transaction make it difficult for Japan to prevent almost any important bilateral arrangement from becoming a source of potential tension in the highly complex diplomatic balance in Northeast Asia. It is unlikely that the Japanese economy will become significantly dependent on either China or the Soviet Union: Japanese world trade is and will be so large in relation to both China's and the Soviet Union's trade possibilities that the overwhelming preponderance (at least four-fifths) of Japan's trade will be with non-Communist nations.

In contrast, economic dependence on Japan is a foreseeable danger for China. Almost 25 percent of China's international trade now is with Japan. Unless China grows much more rapidly in the future than does Japan (which is unlikely) or, unless China substantially increases the share of its GNP devoted to foreign trade while Japan does the reverse (also unlikely), China's interest in diversifying foreign trade sources will seriously inhibit any increase in the relative importance of China as a trade partner for Japan.

The main possible exception is oil. Even here, the possibilities realistically appear substantially less than some optimists have asserted. There are a whole host of important political, technological, and economic difficulties to be overcome. Very little is known about the extent and nature of Chinese oil deposits, especially those offshore. The claims to offshore oil are tangled, with China, Taiwan, Japan, South Korea, and North Korea making overlapping claims.

China has neither the technology nor the capital to engage in autonomous rapid expansion of oil production. With a will these problems could probably be resolved, pretty much on China's terms regarding ownership and control, but perhaps at a high price for technology. However, it remains unclear whether China is willing to shift its developmental strategy to heavy reliance on exports (and imports), and upon depletable minerals as major export commodities. Moreover, China's industrial development strategy will increasingly require the domestic use of oil. The most reasonable expectation is that while China will expand oil exports substantially over the coming decade and particularly to Japan, the amounts and values involved will not bring about major qualitative changes in Japan's economic relationship with China or thereby with the United States. Japan is unlikely to import more than 10 percent of its oil from China (now about 3 percent).

Japan's Economic Involvement with the USSR and China: Issues for the United States. Perhaps the key question is how the United States should view a fairly substantial absolute, but rather modest relative, increase in Japan's trade with the Soviet Union and China. The issues revolve primarily around political rather than economic desiderata. This is not surprising since the United States, the Soviet Union, and China all link economic and political issues in dealing with each other. Only Japan resists such linkage, and probalby will continue to do so. Greater bilateral economic interdependence is likely to have a more substantial impact on China and the Soviet Union than on Japan. It will integrate them somewhat more into the market world economy, with some sacrifice of autonomy compensated by more rapid growth. Is this in American national interest or not?

Is some increase in involvement with the Soviet Union and China likely to reduce significantly Japan's involvement and identification, economically and politically, with the United States? It seems extremely unlikely. Rather, it appears to be one more component of the international expansion and gradual diversification of Japan's burgeoning economy. In a new world of lessened East-West confrontation, this issue appears much less crucial for the United States than it was perceived in the past.

Some direct economic issues may become significant, though perhaps mainly for their political implications. Suppose Japan decides to lend heavily and on a long-term basis to the Soviet Union and/or China? Suppose further this lending seems to be financed in part by borrowings from Western capital markets (unlikely in fact since Japanese loans are likely to be credits for Japanese exports)? Should the United States regard these flows as a desirable use of Western capital? How should the United States respond to Japanese (or Russian, or Chinese) proposals that natural resource projects on the Asia mainland be joint between Japanese and American firms, using credits from both governments?

The United States-Japan Economic Relationship in Broader International and Political Context

The institutions of and the attitudes regarding the international economic system have changed remarkably in the last half-dozen years. Postwar paradigms have unraveled. Improvements in production and the standard of living in many areas of the world and changes in worldwide distribution of material wealth have reduced, though by no means eliminated, American dominance of the international economy. These, together with changing political values, have altered the American foreign policy-making elites' earlier conception of foreign economic policy as only a subordinate component of American global political strategy. This changed perspective has meant increasing unwillingness in the United States to give ground on foreign economic issues in return for a strengthening of an anti-Communist political alliance, while the rising power of other nations has meant an increasing ability to withstand American pressure.

In international commercial policy, the momentum for further reductions in tariff and nontariff barriers has declined in the face of new, if entirely appropriate, American demands for full reciprocity; while the occasional erection of barriers to exports have created new threats to the legitimacy of what has already been achieved on the import side. In international financial policy, the end of the Bretton Woods system has left Western Europe and Japan struggling to circumscribe America's role as world banker while, by way of compensation, the United States is attempting to ensure that it will be afforded ample opportunity to influence the exchange rate for the dollar. In international direct investment policy, the growing economic power of Europe and Japan which have the means to adapt, produce, and diffuse technology, has reduced the bargaining power of American-controlled transnational corporations sufficiently to allow the countries which are host to the international activity of these firms opportunity to shop around, and thereby to extract a growing proportion of the rents associated with their activities.

OPEC's success to date in increasing sharply the relative price of oil has raised a whole set of problems: conservation, alternative sources of energy supplies, and large-scale transfer of financial resources to OPEC nations with the attendant recycling of petrodollars and financing of oil-induced balance of payments deficits, especially for the non-oil developing countries. OPEC's success has encouraged the developing countries to raise sharply their demands on the economically advanced nations, with ongoing confrontation a real possibility. Trade in basic commodities features heavily among the relevant issues. The Sino-Soviet dispute, decline of the cold war, and possibility of détente make old paradigms for economic relations between East and West less relevant.

What do these many changes augur for the evolution of the international economic system and the position both of the United States and Japan within the evolving system? There is small prospect in the foreseeable future that the world economy will return to an American-run system, even if it continues to be a liberal system. American banks and corporations are economically incapable of regaining their sheer dominance of the past, and the American government is politically incapable of perpetuating the trade-off which permitted the accommodation of the economic needs of other nations without great economic *quid pro quo*.

Neither is it likely that the world economy will break down into antagonistic regional blocs. The enormous trade in manufactured products among industrialized countries, the universal desire for access to the American market, and the increasing trade between Japan and Western Europe, together with the virtual necessity of American-led cooperation among industrialized nations on international energy policy make such a development most improbable. Japan will be economically preeminent in the Western Pacific and the Common Agricultural Policy of the European Community will survive, but these conditions will be but facets of the industrialized economies' relations with each other, with the developing nations, and with the Communist nations.

More likely, the evolving international economic system will come to resemble twentieth century pluralism rather than nineteenth century-style liberalism or 1930s style regionalism. Like nineteenth century liberalism the international economic system will be increasingly global in participation. Like 1930s regionalism, the spreading lack of shared values among major participants in the international economic system will leave the coordination of international economic activity less in the hands of markets and private initiative than had been the case throughout much of the postwar period. An increasingly narrower conception of national self-interest on the one hand and an increasingly greater appreciation of the role of international oligopoly and international cartel will mean greater political intervention in international economic relations and, in consequence, an inevitable intermeshing of international economic issues with other international issues.

How will the United States-Japan relationship evolve in this context? The relative power relationship between the United States and Japan has undergone substantial evolution. For some years the relationship was of overwhelmingly greater importance to Japan than to the United States, reflecting the former's weak, dependent position. Even today the relationship is of substantially greater importance to Japan than the United States. This will persist, but decreasingly so, in the foreseeable future. There is no future point at which we can visualize a true parity in both economic and military power between Japan and the United States. But that is not really the issue.

What is of importance to American—and Japanese—national interests is the prospect of continued increases in Japan's economic power in relation to that of the United States. Relatively, Japan is likely to be ever more important for the United States, while, also in relative terms, the United States may well be of somewhat lesser importance to Japan. The past improvement in Japanese position emanated almost solely from economic forces, notably Japan's rapid domestic growth and foreign trade and (recently) investment expansion. Economic factors will also be in the future the main force toward increasing equality in the overall Japanese-American relationship.

It seems unlikely that militarily the present power gap between Japan and the United States will narrow substantially. Economically and technologically Japan does have the capabilities of building a substantial—but relative to the United States modest—nuclear military capacity. However, there appears little reason, much less the political will, for Japan to undertake such an expensive use of resources. One can, of course, conceive of situations in which Japan would go nuclear—perception of a direct threat to Japan, or worldwide proliferation of nuclear weapons in such an environment that Japan feels it has to join the crowd—but neither seem very likely. One suspects that any major Japanese military build-up, if indeed it ever occurs at all, will be founded on post-nuclear military technologies, many years away. Directly or indirectly, Japan will continue to rely on the American nuclear umbrella.

But sheer military power is likely to be much less immediate in its global importance in the future. It is quite clear that direct involvement in war will not provide solutions to the sorts of world problems Japan or the United States will face. Nor is gunboat diplomacy—threats of military action—likely to be effective. As discussed above, détente may well reduce potential military tensions.

As emphasis on military security issues recedes somewhat, economic issues will become of increasing importance in the international system. As more of a factor in the world economy than world military security system, Japan's role will rise, while that of the United States will be relatively reduced. Moreover, the bilateral gap in direct economic power will continue to narrow. Japan certainly will not grow as rapidly as before, and the differential between Japanese and American GNP growth rates will narrow substantially. However, size of growth now replaces rates of growth; a 6 percent increase in a $450 billion economy is absolutely far greater with more global impact than a 10 percent increase in a $100 billion economy. Perhaps equally important, Japan's economy and technology are now highly developed and sophisticated, and improvement will continue absolutely and relatively.

Americans should view the continued rise in Japanese economic power as something healthy and to be desired, rather than to be viewed with alarm or even feared. Rich, interdependent friends are better than poor, dependent ones. A final ending of the yet-persisting patron-client relationship will be beneficial to both nations. After all, the economic as well as political complementarities between the two are great. Both have a global perspective—Japan economically, and the United States both in economic and security terms. Both have advanced, technologically sophisticated, and ambitious economies. Each offers large and increasing economic and technological opportunities for the other.

At the same time, it should be clearly recognized that certain Japanese and American national interests are competitive, even though others are complementary. For this reason the United States faces a number of critical choices in its economic policy vis-à-vis Japan. Some issues will be predominantly bilateral in nature, others will arise as a consequence of differing national interests in essentially multilateral issues. And some issues will be considerably more important than others.

It is not possible to predict the future course of events well enough to know which in fact will be the most critical. Among the host of choices for American policy vis-à-vis Japan raised in this chapter, four appear to stand out as the most critical: (1) the cutting edge problem of large-scale imports from Japan injuring certain important American industries and, causing substantial adjustment problems for American workers and capital in those industries, (2) trade in agricultural products, (3) the mechanism for exchange rate adjustment for balance of payments disequilibria, and (4) the pricing of oil once alternative energy sources become available.

Given these various potential sources of tension, there certainly is no reason to be especially sanguine about future prospects for the American-Japanese relationship. Much depends on the future shape of American foreign economic policy. The textile confrontation of 1969-1971 in which the United States crudely linked a political issue with an economic issue in order to gain satisfaction might well be the harbinger of a new era in bilateral relations. By contrast, the American negotiation stance during the Kennedy Round negotiations in mid-1960s might become regarded as the last high-water mark of American postwar liberalism.

Because Japan is a great economic power but not a great political power, and because Japan is heavily dependent upon the United States for its political security, the sense of Japanese frustration might grow considerably over the years. With increasing power, Japan's frustration (shared probably by others) could result in substantial alteration of the international economic system during the last quarter of the twentieth century. As American foreign policy feels its way through a pluralist global community which it no longer dominates, it would do well to keep in mind the significance of Japan's participation in the international system and the special resolution of forces which condition Japan's position.

V The Constraints on Chinese Foreign Policy

Dwight H. Perkins

Most predictions of China's foreign policy a decade or a quarter-century hence begin with an attempt to discern the intentions or goals of a future Chinese leadership. The task of assessing some future leaders' objectives, however, is a formidable one. In the case of the People's Republic of China, it is, for all practical purposes, nearly impossible, at least when approached directly.

China today is clearly at the end of an era. The men who have ruled the nation since the revolution of 1949 are passing from the scene. Lin Piao and Chou En-lai are dead. Liu Shao-ch'i is nowhere to be seen. Others are in their late 80s and Mao himself is virtually retired. Who will follow these men into the ruling seats of the Standing Committee of the Chinese Politburo no one in or out of China really knows. Everyone concerned, however, does know that there will be no one who can take over the role of Mao Tse-tung. A revolution or a new nation has only one founder or creator and no amount of historical rewriting can give some future Chinese leader the sense of legitimacy that comes from being the very embodiment of the revolution.

New leaders, therefore, will have to seek new bases of power or support, in the Party, in the army, in Shanghai or Szechwan or the Northeast. What the winning combination will prove to be I certainly do not know nor I suspect does anyone else. But whatever the combination, the man or men in charge will have constituencies which will have to be listened to in the making of foreign as well as domestic policy.

Domestic politics will impinge on China's foreign policy just as it has on the foreign policy of the United States. But there is relatively little experience to go

159

on which tells us which domestic issues are likely to spill over into the foreign arena or precisely what influence they will have once they do. The Cultural Revolution is one of the few internal movements which has had an observable effect on foreign affairs that can be readily traced (in some areas at least). Most other struggles over policies or power have taken place behind closed doors and we have only the statements of the victors as to what occurred, and often we do not even have that. The facade of Party unity was maintained with relatively few cracks well into the year 1966.

But there is another approach to the dimensions of Chinese foreign policy in 1985 or the year 2000 that does not involve predicting who will then be the chairman of the Chinese Communist party and whether he will be a "pragmatist" or a "Maoist," whatever those terms may mean. Whoever that man is, he will have to use the foreign policy instruments available to him and the strength of two of those instruments, trade (including aid) and the military will depend to a large degree on what happens to the economy. Predictions about where the Chinese economy will be ten or twenty years hence, of course, are not easily made either. But the range of possibilities is limited and, in large part, known.

The economy also has an important indirect impact on foreign policy as well. Politicians, particularly those in states where the government has taken responsibility for much of the economy, are expected to provide the people with jobs and a steadily rising standard of living. If performance does not match the people's expectations, pressure is thereby exerted on the political leadership to do better. And one option open to a future Chinese leadership under such circumstances would be to move toward greater economic involvement with the outside world—not to jettison the policy of self-reliance, but to modify it in important ways in order to speed the importation of technological progress around the world.

Projections of economic performance, even if accurate, aid in the process of predicting future foreign policy options only if the economy does in some way limit these options. American economic wealth, for example, is already so vast, that a growth rate of 4 as against 3 percent will have little effect on the United States' ability to pay for an arms budget large enough to enable the government to project American power anywhere abroad. But the difference between 4 and 3 percent may have a major impact on the American people's willingness to pay for additional outlays.

In China the difference between a growth rate of, for example, 7 percent and one of 4 percent would also have some impact on the ability of Chinese leaders to divert resources to the military without generating popular discontent. In China, however, the effect of the economy on the size of the military budget is more direct than that. Because China is still comparatively poor, arms expenditures approaching the levels of the United States or the Soviet Union are simply beyond China's capacity. And in China there is also a very real trade-off between a large arms budget now as against an even larger one in the future, because military expenditures today cut into investment and hence into future growth. Furthermore, it is not in the field of arms alone that China's comparative poverty limits the strength of various instruments of Chinese foreign policy. A major objective of this essay, therefore, is to attempt to be more specific about the nature and degree of these limitations as they exist today and the extent to which they are likely to change a decade or two hence.

Even if there were no meaningful limitations on the size of China's military or aid budgets, of course, it would not necessarily follow that China would acquire enormous power or influence over large parts of the world (assuming that a future Chinese leadership wanted such power or influence). The world, including the less developed world, is not a blank sheet on which the great powers can write what pleases them as they could before 1914 and even 1945. Nationalism has proved to be a powerful stimulant for Asian as well as European peoples with the result that many states of the less developed world are quite capable of defending their own sovereignty and territorial integrity against all but the most massive military effort from the outside. The arena where the instruments of power can be exercised, therefore, is much more constricted than it was thirty years or even only a decade ago. In 1985 or the year 2000, this process of constriction is almost certain (barring a catastrophe such as World War III) to have proceeded even further. Power, however, will not be irrelevant in the year 2000 and one objective of this essay will be to identify where in Asia power, whether Chinese, American, or other, can influence significantly the outcome of events both today and for decades ahead.

The initial focus of this essay is on what is happening to China's economy and how that in turn influences China's military capacities and its economic programs abroad, whether in the form of aid or trade. China's ability to make use of its growing capacities is then appraised against the background of what is happening elsewhere in Asia.

Whether or not future Chinese leaders will make use of the nation's growing capacities, of course, is not simply a matter of economics or military power, particularly in as politicized a nation as the People's Republic of China. Current Chinese leaders define their goals largely in political terms and there is every reason to believe that future leaders will behave similarly. But China's political goals are the subject of other essays in this volume. Furthermore, as pointed out above, when writing about events ten or twenty years in the future, statements about economic-military capacities are subject to a narrower margin of potential error than those dealing with political goals. One may learn more about likely future political goals, therefore, by looking at capacities than by attacking the subject directly.

The relevance of these discussions of China's capacities to Americans and to American government policy is straightforward. What matters in United States-China relations is not which of us is winning the battle for the allegiance of the other peoples of Asia. If that is either of our objectives, we have both already lost and the Russians will lose too, although it is not clear that they yet understand this. What is important is not to allow the competition for allies, friends, or spheres of influence to lead us into situations where the great powers end up confronting each other. The goal instead should be to speed the process whereby the states of Asia can stand alone without external assistance of any kind except where a nuclear deterrent is required. In short, it should be the goal of the United States to create conditions that will have the long-run effect of reducing the influence of American power in Asia, not by substituting some other power, but by decreasing the influence of all the major powers. In this effort, there may be more areas were America's and China's interests run parallel to each other than is commonly supposed.

The above statement, however, is only an assertion. The argument that supports it requires first going back to an analysis of China's economy and proceeds from there.

Projecting China's Economic Growth

Most projections by economists involve the use of the past to predict the future. For China, the years that are of most relevance to the future are those beginning with the early 1960s and continuing on up to the present. However, let us begin with the background formed by the preceding decade.

Chinese growth in the 1950s, to be sure, was quite rapid and the foundation for much of the modern sector of China's economy that exists today was laid in those years. But it is difficult to see China in the near or distant future able or willing to recreate the key conditions of the 1950s. Industrial capacity in China at the beginning of the decade was underutilized and factories were filled with inexperienced personnel. Some growth in the period, therefore, was the result of making better use of existing capacity and of rising productivity as workers learned rapidly on the job. The 1950s was also a period when China was dependent to a limited degree on Soviet aid (in the form of low interest loans) and to a very large degree on the importation of hundreds of Soviet and East European industrial plants (and thousands of foreign technicians to help set them up).

Perhaps most important, prior to 1960 the leaders of the Chinese Communist party felt that they could minimize modern investment in agriculture and use the funds instead for producer goods industry (steel, machinery, etc.). Agriculture would pull itself up and would be reorganized in order to facilitate this task. Cooperatives of one hundred to three hundred families each were formed in 1955-56 throughout the countryside and these in turn were combined into individual communes of four to five thousand families in 1958. The main economic objective of these new rural units was to make it possible to mobilize great numbers of rural laborers for construction of irrigation, flood control, and drainage works. In effect, the capital stock in agriculture was to be increased dramatically without having to divert funds from machinery and steel.

Chinese economic development efforts in the 1950s, therefore, were a modified version of the Stalinist model of growth of the 1930s. Investment priorities were similar to those of the Soviet Union at that time and rules and regulations governing the economy, particularly the industrial sector, were often little more than translations of Soviet regulations. But the Chinese situation differed from that of Stalinist Russia in at least two important respects. Firstly, the Chinese could draw on Soviet experience in implementing this growth strategy whereas the Russians, for the most part, had to go it alone. And secondly while Stalin could afford to ignore measures to increase agricultural output, the Chinese could not. Chinese per capita grain production was less than half that of the Soviet Union while China's population growth rate was double that of Russia. If China had experienced the kind of stagnation that gripped Russian agriculture for more than two decades after the death of Stalin, the Chinese people would have been dying of starvation and the government would almost certainly long since have fallen.

Even a modified version of the Stalinist model, however, did not work very well in the Chinese context. China's gross national product did grow rapidly throughout the 1950s at over 7 or 8 percent a year.[a] But the developmental strategy of this period was running into trouble in at least two key areas. On the one hand, it proved to be nearly impossible to control all Chinese industry from Peking as all Russian industry was directed from Moscow. There were over 100,000 individual Chinese industrial enterprises many of them operating under very backward conditions and with inadequate records or accounts. Central planners in Peking, therefore, were in no position to know what was going on in a large portion of China's industry and hence could not very well maintain the kind of close supervision over those plants that is required by the Soviet system of planning.

More importantly, the measures that the Chinese hoped would raise farm output failed to work. By 1960, China was in the middle of what proved to be a three-year-long (1959-1961) agricultural crisis which contributed to a major economy-wide depression. Bad weather was partly at fault, but the 1958-1959 form of the People's Communes also contributed in important ways to the decline. Labor had been mobilized in unprecedented numbers, but the vast amount of water control construction that ensued proved to have a negligible impact in many cases and was actually harmful in others. At the same time, the large commune organization proved to be unwieldy causing numerous mistakes in crop management and interfering with the work incentives of the individual farmer.

---

[a]Careful attempts to reconstruct China's gross national product for the 1950s have led to estimates of a growth rate between 1952 and 1957 of between 6 and 8.7 percent (in 1952 Chinese prices). In the years 1958-1959, the growth rate is believed to have risen although precise estimates are impossible because of the poor quality of data available for those years.

The weather did eventually improve (in 1962) and the communes were reorganized so that the basic unit controlling the cultivation of crops and the mobilization of labor had only thirty families, not five thousand. But by 1963 farm output was back only to the level of 1956-1957 (or still 10 percent and more below 1956-1957 levels in per capita terms). Industry, which had suffered greatly from the campaign atmosphere of the Great Leap Forward of 1958-1959 and the abrupt (with two weeks notice) withdrawal of all Soviet technical support, as well as from the agricultural difficulties, was also beginning again to function more or less normally. Recovery, however, was not a long run solution. China needed a new development strategy that would sustain many decades of modern economic growth.

By the early 1960s China had evolved a new economic strategy, one main feature of which is still in effect today and is likely to be pursued for some time. The debate that surrounded the formulation of this new strategy in the years 1959 through 1962 was apparently bitter at times and it has left permanent scars. In 1966, the top leadership split publicly and Mao's then designated heir, Liu Shao-ch'i, fell from power, but the origins of these differences were in the difficult years of 1959 through 1962.

The key to the new strategy was agriculture. Agriculture was to be the "foundation" and industry the "leading factor." What this meant in concrete terms was that agriculture was no longer to be left to fend for itself, but would be allocated a greatly increased portion of available state funds. The new policy did not mean that most or even a majority of state investment resources would go to agriculture. Although the allocation to agriculture was tripled,[b] the lion's share of investment still went to producer goods and increasingly to the military. Military expenditures had been held down in the 1950s because weapons could be purchased cheaply from the Soviet Union and because the Russians were, it was believed, a reliable nuclear ally. The Sino-Soviet break in 1960, of course, deprived China of its main source of weapons as well as its principal ally (although formally the treaty of alliance continues in effect to this day).

Up to a point the new strategy was a success. Heavy investment in the new chemical fertilizer industry led to marked increase in grain and cotton output particularly between the years 1963 and 1967. By the late 1960s, in fact, per capita grain output had fully recovered to the levels of the mid-1950s in spite of a growth in population of over 20 percent during that same interval. Industrial output averaged 8 to 9 percent growth each year between 1957 and the early 1970s (see Table V-1). Overall, China's gross national product between 1957 and 1974 probably averaged about 5 percent *per annum* although uncertainties about the underlying data make it possible for analysts of the Chinese economy to defend estimates slightly below 5 percent.

---

[b]Data on agricultural investment in the 1960s can be derived from the statement that state funds for agriculture were 23.4 percent above agricultural tax revenues in the 1953-1972 period (*Peking Review*, December 15, 1972, p. 17) together with certain official estimates of the agricultural tax and of state investment in agriculture in the 1950s.

Table V-1
Chinese Economic Indicators

	Gross Domestic Product (billion 1957 yuan)	GDP per Capita (1957 yuan)	Gross Value of Industrial Output (billion 1957 yuan)	Grain Output (million metric tons— unhusked grain)
1952	65.9	115.3	34.3*	166
1957	95.7	147.9	70.4	185
1960	n.a.	n.a.	n.a.	150
1962	97.8	136.9	100.0	174
1965	134.2	177.0	141.7	200+
1971	193.4	226.5	237.6	246
1973	n.a.	n.a.	n.a.	250±

*This figure is in 1952 prices. In 1957 1 yuan = U.S. $0.41. To convert these figures into current (1974) U.S. prices, an exchange rate of 1 yuan = U.S. $0.71 to $0.79 would be closer to the mark. The current actual exchange rate fluctuates around 1 yuan = U.S. $0.55, but this rate does not reflect purchasing power parity.

Sources: The grain and gross industrial output figures are official Chinese figures or derived from official reports of percentage increases. The GDP figures are my own estimates based, wherever such data are available, on official Chinese figures. The per capita GDP figures were derived by using the official figures for 1952 and 1957 and assuming a 2 percent rate of population increase since 1957 (Chou En-lai has told a number of recent visitors that China's population is still growing at about 2 percent a year), although there is also scattered evidence that the population growth rate is coming down.

Development during the 1960s and early 1970s, of course, was not steady. As already mentioned, the great spurt of 1958-1959 was followed by a severe recession. From 1962 through 1966 recovery and renewed growth were quite rapid. But in 1967 and 1968 industry was again disrupted by the political turmoil connected with the Cultural Revolution. Agriculture, however, appears not to have been much if at all affected. Even in industry, the degree of disruption was much less significant than that which occurred as a result of the Great Leap and the Soviet pull-out. By 1969 or 1970 full recovery had been achieved and industry was once again growing at rates comparable to those of the mid-1960s prior to the Cultural Revolution.

China's Unresolved Economic Problems

For all its apparent success, however, the "take agriculture as the foundation" strategy left several major problems unresolved. Foremost among these problems was still agriculture itself. The massive efforts of the 1960s had only succeeded in bringing farm output back even with the growth of population. But population was still growing and raising grain output was proving to be an increasingly difficult task.

Chinese agriculture's main difficulty was not that it was hopelessly backward. In a fundamental way, barriers to further rapid increases in Chinese grain production arise because the techniques in use in Chinese agriculture today are already very advanced. Where there is plenty of water for the growing of paddy rice, yields per hectare are beginning to approach those of Taiwan, Korea, and even Japan.[c] China already has fertilizer responsive seeds and considerable quantities of chemical and natural fertilizers. Chemical fertilizers alone average about 60 kilograms of nutrient per cultivated hectare (in 1973) and the addition of organic fertilizers would raise this figure considerably. India, by way of contrast, uses only 10 kilograms of chemical nutrient per cultivated hectare. Japan and Taiwan, to be sure, use far more chemical fertilizer per hectare (over 300 kilograms of nutrient) but the comparison is misleading because of China's far greater use of organic fertilizers, and because China has large amounts of land where water supplies are inadequate for the heavy use of chemicals.

In the rice growing regions of China, yields are beginning to catch up with the nations of the world that possess the most advanced rice technology. There is still room for improvement in China within the limits of known technology elsewhere in the world,[d] but the gap is closing rapidly. This situation would not be a cause for concern if the rice technology of the most advanced countries was continuing to surge ahead thereby demonstrating that further advances elsewhere were not likely to be difficult to achieve. But increases in rice yields in Japan during the past decade have been very modest despite massive Japanese government subsidies. Japan has instead turned increasingly to imports to meet the food requirements of its ever more prosperous population.

It does not follow from the above discussion that China and the world are about to reach some absolute limit on the capacity of the soil to grow food. It does follow, however, that the nations of East Asia, at least, are launched on an unknown sea and getting safely to harbor will depend on the development of an as yet unknown technology. The spurt in Chinese farm output between 1963 and 1967 was achieved mainly by pouring large amounts of chemical fertilizer onto paddy land. New fertilizer responsive seeds did have to be developed for this effort to be successful, but enough other countries had gone through the process so that the basic methodology was well known. The next step, whatever it is, may not be so easy.

The other half of China's agricultural problem is in the north where paddy

[c]In 1970 average paddy rice yields per sown hectare were 5640 kg./hectare in Japan, 4600 in South Korea, and 4000 in Taiwan. In China in 1971 the average was somewhere between 3700 and 4300 kg./hectare.

[d]There is no precise way to estimate the gap between the yield level of today's best technology (in actual use) and that of China, because each country's conditions are different and hence what works in one may or may not be appropriate in the other.

rice, for the most part, is not grown. The nature of the problem is simple—there is not enough water. Solving it is another matter. As already pointed out, during the Great Leap Forward large numbers of water control works were built by massive labor *corvées*, but their net impact on northern farm output was negligible or even negative. North China's water problem simply could not be solved by large numbers of people wielding picks and shovels.

There are a number of technical reasons why highly labor intensive means could not by themselves provide North China with sufficient water for its fields. Notable among these is the fact that China's rivers carry enormous loads of silt. That, after all, is how the Yellow River got its name. It is not possible to use much of the water from the Yellow River (and others) for irrigation purposes because irrigation canals constructed for that purpose quickly silt up and are rendered useless. The only real solution is to take the silt out of the river and that means a massive program of dams and reforestation on the river's upper reaches. Such a program has been underway for some time, but it is enormously expensive (many billions, perhaps tens of billions of dollars) and it takes time. In the meantime deep wells can be dug to provide some areas with water, and reservoirs can (and have been) constructed to make more efficient use of the rain that does fall.

But none of these measures is likely to turn what is, after all, a part of the great dry central Asian land mass into the lush green of the semi-tropical Chinese Southwest. More to the point, the progress that will be achieved will be slow and costly. It may take ten yuan or more of investment to produce a one yuan increase in annual farm output.[e] Industrial development is, by comparison, quick and cheap.

There are events that could change the above calculations in a direction that would reduce the drag that slow agricultural development places on the rest of the economy. A marked slowing in China's rate of population growth would lower the yearly increase in the demand for food. An annual rise in farm output of 2 percent (the average rate for the 1957-1973 period) would mean a 1 percent annual increase in the per capita food supply if China's population growth rate could be reduced from 2 to 1 percent. One percent a year may not seem to be a significant decrease, but within a few decades China's food problem would, for all intents and purposes, be solved.[f]

There is evidence that China's birthrate is declining, but most of this evidence

---

[e]Chinese farm output in the 1960s was rising at a rate of just over one thousand million yuan a year according to official Chinese estimates. State investment, according to estimates derived by the methodology described in footnotes two were around five thousand million yuan a year in the 1960s and early 1970s. To this figure must be added investment by communes out of their own funds, another 10± percent of gross farm output or about six to seven thousand million yuan.

[f]By "solved" I simply mean that China would no longer have to import food in significant quantities and the Chinese people would experience a significant rise in the amount of meat in the average diet.

is based upon trends in the cities where one would expect more rapid progress in this direction. Furthermore, the great numbers of children born in the 1950s and 1960s are only now beginning to come of age and to form families. Thus efforts to reduce the crude birthrate are fighting against natural trends that would tend to raise that rate.

Still, if the currently less developed nations are going to significantly lower their birthrates, one would expect China to be in the lead. Not only is there an effective rural health delivery system which makes birth control devices readily available, but more importantly, the commune form of rural organization, whatever its other strengths and weaknesses, clearly provides everyone with a degree of security in sickness and old age. And security (or the lack of it) was one of the primary reasons why rural families tried to have many sons. But if progress in lowering the birthrate in China seems likely, there is no reason to assume that it will come quickly.

A second method of reducing the drag of high cost rural development in China would be for Chinese scientists to achieve a series of technological breakthroughs like those attained at the International Rice Research Institute (IRRI) in the Philippines. It is not simply a matter of sending a few scientists to visit the IRRI and then returning with the "miracle" formula. Seeds must be developed in accordance with local climatic, soil, and other conditions. But improved seeds are undoubtedly the key, perhaps the only key, that will free China from the constraint of having too many people on too little land and rather poor land at that.

Although it is difficult to project the possibility of a major technological breakthrough (or really a series of breakthroughs), the task will be a formidable one. It will probably require the efforts of some of China's best minds, minds that have had a rigorous scientific training. Furthermore, although the fundamental solutions must be found within China, the process of discovery could probably be accelerated if Chinese scientists were in close and continual contact with people working on similar problems around the world. Therefore, in this one area at least Chinese leaders may feel some pressure to be more open in their relations with the outside world than they have been to date.

A third alternative for minimizing the scope of an agricultural bottleneck is to turn to imports. But this alternative is open to China to only a very limited extent. A few simple calculations illustrate the main point. In the early 1960s Chinese wheat imports of five to six million tons a year cost China about $300 million in foreign exchange. In 1973 and 1974 slightly larger grain import totals (about seven to eight million tons) cost China around $1 billion due to higher prices. But Chinese demand for grain is increasing at roughly five million tons a year just to stay even with population growth. Thus, if China turned to imports as the sole method of maintaining existing grain consumption levels, by 1985 the nation would be importing over fifty million tons of grain. Even if world surpluses could meet such a demand, prices would undoubtedly be driven much higher than they are today and the foreign exchange cost to China might easily pass $10 billion a year (two or three times China's total annual foreign exchange earnings in 1973).

China must, therefore, raise farm productivity or lower population growth. Imports are not a long-term solution to China's food problem. What farm product imports can do, however, is provide relief in areas where Chinese agriculture is particularly deficient. Thus China has for many decades imported long staple cotton to mix with its shorter staple variety. More importantly, wheat imports have been a method of feeding the northern cities without having to increase compulsory grain deliveries from those areas with accessible surpluses. Total Chinese grain output is two hundred-fifty million tons, but the marketed portion (including the agricultural tax) is only around fifty million tons a year. Of that fifty million tons, perhaps twenty or thirty million tons would be marketed voluntarily leaving another twenty to thirty million tons that must be obtained by compulsory quotas and taxes. Five million tons is a tiny fraction of two hundred-fifty million tons, but it is a substantial portion of twenty or thirty million tons. Imports thus provide significant relief to those regions that must supply a surplus for China's cities.

As the income of the Chinese people increases (in per capita terms) during the next decade and beyond, demand for a greater variety and a higher quality of food will also rise. Most of this demand will have to be met by domestic resources, as in the past, but there will probably be an increasing number of specific bottlenecks comparable to the current situation with respect to cotton and grain (and sugar). Increasing farm imports will be at least a partial solution to the problem. Thus the difficulties China is likely to have because of its endowment of poor land will increase pressure to divert foreign exchange to the purchase of farm products in the future. Chinese planners can resist this pressure, but only at a price.

Agricultural development is China's principal unresolved economic problem, but there is another trend that causes almost as many difficulties. The most rapid way for China to industrialize is for the nation's planners to draw heavily on the past century's technological and scientific progress in Europe, the United States, and Japan. It makes no sense for Chinese to invent known modern techniques from scratch, and this conclusion has been obvious to Chinese planners from the beginning. Most Chinese industrial technology, as a result, is similar to that found in the advanced industrial nations.

But there is a major social cost connected with the use of the most advanced technology. I am not here referring to conventional environmental costs, but to the fact that modern techniques arc, for the most part, highly capital intensive, that is it takes a great deal of capital to provide employment for a single worker. These techniques, after all, were developed in nations where labor is expensive and capital, by comparison at least, is cheap.

In China this situation has meant that investment levels of $20 to $30 billion a year have provided employment in the modern sector for only a few million additional workers a year if that.[g] At the same time, however, China's population has been growing at twelve to sixteen million people a year. Even if the increase in population were to stop tomorrow, large numbers of young adults born in the 1950s and 1960s, perhaps seven to ten million a year, will be entering the labor market for the next twenty years. And far less than half of these will be able to find jobs in the modern sector. The rest will have to go to work in agriculture or other more "traditional" occupations.

The effects of this situation are already apparent. Rather than allow tens of millions of people to hang around the outskirts of cities unemployed or semi-employed and living in makeshift huts, the Chinese have systematically shipped such people back to the countryside. In addition, graduates of middle schools must also spend years in the countryside before a privileged few are allowed to return to universities or to urban employment. Unless there is some radical breakthrough in technology, over half of China's population increase will continue to have to be absorbed by the countryside for the next decade; the rural population will still be rising by the year 2000 as well.[h] By the latter date, however, employment in the modern sector should be absorbing most new entrants into the labor force.

To some the fact that 70 percent or more of the population will still be residing in rural areas nearly forty years after the revolution may not seem to be a source of concern. It is unlikely, however, that China's leaders or large numbers of those going to the countryside see it that way. A major problem is that there really is not that much for these people to do in agriculture. Educated youth, of course, can help keep the rather elaborate accounts required by modern agriculture in general and the commune form of agricultural organization in particular. But a quarter century of massive educational efforts has provided China with far more educated personnel than can be absorbed by rural accounts keeping. The surplus majority, therefore, must do ordinary farm and labor *corvée* work, and rather low productivity kinds of work at that. The rural areas, after all, need more capital, not more workers. The marginal productivity of existing workers is already very low, probably below the subsistence level. Thus the addition of workers who produce less than they consume can only be a source of tension.

---

[g]Precise estimates of China's rate of investment in the modern sector in the 1960-1974 period are not available in either dollars or yuan. But there are reasons for believing that this rate of investment has risen well above the levels of the 1950s for which we do have data, or above 20 percent of GNP. The share of producer goods industry in GNP, for example, has risen sharply from 1950s levels. Since Chinese GNP in the early 1970s was over $100 billion (see Table 5-1), investment must have been over $20 billion by an unknown amount.

[h]To illustrate with hypothetical figures, assume that population by the year 2000 is 1,200 million and growing at 1.2 percent or 14.4 million people a year, and the workforce is rising by 10 million a year. If one assumes that an investment of at least $10,000 (1974 prices) will be required to employ a single worker in the modern sector, then these 10 million people will require $100,000 million or 10 to 20 percent of GNP in the year 2000 (see the GNP projections in the next section).

Therefore, although it is probably true that Chinese society is better off locating these additions to its population in rural areas rather than in shanty towns on the outskirts of its cities, this solution is far from ideal for a nation with the goal of bringing everyone into full participation in the "modern age." Keeping people in the countryside saves on urban social services and it eliminates a situation where people in abject poverty (the unemployed) are living in close proximity to those who are comparatively affluent (skilled factory workers, senior cadres, and the like). But it will take an enormous amount of education to convince those who are sent down to a career on China's limited supply of farm land that theirs is a life of hope and progress.

One conceivable solution to this dilemma is to locate more and more industry using labor intensive technology in the countryside. The Chinese have in fact made major efforts in this direction during the late 1960s and early 1970s. Thousands of small cement and chemical fertilizer plants dot the countryside and there are even more shops and small factories capable of repairing and manufacturing farm machinery. But the quality of output from these small factories is not high. Although they appear to be an excellent interim solution to the problem of supplying farms with needed inputs and of providing China's rural population with experience in running and operating industrial technology, these plants are not likely to be the wave of China's industrial future. Even in areas such as chemical fertilizer, Chinese planners had shifted emphasis back toward large-scale imported urea plants by 1974.

Thus China in the mid-1970s has faced some of the major difficulties plaguing its economy (and the economies of many other less developed countries) and has ameliorated some of the worst problems. But the ultimate solution to these problems is likely to come in ways not unlike what has already occurred in the advanced industrial nations. The solution to the lack of adequate numbers of jobs in the modern sector will be found when urban (and suburban) Chinese industry together with the rest of the modern sector has grown to a point where it can absorb all those seeking to leave the countryside. The faster the modern sector grows, therefore, the sooner will be the day when China's employment problem is a thing of the past.

China's Economic Future

If the above analysis is correct, China is under pressure to accelerate what is already a substantial rate of growth in historical terms in both the industrial and agricultural sectors. There are a number of ways in which a more rapid rate of development might be achieved. China could, for example, raise investment and cut back on consumption either by squeezing personal consumer expenditures (food, housing, etc.) or by reducing military costs. In fact there is evidence that China's rate of investment has been rising during the past decade while consumer goods and services have kept just ahead of population growth.[i] Military expenditures, however, have also risen and, thereby, rapidly cut down the rate of increase in investment.

This rising rate of investment should contribute to an increase in the growth rate of the national product providing that the efficiency of the new capital constructed does not fall at the same time. Furthermore, there are reasons for believing that the rate of investment will continue to rise slowly in the future,[j] but it is unlikely that Chinese leaders will feel themselves in a position to greatly accelerate this increase. For reasons that will be discussed at length below, the Chinese government is not going to be in a position to reduce military expenditures for some time to come. And the pressures to raise personal consumption should grow over time, not decline. The Chinese consumer is largely isolated from the force of the "demonstration effect" of high consuming neighbors, television and movies, or rich tourists. But significant increases in the people's standard of living above the level of the mid-1950s cannot be postponed indefinitely.

A second method of accelerating the rate of growth of the national product and, thereby, employment would be for China to increase the pace of technological change by raising the amount of advanced technology imported and by upgrading China's own scientific and engineering capacities. Moves in this direction, however, have clear political implications. A greater dependence on foreign technology contradicts to some degree with China's own image of self-reliance. Such a move would also require China to push export development in order to pay for the imported technology. And export development would in turn require China either to accelerate its petroleum development or become more effective at marketing industrial products, and the latter might involve closer ties with the foreign companies which control the markets for these products.

Improving China's domestic scientific and technology training and research has even greater political implications, at least potentially. China's leaders could, for example, isolate the scientific "establishment" from political campaigns as was attempted in 1966 during the first phase of the Cultural Revolution.[k] But the very notion of a protected scientific elite and even more an educated elite

---

[i]The principal evidence that the rate of investment has risen is that producer goods industries (steel, machinery, etc.) have been growing much faster than consumer goods most of which are directly or indirectly derived from agriculture. Even if one assumes that the diversion of producer goods to military uses increased markedly, there is still enough left over (under most reasonable assumptions) to allow for a substantial rise in the rate of investment.

[j]Not only is it likely that a large portion of Chinese investment resources will be directed toward this sector in the future, but the sector is not subject to the same kind of bottlenecks that plague agriculture (and thus lower the rate of return in the consumer goods sector as a whole).

[k]The main Central Committee directive of 1966 said that scientists and technicians who have worked hard, been patriotic, and made contributions should be treated with "special care."

flies straight in the face of a principal goal of movements like the Cultural Revolution, which is to eliminate class barriers, not create them.

It is possible, of course, that China's various political campaigns will generate attitudes that will accelerate scientific discovery and technological adaptation, and there are examples one can find to support this view. Keeping the scientific community in touch with farmers and workers, for example, undoubtedly does encourage more applied rather than basic research. But this goal can be achieved in other cheaper ways (through rigorous control of the research budget, for example). The direct impact of such campaigns as the Great Leap Forward and the Cultural Revolution is to disrupt laboratories as well as the universities which train people for research. Accelerated growth, therefore, is not compatible with a high degree of political turmoil. Periods of rapid development in China have coincided, without exception, with periods of comparative political stability (1952-1957, 1962-1966, and 1970-1973), an experience that can be witnessed throughout the world.

An economist of rather narrow vision might argue that it clearly follows that China's leaders should make fast work of the choice of a successor to Mao and then get on with the task of development. But the evidence available today suggests that not only is there no agreement on the name (or names) of the new leader, there are fundamental disagreements over the direction Chinese society should be heading. People who care deeply about the creation of a classless society are not going to be impressed by arguments that they must support so-and-so in order to accelerate the pace of growth of China's gross national product. At a minimum they have a different view of how rapid growth can be achieved, but the more realistic among them (Mao included) appear to realize that there is a conflict between the goal of growth and that of equity, at least when the latter goal is pushed too far in the direction of egalitarianism. When conflict over as fundamental a goal as this is added to disagreements in other areas (over foreign policy, personalities, etc.), it is clear that China may be in for a long succession struggle which occasionally spills over into the society at large. Even if there is no disruption emanating from the change in leadership, future heads of the Party and government may still find it necessary or desirable to institute campaigns that will in one way or another prove to be disruptive.

To predict China's future rate of economic growth, therefore, the economist must somehow balance off two potentials: one for political instability against a second for the strong growth that is engendered by a high rate of investment and a disciplined and readily trainable labor force. In addition, some judgment must be made about the ability of China to overcome the drag of the agricultural sector and the willingness of the leadership to make maximum use of imported technology.

For the seventeen-year period 1957-1974, China managed to sustain a growth rate of 5 percent a year under generally unfavorable conditions, and it is reasonable to assume that it can do at least as well in the decade or two ahead, barring some major catastrophe such as a Soviet invasion. If conditions through 1985 or the year 2000 are significantly more favorable than during the seventeen years to 1975 (there is a better than even chance of this being the case, in my opinion), then China's growth rate might well climb to 7 or 8 percent a year over a sustained period. Much, however, will depend on who or what group leads China in the years ahead. Only a growth-oriented leadership is likely to achieve rates as high as 8 percent per annum, if experience elsewhere in the world is any guide.

What are the implications of a growth rate of from 5 to 7 percent? The military implications will be dealt with in the next section, but there are important economic implications as well. At 7 percent, China's national product would double every ten years or would increase by roughly eight times in thirty years. China's national product during the first decade of the twenty-first century, therefore, would reach a level comparable in real terms to that of the United States in 1970. In per capita terms, if population growth averages 1½ percent per annum over the same period, Chinese product per person will be over $700, still far behind U.S. levels today, but well on the way to West European levels of the mid-1950s (in real terms).

If output grows at 5 percent overall and at 3 percent per capita over the same thirty-year period, however, the results are quite different. Instead of being over $1,000 billion during the first decade of the twenty-first century, Chinese national product will be more like $500 billion (more than four times today's level) which in per capita terms amounts to about $350 per head. This latter figure allows considerable room for increases in personal consumption above the levels of the early 1970s even if the share of investment and the military continue to rise. But China would still be a poor or less developed society with a standard of living to match. Thus the difference between 5 and 7 percent, which to the casual observer unfamiliar with the impact of compound interest may not seem like much of a gap, makes a very large difference over even the comparatively short period of three decades.

If China's population remains isolated during these next decades, either 3 or 5½ percent a year in per capita terms may be adequate to keep the people content. After all, Chinese governments survived for centuries during which consumption per person did not rise at all. The twentieth century, however, is not the eighteenth century and China's population is not completely isolated. Many of China's leaders are familiar with what is happening to the economies of the rest of the world. And there are enough Overseas Chinese travelers returning to visit relatives and friends in China so that a significant portion of the general population is not wholly ignorant of outside economic conditions either. Furthermore, the whole philosophy of Marxism and of China's current government stresses economic progress.

If growth in many of the nations surrounding China continues at the rates achieved during the 1960s and early 1970s, China could find itself a still comparatively poor nation, encircled by rich neighbors, a not completely comfortable position. On the other hand, if there is internal instability within these nations or if the freer trade era of the 1950s and 1960s deteriorates markedly, thus stifling these country's export led growth, a 5 percent per annum growth rate in China may be a cause for congratulation. Even Japan and Sweden did not manage more than 5 percent a year for any sustained period prior to World War II.

I shall have more to say about economic development in the rest of Asia in a later section. The point here is that what China's leaders and people consider an acceptable rate of growth (and acceptable levels of underemployment, consumption, etc.) depends very much on their standard of comparison. And that standard, in turn, is bound to be affected by what happens in the world outside China and on the degree to which Chinese society is open to such influences.

The difference between a 5 or a 7 percent rate of growth will also affect significantly the degree of Chinese participation in international commerce. A few hypothetical but realistic examples illustrate the main point. If a 5 percent rate of growth in national product results in part from a vigorous pursuit of self-reliance, then China's trade ratio $(X + M/\text{GNP})$ might stay below 8 percent. Total Chinese trade $(X + M$ in today's prices) might be no more than $15 billion a year, if that, in 1985 and less than $40 billion by the year 2000.[1] If total world trade continued to grow (in real terms) at 7 to 8 percent a year, China would continue to be a minor actor on the world economic stage as it has been for the past quarter century. China's trade in 1973, for example, was not greatly different in size from that of many of its much smaller neighbors (Taiwan, South Korea, Hong Kong, the Philippines, and the like).[m]

If, on the other hand, China grew at 7 percent a year, in part because of a decision to increase Chinese participation in international trade by raising the trade ratio to say 12 percent, then total Chinese trade might reach $30 billion (also in today's prices) by 1985 and well over $100 billion by the year 2000.[n] World trade would have to be growing rapidly too for such an expansion on the part of China to be feasible. But China's share of total world trade would probably be rising steadily from the current level of under 1 percent to over 2 percent. (The United States' share in the early 1970s was well over 10 percent and that of Japan was over 5 percent.)

Under neither set of assumptions would China become a force in international commerce comparable in relative terms to that of the United States, Japan, or Western Europe today. But the absolute level of Chinese trade in the year 2000

[1]These figures were derived by multiplying 0.08 by $170-180 billion (for 1985) and $500 billion for the year 2000. See the text above for why these estimates of GNP were used.

[m]Malaysia's trade $(X + M)$ in 1973 was $6 billion (at an exchange rate of U.S. $1 = 2.39 Ringgit), while that of Taiwan in 1973 was also about $8.3 billion. The trade of the People's Republic of China in 1972 was $5.9 billion while that in 1973 was $9.9 billion.

[n]These figures were obtained by multiplying 0.10 and 0.12 by $250 billion (for 1985) and $1,000 billion (for 2000).

would be larger than that of Japan today under the latter set of assumptions. Whether such trade would contribute to international economic stability or be disruptive, however, would depend as much on its commodity composition as its aggregate size. If current indications are any guide, China is likely to supply a high proportion of its own basic energy and industrial raw material needs. And in a key area such as petroleum the country might become a major epxorter. Thus in one area in which world shortages are acute today and may remain so for some time until adequate substitutes are developed, increased Chinese participation might have a stabilizing effect. Japan, for example, would clearly feel more secure and would act accordingly if it had major sources of petroleum in China, Indonesia, and Alaska (or the Soviet Union) than if it were wholly dependent on the Middle East as it is at present. And major Chinese participation in the petroleum market would also help depress world oil prices.

In the world agricultural market, on the other hand, current trends suggest that future Chinese participation is more likely to accentuate current shortages than to ameliorate them. China, for example, was once the world's major supplier of soybeans. Today it is actually importing small quantities of soybeans from the United States. In the 1950s China earned considerable amounts of foreign exchange from the sale of edible oils and even grain. Today edible oil exports are not of significant size and wheat is being imported in large quantities.

The degree of China's future dependence on agricultural imports, of course, depends mainly on the success that nation has in overcoming its endowment of poor land and water. As already indicated, China can never depend on foreign countries for the majority of its food requirements. But even a small fraction of the consumption needs of a billion people can have a major impact on the world market for food and agricultural raw materials. And if Chinese foreign exchange earnings reach $20 billion (in today's prices) in 1985 and $60 billion in the year 2000,[o] the country could afford to import considerable quantities of farm products, even at prices much higher than they are today. "Large" imports would not solve China's basic food requirements, but they could put enormous strain on the rest of the world's limited food export capacities.

It is clear from the above, therefore, that because China is a large nation and, like all large nations, depends mainly on its own resources. Thus its participation in international trade will not require all other countries to make fundamental adjustments. On the other hand, China's size and probable future growth rate could give it a much greater impact on the international economic scene than it has today, particularly in such key areas as petroleum and food.

The Economics of Chinese Military Power

The size of China's economy today and in the future will also affect the size of China's military budget and through that budget the strength of China's armed

---

[o]These figures were obtained by halving the high estimates of trade described in footnote n (p. 175). This involves the assumption that $X = M$ in 1985 and 2000.

forces. But the relationship between military capacities and the size of a nation's GNP is more complex today than it was during either World Wars I and II. No longer is warfare primarily a matter of who has the most planes, tanks, and ships and the industrial capacity to replace those lost in combat. Nuclear weapons have changed that. Large steel mills and coal mines are of little use in the construction of missiles with nuclear warheads. Whole new industries are required, industries that do not draw heavily from more ordinary industrial sectors except in their use of electricity. Nor is the research and development stage of a strategic nuclear force all that expensive.

Calculating the cost of a Chinese strategic weapons program, of course, is a very uncertain task. But the experiences of Britain and France are in the public realm and provide some guidance. The costs of these programs during their first decade of development ranged between $300 million to $400 million a year.[p] Even if one allowed for inflation and for much higher costs for each operation because of the comparative scarcity (and hence high value) of the relevant skills and resources in China, Chinese costs in the development stage were probably below $1 billion and almost certainly below $2 billion.[1]

Nor would increasing these expenditures much accelerate the speed with which China acquires an operational nuclear force. The United States, for example, attempted to push the pace of missile development by encouraging different organizations to develop the relevant technology simultaneously. The net result of these simultaneous efforts was a large increase in cost and a very modest shortening of the time needed to acquire a strategic force. The bottlenecks were technical in nature, not economic. Until scientists and engineers solved these technical problems, giving them more and more money did little good. In China the problem was similar, but even more complicated. Only a comparative handful of Chinese technicians had the requisite skills and once they were mobilized and given equipment to work with, further expenditures were of little use.

Similar considerations affect some aspects of China's conventional weapons program as well. China some time ago could undoubtedly have raised the rate at which it was producing MIG-19 fighter aircraft. But then what would it have done with several thousand obsolete fighter planes? The need was for planes that could match the performance of advanced Soviet and American models. And the need was not simply for planes, but also the complicated missiles and electronic gear carried by modern planes. Without this equipment and weaponry even advanced airplanes could be blown out of the air with comparative ease. Raising the rate of production of MIG-19's (or the decision not to) was essentially an economic decision. The money or resources could be better used elsewhere. But new aircraft and missile designs and gear to jam enemy radar were mainly technical problems. Until these technical constraints were broken, there was little use for large expenditures.

Without modern fighter aircraft of advanced design capable of maintaining air

[p]These figures are based on annual expenditures on the French *force de frappe* in the early 1960s.

superiority over supply lines and the battlefield, a large navy or a highly mobile land force with enormous numbers of trucks and helicopters also has its limitations. Naval ships and, to a lesser degree, trucks are extremely vulnerable to any nation that is capable of maintaining dominance of the skies. Since China does not yet have the capacity to maintain air superiority against a major enemy force, it follows that heavy investment in ships and helicopters does not make much sense. After the Yom Kippur War in which tanks proved to be extremely vulnerable to new Soviet missiles launched by ground forces, even a significant investment in tanks must now be seen as an expenditure of limited value.

We are not privy to much of the discussion surrounding China's defense budget, but considerations based on the facts presented above must have had an important influence. Chinese military planners have pushed research and development in both the nuclear and conventional spheres, but a massive deployment of modern conventional weapons of the kind that are vulnerable to air attack has not been attempted.

In calculations made ten years ago, it was clear then that China's economy was capable of supporting a considerable research and development effort.[2] If Chinese GNP in 1962 was $60-70 billion (in today's prices), a research and development expenditure of say $3 billion would amount to between 4 and 5 percent of China's GNP. An expenditure of that size (the figure is hypothetical but probably realistic or on the high side) would have had a significant impact on the Chinese economy of the early to mid-1960s, but it could not be described as a crushing burden. Because of China's formidable taxing capacity, state revenues were six to eight times this level (i.e., they were over 30 percent of GNP) leaving a considerable sum for other government expenditures and for investment. For a small less developed economy, research and development expenditures of several billion dollars a year would be impossible or would require the diversion of all resources otherwise destined for investment. A nation of twenty million people and a per capita product of $200, for example, has a GNP of only $4 billion, and most of the less developed nations of the world have smaller populations or a lower per capita product (or both) than this. China, however, is poor but large and hence can afford a major military development program. If China could afford such a program in the early 1960s, it can do so that much more readily today (the mid-1970s) when its national product is double the earlier level and a higher proportion of that product is in the modern sector.

Once a nation moves beyond the research and development stage, the cost of military weapons becomes more serious, even for comparatively rich nations. Strategic missiles are only a part of the problem and not the major part. Although each individual missile is costly, their deployment can be spread out over a number of years. Furthermore, a nation such as China acquires a fairly effective deterrent once it can assure the destruction of several cities of the potential enemy even if that enemy's nuclear forces strike first. A few dozen missiles fairly well hidden, for example, might be more than adequate for this purpose if the missiles could reach the desired targets. China's current medium-range ballistic-missile force has probably already reached this stage vis-à-vis the Soviet Union and the deployment of an intercontinental ballistic missile (ICBM) would give China a comparable capability vis-à-vis the United States. Strategic parity with the United States or the Soviet Union, of course, is another much more expensive proposition and is not within China's economic or technical capacities either today or in 1985. By the end of the century, however, depending on what happens to the technology of strategic weapons, even parity might be within China's reach.

Conventional weapons are another matter. Even if China had the technical capacity to produce modern weapons like those of the United States or the Soviet Union, the Chinese economy could not afford to produce them in comparable numbers. Furthermore, a force in being is not as important in a protracted war as the ability to turn out replacements month after month. Israel, for example, had a considerable force of planes and tanks at the beginning of the Yom Kippur War, but that force was severely depleted within two weeks. If the Yom Kippur War had gone on for six months, the cost could have run into tens of billions of dollars. (The weapons in this case, of course, would have had to come from the United States.) The Chinese economy, although far bigger in the relevant sectors than that of tiny Israel (or Egypt), is in no position to turn out tens of billions of dollars worth of weapons each year.

The case should not be overstated. Even in the early 1960s China's modern industry was significantly larger than that of Japan's of the early 1940s, and Japan fought the United States for over three years (weapons were not so expensive then, however). As of this writing China, with a national product in 1974 of well over $100 billion, could, in an emergency, divert an annual $20 billion or more to a war effort,[q] a considerable figure. What China's capacity will be in 1985 or the year 2000 depends on what happens to economic growth and technical progress in the intervening years. If the Chinese GNP approaches $1,000 billion by the end of the century, then China could obviously pay for a conventional force considerably larger than that currently in existence in the United States or the Soviet Union today if the pressure to do so were great enough. Whether Chinese military technology could match that of the most advanced nations then is a question that is beyond my competence. But if the Soviet Union's experience is any guide, continued Chinese priority to military technology should steadily narrow the gap between China and the "super-powers."

In some areas, of course, Chinese military technology and arms expenditures

---

[q]This figure obviously is not precise and there are problems connected with defining what constitutes a diversion to a war effort. This estimate was derived by assuming that Chinese consumption standards could not be reduced by much, but that a high proportion of resources destined toward investment could be so diverted.

may not have to catch up with that of the superpowers for China to have a comparable level of military strength. Manpower can be a substitute for machines in warfare as well as industry, as the United States has learned and relearned in Korea and Vietnam. And manpower in China is not expensive. The wages and other personal benefits paid to China's three million plus regular army, navy, and airforce probably amount to less than $2 billion.[r] The U.S. figure for a force slightly smaller is $23 billion.[s] But one cannot carry this argument too far. If wages are low in China compared to those in industrial nations, the cost of weapons is considerably higher.[t] And there are many areas where manpower is not a very good substitute for modern armaments. Lightly armed men, for example, might do very well in defensive or guerilla type actions in mountainous or jungle terrain, but their effectiveness declines rapidly across open water and treeless plains or deserts or in offensive actions taken a long way from China's borders and its friendly and supportive population.

Thus in the mid-1970s China's economy does put severe constraints upon the nation's ability to afford modern conventional weapons in great numbers even in areas in which Chinese technology is nearly a match for that of the industrialized world. In the nuclear-strategic realm economic constraints are not so important as the technical ones and even the latter are being overcome fairly rapidly. Ten years from now this picture will be beginning to change. Economic constraints will still hold China's conventional arms budget below that of the superpowers, but the difference will not be so great as it is today. In another twenty-five years, the economic constraints that have dominated the Chinese defense budget for the past two decades and will continue to do so for perhaps another decade will have largely disappeared. The faster China's rate of growth, the more rapidly will the constraints disappear.

China's Ability to Defend Itself

If the above calculations are close to the mark, China today is clearly capable of a formidable defense of its own territory and of areas immediately adjacent to that territory. This conclusion should surprise no one familiar with the history of the past quarter century. In Korea in the years 1950-1953, China was able to maintain a force of fifty divisions in perpetual combat with the United States and South Korean armies where the latter had complete command of the air and

---

[r]China has a regular armed force of roughly three million men. If the average wage plus other benefits per person were one thousand yuan a year or equivalent to that of a skilled factory worker, then the Chinese budget for this category would be three billion yuan or around $2 billion depending on the exchange rate used.

[s]This figure is for fiscal 1972 and does not include payments to retired military personnel nor to civilian defense department employees.

[t]The higher cost of capital and the limited technological development in less developed countries generally lead to a situation and sophisticated technology become much more expensive than in developed nations. Many military weapons are of this type.

the sea. The weapons at that time, to be sure, came in part from the Soviet Union, but they were bought and paid for by the Chinese. Chinese industry was in a severely weakened condition at that time although it was undoubtedly capable of turning out large quantities of infantry weapons. Chinese casualties were enormous, but their armies held their ground.

By the time of the Vietnam War, China's army was a much more formidably equipped force than in Korea. How many men could have been committed to the defense of North Vietnam if the occasion had arisen is anybody's guess, but it would have been a more powerful army than fought in Korea. Statements occasionally heard that airpower could have severely limited this force by cutting China's lines of supply cannot be taken seriously. Manpower is a particularly effective substitute for machines in repairing roads and bridges, or finding alternative routes around damaged routes, as the North Vietnamese themselves demonstrated over and over again. And tens of millions of Chinese lived near the adjacent borders and could have been readily mobilized for such a task. Fortunately, the United States never attempted to find out what the Chinese could have done under those circumstances.

China's major defense problem today and probably for some years to come is on its northern border with the Soviet Union. And China's perception that the Soviet design is to encircle China poses a potential Soviet or Soviet ally's threat from other directions as well.

The nuclear danger from the Soviet Union is straightforward. It is difficult to ascertain Russian intentions, but the Chinese have clearly been worried about a Soviet attack designed to destroy China's developing nuclear weapons capacity. The period of greatest danger was probably when China had the bomb but only a handful of crude methods of delivery. At that time a first strike could have readily eliminated China's facilities. But that time is now past. It is unlikely today that anyone would be confident of locating all of China's delivery vehicles preparatory to a first strike. And the overlooking of only two or three warheads could lead to millions of dead Russians. Thus the danger of nuclear war between China and the Soviet Union today lies more in what might happen during an escalating border war. Even this danger is likely to recede, however, as it becomes clearer and clearer with the passage of time that both sides would suffer enormous and unacceptable levels of destruction.

The confrontation of conventional Chinese and Soviet forces along several thousand miles of border (if one includes Inner Mongolia where Soviet troops are stationed in strength) is more complex. First of all, there is the question of China's ability on its own to withstand a direct conventional attack from the Soviet Union. Speculation about this possibility does not mean that such an attack is likely. This discussion is focused primarily on capacities, not intentions. If one were to get into the area of intentions, however, one would have to go no further than the Brezhnev Doctrine to establish a plausible basis for Chinese fears of a Soviet attack.

Could China defend itself against an all-out Russian invasion with conventional arms? If the issue is whether Chinese forces loyal to the present government could survive in some form and control significant parts of China's territory and a majority of its population, the answer is undoubtedly yes. Except possibly for a few minority groups, there would not be many defections to an alien invader of differing race and culture. Both in open and guerilla warfare China's regular army and its militia could inflict enormous casualties particularly where terrain reduced the advantages of heavier firepower and greater mobility on the part of the invading forces. Chinese forces might even be able to take the offensive in certain areas, thus penetrating Soviet territory.

But the costs to China of such an effort would be enormous and it is unlikely that a major attack would come in this form in any case. Large parts of Chinese territory, notably in the northwest, are lightly populated with Inner Asian people (although many Chinese people have settled in this region since 1949). These Inner Asian people in many cases have ties with their ethnic compatriots on the Soviet side of the border. In addition, the barren terrain of this region is far better suited to heavily armed and mobile regular army forces than it is to guerilla troops.

In a Sino-Soviet war, therefore, China probably could not hold vast areas of the northwest and might soon find itself faced with a new "independent" or "puppet" Soviet state carved out of its former territory. Thus, although the People's Republic of China is strong enough to avoid the prospect of an "unconditional surrender" to Soviet forces on the Czechoslovakian or Hungarian models, it could lose a large and rich (in terms of natural resources) portion of its land on a more or less permanent basis. Although they do not speak about it, such a prospect must be a constant worry for China's leaders over and above the casualties and destruction that a war of that magnitude would entail.

China, therefore, obviously finds the prospect of going it alone against a Soviet Union free to concentrate all its forces against China distinctly unattractive. Chinese diplomatic efforts during the past few years, as a result, have been directed to a significant degree toward tying down Soviet forces and the forces of Soviet allies elsewhere. The most conspicuous example of this change in China's posture is its new found enthusiasm for NATO. It was not long ago that China was encouraging France in its independent stance vis-à-vis the United States and the North Atlantic Treaty Organization (NATO), but no longer.

China's close ties with Pakistan and its firm support of Pakistan during its war with India over Bangladesh were also, to a degree, a part of this effort. A dismembered Pakistan leaves India free to take whatever advantage it could of an outbreak of war on the Sino-Soviet border. Tibet, like the northwest, it also a long way from the centers of Chinese population.

These examples could be readily multiplied, but two are enough to make the main point. A remaining question is whether China is always likely to be in this relatively vulnerable position or whether China's military capacities will evolve to a point where Chinese territory, all of it, could be adequately defended by Chinese armed forces alone. If the calculations in the previous section are roughly accurate, the day when that level of capacity will be achieved may not be more than a decade or two away. A major breakthrough in Soviet arms technology or prolonged political disruption within China, of course, could delay the achievement of such a capability. If and when China attains this level of military might, Chinese leaders' perception of their international position is likely to undergo a significant change.

The Asian Nations on China's Periphery

When one turns away from the Sino-Soviet border to the nations surrounding China to the east and southeast, the situation facing China changes fundamental-ly. These nations, to be sure, are also involved to a degree in the Sino-Soviet dispute. China and Russia have vied at one time or another for the allegiance of the Democratic Republic of Korea and Vietnam, but both these smaller nations have been mainly concerned with their own civil wars and have given allegiance to neither the Russians or the Chinese. Elsewhere in Asia the Soviet Union has made noises about a mutual security pact for the region, but unlike what John Foster Dulles had in mind when he formed the South East Asian Treaty Organization (SEATO). But by focusing on Sino-Soviet issues, one misses the main trend of developments in Southeast Asia and the role China is likely to play in them.

There are two basic trends in Southeast Asia and in the Republic of Korea today that have already had a profound effect on international relations in Asia and will continue to have an impact in the future. One is political and the other economic.

The principal political trend is the continuing rise of nationalism throughout the region. This nationalism, of course, is not a recent phenomenon. It began before World War II and received a major push from the victories of Japan during the war over the various colonial powers in Asia. But at the time that most of the nations in the area received their independence in the late 1940s and 1950s, large parts of the populations within these countries did not identify themselves with the nation. (Korea was a notable exception even then.) Instead one's first loyalty was to one's race or culture as in the case of the Overseas Chinese and Indians or to some other group that encompassed far less than the entire nation. Indonesia, for example, was hardly a nation at all, but rather a collection of Javanese, Sumatrans, and the like.

This situation has been steadily changing in the direction of national cohesion ever since. In Thailand, most Overseas Chinese have become Thais in more than just the formal sense of taking Thai citizenship and Thai names. The term "citizen of Indonesia" now has real meaning for that nation's hundred million plus people. Several minority groups, to be sure, continue to strive for autonomy or independence—the Moslems in the Philippines and the Karens and Kachins in Burma, for example. But these groups are generally not very large in comparison with the dominant populations within each nation. Laos is the only country in the region where a strong sense of national identity seems to have not yet taken a firm hold of any part of the population. And in Malaysia, nationalism is much stronger among the Malays than among the Chinese and Indians. But elsewhere there is no longer much prospect of nations splitting apart because of ethnic separatism as happened recently with Pakistan and Bangladesh and as almost happened with Indonesia in 1958.

Along with this rising sense of national identity has come an increasing amount of experience within each nation in the handling of its own affairs. At the time of independence few countries in the region possessed leaders with any significant level of experience in running a national government. (Thailand was the only exception.) It was natural for these new governments to feel insecure about their ability to defend themselves against efforts perceived of as attempts to deprive them of their independence. After all, a comparative handful of colonial troops and administrators only a few years before had deprived them of self-determination often for a hundred years or more.

Today (mid-1970s), however, these nations have had seventeen to nearly thirty years of experience in managing their own governments.[u] In the process they have developed political styles and procedures of their own. Many Westerners (as well as many people within these countries) may have a low opinion of some of the procedures adopted, but at a minimum these procedures were and are in a very real sense indigenous. The prime minister or president of each nation in the region holds office today not because he has powerful friends in Britain or the United States or elsewhere, but because he has built a political base of power within his own country and because he knows how to maintain and nurture that base.

Thus the primary political activities in Southeast Asia and Korea today are internal. Where external forces are present, whether in the form of support for guerilla warfare or for foreign military bases, it is mainly the internal political groups that find it convenient to draw on outside support rather than the outsiders who are using and manipulating the internal forces.

Although the dominant political forces in the region will be those internal to each nation, it does not follow that Southeast Asia and Korea will be free of international conflict. The recent history of the region together with earlier experiences of the difficulties created by rising nationalisms in Europe make it appear likely that wars over boundaries and similar issues will never be far below the surface. The argument here is not that there will be an absence of armed conflict between nations in the region, but that such conflicts will be of

[u]India and Burma gained their independence in the late 1940s while Malaysia the last Asian nation to achieve independence, did so in 1957.

secondary importance in shaping these nations' futures. However, if local conflicts are allowed to escalate into great power confrontations, they could clearly reach a point where they dominated or profoundly influenced internal political developments.

The economic trends in Southeast and East Asia are no less profound than those occurring in the realm of politics. But not all the nations of the region are undergoing similar economic experiences. The nations of Indochina have only just begun to recover from their civil wars. In Burma, Burmese socialism and isolationism have managed to remove the nation from some of the international pressures that have buffeted the rest of the region, but the price has been a declining and highly inefficient economy.

Another group of nations, however, has been undergoing an extraordinary economic boom for more than a decade. This group includes the Republic of Korea, Thailand, and Singapore together with Taiwan and the colony of Hong Kong. Malaysia may also belong in this group, although it is somewhat of a special case.

In these nations rates of economic growth have ranged from 6 or 7 percent a year to over 10 percent. Per capita incomes, in spite of rapid increases in population, have more than doubled since 1960. Singapore and Hong Kong, at one extreme, have per capita incomes of over $1,000 and can no longer be considered less developed. Taiwan has passed $500 and other nations in the region are approaching that mark (see Table V-2). Considering that these countries in the early 1950s had per capita incomes ranging from less than $100 to no more than $300 (in 1974 prices), this is an extraordinary transformation. No nation anywhere in the world prior to World War II came close to this level of performance, although there are others that have done so since the war, notably Japan.

There are a number of reasons why rapid growth has occurred in these particular countries, but many of these have little relevance for Chinese foreign policy.[v] Other aspects or causes of this performance, however, do have significance for China. Notable among the latter is that growth in each of these countries has been export led. That is, instead of following a policy of autarky, which would have been impossible for most of these countries in any case because of their small size, they have relied heavily on an expansion of both their exports and imports. Thus the future growth and present standard of living of these nations is heavily dependent on the outside world.

A major beneficiary of this development has been Japan. Japan's share of the imports of these countries rose steadily throughout the 1960s and early 1970s to a point where Japan became by far their largest supplier.[w] In the last few years,

---

[v]Any careful analysis of this performance would have to take into account the past role of American aid, the entrepreneurial skills of Chinese businessmen, and other "sources" of this growth.

[w]In 1969, for example, Japan's trade with Asia (excluding the Middle East) constituted 34 percent of the total trade of these other Asian nations.

Table V-2
Per Capita GNP, Level and Rates of Growth

Country	Average Annual Growth Rates of GNP Per Capita (%) (Constant Prices)			Per Capita GNP (in 1970 U.S. $)	
	1960-1970	1971	1972	1960	1970
Japan	9.6	5.2	8.0	768	1,920
Hong Kong	8.4	4.8	8.2	433	970
Singapore	5.2	15.0	12.0	554	920
Taiwan	7.1	9.3	9.4	196	390
Malaysia	3.1	1.4	1.7	280	380
Korea (South)	6.8	7.2	4.7	129	250
Philippines	2.9	2.8	1.6	160	210
Thailand	4.9	1.4	−0.1	124	200
China	3.6−	4.4	n.a.	100+	160
Sri Lanka	1.5	−0.9	n.a.	95	110
India	1.2	n.a.	n.a.	98	110
Pakistan	2.4	3.1	n.a.	79	100
Indonesia	1.0	n.a.	n.a.	72	80
Burma	0.6	n.a.	n.a.	75	80

N.B. All GNP figures in U.S. dollars are subject to a wide margin of potential error because of the crude techniques used to make such estimates. The growth rate estimates, particularly those for 1971 and 1972, are also crude approximations and subject to revision when more complete constant price series become available.

Sources: The 1960-1970 per capita growth rates and the 1970 per capita GNP figures are from, World Bank, *Atlas: Population, Per Capita Product, and Growth Rates* (Washington: 1972). The 1960 estimates were obtained by applying the 1960-1970 growth rates to the 1970 figures and working backwards. The 1971 and 1972 growth rates were taken from a variety of sources too numerous to mention here.

The Chinese data (except for the 1970 dollar figure which is a World Bank guess, but a reasonable one) are from data in Table V-1 and other estimates I have derived for 1970. The 1960 per capita figure used here is actually based on Chinese GNP in 1957.

the liberalization of Japanese importation policy has meant that these nations have been exporting more and more to Japan as well, although the United States in most cases remains the principal market for their manufactures.

As a result of these trends, the daily concerns of the governments of these nations involve not so much how to deal with their gigantic neighbor China, but how to secure expanding markets for their products in the rest of the world. More recently they have also had to be concerned with how to obtain reliable sources of fuel and how to increase exports in order to meet higher fuel bills. Most of these nations, therefore, have had to devote considerable amounts of energy to negotiating textile quotas with the United States, for example. And each has had to decide how far to go in welcoming foreign capital because one of the best ways to sell in foreign markets is to be tied into an established marketing network of some large multinational firm.

Close economic contact, of course, does not necessarily lead to good and stable relations between the countries involved. American textile import policies in recent years and the Arab oil embargo, to mention only two of the more conspicuous cases, have been the cause of considerable tension between former friends or allies. The point, however, is that these fast-growing nations in Southeast and East Asia must worry constantly about their relations with the United States, Japan, the Arabs, and other countries because their economies are to a degree dependent on these nations. As will be argued at greater length below, they have no comparable need to worry about Chinese economic policies, the fanfare surrounding the recent establishment of diplomatic relations with China not withstanding.

Another relevant issue concerning these fast growing Asian states is the question of whether or not they will do equally well in the future. There is not enough room in this essay to deal with the issue in depth, but a few brief remarks are in order. The principal economic event that might bring rapid development to an end would be the gradual closing off of export markets abroad. The United States and other industrialized nations have not found it easy to adjust to the extraordinary economic rise of Japan. The population of the other fast-growing Asian states is roughly comparable to that of Japan and their combined economies are growing almost as quickly. It is not inconceivable, therefore, that difficulties in adjusting to this new "economic giant" could generate protectionist sentiment that could contribute to existing trends in the world toward greater restrictions on international trade.[x]

The greatest danger to future growth in these states, however, lies in the political realm. Rapid development is not consistent with a high degree of political instability and certain features of these nations' current economic policies could join with other political forces to undermine the stability that they have enjoyed over the past decade. The conspicuous role of foreign investment, for example, is bound to be again a source of tension in an increasingly nationalistic region. And the high living of the new rich who have been major beneficiaries of the current boom has not gone unnoticed by those who have been less fortunate. When tensions from these sources are added to traditional hostility between certain ethinic groups and to the instability of political institutions that have not yet taken root, it is clear that political stability and hence a future of uninterrupted economic growth cannot be taken for granted.

---

[x]The problem is made all the more acute by the fact that other nations in the world have been experiencing similar booms involving the rapid expansion of industrial exports (e.g., Brazil).

If growth does continue at current rates for another two decades, however, most of these states will have left the ranks of the less developed nations far behind. By the year 2000 China would be surrounded by half a dozen states (plus Japan) with per capita incomes ranging from around $1,000 (in today's prices) to $3,000 to $5,000 (not far below the current American level).[y]

Finally, mention must be made of those nations of the Asian region which are rich in natural resources—notably Indonesia, which is by far the largest. (Malaysia could also be included in this group along with the Philippines, but each of these nations differs in fundamental ways from Indonesia.) Indonesia is and probably will remain a poor country for some time to come. Most of its people are farmers crowded onto too little land on the island of Java. Nor is Indonesia likely to make a major success in the immediate future, at least of an industrial-product-based export drive comparable to that of Taiwan or Hong Kong. There simply are not enough trained technical and managerial personnel available, largely because of the Dutch colonial heritage that de-emphasized education and excluded Indonesians from management positions of any kind. Indonesian development over the next decade or two, therefore, is likely to depend heavily on the exploitation of its vast natural resources and the sale of those resources to the world's industrialized nations. Indonesia's international relations, as a result, are likely to be increasingly concerned with seeking ways to combine with other nations in order to obtain the best price for its exports and devising means of controlling those foreign companies that are handling the development of these resources. Finding markets for their exports, of course, will not be much of a problem.

China's Role in its Asian Periphery

In Asia there are leaders who worry about the possibility of China suddenly turning outward and becoming a major competitor with them for world markets. There are others who see China as a land of 800 million potential customers as have so many traders before them. But neither the danger nor the opportunity are in reality very great, and China will have but limited influence over the economic paths taken by the various nations in the region.

The current state of Chinese economic relations with East and Southeast Asia (excluding Japan) is clear. Total Chinese trade with the region in 1972 was $905 million, and of this total, a large portion ($513 million) was with Hong Kong.[z] Furthermore, China has a large balance of payments surplus with these nations.

---

[y]Even today (1973-1974) Singapore and Hong Kong are over $1,000 per capita (GNP in 1973 prices) and Taiwan and Malaysia are over $400. At the 10 percent real annual rates of growth prevailing in many of these countries, these figures would double in seven years.

[z]Chinese trade figures are compiled by adding up the figures published by China's trading partners. These estimates were taken from U.S. government publications and exclude North Vietnamese and North Korean trade with China.

The Chinese earn foreign exchange from the region from remittances and from the sale of food and other consumer products, much of which are destined for Overseas Chinese use. China, in turn, buys very little from the region; the largest single item purchased is rubber from Malaysia. Chinese foreign exchange is spent mainly on high technology and other producer goods manufactured in Japan and the West. There is no significant market in China for the major exports of these other Asian nations, which are mainly manufactured consumer goods and natural resource products (except rubber). China does import food, but the rice surplus of Southeast and East Asia is rapidly becoming a thing of the past.[aa]

Nor is China a major competitor for the export markets currently enjoyed by other nations in the region. China is a competitor, but only one among many. Current Chinese exports are no larger than those of such countries or regions as Malaysia or Taiwan.[bb] And China's ability to expand these exports, as already pointed out, is limited by the problems of raising farm output. In addition, if China did decide to move in the direction of becoming a major exporter of electronics goods and the like, it probably would have to become more closely involved with the international companies that control the relevant markets, a step China has shown little willingness to take. However, foreign exchange pressures could push China in this direction.

As China's foreign trade grows along with Chinese national product during the coming decades, trade with the Asian region and in competition with that area will also increase. However, unless economic growth in these other states stops, there is no reason to believe that China's share of trade will increase. On the contrary, if trends of the past decade continue, China's share would decline still further.[cc]

Far from being a major economic influence on East and Southeast Asia, actual or potential, it would be closer to the truth to say that economic influence moves in the other direction. The nations of the area could get along easily without importing Chinese consumer goods (or allowing remittances to China), but China would find it difficult to maintain a balance of payments surplus elsewhere with which to offset its deficits with the industrialized nations.

China's one source of economic influence on the Asian region, in fact, is as much political as economic. China is, in a fundamental sense, an alternative model to the kind of developmental programs currently followed elsewhere in Asia. There are no Chinese owned Mercedes on the streets of Peking nor are there reports of high level financial corruption. Much of the Chinese "model" is not transferable, but China's ability to narrow the gap between rich and poor is a

---

[aa]In 1934-38, all of Asia had a net export of grain of two million tons, whereas in 1973, the region had a net import of thirty million tons. (Lester R. Brown, 'Food: Growing Global Insecurity," in *Food and Population*, Report No. 19 of the International Planned Parenthood Federation, Summer-Fall 1974, p. 30.)

[bb]See footnote m (p. 175).

[cc]In 1958, for example, China's total trade represented about 1.7 percent of total world trade. In 1969 this percentage had fallen to 0.7 percent.

constant challenge to the leaders of those nations who have made few efforts in this direction.

The influence of the respective "models," however, is felt in the other direction as well. As already suggested, if growth in East and Southeast Asia continues at the rapid pace of the past decade, the advantages of a larger pie in the future may seem greater than a more equal division of an existing pie in the present, both to the people in the regions undergoing rapid development and to future Chinese leaders observing the phenomenon.

The performance of Taiwan's economy is a particularly serious problem from this point of view. If economic conditions on Taiwan were gradually converging with those of the mainland provinces of China, eventual rapprochement between the two regions would be greatly simplified. There would still be many fundamental political differences to overcome, but at least the people of Taiwan would not have to take a substantial cut in their standard of living. Equally important, the province of Taiwan could be allowed to retain considerable autonomy for a time and travel between the island and the mainland in both directions could be encouraged. There would be little danger of Taiwan becoming either a magnet for the discontented on the mainland or an alternative model for some Chinese planners. However, if Taiwan's product per capita is well over $1,000 a decade from now while that in the rest of the nation is below $300, and the gap is widening, a degree of freedom of movement between the two regions could have a powerfully disruptive effect. The far greater prosperity of Taiwan would then be apparent to all and some people both high and low would begin to draw unfavorable conclusions about the mainland provinces' economic performance.

Political sources of Chinese influence on East and Southeast Asia (in addition to whatever influence the Chinese model might have) are not much greater than those in the economic realm. There are people, however, who would challenge this view. It was not long ago, after all, that it was widely believed that outside forces could readily create powerful minority parties backed by guerilla armies that could then be used to topple existing governments. One interpretation of Lin Piao's famous article, "On People's War," was that this work was a blueprint for a world revolution directed from China.

This interpretation of Lin Piao's article is now generally discredited. The accepted view is that he was saying to revolutionary movements in general and to the North Vietnamese in particular that victory depended on the internal situation in each country, and that outside forces could have only a limited impact on the outcome. But the reasons why outside forces cannot readily either create revolutionary movements from scratch or determine whether they will succeed or fail are not well understood.

To begin with, in countries like those in Asia where the spirit of nationalism is strong, revolutionary groups gain little from being associated with nations other than their own. When the other nation involved is China, nationalistic hostility toward foreigners and people closely tied to outsiders is compounded by the widespread prejudice in the region against their own ethnic Chinese minority.

The Indonesian Communist party, for example, appears to have suffered from its association with the People's Republic of China, and the anti-Communist wave that followed the 1965 coup had a strong element of an anti-Chinese pogrom within it. All the Chinese government can offer an organization such as the Indonesian Community party is advice and material aid. Moreover, such advice is of limited use because each nation's political condition is to some degree unique. Material aid is not much more valuable because most revolutionary movements of any size have internal sources of finance and weapons of their own (and the weapons involved are not very sophisticated in any case).

As one moves closer to China's borders, China's ability to aid local guerilla movements increases, but not in any dramatic way. China, for example, can more easily supply arms to and provide sanctuary for guerilla movements operating near its border. And Chinese troops can pose an implied threat to anyone attacking areas in the neighboring country that are under Chinese protection (as in northern Laos). But to state these advantages is to underline their limited significance. All of the various dissident groups operating near the Burma-China border with Chinese support, for example, pose little threat to the present Burmese government.

Nor in a highly nationalistic world would overt Chinese military action accomplish what cannot be handled by more indirect means. If there were no Soviet troops on China's northern borders and no likelihood of an American response to an unvarnished invasion of Southeast Asia, it is quite likely that Chinese troops could conquer much or all of the region. After all, except for Vietnam and Indonesia the opposing armies are quite small.

But what would China do with the region once its armies occupied it? The rise of local independence forces would require a constant effort of suppression and to what end? Southeast Asia has some natural resources in abundance, but it is far cheaper to buy them than to pay for a large occupation army to seize them. The Soviet occupation of Eastern Europe at least creates a buffer between Soviet and Western forces, but for what would Southeast Asia be a buffer zone? The one area where conventional Chinese armed forces can play an important role in Southeast and East Asia is in the defense of existing friendly governments. This capacity was demonstrated during the Korean War, and it had an important influence on the development of the Vietnam War.

From the economic, the military, and even the political perspective, therefore, China's ability to influence the course of events in East and Southeast Asia is limited. Internal events within these countries are going to be the dominant determinants of their futures. China, as a result, is in no position to create societies in its own image throughout the region, if that was ever a Chinese goal. It can, however, contribute in a small way to the establishment of strong independent nations within the area that can stand on their own feet and thereby resist the temptation to seek security in the arms of powers actually or potentially hostile to China. One can observe clear moves in this direction somewhat further afield in China's firm support for a strong Pakistan and its close ties with Iran. That Chinese policies toward Southeast Asia may be moving in the same direction can be seen in the recent exchange of ambassadors between China and Malaysia, Thailand, and the Philippines and China's apparent tolerance for a continuing U.S. military presence in the Philippines.

A future Chinese government, of course, may not follow policies similar to those of the present. There could be a concerted Chinese attempt to foment revolution throughout Asia. However, the foundation of the above analysis was not based upon the intentions of a particular set of Chinese leaders, but upon the capacity of the Chinese state under any leadership to influence events in the region. Of course, there is the added factor that particular Southeast Asian leaders with greater or lesser friendship for China will rise and fall. There is no evidence that nationalism in the various states will get weaker—to the contrary. Nor will China acquire a dominant position in the region's trade. Thus the elements limiting Chinese influence in the region today will probably exist a decade or two hence as well.

Implications for the United States

China, therefore, is a nation sovereign at home, but with limited opportunities for extending its influence abroad. To the north and west Soviet armies not only block any extension of Chinese control or influence in those directions, but actually threaten China with loss of pieces of its existing territory. In addition, these same armies limit Chinese maneuverability in other directions as well. Any Chinese military move whether in aid of a nation like Pakistan or as part of an effort to extend Chinese control to the south or east must reckon with the danger in China's rear.

Even if there were no Russian troops on the northern borders, some future Chinese leadership intent on extending China's "sphere of influence" would not have an easy time of it. China has the military muscle to conquer nearby foreign lands or will have it soon, but the day is long past when foreign armies and foreign administrators (or their puppets) can easily and cheaply rule alien peoples. The Soviet Union continues to make efforts in this direction in Eastern Europe, but the price to its international reputation has been high. And the "gains" must largely be measured in terms of the enhanced ability of the Soviet State to ward off internal liberalizing influences and to create a military buffer with the West.

Nationalism is a powerful emotion today virtually everywhere and the Chinese Communists, beneficiaries of this spirit within China, seem to be well aware of its implications elsewhere. A series of Chinese puppet states in Southeast Asia would add little or nothing to Chinese security and would be a steady drain on China's limited resources. In fact, the attempt to create puppet states would probably elicit responses (military or other) from both the Soviet Union and the United States. The net result, therefore, might actually be a reduction in Chinese security.

The position that the United States finds itself in in southern and eastern Asia is not radically different from that of China. Whatever other lessons we learned from the Vietnam War, Americans should know by now that the price of shaping governments and societies to our liking in that region is extremely high and does not succeed in the end in any case.

Nevertheless, both the United States and China have some influence over the course of events in the smaller nations of Asia. Both countries also have interests in developments in the region. The Chinese do not want to see countries in the area become bases of operations against China as they have been, to some degree, in the past. The United States does not want to be cut off from the benefits of trade with the region, nor does it want to see a rising level of political instability and foreign attempts to exploit that instability. Not only would these attempts involve hazards of their own in the form of great power confrontations, but powers such as Japan could be driven once again to build large military forces.

It would appear, therefore, that it is in the interests of both China and the United States that southern and eastern Asia be a region of strong independent states beholden to no one. And there is every reason to believe that such an achievement is now possible. The United States has already taken major steps in this direction even if some of these steps have been involuntary. The United States' withdrawal from Vietnam has been followed by the removal of American combat aircraft from bases in Thailand and a continued reduction of the forces on Taiwan. Where U.S. military bases continue to exist (principally in Korea, Japan, and the Philippines), their presence appears to be tolerated if not actively supported by the Chinese. However, nothing will be gained and something will be lost if reduction of United States involvement in Southeast Asia is followed by an increasing Soviet military presence. Furthermore, some of the East Asian nations may well turn to the Soviet Union if they continue to perceive as China as hostile and the United States as unwilling to help. The Chinese decision to establish diplomatic relations with Malaysia, Thailand, and the Philippines is, in this respect, a welcome step in the right direction.

This parallelism of American and Chinese interests, of course, does not mean that these nations will see eye to eye on the precise nature of the desired independent states of Asia, far from it. But attempts on our part and theirs to give diplomatic and economic aid to one government or another or to rival political claimants need not spill over into the military arena. In this kind of rivalry, China and the United States have different strengths and weaknesses.

American economic power in the region is, for example, much greater than that of China, but this is not an unmixed blessing. The net effect of Japanese foreign investment in Asia on Japan's relations with the nations of Asia has been negative, and the United States could easily find itself in a similar position.

China, unlike the United States, is a revolutionary state and as such can confer its blessing on governments and groups thereby giving them a degree of revolutionary legitimacy. But this too is a mixed blessing because for everyone who is happy at receiving such support there are usually others who feel threatened by it.

This list of foreign policy instruments available to China and the United States could be readily extended. The main point, however, is that there is plenty of scope for rivalry without armed confrontation. And more importantly, no matter how hard China and America attempt to shape other Asian nations to their liking, it will be internal forces within these nations that will have the greatest influence on the ultimate outcome.

When one moves beyond the Asian region to confront some of the major issues facing the whole world community today, China's role is central in only one important area, disarmament. From the discussion earlier in this essay, it is clear that there are no major economic barriers to prevent China from becoming a near superpower in military terms within the next two or three decades. It follows that no serious attempts at disarmament will be possible without full Chinese participation. There is little point now in speculating about the shape of some future agreement, but a brief word is in order about China's attitude towards disarmament. China's current posture is one of disinterest or outright hostility toward most efforts in this area.

Peking's stance towards world arms control and disarmament issues today is a product of its own relative weakness and a belief, that is not without some basis in fact, that many attempts at arms control agreements have been directed at keeping China in an inferior military position. But, if the analysis above is correct, China is gradually reaching a point where its relative military strength will be much greater. As that development takes place, there is every reason to believe that the Chinese will worry less about freezing the status quo and more about the dangers of a world full of nuclear weapons. Taiwan, for example, might attempt to offset its deteriorating international position by developing its own nuclear force, and fear of a U.S. withdrawal from the region might have a similar result in the Republic of Korea. Either event would pose very real dangers for China. For the United States, therefore, the task is not to be discouraged by current Chinese refusals, but to continue to design proposals that the Chinese someday ought to find attractive.

When one turns to the major economic issues facing the world today, China's actual and potential role is much more modest. Because China is not a major trading nation, and is never likely to be among the top ten nations in this respect, its influence on the outcome of world balance of payments issues, for example, is not likely to be significant. Nor can China play much of a role in world efforts at trade liberalization since China's system of state trading must always remain outside of the mechanisms designed to promote the freer international exchange of commodities.

China may play a significant role with respect to specific commodities, however. The Chinese are already a major factor on the world grain market. Whether their position in agricultural trade will become greater or smaller over time will depend on what happens to domestic Chinese farm output. But the formidable difficulties facing China's land-short farmers make it more likely that Chinese agricultural imports will rise then decline. On the more positive side, Chinese exports, as pointed out earlier, could help ameliorate the world oil shortage, although Chinese domestic requirements are bound to be large and growing thus limiting the surplus available for sale abroad. United States policy, of course, will not be the major determinant of what happens to China's farm and natural resource output. But at least it should be clear that whatever the United States can contribute to raising the rate of growth in these sectors in the form of advanced technology and the like, it is in the American interest to do so.

There is an underlying theme throughout this essay that should provide a background for all discussions of specific issues in this area. That theme is that China, already the world's most populous country, is steadily moving toward near superpower status, at least in the military realm. That movement should not be a cause for panic, but neither should it be ignored. American security is increasingly tied to the ability of the United States and China to find ways of settling their differences by peaceful means in an atmosphere in which each side finds the other predictable and reliable.

The United States and China are not yet at a point of trust, although there is movement in the right direction. What is needed now is not some short-term tactical maneuver on our part that will please the Chinese (or vice versa). At a minimum, stability in the United States-China relationship will require a far higher understanding of each other's point of view than is presently the case, and that in turn will require far greater mutual contact and openness than is currently the case. Such efforts must be stepped up now, not because a crisis is imminent, but because the process, if it is to succeed at all, will take a long time. There is urgency to efforts to improve United States-China relations, but it is an urgency based on our having a long way to go before we reach a reliable basis for the good relations which will be essential a decade or two hence. There is no immediate crisis between China and America that must be solved now or next year.

Notes

1. For a discussion of the methodology used in arriving at this very rough estimate, see M.H. Halperin and D.H. Perkins, *Communist China and Arms Control* (New York: Praeger, 1965), pp. 34-35.

2. Ibid., pp. 28-40.

VI Political and Strategic Aspects of Chinese Foreign Policy

Thomas W. Robinson

The General Setting of Chinese Foreign Policy

By 1976, the political history of the People's Republic of China stretched to over a quarter century, and, counting the pre-1949 quarter century of struggle for power in China, the Chinese Communist party had been an international actor for over fifty years. Sufficient time has passed, therefore, to judge by what operative principles of foreign policy the Peking leadership have governed their international behavior and what factors have diverted Chinese goals from ideologically desired ends.

Chinese policy as a whole has been determined by four major elements: the panoply of domestic determinants; Chinese national interests, modified by its power compared to that of other states; the foreign policies of other states and parties; and the changing character of the international political and economic system. Since each of these in turn is composed of a number of subelements and the whole is interconnected in such a complex manner, at any given time, it is impossible to predict with great accuracy what course China will take internationally. Nonetheless, we know enough about each of the elements and their linkages and about Chinese intentions and actual foreign policy behavior to advance a number of generalizations. We are able to make certain assumptions about Peking's future relations with important foreign states and about its policies toward important issues of international politics and economics.

Domestic Determinants

Perhaps the most important element in forming Chinese foreign policy is the series of domestic determinants. These include: the "lessons" that the history of China and the Chinese Communist party are thought to hold for the conduct of foreign relations, the constraints and opportunities stemming from China's unique population and geography, the level of economic development and the sociological character of the Chinese people, and the operational characteristics inherent in Communist China's political decision-making. The essential elements in decision-making are the influence of Chinese "political culture," the nature of Chinese politics, and the political "style" of its chief policy-makers. Although the features which determine the form and content of China's foreign policy can be identified, there is no general agreement on the manner in which these factors interact to affect Chinese foreign policy. Nonetheless, any sound approach to an explanation of Chinese foreign policy must take into account the interplay of internal elements with international forces, and the unique importance of domestic considerations.

There are attempts to analyze China's international posture by one factor. Thus we find that "Chineseness," the longevity and cyclical character of Chinese history, the personality and philosophy of Mao Tse-tung, the operation of Leninist style politics within a Chinese framework (i.e., Machiavellianism plus a conspiratorial Party), and the workings out of the "lessons learned" and the habits developed during the Party's formative past have served, individually, to explain Chinese foreign policy. Each of these explanations is an important influence on China's conduct on the international level, but none is powerful enough to stand alone or to act as a dominant concept under which all others might be grouped.

Indirect explanations also exist. These approach the subject from the perspective of the social sciences, importing and introducing needed theories of behavior into the field. The theoretical concepts so contributed are of value in analyzing Chinese conduct. They provide avenues of approach to the subject through the use of various models. Specifically, the studies on the politics of bureaucracy offer insights into small group processes and the politics of decision-making. Equally, the work done on such subjects as the modernization process and its implications for foreign policy, and on "regime-types" and their effect upon the rhythm of a nation's external political behavior are aids to analyzing China. However, while these concepts bring out important influences, they move us only to the first stage of analysis.

An integrated approach must unify China-derived and social science-related factors; it must, in addition, provide the links between domestic and international elements that shape Chinese foreign policy. The problem is complex because international systemic factors and domestic processes influence each other directly as well as through the medium of foreign policy. Any realistic approach to the subject must therefore include "feedback" elements and place the study of domestic determinants in a larger schema.

Given these problems, it is perhaps useful to adopt the approach of successive approximations in order to produce a realistic and workable understanding of Chinese foreign policy. A first, additive stage tallies up relevant domestic factors and includes ideas from the social science and literature on China as well as propositions, based upon past experience with the Chinese. All these elements are then welded together to form a comprehensive explanation.

One list that covers most of the "causal space" allotted to Chinese domestic factors is:

1. Political culture
2. Ideological attitudes (including historical memory and philosophical code)
3. Institutional and procedural requisites
4. Struggle for power (including issues, means, and arenas)
5. Personality variables.

Although seemingly small, this list actually contains, through subcategories, most of the domestic ingredients of Chinese foreign policy.

These factors fit into a workable scheme, which shows their interrelationship. Figure VI-1 is a diagram of how we consider these factors to be interrelated. Chinese foreign policy is thus the joint product of the five factors, now joined together in a definite manner. The struggle for power, for instance, is hypothesized to be the central variable of the domestic political process. Personality variables are judged to operate both directly on foreign policy formulation and indirectly according to their influence on the struggle for power. Institutional and procedural requisites influence foreign policy formulation at several different levels (as shown in Figure VI-1). Various and changing arenas, issues, and means of conducting the struggle for power exist, while ideological attitudes are subdivided into historical and philosophical components, each of which has further divisions. Such well-known factors as the historical legacy, which confronted the Communist regime in 1949 can be included in this scheme at several points: historical memory, domestic and foreign policy issues, and administrative levels on which the struggle for power is conducted. Provision is made for "feedback" of other states' foreign policy by including foreign policy issues among those over which the domestic struggle for power is fought (such issues may, of course, enter the policy-making process at other spots, as noted below).

The third stage is reached by introducing propositions, hypothesizing dependency relationships among the variables or by importing whole explanatory concepts. Limitations of space constrain us to provide only general indications of relevant ideas and how they help us understand Chinese policy formation. Below are a number of propositions on foreign policy keyed to the five domestic factors.

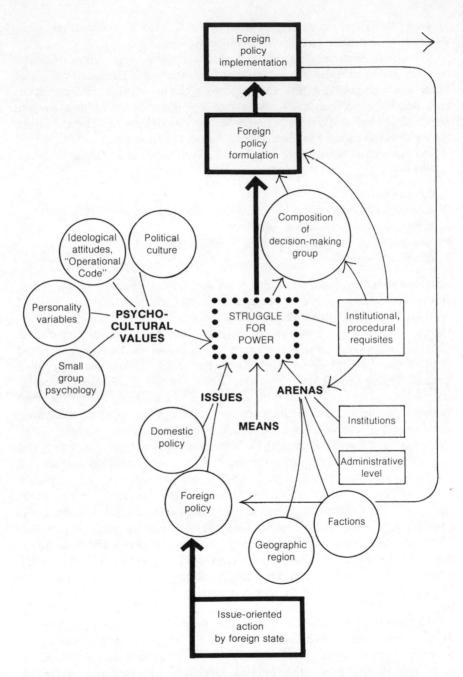

Figure VI-1. Diagram of the Domestic Ingredients of Chinese Foreign Policy

Political culture

1. A contradiction exists between traditional Chinese political culture (which emphasizes subordination of the individual to the group, repression of hatred and emotion, fear of authority but also of disorder, and dependence on external political direction) and Maoist political culture (which stresses confrontation with authority, self-assertedness, activism, controlled struggle, and disciplined release of emotion into aggressive political action).

2. This contradiction imparts a tension to Chinese politics, since Mao and his supporters must fight against traditional modes of organization and behavior. This tension, coupled with the Party's emphasis on military virtues, imposes a campaign style on Chinese political and economic life.

3. While Maoist political culture has succeeded in transforming the nature of politics in China, it could prove to be a temporary phenomenon that might atrophy after Mao's death and gradually be replaced by a political culture, which will combine Soviet-style bureaucratic communism and authoritarianism based on traditional Chinese political values.[1]

Ideological attitudes

1. Ideology serves five political functions in China: legitimacy, solidarity, agitation, communication, and goal specification.[2] In each case, Maoist ideology competes with such other philosophical codes and loyalty structures as elitism, professionalism, family and other primary group affiliations, and institutional ties. Moreover, the "thought of Mao Tse-tung," officially regarded as the practical application to China of Marxist-Leninist theory, is being transformed into abstract theory used to justify policies and practices promulgated for other reasons.

2. There is nonetheless an enduring core of Maoist ideological beliefs that, together with accumulated memories of the past, constitute an "operational code" of the Chinese Communist party. Five components comprise that code:

a. A basically Marxist outlook, emphasizing in particular the Maoist theory of antagonistic and nonantagonistic contradictions, but modified by

b. A pessimistic view of the inevitability of progress in history—sliding backward from socialism to capitalism is explicitly acknowledged—and a reversal in the importance of the economic base and the political-social superstructure;

c. Leninist-Machiavellian assumptions about people, politics, and organizational structures;

d. A tendency to think and act in military terms, even with regard to essentially nonmilitary operations, and thus to transform programs into campaigns and denote relevant actors as allies, neutrals, or friends;

e. A "Yenan complex," the legacy of the lessons learned during the quarter
century of struggle ending in 1949, including:
  i. A united front strategy toward the non-enemy
  ii. Mass line mobilization techniques applied to the populace
  iii. An assumption that any obstacle can be overcome through a combination
     of force, stratagem, and time
  iv. Emphasis on the virtues of self-reliance
  v. Insistence upon Party control over every sphere of life, even the most
     nonpolitical.

3. Maoist ideology is progressively out of tune with the demands of public
administration in China and with the structure and trends of the international
political/economic system. It is, in fact, being challenged internally by an
inchoate alliance among Party pragmatists, governmental administrators, and
regional military commanders. It is possible that, after Mao's death, this
challenge could result in revisionist practices and, eventually, revisionist ideological changes in orthodox Maoism.

Institutional and procedural requisites

1. The Chinese Communist party is basically a Leninist organization, that is,
centralist with a few democratic amendments. However, there are a number of
differences from the Soviet archtype:

a. The People's Liberation Army exerts much influence over Party decisions;
b. Major aspects of Party structure and policy are the product of the personality
   and preferences of one man, Mao Tse-Tung;
c. Intra-Party politics is largely factional in nature, reflecting not only the
   normal range of issues but regional and institutional loyalties;
d. The Party is periodically called to account for its actions, which makes it
   somewhat more responsive to popular desires and Mao's own dictates.

2. The locus of power in the Party is never stable because of the great
influence exerted by individual personalities and the lack of a tradition of
obedience to written constitutional documents. This provides the leadership
with institutional flexibility of decision-making, although it does make an
analysis of Chinese politics difficult.

3. Decisions normally are taken by the Party's Politburo. Membership in this
group is the political result of the struggle for power and, in addition, reflects a
combination of three factors: Mao Tse-tung's desires, the necessity of representing such important institutions as the army, the government apparatus, and the
ideological directorate, and such regions as Peking and Shanghai. Often,

however, the shape of the decision-making group changes. It is narrowed to the Standing Committee of the Politburo, broadened to the Central Committee, or even changed entirely in number and composition to reflect the exigencies of the factional struggle for power and Mao's own proclivities.

Struggle for power

1. Since the Party considers the regulation of every aspect of life in China to be within its purview, any issue can come before its decision-making organs. In general, however, two types of issues are addressed. One is political: that is, who is to make decisions (Mao and his followers, the bureaucrats, the regional military, etc.); who should be excluded from sharing in decisions; and how decisions are to be made (e.g., institutional vs. regional representation, by what body, and by what method). The other type of issue is substantive, chiefly: the pace and priorities of economic policy, foreign policy, and questions of intra-Party life—e.g., rules and purges—timing and direction of mobilization campaigns, and social/literary/educational policy. The latter often serve as surrogates for, and lead to, the former.

2. The resulting open-ended nature of Chinese decision-making brutalizes the political process within the Party and calls into question China's future political unity. The critical time will be when Maoist helmsmanship is no longer available or when the restraints imposed upon the pursuit of divergent views by the commonality and longevity of the leadership's experience is gone. However, the necessity to deal with continually severe environmental limitations (principally the food/population balance), the awesome alternative of civil war and possible warlordism, and the Marxist propensity to stress unity in times of danger— internal or external—all argue against the emergence of a political free-for-all after Mao. More likely, in fact, is a collective leadership based on an uneasy and shifting compromise between powerful institutions, regions, and individuals.

3. The means by which a person or group attempts to attain, or preserve, a share in Party decision-making runs the gamut found in every political entity, from alliances (usually unwritten or inchoate) to logrolling, bribes, violence, and rational argumentation. In general, however, Chinese politics tend to follow two courses. One is the subterranean channel of conducting political struggle without openly admitting it, since formation of political interest groups is expressly forbidden and since all discussion must be conducted within the general framework of Maoist philosophical categories. This imparts a superficially unreal character to Chinese politics. The other is the formation of political factions, however informal, on the basis of some kind of tie, be it personality, common experience, issue, or fear. Chinese politics is factional politics, the "rules" of which are by now rather well understood. Although usually formed around a given leading personality, factions are often institutionally based (as in various

military factions), regionally related (as with the so-called "Shanghai Group"), or ideologically separable (as "left-wing ideologues" versus "pragmatists"). Since Chinese politics must be conducted within the framework of Party rules and institutional requisites, and since Mao's philosophy pervades all written communications, it must be assumed that factions always exist, that the factional structure is constantly in flux, and that all pronouncements emanating from high Party organs contain hidden, but still discernible, indications of the state of the political process in China.

Personality variables

1. For at least four decades Chinese Communist politics has been dominated by the personality and philosophy of Mao Tse-tung. Despite the fact that Mao is physically declining, his influence will not cease after his death. Mao is China's Lenin and Stalin and it is improbable that another such leader will arise soon to rival his authority. Mao has attempted to transmit not only his philosophy to the Party and to the Chinese people but his "style" of political behavior as well. While the latter is a complex phenomenon, being the political reflection of an extraordinary personality, it can perhaps be summarized as follows:

Mao believes in individual initiative and dynamic individual activity, as opposed to passive execution of orders from above or over-intellectualization of a problem. Social institutions, particularly bureaucracy, should not hinder such initiative. The way to do things is to do them. If obstacles present themselves, they should be pushed over. This implies an emphasis on martial virtues, military solutions, guerrilla warfare, and highly flexible, pragmatic, and autonomous political activity. Politics must be given priority over economics or personal desires. When others hinder the attainment of ones goals, they must be humored along (if they are too powerful) or cast aside (if they are not). Rapid social change is advocated as a good in itself, to be attained by great popular effort in a relatively short time. The Chinese people possess the national greatness and revolutionary potential for attaining these goals. Marxism is a vehicle for implementing national goals and a convenient framework for rationalizing Chinese populism and revolutionary activism. It is, moreover, imperative to oppose wavering and backsliding and to prevent such tendencies from snowballing into serious impediments to the implementation of the permanent revolution. The result is a positive emphasis on indoctrination, and a negatively one on thought control, organized coercion, and purge. Once these intermediate goals have been assured, one can push forward vigorously the revolutionary struggle against the ideological enemy within and without the party, for the good of the "people," the country, and nature itself.

2. The Maoist operational style is not the only expression of the role of personality in Chinese politics. There are at least three others, associated respectively with Chou En-lai, the late premier; Liu Shao-ch'i, the former state chairman and Mao's Party successor-designate until the Cultural Revolution; and

Lin Piao, the former defense minister and Mao's second successor-designate until his demise in 1971. While there are differences among their operational styles, in the context of Party administration policy-making styles, and orientation toward specific issues, they all stand in contrast with the Maoist attitudinal structure. Moreover, because Chou's and Lin's operational styles summarize philosophies stemming from their roles as former heads of the governmental and military structures, respectively, and because Liu's political style was an intra-Party alternative to Maoist extremism, each can be seen as an archtype of the possible future biases of their respective institutions.

Chou En-lai's operational style can be summarized as follows:

Chou emphasized his roles as problem-solver, trouble-shooter, negotiator, administrator, and policy enforcer, rather than as an initiator of new policy ideas. His purposes were essentially two: (1) public—dispute settlement, policy implementation, and steerage of issues through the decision process and (2) private—preservation of public order, preserving and adding to China's store of industrial and human capital, and safeguarding the state bureaucratic apparatus from attack. He utilized four clusters of techniques to attain these goals: moving with the political tide when his purposes were served and opposing it when not until the point was reached when further delaying tactics were disfunctional (then he turned around to move *with* the formerly adverse current in order to foreshorten its period of influence); obfuscation of undesirable tendencies by drawing distinctions, making simple matters complex, and providing practical interpretations of theoretical pronouncements that limited the latter's effects; relying on personality and energy to enhance political maneuverability; and stressing personal contact as a means to make himself *persona grata* with all factions.

Lin Piao's political style can be described in somewhat different terms:

Lin was a behind-the-scenes administrator-politician-general who combined a public image of quietude, reserve, calmness, coolness, and modesty with such private qualities as cleverness, calculation, deliberation, and astuteness. Lin did not think in political terms. He learned Marxism-Leninism but depended upon his superior, usually Mao, for guidance. His most outstanding political characteristic was intense nationalism. Lin saw political problems in military terms; consequently, he had a penchant to seek military solutions to political issues and a propensity to overcome obstacles by military tactics: indirect, delaying, or guerrilla-like action. There was a military cast to his style of activity. He would prepare and plan his actions for a lengthy period before he embarked upon a venture. Then he would strike quickly, with a large percentage of his forces, at his opponent's weakest point and, finally, retreat rapidly, if necessary, to previously prepared positions.

Liu Shao-chi'i's operational style is somewhat better understood:

Liu emphasized organization and discipline as keys to success. He favored an orderly and meticulous work style and devoted his skill to organizing the Party, the economy and mass campaigns. He insisted on thorough preparation of Party initiatives or of any departure from established procedures. He stressed the virtue of keeping things under control and was, indeed, opposed to Mao's emphasis on voluntarism. Liu was skeptical, and Mao was not, about the perfectability of human nature. He would rather strive for intermediate goals attainable with present resources than risk failure by reaching too far. Liu strove for equilibrium in all that he did, stressing balance and realism as virtues, especially in Party life and economic policy. Two expressions of his preference for orderly development were that industrialization and, therefore, mechanization were pre-conditions to collectivization and that organizational solutions were better than voluntaristic ones. Liu was a thorough-going Marxist-Leninist: he preferred proletarian to peasant leadership; Party rule to personalist rule; city over countryside; limited inner-Party democracy over extensive mass-directed democracy. He was also a Bolshevist, in the Soviet sense of stressing Leninist Party norms, and he was a believer in following the Soviet example, since he viewed the Soviet present as China's future and the Soviet path as China's preferred road.

These five groups of variables operate on all Chinese political decision processes, domestic or foreign. Foreign policy decision-making in China is similar to that of other states in at least one respect, however. The actions of other states influence the Chinese domestic political process at more than one point, but not necessarily at the same time nor with the same degree of strength. This is evident if, assuming that the domestic political system in China has been able to decide who should comprise the foreign policy decision group (i.e., the leadership of the Party), we consider the three stages of foreign policy decision-making themselves. This is illustrated in Figure VI-2, which, as shown, is organically connected with the domestic political process at the level of foreign policy formulation.

The decision-making group selects the problems which it will consider. This selection is determined by an appraisal of the actions of foreign states as well as by the nature, both in terms of function and personality, of the group. Choosing an issue is, therefore, relatively straight-forward but the process of selection does not imply that there is harmony of definition. Perceptions and appraisals of the same issue may differ at various times because of the domestic pressures upon and past experience of each individual member.

Once the issue is defined, the Chinese leadership group can consider what options exist. Aside from the "definition of the situation," which is the chief product of the formulation stage, two other important variables influence this second, decisional, stage. These are the power at the disposal of the state and the nature of the country's national interests, as historically perceived. Both variables are modified by the group's perception of them; thus, there exist both objective and subjective definitions of power and interest. It is, however, the subjective appraisal that weighs more heavily in the formulation of policy. Before power and interest can be utilized as concepts for understanding the operational characteristics of Chinese foreign policy, they must be broken down into their components and related to specific issues and situations.

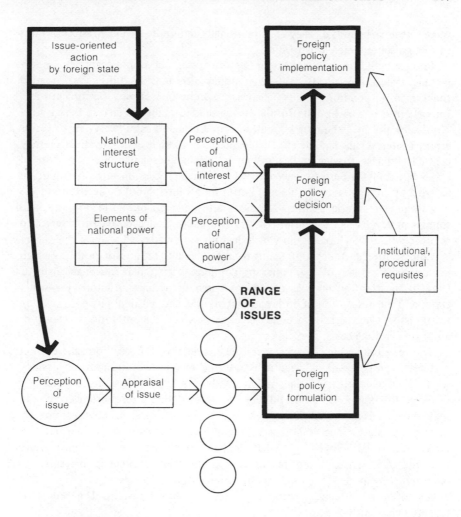

Figure VI-2. Diagram of the Three Stages of Chinese Foreign Policy Decision-making

Power and interest are relative terms; their specific meaning changes over time and space. While it is not, therefore, possible to speak in terms of an unchanging aggregate Chinese "power" or of some objectively existing, timeless Chinese "national interest," nonetheless, no analysis of Chinese foreign policy options is complete without the inclusion of the specific operational content of these two factors, simply because decisions depend upon the Party leadership's perception of their nation's interests and of its power. These two variables are thus relevant to the issue at hand (i.e., they are situationally determined) and to those actions of foreign states which affect China.

Foreign policy implementation, the third stage of Chinese foreign policy-making, flows directly from foreign policy decision. It fulfills its intended function of responding to the challenges posed by the actions of a foreign state. Importantly, it also has the (usually) unintended ability to affect the internal political scene by becoming a domestic (in China, an intra-Party, Party versus army, center versus region, etc.) issue itself. A foreign policy cycle is thereby created. Chinese foreign policy influences the actions and policies of foreign states but it also affects China's domestic political process. In sum, international activity by foreign states influences both China's foreign policy decision process *and* Chinese domestic politics. Decisions are made on both the domestic and foreign policy levels. The result of this process is that each decision serves to reinforce the cyclical manner in which decisions are made.

Chinese foreign policy thus stems from four factors: domestic politics (which in turn is made up of a number of complex parts); perception of an issue brought to attention because of actions taken or policies adopted by another state; and the perception of both national interest and national power in relation to the issue. Chinese foreign policy changes as a result of alterations in some or all of these influences.

The resulting action also influences the character of Chinese domestic politics and, although delayed, will eventually return ("feed back") to the foreign policy level. It influences the foreign nation involved in three ways: by becoming a factor in that state's domestic politics; by necessitating a response according to that state's self-perceived ideological and psycho-cultural proclivities; and by forcing the state's decision-makers to consider what aspects of the national interest are to be invoked, and what elements of power, in consequence, are to be employed. These three reactions combine with domestic pressures to determine the policy response of the foreign state. This response to Chinese policy initiatives affects, in turn, the Chinese political system. The process is repeated constantly.

Time is a constant factor in the Chinese foreign policy cycle, since each of the stages of perception, policy decision, and implementation requires time to complete, and since there are delays between an action taken by foreign states and its perception by the Chinese. More importantly, time differentials are not equal, so that as the cycle is repeated, actions, perceptions, and decisions may occur at different (or even simultaneous) times. Thus, a given Chinese foreign policy action (for instance, Peking's decision to threaten, but not actually to intervene with ground troops in the Vietnam conflict in 1965) may affect the domestic and foreign policies of other states (the United States did not directly engage China militarily in Vietnam and avoided provoking China along its border), which later take action according to their perception of interest and power (the United States did not mount a ground invasion of North Vietnam).

At some further time, the policies thus adopted enter the domestic political processes of China as one of the issues in the internal struggle for power. (For example, Mao's decision not to intervene precipitated a domestic debate on Sino-Soviet relations and delayed the onset of the Cultural Revolution for at least a half year.) There may be a lag between the time at which China's foreign policy actions are taken and the point at which they enter the domestic political arena as a disputed issue. The fact that the domestic strategic debate on Vietnam began only in June, 1965, although the foreign policy decision was taken very early in the year, illustrates this tendency. Thus, the policies of both China and foreign states may influence Chinese domestic politics simultaneously, or the actions of a foreign state may trigger a debate in China on the merits of actions taken some time previously. (The latter is what occurred in the summer of 1965.)

The Chinese foreign policy-making process is in fact largely made up of the differential effects over time of the various causative factors outlined above. While the relation of causes, processes, and effects appears rather simple, the reality it is designed to represent is quite complex. Moreover, Chinese foreign policy is not merely the sum of its actions and policies taken in relation to single foreign states or to individual issues. Policies toward many states and multiple issues must be adopted, carried into effect, and monitored simultaneously. This further complicates the picture, even more confuses cause and effect in the minds of Chinese decisionmakers, requires trade-offs between sometimes incompatible national and ideological interests, and makes necessary a differential evaluation of the utility of the several elements of national power. Thus, Chinese foreign policy (no different, in this respect, from that of other major states) becomes an art in terms of management and a nightmare in terms of analysis.

Chinese Interests and Power

In addition to coping with these normal, if complex, processes of foreign policy management, the Chinese leadership must deal with domestic constraints rooted in its historical legacy and the requirements of its physical environment. One goal of Chinese foreign policy is to turn such present limitations on its freedom of external action into positive conditions for supporting longer-term goals. China's enormous population is today a restraint upon current policy and Peking would like to see either an easing of the population/food balance or such a high level of economic development that a much larger proportion of the population would be free to contribute to foreign policy goals. China's per capita level of economic development (which is one measure of the degree to which it is able to apply internal economic resources to pursuing external interests) is currently low and prevents the adoption of desirable policies. However, the continuation of the current reasonably rapid rate of economic growth (upwards of 5 percent per annum) does provide an increasingly large absolute amount of hardware that can be utilized in support of Chinese foreign interests. Moreover, there is a close relationship between the level of economic development, and hence aggregate national power, and the discovery of new national interests; thus, Chinese involvement in the international political system should increase in the future, even if present population/food margins continue to be rather precarious.

China's geographic setting exerts a similar influence on Peking's foreign policy: so long as the country is not highly developed, economically and educationally, natural conditions restrain the Party from pursuing fully its international goals. A long seacoast presently means a difficult area to defend from foreign invasion, just as does a long land boundary with the Soviet Union. Relatively poor means of internal transportation tend to divide the country into semi-autonomous political satrapies and make it difficult for the regime to shift resources quickly from one sector to another. A low level of economic development necessitates the concentration of the population on a relatively small percentage of the total land area that is neither mountain or desert.

As China moves ahead economically, these liabilities will tend to become assets. Its enormous frontage on the Pacific Ocean will, with a modern fleet, enable China to gain seaborne access to the world, while the enormous frontier with the Soviet Union will be increasingly easy to defend as industrialization and population dispersal gain momentum. The unification of internal transportation will mitigate regional dissociative tendencies and make it possible for China to take advantage of its geographic shape: being essentially circular, China will be able to shift resources at will from one extremity to another (contrast this with the Soviet Union, which feels vulnerable partly because of its elongated shape). The development of the economy and the means of transportation will also enable Peking to overcome sometimes severe differences in climate: if one region's harvest fails, another's success can make up the loss. China's natural environment, hitherto a major limitation upon its freedom of maneuver in foreign relations, may therefore become increasingly an asset. Thus, environmental limitations upon Chinese foreign policy should be progressively downgraded.

The future influence of historic constraints upon Chinese foreign policy will be determined by China's success in two areas of the economy. The first need is to overcome poor harvests and thereby eliminate starvation by modernizing agriculture and producing food surpluses. The prospects of success are virtually dependent upon China's ability to limit the growth of its population. A population growth rate of even 2 percent will suffice to short-circuit major increases in agricultural output. Even a much lower, but still positive, rate of growth would result in a population of 1.3 billion by 1985. The range of foreign policy goals cannot be constantly broadened if the leadership must fear the consequences of agricultural downturn. Indeed, failure to solve the food/population problem in a definitive manner might lead to a reinterpretation of China's national interest to permit the "defensive" acquisition of agriculturally produc-tive land outside its present borders or to allow the mortgaging of other vital interests or resources to assure a supply of food from foreign sources.

The second area in which China must be successful is in the progress of industrial development. Industry must be able to keep ahead of the demands imposed by population growth and to stay abreast of technological develop-ments elsewhere. If, as seems likely, the rate of technological change throughout the world is increasing, it will become correspondingly difficult for China to catch up with world standards. Concommitently, freedom of maneuver in foreign policy will decline. It is not enough, therefore (although it remains a most important condition), for China to increase its production of steel, electric power, and oil to levels where, by restraining domestic demands, it can devote increasing amounts to the support of foreign goals. It is equally important that the technological quality of its production increase *faster* than average world rates.

The Sino-Soviet-American Triangle

Chinese national interests, which are inextricably intertwined with the domestic political situation as outlined above, are also organically linked to the level of resources that Peking can apply in pursuit of those interests in any given situation. Equally, Chinese interests are primarily directed to its relations with the five or six states that are important in the sense of requiring a response at the foreign office level and of being able to influence domestic Chinese develop-ments. They are the United States, the Soviet Union, Japan, North Korea, North Vietnam, and (possibly) India. However, the two superpowers, America and Russia, have so vastly affected Chinese foreign policy that post-1949 Chinese policy can largely be analyzed in terms of Peking's relations with them alone. Indeed, most post-War diplomatic history concerns triangular relations among the three, which form a subsystem dominating international politics in form and in content. Relations between China and all other states depend upon the state of relations between Peking and Moscow and Peking and Washington and, indirectly, between Moscow and Washington and their respective relations with the other states in question.

North Korea, North Vietnam, and India are included among those of central importance to China because Peking has been militarily involved on each of their territories and because India now possesses a nuclear capability, if still relatively small. Japan is also of central concern to China. But because of Tokyo's lack of offensive military potential, its alliance with the United States, and China's inability to influence Japanese domestic developments decisively, Peking has tended to treat Japan as a Far Eastern appendage of the United States.

However, even Chinese policy towards India and the two Asian Communist states, is largely determined by the character of its relations with the two superpowers—until the early 1960s by relations with the United States, since then by relations with the Soviet Union. So Chinese interests in regard to these states, too, can be reduced, for expository purposes, to a status of dependency upon the character of its interests toward, and relations with, America and Russia.

From China's point of view, the following appear to be reasonable propositions.

Power

1. When China perceived the United States to be more powerful than itself or the Soviet Union, it allied with Russia against America. This was the major reason for the Sino-Soviet alliance in 1950.
2. When China considered the Sino-Soviet alliance to be more powerful than the America-centered alliance system, it acquiesced in attempts by other Communist states at military expansion in peripheral areas. This was a major cause of the Korean War.
3. When all three parties considered Soviet and Chinese power to balance that of the United States, the resulting equilibrium led to relatively peaceful relations within the triangle. This was the situation from 1953-1960.
4. When mutual fear of nuclear war drove Moscow and Washington to seek détente, and the Sino-Soviet alliance began to dissolve for internal reasons, China could adopt a policy of opposition to both superpowers. This was the case from 1961-1965.
5. When the Soviet Union threatened China militarily, Peking resolved some of its differences with Washington to construct a proto-coalition against Moscow. This describes the situation from 1969 to the present.

Domestic

6. China has occasionally refused to pursue *any* foreign policy because of domestic priorities. It has then pretended to ignore Soviet and American policies as factors influencing Chinese domestic politics and foreign policies. This is what occurred during the Cultural Revolution, 1966-1968.
7. Peking's propensity to involve itself actively with the United States and the Soviet Union is directly related to the intensity of campaign-style economic development programs and inversely related to the level of political disagreement in the Party leadership. The former tendency is illustrated by the Great Leap Forward in 1957-1959, and the latter by the P'eng Teh-huai affair in 1959-1961 and the emerging Cultural Revolutionary differences in

1964-1966. Both aspects of this propensity impart a cyclical character to Chinese domestic politics, and hence to Chinese foreign policy, albeit attenuated and with a varying time lag.

8. Given the Party's greater interest in domestic matters and its tendency to pursue a foreign policy course, once established, until it is in obvious need of revision, Chinese relations with the United States and the Soviet Union often are not amenable to rapid short-term alternation. Two examples are the overly-slow improvement in Sino-American relations after 1969 in the face of Soviet military threats, and the continued decline in Sino-Soviet relations after 1963 below the point where China retained control of the situation.

Interests—Security

9. To permit no loss of national territory through military or other action of any hostile nation, especially the Soviet Union.

10. To recover "lost" national territory, especially Taiwan but not excluding, in the long run, Mongolia.

11. To settle outstanding border problems with the Soviet Union and India on Chinese terms (which does not exclude some trading of land on an equitable basis).

12. To establish a favorable military balance in two spheres: (a) nuclear—deterrence (first counter-city and later counter-force) against the Soviet Union, the United States, and other potential nuclear powers, particularly India and Japan; (b) conventional—protection of all Chinese borders without reliance on the outset on nuclear weapons, first the Sino-Soviet border, second the Fukien front against Taiwan and the United States, and third the Sino-Indian border.

13. To agree to controls on nuclear weapons production and disposition only if and when the Soviet Union and the United States disarm to Chinese force levels. Failing that, to build up to their own levels.

Interests—Diplomatic

14. To oppose the creation of a hostile combination of foreign powers, especially the United States and the Soviet Union. To that end, China desires to establish balances of power, globally and regionally:

    In East Asia: to play the United States off against the Soviet Union; to recover Taiwan; to isolate Japan, separate it from the United States, and prevent Tokyo from joining with the Soviet Union; and to keep North Korea neutral in Sino-Soviet competition or pro-Chinese by supporting North Korean ambitions toward the South without becoming involved militarily.

In Southeast Asia: to force the United States out as the primary security guarantor and to forestall the Soviet Union from replacing the United States in this role; to keep North Vietnam either neutral in Sino-Soviet competition or pro-Chinese by supporting its territorial ambitions without becoming involved militarily and assisting in its economic development.

In South Asia: to prevent or forestall the Soviet Union from becoming the primary security guarantor, and to cooperate with the United States to this end; to oppose Indian regional hegemony through support of Pakistan; and to break up the Indo-Soviet alliance.

Toward the Ruling Communist Governments in East Europe: to hinder Soviet efforts at building anti-Chinese unity, especially by supporting the continual autonomy of Rumania and the independence of Yugoslavia and Albania.

In the Developing World: to improve relations with local governments whenever it appears that such acts will outflank Soviet and American efforts; to take sides in local conflicts whenever it appears that to do so will precipitate or exacerbate Soviet-American conflict; given progress toward these ends and given limitations of distance, to support local revolutionary groups through adoption of the Maoist path of revolutionary violence.

In the West: to develop state relations to the extent it creates support for Chinese programs elsewhere, as it serves to drive the Soviet Union and the United States apart, and as it aids Chinese security interests against the Soviet Union.

15. To keep Japan off balance, to encourage anti-Liberal Democrat forces in Japanese politics, to prevent Japan from replacing the United States as the new protector of Taiwan, and to forestall Japanese nuclear armament.

16. To extend diplomatic influence into Soviet and American spheres, weakening Soviet-American abilities to deal with China from positions of strength.

17. To establish a record of support for allies and to pose as the leader of Third World states united against the superpowers.

18. To avoid wars, not related to primary security interests, with the United States and the Soviet Union, and to engage in military actions abroad against smaller powers (India, Southeast Asia, Korea) only for good cause, on its own terms, its own initiatives, and with high probabilities of success.

19. To isolate Taiwan from the United States and from Japan, to deal with it without fear of outside interference, and eventually to bring her under Mainland rule.

Economic

20. To arrange international trade and aid conditions to promote rapid domestic economic growth, but not at the expense of the more important principle of economic autarky.

21. To direct trade away from the Soviet Union and the United States, except where trade promotes Soviet-American disunity or where it promotes domestic economic growth in critical areas.
22. To utilize trade in gaining the favor of developing countries and in outflanking the Russians and the Americans.

Ideological

23. To demonstrate the universal validity of the Chinese path to power and the Chinese mode of social-political-economic organization.
24. To demonstrate the corruption by latter-day Russian leaders of the Leninist ideal by pointing out shortcomings in contemporary modes of Soviet social-political-economic organization and, consequently, of Soviet foreign policy.

Soviet and American domestic conditions and foreign policies are addressed in other volumes in the Critical Choices for Americans series (including one chapter by this writer, "Soviet Policy in Asia").[3] They are major determinants of Chinese foreign policy—indeed, they affect Chinese domestic politics and economic development and hence influence Chinese policy "from below" as well as call for a Chinese response more directly at the foreign office level. Because American and Soviet levels of aggregate power are so high, Chinese decision-makers must devote inordinate attention to Soviet and American policy initiatives, as the above listing of generalities concerning Chinese foreign policy objectives indicates. The differential perceptions on the part of Soviet, Chinese, and American decisionmakers of the relative power of the three states, the vastly different domestic circumstances in America, China, and Russia, and the varying perceptions of interests among the three, determine the character of their triangular relations. The history of the triangle, since the founding of the People's Republic of China in 1949, indicates that the basic direction of, and most of the specific departures in, Chinese foreign policy have been determined by the character of Chinese relations with the Soviet Union and the United States, no matter what aspect of relations—diplomatic, military, economic, or third state policies—are considered.

In the diplomatic, the most general, realm, Chinese policy is divisible into three periods. In the first, covering the initial decade of the new regime's existence, China leaned toward the Soviet Union, because it perceived a wide gap between Soviet and American power (to say nothing of Chinese and American power). Chinese policy was the result of the understanding gained from its newly-adopted Marxist-Leninist outlook of the vast gulf between Chinese and American societies, as well as differences in national interests (e.g., over the future of Taiwan), which quickly became evident. The Sino-Soviet Treaty, the Korean War, and the two Taiwan Straits crises were the result.

In the second period, covering most of the 1960s, China strove to attain its independence from Moscow while it continued to maintain a policy of intransigence toward Washington. Peking took note of the increasingly equal balance between Moscow and Washington and realized that all-out Chinese support of the Soviet Union was no longer imperative. China discovered that Soviet-American détente was not in its own interest since Moscow would no longer support Chinese goals as a matter of necessity in the Kremlin's competition with the United States. And China found it could overcome the destructive efforts of the Soviet Union. The termination of Soviet military and economic aid and the attempt to impose ideological isolation could be countered by internal efforts and by emphasizing the growing solidarity of the Third World as a counter to Soviet-American hegemony. Equally, China realized it could ignore trends in the external world, as it did during the Cultural Revolution.

In the third period, beginning with the Soviet-Chinese border clashes in 1969, China leaned toward the United States although not nearly so much as it had previously inclined toward the Soviet Union. Like Washington, Peking became alarmed at the growing power of the Soviet Union and the declining ability of the United States to cope with its own problems and deal, at the same time, with the Soviet threat. China was also frightened at the prospect of a Soviet military onslaught that could not be handled without very large losses of life, property, and territory. But the resulting Sino-American détente could not proceed to the point of open coalition because of the immense differences in domestic societies and ideological outlook, and the inability to settle the Taiwan question, the most important outstanding territorial difference.

Chinese military, economic, and third state policies followed closely the outlines of its diplomatic policies. In the military sphere, close cooperation with Moscow during the 1950s was succeeded in the 1960s by emphasis upon independence from both superpowers in every area. China soon produced its own nuclear weaponry, gave renewed emphasis to its own strategic and tactical military philosophy, began producing all components (even the most sophisticated) of a modern military machine, and became a not-insignificant factor in the world nuclear deterrent equation. By the beginning of the 1970s, instead of attempting to use its new military power to drive the Americans gradually from the Taiwan Straits and Southeast Asia, China found itself threatened by the Russians from the North and, in league with the Indians, from the Southwest, while the Americans were still firmly in place in the Northeast (i.e., Japan and Korea) and the East (Taiwan and the Philippines).

Exiting from their Southeast Asian disaster, the Americans nonetheless left behind a divided, if still Communist, Indochina, a North Vietnam leaning visibly toward Moscow, and the strong possibility of continuation of non-Communist rule over the rest of the region. China had to protect its homeland against the more obvious Soviet threat and thus felt obliged to agree with Washington to neutralize the Taiwan Straits region, to cease opposition to the American-Japanese security tie, and to acquiesce in a slight (and perhaps short) lessening of tensions in Korea.

Economically, much the same pattern prevailed. Reliance upon Soviet assistance during the 1950s, even to the extent of temporarily adopting the Soviet model of economic development, was followed, in the 1960s, by an emphasis on autarky and self-reliance at home and the diversification of foreign trade abroad. Melioration of Chinese relations with the United States following the Sino-Soviet border clashes accentuated the latter trend by opening trade relations with Washington. Perhaps more importantly, Peking attempted to prevent the development of close Soviet-Japanese economic relations by offering to sell to Tokyo virtually all of China's increasing supply of surplus oil. At home, the Soviet threat was felt so deeply that the principle of near-total self-reliance was dropped and even the policies of avoiding long-term external debt and not paying interest on short-term loans were laid aside. In general, leaning economically to one side or another meant that the development of the Chinese economy as a whole would be faster and more efficient; isolation, as the 1960s had shown, meant economically difficult times at home and a general decline in economic contacts abroad.

Chinese policy towards other states and international actors also depended greatly upon the state of Peking's relations with Washington and Moscow. During the period of near-total enmity with the United States, from 1950 to the late 1960s, friends and allies of America were *ipso facto* enemies of China. Japan and India are good examples: when Tokyo signed an alliance with Washington, China declared every successive Japanese government to be unfriendly; the warmth of Peking's relations with New Delhi was inversely related to the ups and downs of India's friendliness with Washington. To overcome its isolation in international affairs, the Chinese devised "people's diplomacy" as a means to establish unofficial relations with unrecognized states, and thereby, to put pressure from below on pro-American regimes to change their policy. "National liberation movements" were not supported in states of neutralist or pro-Chinese persuasion but were supported in states ruled by governments considered to be pro-American.

Once Peking and Washington began to seek détente, however, Chinese policy changed nearly overnight. Japan is again a good example: Peking quickly worked out with Tokyo the terms of recognition; it greatly increased the level of Sino-Japanese trade, and even encouraged the Japanese to continue to keep the Security Treaty with the Americans in force. The reason was the decline in Peking's relations with Moscow (as well the Chinese realization after the Cultural Revolution that Japan, not China itself, was the world's third economic power). The last thing Mao Tse-tung and Chou En-lai wanted was the replacement of a conservative and anti-Soviet Japanese-American connection with a more radical and anti-Chinese Soviet-Japanese arrangement. Once the Sino-Soviet break came in 1960, moreover, an increasing amount of Chinese energies went into countering Soviet influence in those areas and institutions to which it had access. Given the lack of Chinese influence in both Eastern Europe and the America-centered alliance system, Peking concentrated on battling the Russians ideologically within the nonruling Communist parties throughout the world and on competing for the favor of newly-independent states in Asia and Africa.

Chinese foreign policy for the quarter century of the existence of the People's Republic has thus been the product not only of domestic conditions and of the Communist party's perceptions of China's relative power, national interests, and ideological goals, but also of the necessity to deal with the nuclear superpowers. Most other states did not count in Chinese eyes as factors of major causative importance in formulating Peking's general foreign policy direction. Partial exceptions do occur in the cases of North Korea and North Vietnam, two contiguous Communist Asian states that, when threatened with external attack, forced Peking to put aside other goals to assure their defense and continued existence. Even here, however, the "rule" that the essence of Chinese policy can be found in the triangular interplay between itself, America, and Russia is confirmed, since in each instance the United States was perceived to be the external threat and the Soviet Union was the alternative guardian within the Communist system. For all intents and purposes, then, it would seem that Chinese policy is the product of events that occur not only in the People's Republic but of what emanates from Moscow and Washington. The rest is largely derivative.

The International System

If one is seeking a parsimonious explanation of the essential elements of Chinese foreign policy, therefore, he could well concentrate on the interaction among Chinese domestic politics, the perceptions in Peking of the country's power, interests, and ideology, and the policies of America and Russia. This approach can explain much of past Chinese policy because it encompasses the domestic, foreign office, and triangular political levels of policy formation within a single framework. But it neglects the influences upon Chinese, American, and Soviet policy of the structure of and trends within the international political-economic system as a whole, without which any explanation is incomplete.

A series of systemwide factors exists that operate parametrically upon all members and that, taken together, constitute a fourth level of analysis. Many of these factors change rather slowly and for this reason, together with their tendency to affect most states equally at any given time, they are often ignored in short- to medium-term analysis. Yet they are responsible for much of the general direction of world policy activity and as such are the prime agents responsible for longer-term change in the nature of the international system itself. There are four groupings of such factors: the distribution of power around the globe; the number and kind of economic actors comprising the system; the role of technology; and the part played by the relation of man to his natural environment. While there is a massive literature on each of these subjects, here we must confine ourselves to their impact upon Chinese foreign policy.

Distribution of Power. Power within the international system is obviously not distributed evenly, a fact for which history, geography, climate, and other relatively invariable factors are responsible. Power relevant to global politics is distributed laterally across the Northern Hemisphere, and concentrated in five specific areas: North America, Europe, the Soviet Union, East Asia, and the Middle East. In Europe and Asia, power is bifurcated into eastern and western sectors, either by geography or politics. The situation was not always thus: as short a time ago as 1870, global political and economic power was concentrated in Western Europe. Within one century, therefore, power has been dramatically dispersed laterally throughout the globe. But the process, so speedy during the first two-thirds of the twentieth century, is now dramatically decelerating: only India and Brazil remain candidates for great power status, and the case in favor of the former is dubious at best.

Thus, the twentieth century revolution in world politics, to the extent it has been linked with the changing distribution of power, is over. Implications follow for Chinese foreign policy. Peking cannot, for the most part, realistically depend upon defining the Third World into existence as an entity with natural unity, possessing the necessary potential to counter the established centers of power, and holding a set of interests naturally in harmony with those in China. China may well seek unity of policy with Third World states and may even emerge as the natural leader of such a politically disparate, geographically dispersed, and relatively powerless group to act as its chief international supporters in playing the balance of power game against the Soviet Union and the United States. However, China must take the world much as it is, which means that, although the theoretical combination of power among five relatively autonomous geographic centers is large enough, ideology, geography, and interest severely limit the range of Chinese political choices.

Modern advances in transportation and communication have made the world, for the first time, a unity in the sense that power can be applied almost instantly at vast distances, while information is no longer slow to spread nor facts easy to conceal. This means that, for the first time in man's history, world politics is also an entity and, although it is still possible to speak of regional politics, what happens in one part of the globe may affect, and therefore must be taken into account in, any other area. Moreover, decolonization has brought the number of states of the international political-economic system close to its potential maximum. Previously, only during the Second World War were these conditions approximated. Now they are all permanent features of world politics. But although global politics is unified in this sense, it is also fragmented along several lines over which China, like the other participants, has little control. The divisions are no longer simply ideological, as during the cold war (although the Soviet-American competition remains and the residual division of the developed world into America-centered and Soviet-centered alliances continues). Rather, they are ideological, economic, military, and—to some extent—geographic.

Economic Actors Comprising the System. Not only is there the Sino-Soviet-American triangle, which dominates the political and military aspects of world politics, but there is also an economic split into industrialized/developed and the agricultural/developing countries. This split is further divided into the Western industrial triangle of nations (the United States, Western Europe, and Japan), the Soviet-led Socialist group (i.e., the Soviet Union, Eastern Europe, and Mongolia), the resource-rich developing countries (mostly the Middle Eastern oil producers but also including Venezuela and Indonesia), and the residue of poor states located mostly in Africa and Asia.

China does not fit easily into any of these groupings: it is neither fully industrialized, nor basically agricultural, nor essentially resource-exporting, nor basically poor. China must pay attention to these divisions and cannot make policy merely by acting as if it were the natural leader of the "world countryside" against the "world city." If anything, China risks isolation within the contemporary economic world because of its in-between developmental status, to say nothing of the fact that since its economy, which is state-controlled although no longer on the Soviet model, and its polity, which is Communist but, again, no longer classifiable as Soviet-style, make it difficult to deal with Peking in terms of known parallels. The Chinese economy has much to offer in terms of its inventiveness, but its special character—to say nothing of the uniqueness that derives from its very large size—makes it doubtful that China can for long continue to participate in world economic activity merely as a self-proclaimed Third World developing country.

Role of Technology. Technology is one of the driving forces of change in the contemporary world. Technology passes national boundaries with relative ease and in certain spheres, e.g., military hardware, technological change makes it imperative that states keep abreast of their opponents. Most observers agree that, if anything, the rate of technological innovation is increasing. For China, it is essential to move even faster in order to absorb foreign technology and to accelerate the rate of innovation within national boundaries, for its entire program of economic development and military modernization depends largely on catching up with the outside world. It will not do for China perpetually to be one or two technological generations behind the most advanced countries, for each succeeding wave of technological progress quickly makes preceding modes of production obsolete. Equally important, each higher level of technology is much more costly than the previous level, so that the price of remaining competitive rises at increasing rates.

China has no choice but to "stay in the game," because it must compete with the Russians and the Americans and must overcome its legacy of backwardness. But the technological race imposes increasingly severe constraints upon the economic investment choices and the domestic and foreign political options open to the Peking leadership. Because the world centers of technological innovation are located for the most part in the developed nations (America, Europe, and Japan), Chinese decisionmakers must always keep open channels of communication, information exchange, and trade with these states; this necessity can only constrain Chinese policy within a more narrow set of policy options than the Party leadership would prefer from the ideological standpoint. It is true that, as the Chinese economy develops more fully, a higher percentage of today's available technology will be able to be produced within its national boundaries. But by the time China is able to reach this level, the next several technological revolutions may have occurred, and Peking may find itself relatively further behind.

Indeed, China under Communist rule must display a much greater degree of native inventiveness than it has done so far and become increasingly open to the influx of new ideas from abroad. Both needs carry implications for the nature of Communist political rule in China and for Chinese foreign policy. Domestically, greater autonomy must be provided to intellectuals and scientists to pursue topics which they themselves determine to be important, while the educational system must teach the virtues of freedom of creative inquiry. In foreign policy, China must stay in close contact with Western centers of technological advance, not merely by reading their publications but by entering into mutually cooperative research and development endeavors. This will obviously restrain the international maneuverability of the Peking leadership even as it aids in achieving important technological breakthroughs.

China's Environment. The final group of exogenous factors is perhaps of the greatest relative importance to China. The natural conditions within which the Chinese people must exist exert an exceedingly important constraining influence upon their ability to pursue their interests abroad. We have already alluded to the constraints of a very high population, a relatively low level of economic development, and a presently disadvantageous geographic setting. These factors also limit the effectiveness of many other countries, particularly in Asia and Africa, and thereby impinge on the direction and the probabilities of success of Chinese foreign policy. Thus, for instance, the growing global shortage of food per capita affects China directly by making it both more difficult and expensive to purchase grain and other commodities when needed. Since China's own production occasionally falters as a result of uncontrollable circumstances (weather, etc.), and since China's own population is still increasing by large yearly amounts, that nation must constantly be ready to enter world markets to cover shortfalls. In extreme circumstances, China would not only be unable to aid other countries more or less constantly in need of food but would even have to compete with them for available stocks. And since the Western countries, principally the United States, are likely to continue to be the main suppliers of food stuffs, China must continue to modify its policy of opposition to Washington longer, and with regard to more issues, than it would otherwise prefer.

Another case in point concerns oil policy. China supports the Organization of Petroleum Exporting Countries (OPEC) states' policy of large increases in prices to near-monopoly levels, because it wishes to gain influence in the Middle East and the Third World, and because it views these measures as generally anti-American. But to the extent that such support prolongs the OPEC-imposed price levels, China contributes to higher costs to the very Western industrial goods that it desires to acquire, and it aids in weakening the West in general, which Peking now wishes to strengthen for anti-Soviet reasons. In the longer run, this policy contradiction could redound to Peking's disadvantage, leading possibly to having to choose among the following policies: supporting OPEC, selling oil to Japan at less-than-OPEC prices, waffling in that support, or even changing it entirely.

Any realistic examination and forecast of Chinese foreign policy must take into account the complex connections between four sets of factors: domestic, foreign policy (power and interest), international political (in our case, Sino-Soviet-American relations), and international systemic. Each category forms a part of Chinese foreign policy and each is partially the product of the factors comprising the other three domains. The basic direction of Chinese foreign policy is provided by the structure and trends in the domestic political-economic-social-cultural system, specifically by the melding together of Chinese political culture, ideological attitudes, institutional requisites, the political struggle for power, and personality variables. The Chinese decision-making body thus formed must consider specific domestic and international issues in terms of the group's perceptual evaluation of China's ideological and national interests as well as the country's aggregate national power both in relation to a given problem and to foreign states. This process produces a foreign policy.

The two states most important for Chinese foreign policy are the Soviet Union and the United States; interaction with these two states has largely determined Chinese policy since the establishment of the People's Republic. Thus, instead of inquiring into Chinese relations with a large number of foreign states and inducing generalities from the product of all such relationships, great accuracy about the operational characteristics of Chinese policy may be gained by investigating the triangular Sino-Soviet-American relations. This inquiry reveals that for a quarter century Chinese policy has possessed relatively little freedom of movement. It was constrained initially by fear of the United States, bound later by the confines of the alliance with Moscow, kept back by domestic disturbances and problems during the late 1950s-early 1960s and during the Cultural Revolution, threatened by overt Soviet military attack and the subsequent conventional and nuclear buildup, and, throughout the period, constricted by China's relative lack of national power vis-à-vis America and Russia. Only during the two years from the second Sino-Indian border clash (October 1962) to the initiation of American ground intervention in Vietnam (early 1965), and during the period after the Nixon visit in early 1972, did China possess any significant freedom of policy maneuver. Even at those times, China could not go very far in pursuing its longer-term goal of spreading the word of the general verities of the Chinese path to revolutionary power and of Maoist sociocultural development, and was unable to contribute much assistance to "national liberation movements" in developing countries. It is significant, however, that in both these periods, China concentrated on improving relations with the Third World and felt at least marginally safe in steering a course relatively independent of either Soviet or American policy goals.

Throughout the entire period, however, exogenous, systemwide variables affected Chinese policy, as they did all other international actors, by skewing policy goals away from desired directions. Global power continued to be dispersed well away from Europe but tended to reconcentrate in a small number of new centers. Intra-Western politics became global politics, thanks to the increase in the number of independent states too close to its theoretical maximum and the unity provided by near-instantaneous transportation of the means of power, communication, and information diffusion. Accelerating technological progress partially enslaved all societies, forcing them to press ahead lest their competitors catch up or, if they were obviously behind, decreeing that they work very hard to remain competitive. Environmental constraints, ranging from too many people to maldistribution of critical natural resources, increasingly drove states to restrain their longer-term policy ambitions and to adopt unpalatable interim measures.

On balance, then, Chinese foreign policy turns out to be not startlingly different from those of other major states in terms of causal factors, and even, generally, in terms of results. Despite ideological pretentions and a number of laudatory goals, processes and trends over which Chinese policymakers have had little control, much less knowledge, have determined a large part of the course of Peking's relations with the external world. Like the rest of the world, China is being pushed along by the press of events and unforeseen contingencies. Despite a very strong domestic government ruling over a state united (with the exception of Taiwan) for the first time in over a century, China in reality has had surprisingly little control over the course of its international relations.

From the very beginning of the existence of the new regime, China was a major participant in world politics, playing a major part in precipitating, solidifying, and continuing the East-West split. As time progressed, and as it moved more surely onto the international scene, Peking found to its dismay that its freedom of initiative tended to decline instead of expand. Although China's advancing power allowed it the comparative luxury of ceasing to fear invasion, foreign control of its economy, and unequal legal status, the more active Peking became, the higher were the barriers that designated enemies, not unnaturally, threw up before her. China could gain reasonable military security in the nuclear missile age by providing itself with at least a minimal deterrent capability. Given the country's enormous size, reasonable prospects for economic development could be provided by a program that stressed self-reliance and autarky. These were programs that any forward-looking Chinese regime, Communist or not, would rationally have adopted.

At the end of a quarter century, then, Peking's foreign policy appeared to be increasingly the product of a rational response to external demands, subject to the same forces and obeying the same "rules" of power politics as did other states. This is not to say that Chinese foreign policy would be exactly the same were a non-Communist government suddenly to appear in Peking; but China's ideologically-induced departures from the established norm of international behavior appear to be declining in number and importance. The "style" and many of the goals of Chinese foreign policy remain undeniably Communist, as do at least some of the means. But an increasing proportion of both goals and means are relatively indistinguishable from those that China *qua* China would adopt, while many of the twists and turns of policy, as well as the general drift of things, seem explicable on the same grounds that serve as the basis for most other states' behavior.

Two Case Studies

Chinese Revolutionary and Third World Policy in an Era of Détente

The one component of China's foreign policy that has aroused the most controversy is her policy toward "national liberation movements" in foreign countries and the use of violence in support of revolutionary, as opposed to national interest, goals. It is particularly important to evaluate that aspect of her overall policy, for it seems recently to have become embedded in—even superseded by—what is now termed Peking's Third World policy. Since 1949, Chinese revolutionary policy has gone through two rather distinct phases. From 1949 to 1969, it varied considerably with the see-saw nature of the general approach of Mao and his associates to foreign affairs, although its theoretical base remained more or less constant. From late 1969 onward, fear of military attack from the Soviet Union began to dominate nearly every aspect of Chinese foreign policy, and China's revolutionary policy changed along with other components of its approach to the external world. Western evaluation also went through two distinct phases, differently timed than the Chinese stages as a result of the accumulation of experience with Chinese support (or nonsupport) of local insurgent groups and as attitudes in Washington and other capitals evolved. Let us use Western evaluation as a means of approaching Chinese policy itself.

China's "Export Revolution" Policy: Interpretations. This interpretation held sway from 1949 until the Sino-Soviet dispute came into the open in the early 1960s. This view held that China was a dangerous revolutionary state, seeking at every turn to "export its revolution" and to intervene in the internal affairs of as many fledgling states as possible around its periphery and farther away. Peking had shown the world that the Maoist gospel led to a revolutionary seizure of power in China itself. Now Mao would establish and support like-minded insurgent groups striving to overthrow their own governments in the many states—what we now term the Third World—where socioeconomic-political conditions seemed similar to those in China and hence indicated that these countries were ripe for revolution. The Chinese would thus demonstrate that their path to power was the correct and superior one, while the capitalist-imperialist system would suffer its inevitable demise more quickly and efficiently than would be true if one waited for the long-term effects of internal decay to work.

This interpretation of Chinese motivations, along with the American experience in the Korean War, was the basis of the Western policy to isolate China as much as possible, to contain that country, and to defend whatever state seemed in need of assistance against Chinese-inspired insurgency. Alliances were signed, bases constructed, military aid rendered, and counterinsurgency operations mounted. China was seen to be behind every domestic rebellion in Southeast Asia, was rapidly penetrating Africa, and was even casting its eyes on the Middle East and Latin America. The American role in Vietnam was specifically justified as an attempt to stop a Chinese-sponsored insurgency. Hanoi, for instance, was regarded as no more than a staging ground for a Chinese operation. It was felt that if counterinsurgency techniques in Vietnam were successfully applied, the West would have learned, once and for all, how to cope with this new form of warfare, and that the last link in the *cordon sanitaire* surrounding the Communist camp would have been forged. Consequently, the lie would have been given to claims of Chinese invincibility and historic inevitability.

About this time, however, controversy arose concerning the theory of Chinese revolutionary policy and the facts of, and the reasons for, Peking's support of certain revolutionary movements. Some now said that both theory and fact had been misunderstood, that the level of Chinese support to "national liberation movements" was low not merely because of logistical and other presumably temporary constraints but because China had no intention of becoming, everywhere, the international perpetrator of domestic rebellions. Moreover, it was stated that, in practice, China's revolutionary policy differed considerably from what revolutionary theory and declarations would indicate, and that this aspect of Peking's foreign policy was almost wholly dependent upon other, more central, factors such as the desire to see the United States evicted from the Asian periphery and the decision to compete with the Soviet Union for primacy within the Communist movement. Thus, even as the Vietnam War was being justified in terms of the former thought pattern, a new orthodoxy arose that sought to understand Chinese actions on their own terms and for its own sake.

Since earlier interpretation had sometimes gone to the extreme of suspecting Peking to be behind every anti-Western move by Third World regimes as well as responsible for nearly all acts of violence and propaganda against those same governments, the new interpretation served as a healthy antidote. But it also erred by whitewashing Mao's statements concerning the desirability of violent revolutionary change and by justifying each instance of Chinese support for local insurgent groups and anti-Western governments. In this view, not only were Chinese activities understandable and reasonable in their own terms, but Western, particularly American, policy was morally reprehensible and the reason for Chinese offensive-defensiveness. Thus, if American policymakers were anxious to secure the future of local governments in Southeast Asia and elsewhere, the way to do so was not to prop them up with American guns, advisors, and dollars, but to refrain from intervention and leave the area entirely. China would henceforth feel less threatened and would not consider it mandatory to counter the imposition of American power by expanding its own influence.

Then came the watersheds of the Cultural Revolution, for China, and the peak of Vietnam involvement, for the United States. Together with Chinese foreign policy defeats in late 1965, these events made it possible to evaluate China's revolutionary policy with somewhat greater objectivity. China isolated itself for several years, so that, despite some involvement of Red Guard elements in Hong Kong, Rangoon, and elsewhere, the revolutionary component of Chinese policy was essentially moribund. The ever more serious nature of the Sino-Soviet dispute skewed Chinese declarations and actions in the Third World from its "normal" anti-American direction. And the tacit agreement with the United States over Vietnam—trading no American invasion of the North for no greater Chinese involvement than arms supply to Hanoi—plus the very nature of the American involvement in the South, meant that a reasonably objective evaluation of Chinese policy toward, and its role in, the most important case of "national liberation war" since the Chinese revolution itself could finally be made.

That reinterpretation, completed by 1969, found that Chinese policy had, for the past twenty years, been flexible; that Chinese practice was to give declaratory support of insurgent groups abroad but surprisingly little material aid; and that the apparent contradiction between theory and practice was explainable in terms of the combined influence of internal, external, and historical constraints upon policy. The conclusion was that it would probably be best to take a relaxed, although by no means *laissez-faire*, attitude toward future prospects for Chinese revolutionary policy.

Détente and the Export of Revolution. The year 1969 was a watershed for Chinese foreign policy as a whole. Above all, the violent turn in Sino-Soviet relations caused China to restructure every aspect of its external relations to take account of the perceived military danger from the north. In addition, the end of the Cultural Revolution signified that, internally and externally, China could return to some kind of "normalcy." Rapid economic growth could resume, socio-political regularities be reconstituted, and the many discontinuities produced by the Cultural Revolution be adjusted. Externally, China could again think about carrying out its declaratory policy, reestablishing working relations with Third World states and revolutionary movements, and even replacing Nationalist embassies in some countries and at the United Nations. Moreover, the approaching end of major American involvement in the Vietnam conflict, together with what appeared to be a more positive attitude toward Peking by the new American administration meant that, for the first time since early 1950, China and America could approach each other with some degree of objectivity. Finally, the new economic power of Japan, and the growth in military power of India, indicated that an entirely different situation existed in Asia.

Chinese revolutionary policy also changed. If China now had to govern every move by its effect upon Peking's defense against the Soviet Union, Chinese relations with local governments in the developing world and with insurgent groups would have to vary accordingly. Now the important question for Peking was whether a given government was *pro-Soviet* (not pro-American) or not, and if so, what could be done to weaken that government or, more realistically, wean it from its orientation toward *Moscow* (and not Washington). Chinese support of local revolutionary groups would then be determined by the besieged government's relations with Russia, not America. But Peking also found that, during the interval of the Cultural Revolution, the fires of revolution had burned low (whether for lack of Chinese support or not is not clear) and that the Soviet Union had stolen a march on the Chinese by maintaining good or improving relations with many Third World states. In this situation, it was all China could do to return its ambassadors (called home during the Cultural Revolution) and attempt to compete with Moscow for favor of local governments. Revolutionary movements, where they existed, had to take a back seat, while the option to weaken pro-Russian governments through revolutionary means did not, in reality, exist.

One corollary, as we saw in the first part of this chapter, of the principle of universal anti-Sovietism was rapprochement with the United States. Hence, Peking would have to change its treatment of American allies in Southeast Asia and elsewhere. These nations (with certain exceptions such as South Vietnam) would now be approached on the basis of peaceful coexistence, which meant, in turn, that local insurgencies would not be supported as fully as in the past. (Not that they would be sacrificed entirely upon the altar of Sino-American rapprochement. China attempted to preserve the movements at a fairly low level, presumably until the crisis with Moscow was over or until Sino-American relations entered a new and less friendly phase.) Thus the oft-noted duality continued in Chinese revolutionary policy toward states allied with America, but now there was an emphasis placed upon improving relations. A good example is Thailand, where Peking and Bangkok exchanged ping-pong teams (accompanied by high foreign ministry officials who held extended talks), looked to increased trade, and eventually established diplomatic relations. At the same time, however, Peking's support for local Thai insurgent groups, although muted in the declaratory sense, continued.

Chinese energy in the years after 1969 was thus divided between defense against Soviet attack, working out the new relationship with the United States, and reconstituting and extending relations with Third World governments. There was correspondingly little time to devote to the support of revolutionary groups, although they were by no means overlooked. China, since 1949, has considered itself to be a "developing country," and thus, at least implicitly, to have much in common with former colonies and other "non-Western" states. But it was not until the Sino-Soviet split drove Peking to search for allies in the emerging struggle with Moscow that China paid serious attention to Third World states in their own right.

During most of the 1950s, the Stalinist, two camps, socialism-versus-capitalism view permeated Chinese outlooks, and it was really not until the last year or two before the onset of the Cultural Revolution that the Chinese leadership sought to appeal directly to the governments of Third World states. Even then, the contradiction between encouragement of antigovernmental rebels, as in the 1965 Lin Piao pronouncement, and support for established governments (itself an element in Peking's struggle against Moscow and Washington) rendered the claimed disinterestedness of China's policy rather suspect. The problem came to a head, in fact, just as the Cultural Revolution began and was symbolized by policy defeats in Indonesia, Algeria, Nigeria, and other states in Sub-Saharan Africa, and in abortive Third World leadership conferences in North Africa. During the Cultural Revolution itself and for two or three years thereafter, China's prestige among Third World states sank to an historic low.

Only with the beginning of the 1970s did China awake to the realization that it was isolated politically and economically, since Peking was a member neither of the Soviet-led Socialist camp, the American-led capitalist group of states, nor, in fact, of the still ill-defined conglomerate of developing states. Having chosen to be outside the former two groups, China could only attempt to maximize its credentials for membership in the latter. It did not matter so much that none of the Third World states were led by Leninist-style Communist parties—although many espoused some form of socialism—nor that many indeed had intimate ties (such as military alliances) with the United States and its allies. It did matter that the group formed a potential alternative to both the superpowers, that it was composed of a large number of states which had economies not dissimilar to China's, and that it appeared to be in need of leadership, which China could hopefully provide.

China's definition of the Third World was as political as its motivations for joining the bloc. To Peking a state is a member of the Third World: first, if it is not militarily allied to the United States (or, if it is, is moving away from Washington, as in the case of the Philippines); secondly, if it is dependent upon the West economically but desirous of becoming less so (as in the case with Latin American states); thirdly, if it is not tied militarily to the Soviet Union (hence, India, the classic Third World state of the 1950s, is excluded); fourthly, if it is actively pursuing an anti-Western and hopefully anti-Soviet policy. Even states in which the regimes are avowedly anti-Communist, such as Iran and Saudi Arabia, are to be included as long as they meet these criteria, and the obvious requirements of insufficient industrialization and low per capita income.

China might have had a rather difficult time persuading other developing countries of its worthiness of membership were it not for several developments and conditions. The most important condition was the common interest of China and other developing countries in gaining a greater proportion of the world social and economic product and hence, in the short run, reducing the shares of the West and even of the Soviet-led East. The pursuit of this interest had nothing to do with the Leninist theory of imperialism, although this theory obviously made the Chinese more receptive to participating in anti-Western declarations. The most important motivation was the Arab oil embargo following the October War in 1973; this development demonstrated the utility of withholding raw materials from the West, or selling them at a premium, as a means of forcing a transfer of resources from the more industrially developed world. These conditions and developments gave some objectivity to Chinese claims of confluence of interests between itself and other developing countries.

It should be noted, however, that from a Marxist-Leninist ideological point of view, there are only some arguments in favor of cooperation between Maoist China and the bulk of the Third World states. After all, they pursue economist policies based on an amalgam of ultra-nationalist, often religious, and nonclass or narrowly bourgeoisie goals, all of which Peking has often denounced. There is the possibility, therefore, at some future point of a breakdown of this confluence of interests and a redefinition of the situation by the Chinese. Intra-Party ideological criticism could be the catalyst for such a change; world political changes could be its impelling rationale.

Future Policy Toward the Third World. How long will the present phase last and what factors will work toward a change in Chinese policy? One part of the answer lies in the realization that anti-Sovietism and, concomitantly, rapproche-

ment with America are only two parts of Chinese policy. A third aspect is
Peking's attempt to place itself in the forefront of (or help to create) a new
coalition of Third World states against the two superpowers. There are obvious
contradictions between this aim and the other two elements, but China, as other
states, can often pursue contradictory policies in the short run. Still, as long as
China chooses to regard itself as the (to be sure undeclared) leader of an
anti-superpower coalition of states, whether that coalition is real or not, its
support for local insurgencies will probably be muted.

The question might even be raised as to whether, if the present orientation
continues for a considerable period, Chinese revolutionary theory might have to
be revised to accord with Chinese foreign policy practice. That is, if Third World
people are generally regarded as adequately represented by their governments
and, at the same time, considered to be in rebellion against the neo-colonialism
of the superpowers, then the idea that class relations within these states are of
overwhelming importance (and hence that revolutionary movements of the
proper—Maoist Communist—type must be supported) will have to be modified
or even discarded. Evidence of this shift may be seen in Chinese statements at
the United Nations. In the Security Council debate in Panama on the future of
the Canal, for instance, Huang Hua equated the struggle of the Panamanian
people against the United States with that of its government; nothing was said of
class relations within that country or about the nature of the government.

Another part of the answer is to recognize that China has tended increasingly
to drop its dual policy of support for a government that is pro-Chinese while
often working behind the back of that same government to support local
dissidents. The best example is Tanzania, where the Chinese are attempting to
make a showcase of their neutrality in Tanzanian affairs, despite the presence in
the country of large numbers of Chinese technicians constructing the new
railway. They could well have carried out subversive missions but apparently
have not. Lest this be thought to be a universal pattern, however, it should be
noted that in Burma, where the government is also pro-Chinese, Peking
continues to support the White Flag Communists, whose lack of success is to be
attributed as much to disunity within the movement as to the relatively low level
of Chinese support.

Of equal importance in assessing Chinese policy are two other factors. One is
the question of how China will evaluate the results of the Vietnam experience
and the extent to which Peking will continue to feel that it is necessary and
desirable to support insurgencies in Southeast Asia. The complex of insurgencies
and interventions that comprise the Vietnam imbroglio has now been resolved.
Peking continued to the end to play an important part in supplying arms and
other supplies to Hanoi, which then used them to conclude the war in the South.
China could hardly have withdrawn from the situation, despite the probability
that it pressured North Vietnam into signing the truce agreements with the
United States, for it had to continue to vie with the Soviet Union for Hanoi's

allegiance. Of equal importance, Peking saw the Vietnam victory as the best proof so far of the veracity of the people's war concept, however distant the actual conduct of fighting was from the Chinese ideal. In this regard, the arrangement of elements in the Maoist theory is flexible enough to fit any particular situation. For example, in 1965, Lin Piao argued that American intervention in force in the South completed the analogy with the revolutionary past in China. In 1972, Peking argued that withdrawal of those same American forces would also enhance revolutionary prospects.

Finally, one result of the war has been to link, in Chinese declaratory pronouncements, all the otherwise separable dissident movements in Indochina and Thailand. By sponsoring conferences of Indochina people (however unrepresentative they may be), by keeping Sihanouk in Peking and supporting first the Khmer Rouge insurgency and then the new rulers in Cambodia, and by supplying the Thai revolutionary movement with enough arms to threaten the regime in Bangkok at some future time, China assured itself a role in Southeast Asia that may continue to gain the enmity of local non-Communist governments and that risks ruining its budding relationship with the United States. China can, in fact, do little else than remain committed to the Communist regimes and movements in the area. To abandon them now would be to lose the mantle of revolutionary virtue China wears so proudly and to risk losing control of the future of Southeast Asia to a much enlarged (and possibly pro-Soviet) North Vietnam or to a coalition of non-Communist, neutralist governments, or to enhanced Soviet and/or Japanese influence. Thus, continued Chinese involvement in Southeast Asian military and political developments assures that Peking will not soon forget its revolutionary heritage nor be tempted to dampen its support for local revolutionaries completely, merely to satisfy the demands of state policy. For these reasons alone, China is likely to continue its dual policy, albeit on somewhat shifting grounds.

It still must be realized that the opportunities for Chinese support of revolutionary groups is declining as there is an increase in the number of states governed by leftist, radical, or even anti-Western groups not necessarily Socialist in inclination. As long as China continues to find it politic to view the world as divided into American, Soviet, and Third World spheres, it will be difficult, to continue pursuing a dual policy with the same emphasis on antigovernmental violent revolution as in the past. "Revolution," in fact, is taking on a quite different meaning in Chinese pronouncements: revolution now means government-sponsored social change in the socioeconomic sphere, some version of national cultural renaissance, and state-led opposition to the economic and cultural presence of the West through such devices as nationalization of foreign-controlled industry.

China will probably continue to support revolutionary groups in southern Africa, the Middle East, non-Communist Southeast Asia, and perhaps even Latin America. But even in these regions, opportunities are declining. The former

Portuguese colonies are now independent; the Palestine Liberation Organization plays China off against the Soviet Union but realizes that only Moscow and Washington, not Peking can in the end provide it what it wants. In Latin America, antigovernmental insurgencies have not been successful in recent years, while there is more for Peking to gain from improving its relations with those governments that take an increasingly anti-American stance (Mexico and Allende's Chile are good examples of this trend). In Southeast Asia, future assistance to guerrilla groups in non-Indochina must be funneled through Hanoi or, possibly Pnom Penh. Thus, the revolutionary component of Chinese Third World policy has lost much of its weight in recent years.

The final factor in evaluating the trend in future Chinese revolutionary policy is the reciprocal relationship between Chinese policy goals and policy means (that is, intentions and capabilities). As we have seen, intentions seem to change, depending on a host of factors, although there continues to be an irreducible core of beliefs common to all Chinese revolutionary policy since 1949. But capabilities also change. Since 1949, most analysts of the first school of thought mentioned previously have tended to maximize their evaluations of China's capabilities to involve itself in domestic disorders abroad, while those of the second school tended to minimize Peking's ability to do so. It seems, in fact, that until very recently China did not have the range of physical wherewithal sufficient to assure it a major voice in distant revolutionary movements. This is one reason why the Chinese have emphasized the necessity of local self-reliance and stressed Mao's thought as a catalyst to action. It was comparatively easy to use the diplomatic pouch, the ether, and the mailbag to overcome the disadvantages of distance and transportation.

But is not the situation now changing rapidly? China is providing itself with a sizable merchant marine, a blue water navy, and its own channels of international air communication. The Chinese are gaining experience in building roads and railroads adjacent to, and sometimes at great distance from, their borders. As we discuss below, China will soon have much more than the minimum strategic retaliatory power necessary to ensure a high probability that nuclear weapons will not be used against the country (meaning that, among other things, were China's problems with the Soviet Union ever to be solved, its very large ground force would be freed for use elsewhere). And, through the media of foreign aid and military assistance, China is gaining the experience necessary to become knowledgeable in the linguistic, cultural, and political details of distant lands.

Capabilities and intentions are closely related. With enhanced capability for intervention, it may be that Chinese revolutionary doctrine and practice will change in the same direction. Experience has shown that it often takes only a minimum of external assistance to kindle and maintain a revolutionary movement (although the Cuban experience in South America, as well as the Chinese and Vietnam conflicts themselves, should be proof that external aid is by no means a necessary, nor even a sufficient, condition for a successful movement).

But if external assistance is an important adjunct, there may be a resurgence of Chinese interest and involvement in supporting national liberation movements in the not-too-distant future.

It is true that the constraints upon Chinese policy noted earlier will, if anything, become more severe with time, and that new constraints (such as declining revolutionary propensities after Mao and his generation leave the scene and changing domestic/foreign priorities stemming from the exigencies of economic development) will be added to an already formidable list. It is also true that the supply of revolutionary situations may tend to decrease with time as newly independent regimes learn how to cope with their problems. But one cannot be sure of that: political "development" has often not been forward at all and economic "development" has frequently been distressingly slow.

There are, moreover, a number of classic cases of national liberation that, despite their distance from China, could still provide fuel for Chinese involvement, or at least keep revolutionary hopes burning. The situations in the southern third of Africa come readily to mind, while the Subcontinent retains enough volatility to provide China with ample opportunities to exploit were it ever to free itself from overdependence on the anti-Indian, anti-Soviet necessities of her present state policy. Even in the Middle East, the perpetually dangerous status of the Arab-Israeli confrontation, together with the disinclination of the Soviet Union to take great risks in the area, may eventually provide a greater opening for Chinese involvement.

But it remains true that the many constraints upon Chinese revolutionary propensities are, on balance, probably increasing. The trend, if history is any guide, is against vastly increased Chinese involvement. In this regard, the events of late 1965 may prove to be decisive. However, history also plays tricks, while trends, statistical concepts at best, are often modified or reversed by single events. Thus, continued attention to the details of Chinese revolutionary theory and practice is warranted. Certainly they are of more than academic interest, since more than in any other sector, all the contradictions and complexities of Chinese foreign policy are united here.

Chinese Nuclear Strategy, 1965-1985

By early 1976, China had been a member of the nuclear club for nearly a dozen years and a nuclear power of consequence since it exploded a thermonuclear device in 1967 and demonstrated a clear delivery capability. Since that time, many in the West have attempted to sketch the likely directions of China's nuclear strategy; indeed, over the years the Chinese themselves have provided some of the elements necessary to conduct a relatively definitive analysis. However, no authoritative statement of nuclear deterrent policy has been issued by the Chinese; no literature of Chinese authorship has appeared indicating acceptance of the basic precepts of nuclear deterrence; and even the evidence of deterrent strategy stemming from force composition and disposition is neither fulsome nor convincing. The many problems produced by this lack of defensible conclusions drive the analyst to lower his standards of judgment, to look perhaps too closely at the "esoteric" literature, to substitute logic, extrapolations, and scenario-writing for fact, and to consider possibly inappropriate parallels from the Chinese past or from other states' histories.

But it is possible to derive a reasonably accurate statement of what Chinese nuclear strategy has been and to set forth a useful set of alternatives that Peking might pursue in the medium-term future. There have been policy discussions in China on this subject, some of the facts of which have emerged. In addition, force dispositions and other hard evidence can be matched with programmatic Chinese statements. Moreover, the influence of delivery system technology and the nuclear weapons development programs of the United States and the Soviet Union forces the Chinese to concentrate their work to prescribed areas. And, finally, the military propensities of the Chinese political and defense establishment (determined by past activity and selective memories of that past as indicated by Maoist writings and statements) can be inspected for clues on how the Chinese might perform in deterrent-related situations in the future. This material can be combined to form a composite statement of Chinese nuclear strategy, past and future.

Past Strategy. The declaratory and operational aspects of Chinese nuclear strategy must be placed within the context of three sets of constraints: domestic, technological, and international.

Domestic Influences. Domestically, the dozen years since 1964 have witnessed major shifts in political alignments within the country and equally great variations in the tempo of economic growth and educational progress. All of these are of commanding importance for Chinese nuclear strategy. The Cultural Revolution, for instance, brought to the fore, even more than previously, the Maoist world outlook, which included: a strategic theory stressing voluntarism; "people's war"; derogation of the importance of technology; an emphasis upon a defensive, piecemeal defeat of an enemy intentionally allowed to occupy large stretches of territory; and deliberate scorn for the obvious destructibility of nuclear weapons and for the delivery capabilities of the Russians and the Americans. The Chinese could pretend that their own shortcomings in the nuclear realm were of no great importance, while declarations concerning the efficacy of people's war could provide a cover for the continued accumulation and deployment of a credible, if still minimal, nuclear force. In this sense, what appeared to be unrealistic braggadocio, combined with almost total silence concerning the details of force planning and disposition, was perhaps a deliberate gambit to dissuade the nuclear superpowers from attacking China.

At this time, China was in a period of great strategic inferiority, because of the removal of the Soviet nuclear umbrella, domestic turmoil, and the threat of unwanted involvement in the Southeast Asian war. Chinese strategic inferiority probably increased after the end of the Cultural Revolution, despite the beginnings of a deployed, credible nuclear strike force. Indeed, the 1969 border clashes with the Soviet Union, the necessities of military rule following the collapse of the Party's political authority, the wranglings over the Maoist succession, and the emergence of intra-army and Party-army fissures attendant upon the Lin Piao-led coup attempt, all weakened Chinese unity and caused the Soviet Union at least to think in terms of preemptive attack against Chinese nuclear facilities. Therefore, it is not surprising to find a relative absence of sophisticated and detailed Chinese statements on the role of nuclear weapons in foreign and military policy and on the direction they intend to move in terms of force structure and deployment.

This is not to say that the Chinese had no declaratory policy whatsoever. A statement on such matters was forthcoming after nearly every one of China's eighteen nuclear tests, as well as on other occasions such as the various Soviet-American disarmament talks and the opening sessions of the United Nations General Assembly. Chinese statements, until the end of 1971, centered around five themes: a pledge not to initiate nuclear war (the "no-first-use" pledge); justification of the Chinese program (and some, but not all, attempts by other states) on grounds of self-defense and the need to break the superpowers' "nuclear monopoly"; denunciation of all collective efforts to engage in control of nuclear weapons, on grounds of superpower domination (even though the *results* of such efforts as the Non-Proliferation Treaty dovetail with Chinese policy and Chinese interests); a few suggestions, however impractical, on how states should deal with nuclear weapons for example, China advocated the complete prohibition and destruction of nuclear weapons be adopted by an all-states' summit conference; and the claim that Chinese tests and deployment gave encouragement to revolutionary movements throughout the world. Although such statements were not unexpected, given the Maoist *Weltanschauung* and Peking's position of acute strategic inferiority vis-à-vis the Soviet Union and the United States, they did not in themselves constitute a nuclear strategy.

The post-Lin Piao period (e.g., after September 1971) gave evidence of several other aspects of Chinese policy that stemmed from domestic considerations. One was clearly economic. Shortly after the Lin Piao events (whether directly related to them or not is not known), China began not only to shift investment from the military sector but also to decrease the amount of military equipment flowing to army units. The reasons are complex, but they reflect the state of the economy as a whole (particularly the role of agriculture); the apparent belief that the Soviet Union would not attack; and the desire to invest scarce resources in areas (such as petroleum and high technology industries) that would in the long run quicken China's rate of industrial growth. It is not clear whether the ensuing general slowdown in procurement extended to the nuclear/missile/high technology field, but surely the influence was felt, if in no other sense than that the military as a whole had to compete for relatively more scarce resources. Moreover, if the obvious slowdown in progress toward the development of an intercontinental ballistic missile an (ICBM) that could hit the United States and the deployment of a nuclear-powered submarine (the first step toward a sea launched ballistic missile (SLBM) is related to the economic issue, then there is direct evidence that the 1971 decision included the nuclear realm.

A second post-1971 domestic factor was the resuscitation of the Party, and concomitantly, its ability to command the army (or be able to acceed to the army's request) to return full time to national defense duties. Both of these factors, together with emergent Sino-American détente, meant that Chinese nuclear strategy would henceforth be more closely integrated with conventional defense against the Soviet Union and be directed away, over the short run, from the United States and its principal Asian ally, Japan. Thus, domestic factors assisted in altering, geographically, the direction of Chinese nuclear strategy.

A third post-1971 domestic factor helped to change the emphasis of Maoist military thought from the "people's war" (allow-the-enemy-to-penetrate-deeply syndrome) to a much more conventional strategy stressing defense at or near the border, and mass, set-piece battles of annihilation on the order of the Chinese civil war period after 1945. While the influence of the Soviet threat on this change is obvious (Manchuria, still the center of Chinese industrial strength, could not be abandoned to the Soviets without dealing a fatal blow to the state nor, for that matter, could such a large and mineral-rich province as Sinkiang be let go without a major fight), the general weakening of Mao's role after the Lin affair and the concomitant strengthening of the Chou En-lai-Teng Hsiao-p'ing "modernizers" probably contributed to the change.

Post-1971 policy showed some modifications from the line established in 1964, some aspects of which seem to be related to internal developments. The campaign against Lin Piao contained a number of interesting features that provided evidence of the resolution of a debate on military policy. Not only was there the shift (noted immediately above) from guerilla to conventional defense in case of Soviet ground attack, but the alleged Lin Piao theory that nuclear wars were too destructive and hence should be avoided at all costs was rejected in favor of continued participation in "just" wars (e.g., wars of "national libera-tion" and wars of defense against such "reactionary" states as Russia and America). The very fact that the Lin Piao line had to be criticized indicates, however, that at least part of the military favored modifying Chinese nuclear strategy to the Khrushchev-like approach of casting nuclear conflict into the category of unjust wars, to emphasis upon the relative safety to be found in a balance of nuclear weapons, and to opening discussions and concluding agree-ments with the West (and presumably the Soviet Union) on the control of strategic arms.

Although these contentions were rejected by the Mao-led leftists, the controversy was evidently still unsettled, since neither of Chou En-lai's major reports (to the Tenth Party Congress in 1973 and the Fourth National People's Congress in 1975) contained a single word about the issue. Not wishing to support openly the "rightists," but refusing to repeat the words of the "leftists," Chou apparently chose to remain silent. With such a history, the controversy is likely to reemerge in the future, most probably after Mao's death.

A second aspect of post-1971 nuclear declaratory policy traceable to domestic developments is the subtle toughening of the Chinese conditions for cessation of its nuclear test program. The five points noted above were repeated, but now were made conditions to which *all* nuclear states would have to adhere. *All* nuclear stockpiles would have to be destroyed, *all* tests stopped, *all* nations would have to pledge not to be the first to use nuclear weapons and to promise never to use or threaten to use nuclear weapons against nonnuclear states (a new condition), nor to emplace them in or transport them across designated nuclear-free zones (for the most part, coterminal with the Third World), and *all* would have to evacuate all foreign bases of whatever kind. While much of this more stringent listing of conditions is directly related to fears of an eventual Soviet attack, clearly the higher degree of military readiness of the country and the larger stockpile of deliverable nuclear weapons enabled the Chinese leadership to take a harder line. Thus, China rejected all proposals to participate in arms control discussions, turned down out of hand any moves in whatever forum that would have limited the forward momentum of its nuclear program, and attempted to turn discussion from its own acquisition of nuclear arms to Soviet-American (particularly Soviet) blame for the existing situation. Finally, the post-1971 period gave evidence that China was beginning to acquire the vocabulary of nuclear deterrence while still rejecting the concept. By 1976, Chinese spokesmen talked in terms of throw-weight, multiple independently-targeted reentry vehicles (MIRVs), quality of weaponry, mobile launchers, and degrees of hardness. Such relative sophistication was in marked contrast to the range of public pronouncements in the prior period.

Technological Influences. Technology, and related aspects of the Chinese economic situation, has been the second major constraint upon Chinese nuclear policy in the period 1964-1976. The technological/economic gap influenced the Chinese program in at least five ways. Perhaps the most obvious was the absolute shortage, relative to China's perceived defense needs, of the base and matériel critical to the production and deployment of nuclear weapons/delivery systems. Shortages of missile material, electrical power, heavy industrial capacity, scientific and technological capability, and the relatively slow adaptation of foreign technological innovations (the result of Maoist insistence on self-reliance and the effects of the Cultural Revolution) all constrained the Chinese and forced them to move more slowly than they would otherwise have wished. The resulting, small margins for error, along with the necessity to move rapidly in order to acquire the beginnings of a minimal deterrent, combined to produce a conservatism and a caution that slowed overall growth once the period of the initial explosions, 1964-1967, was past.

Perhaps of greater importance, however, was the quickened rate of nuclear innovation in the United States and the Soviet Union. The Chinese had not only to provide themselves with a minimal defense capacity, but also to catch up to American and Soviet levels in terms of quality if not numbers. The concentration of scarce resources on obsolescent techniques or old models would mean that China risked being even farther behind than it was at the beginning, thereby jeopardizing its overall defense. China responded by attempting to raise its internal rate of innovation (probably with success) by purchasing or otherwise acquiring technology from abroad (principally from the West, including the United States), and by buying numerous copies of some systems rather than going through the time-consuming and risky process of prototype copying. Whether successful or not, the point is that the accelerating rate of change forced by the Americans and the Russians impelled the Chinese to change their "mix" of research/development versus production/deployment so that the former received priority, and thereby, risked, in the short run, basic security requirements. This was especially true in the 1969-1973 period.

A third, related factor is that America and Russia also determined the direction of technological change in the nuclear/missile field. When the United States decided to adopt highly accurate, dispersed, and hardened missiles fuelled by solid propellents and backed up by satellite warning systems, the Soviet Union felt compelled to do the same and, hence, so did the Chinese. If the Americans and the Russians competed in terms of triad systems (e.g., land and sea-launched missiles and aircraft delivered bombs), the Chinese believed it necessary to produce both a family of missiles and a bomber and to develop a nuclear-powered submarine, however costly this dispersion of effort was. If the Russians and the Americans developed MIRVs and other penetration aids, the Chinese would have to do the same. One reason, perhaps, for the near total absence of Chinese discussion on proper strategy is that the Americans and the Russians set it for them. In this regard, it may be said that the United States has been teaching nuclear strategy to the Chinese through its own research, development, and deployment decisions.

A fourth technological factor is the tendency of weapons systems to be mutually interdependent for maximum effectiveness. If China is indeed to convince the Soviet Union and the United States that its strategy is that of "no first use" (i.e., second strike and not launch on warning), it needs large and sophisticated radars and early warning satellites, solid propellents, effective command and control systems, hardened (perhaps even hidden or mobile) sites, and sophisticated guidance systems. Thus, taking a decision to develop one system locked China into developing several others simultaneously. Again, this tended to make Chinese strategic planning more conservative, to drive up costs, and to follow the Soviet-American lead as the tried-and-true path. It also meant that systems acquisition had to be undertaken in an integrated manner, so that resources tended to be strained by a bunched, rather than a sequential, development and deployment scheme. Hence, China found it lacked critical components of an overall nuclear defense, such as communications satellite technology, certain types of computers and programs, and guidance systems. The necessity to acquire these compelled Peking to approach the United States and to make political compromises in order to obtain them.

Finally, there were trade-offs, in the Chinese economy: between investment in a large research and development effort versus a substantial procurement program; between nuclear and conventional weapons programs; and between military procurement as a whole and the civilian economy. Despite the size of the Chinese industrial plant and the relatively rapid progress that had been made in the nuclear field, the country still could not afford to produce all the guns and all the butter it would like, and because it continued to live so close to the margin, given the land/population ratio, the resources available to defense and civilian economies perforce had to be calculated rather closely.

International Influences. International factors are perhaps the most important of the three constraints upon Chinese nuclear policy in the period after 1964. China would not have felt the need to develop nuclear weapons so intensively had there been no split with the Soviet Union and had Moscow not abrogated the nuclear assistance treaty of 1957. China might not have felt the need to acquire such devices at all had it not been for the Korean War experience with the United States, the American nuclear threat near the end of that war, and the entire range of differences—historical, perceptual, and territorial—that emerged in the half-decade following Communist conquest of the mainland. The split with Moscow and the continued separation from Washington isolated China in the international community; and, while that isolation alone did not cause China to set about producing nuclear weapons, it provided an additional, practical reason for doing so.

Given the existence of nuclear weapons, moreover, and their possession in large numbers by America and Russia, postwar history had clearly demonstrated by the mid-1950s that the degree of a state's international influence was closely linked with its nuclear status. If China wished to attain international standing, if its Communist government desired to have a say in the councils of Communist power, if Peking hoped to attract revolutionary movements not merely by the presumed verity of Maoist thought, it would have to have a credible, even if relatively small, nuclear force. Indeed, the prestige derived from the possession of nuclear weapons alone would have been enough to attract China into making the initial investment. To China, as to others, nuclear weapons were thus part of an historic drive for equality with the West. They were also an indispensible political tool for dealing not only with the two superpowers but also with such would-be Asian competitors as India; for impressing Third World states such as Sukarno's Indonesia; or for convincing newly independent African states to side with Peking on international issues.

More importantly, the status of China's relations with the United States and the Soviet Union affected centrally the nature of its nuclear program. Given the Mao-determined policy of emnity toward both, there seemed to be a need for a nuclear capability that could deter attack from either or both. This would have meant the creation of a very large stockpile of warheads and the emplacement of a large number of diverse types of delivery vehicles with extreme range, which would have been an exceedingly expensive and demanding task. The alternative was to adopt a minimal deterrent posture, direct it against the more threatening and easily reached opponent while making temporary compromises with the other superpower. At the same time, the emergent nuclear force would be combined with a conventional strategy which stressed the invincibility of Chinese ground forces armed with Maoist thought and tactics. Such an alternative, the one adopted once the choice had to—and could—be made after early 1969, had the added virtue of being cheaper, quicker, and more effective in terms of utilization of existing forces and did not force the leadership to renounce all-around deterrence. Also, relatively greater investment could be directed toward acquiring advanced technology and thus catching up to the American-Soviet levels without having to spend large resources on deployment. Such a minimal deterrent posture thus made sense from every point of view, including that of Mao, who was not only on record as having denigrated the role of nuclear weapons but was also quoted as saying: "all I want are six atom bombs. With these bombs I know that neither side will attack me."[4]

Postponement of acquiring an all-around deterrent capacity also possessed the virtue of not frightening Japan into building its own force. Although Chinese medium range ballistic missiles (MRBMs) and aircraft have been capable of blanketing Japan for some time, they remained on Chinese soil and out of sight. One reason for stretching out China's program to develop nuclear-powered submarines was that the eventual capability that such boats possess to launch missiles would be provocative to Japan. For that reason also (although not solely so), Chinese pronouncements on nuclear doctrine have been minimal and Peking's testing program has been conducted with circumspection. The present configuration of the international political landscape is thus convenient to China in terms of the room it provides to the Chinese nuclear weapons policy. A United States partially withdrawing from Asia—with a problem parallel to China's of staving off Soviet expansion, a United States still in alliance with Japan, and holding back South Korean and Taiwanese nuclearization is obviously pursuing a policy advantageous to China in a period of rapid growth of its relatively small and still vulnerable nuclear weapons capacity.

The development of Soviet-American strategic arms control talks was a further international factor influencing the Chinese program. The fact that China was not a member of the United Nations for most of the 1964-1975 period, and was out of favor with both America and Russia, meant that Peking was not asked to participate in international arms control negotiations. That circumstance was most agreeable to China because it did not, therefore, have to face international pressure to constrict its weapons development effort, to limit its tests, to permit inquiries into its military budgets, or to declare itself on important details of its strategic policy. A policy of "strategic ambiguity" depended in the interim period on relative silence, and isolation from international arms control and disarmament forums aided materially that policy. If China has had a "problem" in this area, it has emerged only since joining the United Nations and since achieving its *modus vivendi* with the United States. Peking has had to justify to a broad audience why it has continued to refuse to join at least in a strategic dialogue, and its excuses, generally based on the perfidity of the Soviet Union, have been forced and unconvincing.

The last international influence was the perceived opportunity to forward the Chinese version of the Marxist-Leninist revolutionary cause through assistance to "national liberation movements" in the developing world. Although Chinese aid was always low-key, often merely hortatory, and never a major element in day-to-day policy, it did affect Peking's long-term global outlook and thus directed its general foreign policy away from purely national interest directions.

The acquisition of nuclear weapons contributed to Mao's revolutionary policy, since Chinese possession was supposed to prevent the United States from escalating its response to guerrilla attacks against its client governments and to forestall attack against training bases inside China itself. More to the point, Chinese nuclear weapons, once deployed in sufficient numbers, could stabilize a balance of terror that would increase the importance of nonnuclear wars. A kind of Chinese nuclear umbrella would thus extend to revolutionary groups and make their ultimate victory more probable. American strategic impotence in the Southeast Asian conflict was probably viewed as confirmation of this analysis. Thus, nuclear weapons were brought in, as it were, to restore the primacy of the Maoist emphasis upon revolutionary war on the Chinese model as the means by which the non-Western, non-Soviet world will embark upon the path of true socialism-communism. There is thus a specific nuclear weapons assumption to the Maoist slogan: "countries want independence, nations want liberation, and the people want revolution," and to the assertion that wars will give rise to revolution unless revolution occurs first. China sees its possession of nuclear weapons as both preventing international war and assisting local revolutionary war, thus making the world safer for itself and quickening the presumably inevitable pace of history.

Future Strategy. Given the role of domestic, technological and international factors in determining the main outlines of present Chinese nuclear strategy, what can be said of the future? Will the relative weight of the components of each factor remain nearly the same as in the recent past, so that the most likely future strategy would be a continuation of the present policy? Or will, as so often happens in Chinese politics, in technological development, and in international relations, major variations occur? And if so, in what directions can Chinese policy be expected to move? Since many changes can be expected, including the occurrence of random events, and since the sequence of predictable events cannot be known, recourse must be had to reasoned presentation of a small number of well-defined alternative futures. The definition of such futures will depend upon how changes in components of the three factors are assessed, and the details of the alternative futures will stem from the manner in which their components are grouped. Before addressing that task, however, we must ascertain what aspects of Chinese nuclear strategy are to be included within that term. The following are some critical variables:

1. size of nuclear force (minimal: 20-100 warheads 20 kiloton (KT) equivalent for larger; intermediate: 100-1000 warheads; large: 1000-2000 warheads)
2. kind of delivery systems (missile only; missile and bomber; missile, bomber, and submarine)
3. quality of system (presence or absence of MIRVs and penetration aids; degree of variation in warhead size—20KT to 3,000KT equivalent; sophistication of guidance system in terms of circular error probable (CEP) two miles to less than one-half mile; kind of ballistic missile early warning system—(BMEWS) to satellite system)
4. strategic doctrine espoused or assumed (counterforce, countervalue, or mixed; first or second strike; kind of provocation necessary to trigger nuclear response—nuclear attack, conventional attack, attack against ally)
5. direction and range of weaponry (Asia regional only; European Russia; Continental United States)
6. arms control measures (hot lines, test bans, nuclear free zones; no first use pledge; non-proliferation policy; participation in strategic arms limitation talks; inspection, military budget disclosure)
7. connection with overall military policy (use of tactical nuclear weapons; coordination of strategic and tactical nuclear weapons; coordination of nuclear and conventional strategy; coordination with Maoist "people's war" tactics, as concerns both national defense and assistance to revolutionary groups abroad)

Continuation of the present strategic nuclear policy would thus be described as follows. The Chinese force, at present of intermediate size (circa 300-400 warheads) would by 1985 be well over 1,000 and likely be closer to 2,000, thus posing as a distant rival to the Soviet Union and the United States, far ahead of any fourth power. Having entered the realm of nuclear plenty, China would face a decision whether to curtail further acquisition or continue to chase Soviet and American increases. Having a combination missile/bomber deterrent at present, by 1985 China would have a family of second generation missiles, possibly a B-1 type supersonic bomber, and a SLBM capability equivalent to that of France or Great Britain. Peking's missiles, at present tipped with a variety of warheads for the most part near the lower end of the spectrum of destructiveness, could be mainly configured with hydrogen bomb (1,000 kiloton [KT] equivalent and above) or, more likely, with a variety of differently-sized warheads suitable to a multiplicity of tasks. Some of the heavier missiles, equivalent to the Soviet SS-9, would be MIRVed, although technological difficulties would preclude recasting the entire force in that mode. Sophisticated guidance systems would give a CEP of at least one-half mile and China would have enough ICBMs and SLBMs to target the fifty largest cities in America and the one hundred largest population centers in the Soviet Union, and the major cities of Japan, India, Southeast Asia, and the Middle East.

Given nuclear sufficiency, Peking would feel less inclined to refuse participation in arms control talks, although—given probable continued Soviet and American technological progress and new systems acquisition—it is doubtful that China would sign any agreement placing absolute limits on numbers and kinds of warheads and delivery systems. It might, on the other hand, agree to set up hot lines, exchange technical data leading to better national means of verification of systems deployment, participate in Pugwash-type exchanges, and might even sign specific agreements pledging say, no first use of nuclear weapons.

China would be able to target most of its warheads on military installations and Soviet and/or American missile sites, thus moving from a counter-city to a counterforce strategy or perhaps a mixed strategy weighted toward the counterforce end of the spectrum. Since its missile/bomber/submarine systems would be dispersed and hardened, and since China would possess adequate satellite reconnaissance technology, it could move to an explicit second strike strategy. Nuclear plenty would allow the production and deployment of several hundred tactical nuclear warheads, thus making it possible to defend the country at or near the borders and to decrease the probability of foreign—specifically Soviet—invasion close to the vanishing point. The emphasis in defensive strategy could thus change almost entirely from "people's war" tactics to entirely conventional ones.

Domestic Influences. Much, however, depends on the political context, in China and internationally, as well as on the rapidity of technological change, and there is no reason to imagine that such a straight-line extrapolation of current Chinese capabilities would necessarily result in this strategy and force mix. It is essential, therefore, to sketch out several alternative futures in each of the three realms before evaluating the probability of the above, and alternative, eventualities. In the past, *domestic* developments have been most important in determining the course of Chinese foreign relations, including its military policy. For the future, as in the past, the state of the economy (and hence the nature of the Party's economic policy) and the question of Party leadership (and thus the problem of the Maoist succession) are the major determining variables. Economically, there seem to be three options related to military affairs. One is the so-called balanced growth benchmark projection,[5] wherein approximately the present mix of investment in defense, consumer, heavy industry, and agriculture is maintained indefinitely. This would continue to allocate about one-fifth of industrial production to the defense sector and provide for the equivalent of a defense budget of nearly $50 billion by 1985. This would clearly give China the status of a superpower in the 1960s sense and, in absolute terms, would enable it to surpass any other state save America and Russia. It would allow the production and deployment of a number of new weapons systems, as well as make it possible for China to upgrade its conventional defense capability.

One of China's alternatives is to put more into the defense sector—in an effort to catch up to the Soviet Union and the United States in the qualitative, if not the quantitative, sense. Presuming that China continued neither to wish to borrow hugely from abroad nor to accept large-scale foreign aid from the West (including Japan) or the Soviet Union, the only way to accomplish the task would be to provide for a defense budget by 1985 of between $75 and $100 billion and to permit the defense industry to take half of all industrial production. That probably could be done in China, but only at tremendous, and in the end ruinous, cost to the agricultural economy and to overall standards of living, both of which would decline precipitously. Given the buildup of popular expectation for a gradually improving standard of living, together with interest group pressures from bureaucrats and others within the Party favoring balanced growth, it is doubtful whether any post-Maoist leadership could stay long in office if it followed this sort of program. The only condition under which such a program would be feasible politically would be the perception, or the actuality, of acute and continuing military threat over the entire 1976-1985 decade. Although the Soviet threat could well move to that level, neither current or projected Soviet policy nor the continuously increasing probability of post-Maoist settlement of the Sino-Soviet border dispute lend support to such a possible threat level.

A third economic option, relating to military procurement, is to proceed at a slower pace than is projected in the balanced growth scheme. This would provide a military budget, by 1985, of between $25 and $50 billion equivalent. The pace of procurement of strategic systems would slow (say, dispensing entirely with a SLBM system), concentration would be on conventional modernization of existing forces (particularly with the next weapons revolution, involving precision guided munitions, necessitating heavy research and testing costs), the number of warheads would be limited and the kinds of missiles that would deter Soviet attack but not an American nor a combined Soviet-American strike, would be produced.

Such a slowed rate of military procurement would be possible under certain international political and strategic conditions, which are discussed below, but might be forced upon a post-Maoist regime independently of such considerations if the economy as a whole were to falter. This could well occur were there a number of bad harvests in a row, were China to find itself isolated economically from the rest of the world, were domestic disorders of the type of the Cultural Revolution (or, worse, post-Maoist regional military fratricide developing in near-civil war) to affect adversely production, or were a new Great Leap attempted with resulting economic depression. Although the post-1969 history of Chinese economic development supports the likelihood that political interference will not again knock the bottom out of the Chinese economy, and although the leadership has done well to direct an increasing percentage of resources into agriculture, it is still possible for a Mao-like charismatic figure to wreak economic havoc.

On grounds of economic rationality alone (that is, putting aside political, technological, and international factors), it would seem best for China—in terms of maximizing real industrial growth, gradually pulling away from the specter of starvation, modestly increasing living standards, and providing for a viable but not ruinous defense—to continue the present mix of industrial, agricultural, consumer, and defense investment, e.g., the balanced growth projection noted above. If the international situation were to improve—if, for instance, the border dispute with the Soviet Union were settled and relations with the United States and Japan did not thereby grow worse—the third option would be attractive. On the other hand, if relations with Moscow deteriorated even further, and Peking and Washington failed to improve their own ties as well, the option of recasting the Chinese economy to maximize military growth might have to be taken, at least in the short run, however unpalatable the consequences for longer term growth in other sectors might be.

Domestic political factors, however, seem to be the controlling ones, in the sense that Chinese relations with Moscow, Washington, and Tokyo are dependent principally on what happens in the Chinese capital, not abroad. The reasons are several. One is the imminence of the Maoist succession, together with the strong possibility that there could be changes in the manner by which the Party governs the economy and conducts its foreign policy. Although there are many possibilities, only four general alternatives seem likely: (1) radical leftism of the sort associated with extreme, utopian Maoism shown during the Great Leap Forward and the Cultural Revolution; (2) bureaucratic pragmatism, paralleling the set of practices seen between 1960 and 1965, and after 1971, and associated with a philosophy of class harmony, national unity, incremental economic progress, and balance of power foreign policy connected (whether accurately or not) with the policies of Chou En-lai; (3) more or less direct military rule, paralleling the situation during the latter stages of the Cultural Revolution and, to some extent, the early 1950s, and following a period of turmoil induced by leftist rule or radical-pragmatic tussling; and (4) alternation between left-right, radical-pragmatic primacy, resulting in an oscillating political/economic situation.

There is, of course, no way of assessing definitively which of these political situations is likely to ensue. More than likely, the next decade will see more than one of the four possibilities. Thus, in the period before Mao dies, as well as in the two to three years thereafter, there is likely to be a continuation of the oscillating left-right politics that has become the hallmark of the Maoist operational style. If attendant problems become too great, and depending upon the propensity of the Soviet Union to intervene or refrain from involving itself in Chinese domestic matters, the military could "take over," whether temporarily (as seems more likely) or permanently. Over the longer term, however, it seems likely that a second general determinant of the Chinese political future, "modernization," will gradually tilt the balance to the "pragmatists," who would put into practice a series of policies that would appear less and less distinguishable from post-Stalinist (perhaps even post-Khrushchevian) Soviet modes of rule. The innate forces of modernization will gradually change the nature of Chinese politics, (i.e., by smoothing out oscillations, making it more difficult for charismatic figures to emerge, routinizing political careers and turning politics into administration, bureaucratizing Party, military, and governmental hierarchies, generally rationalizing domestic decision-making, and formulating foreign policy on the basis of national, as opposed to personal, interests) and such changes may come with increasing rapidity after Mao. Already in the military and foreign policy sphere, there have been a number of attempts to modify policy in more rational directions (pressures toward professionalization in the army and toward settlement of the Sino-Soviet border conflict are two outstanding examples), and Mao's demise will probably see these pressures increase.

Although there is no one-to-one correspondence between the three non-oscillating political possibilities and the three alternative economic paths outlined earlier, it does seem reasonable to associate, in a general way, the pragmatic-bureaucratic political possibility with the balanced growth projection of the economy. The radical-leftist political path is likely to be linked to an economic outcome of lowered rates of growth stemming from political turmoil; and military rule would be tied to the option of extracting as much as possible from the economy to finance very high levels of military hardware acquisition. Since each of these possible political forms is associated with a particular nuclear strategy, in this scheme, forecasts of likely Chinese strategy would depend on evaluations of the relative probability of each of these alternatives, presuming, of course, that technological and international factors are of little consequence or that, in each case, they balance each other out. These other factors are not, however, of little consequence, and there is very little probability of their working in a constant direction over the three political-economic alternatives.

Technological Influences. Let us consider the technological aspect first. As noted, the Chinese nuclear program historically developed in its present direction, pace, and size because of the very manner in which the American and Soviet nuclear programs had developed. This would have been the case even had there been no Sino-Soviet split or Sino-American tensions.[a] Most writers in the field agree that, if anything, the pace of nuclear/missile technology has accelerated in recent years, despite (or even because of) the series of Soviet-American strategic arms and other agreements, and that it is likely to continue to do so for the foreseeable future. MIRVs, very accurate guidance systems, cruise missiles, ABM and associated radar technologies, directed energy (e.g., lasers), electronic miniaturization, and satellite reconnaissance photography are only the most important manifestations of this process of acceleration, a process, it should be noted, that requires much more than mere capital-intensive industrial input. China has no option, if it wishes merely to maintain the present technological gap between itself and the Russians and the Americans—to say nothing of closing the gap—but to make the necessary investments to produce such technologies.

The decision to remain competitive (which is really not a single decision, but a series of technological, incremental, politically unnoticeable choices) holds many implications for the nature of the domestic economy and politics. There are only two ways of accelerating technological progress: engaging in a larger effort internally and importing technology. China has shown the ability, and sometimes the desire, to do both, but in each case there are serious problems. Internally, acceleration of technological progress would mean that the educational system would have to depart dramatically from the present Maoist model stressing class background, rather than intellectual and educational competence, and would have to emphasize specialization rather than all-around learning of a rudimentary sort. Since the present educational system is the outgrowth of much wrangling over the efficacy of the Maoist model, any wholesale changes would have to be made as part of a process severely modifying the Maoist system as a whole. This implies that a radical-leftist political regime would hold a smaller chance of remaining in power over the long run, whereas the pragmatic-bureaucratic or the military variants, each of which would welcome the imposition of an educational system stressing competence and specialization, would be more likely to come to and to remain in power.

The resolution of a second internal problem leads in the same direction. Maoist ideology emphasizes the virtues of self-reliance in all spheres, but technological autarky is out of the question in the strategic nuclear realm. China must provide itself with a flow of ideas, techniques, prototypes, and sometimes

[a]The British, French, Indian, and Israeli nuclear programs have also developed along similar lines (although there are major differences in employment strategy and force size), merely because technology dictates the direction that must be taken and because the Americans and the Russians have been the first to work out how the various systems fit together.

whole systems if it is to close the strategic gap or merely keep up. This involves more than just allowing a small number of top scientists to read copies of foreign journals or purchasing the single copies of equipment displayed at trade fairs. It means a broad opening up of the country to much larger numbers of foreign technicians than at present, allowing a much freer flow of information into and out of the country, and permitting Chinese scientists to travel internationally in much larger numbers and with much greater freedom than is now the case. All of these developments would be dissociative of the Maoist stress upon self-reliance and, hence, weaken the prospects of a leftist-radical political emphasis and strengthen the bureaucratic-pragmatic and military alternatives.

The final internal means to accelerate technological growth is to step up the overall rate of investment in technologically-intensive industries. Once again, however, this would turn emphasis away from the Maoist orientation of agricultural primacy and relatively equal distribution of the social-economic product. In terms of the three economic options discussed earlier, the propensity would be to depart from the balanced growth projection in favor of accelerated investment in industry and certainly to oppose slowing down overall growth and reducing military investment.

The other means of accelerating the pace of technological progress is to acquire it from the external world. Since China is understandably reluctant to magnify greatly its level of indebtedness to the outside, it must procure foreign technology through trade which, because Peking must sell in order to buy, in turn means that China would have to restructure an increasing part of its economy to service foreign buyers. Although petroleum exports may enable Peking to earn a great deal of foreign exchange while not at the same time requiring huge amounts of domestic investment capital for that purpose, it may be that rapidly rising internal demand for oil might consume most of the surplus. Even presuming China finds the means to finance the transfer of military technology through imports, it still must provide the capacity to absorb that new technology, chiefly by moving to a much higher level, and much larger numbers, of skilled labor than at present. But to do so requires, as before, a reversal of the present educational policy, concentration of industry in urban areas rather than dispersal to the countryside, and the granting of absolute priority to high technology industries. Thus, if China is to catch up militarily with the United States and the Soviet Union over the next decade, radical-leftist policies must be eschewed and governance must proceed by either pragmatic-bureaucratic or military regimes.

International Influences. If domestic factors are the most important in determining future Chinese nuclear strategy and technological elements are most constricting, surely the international component is the most complex and difficult to assess. Chinese nuclear strategy is directly influenced by the strategic policies of the Soviet Union and the United States, since these two states could destroy China; by India, as the other Asian nuclear power and regional political rival; and, potentially, by Japan, South Korea, and Taiwan, as the three neighboring political entities that may, over the next decade produce nuclear weapons. While America and Russia are supremely important, China would suffer an enormous political defeat and further jeopardize its security were Japan to develop nuclear weapons. If Taiwan demonstrates a nuclear capability, which is well within the range of possibility, the probabilities of eventual recovery for the mainland drop precipitously. And if South Korea "goes nuclear," the potential for regional conflict rises greatly—and with it Chinese participation—as does the likelihood that Japan would feel forced to embark upon the production of nuclear weapons. In all three cases, China's only hope of exercising leverage is through the good offices of the United States. For that reason alone, there are severe limits upon the length to which China can depart from its present policy of total enmity toward the Soviet Union and modified détente with the United States. Part of Chinese nuclear policy is, therefore, made in Washington.

Although it would be rational to expect a departure, after Mao, from the present one-sided policy toward a more balanced posture toward Moscow and Washington, the fact that the paths to Tokyo, Seoul, and Taipei lay through Washington heavily weights the American side. Intellectually, China has at least three options. One is to continue present policies. The second is to move far enough back toward more friendly association with the Soviet Union to provide additional freedom of action within the emergent triangle of global nuclear powers. The final option would be to reestablish close ties with Moscow, similar to those extant in the middle-1950s, and concomitantly to allow relations with Washington to atrophy. If the nuclear aspect were set aside, it would be reasonable to expect Peking to adopt the second alternative and move at least part way back to Moscow, ideally ending up politically equidistant between the Soviet and American capitals. This is a probable occurrence in any case, since it is Mao, almost alone, who stands in the way of settling outstanding Soviet-Chinese disputes, and since the most important of those disputes, the border differences, could be resolved easily on their merits at any time. Once Mao dies, therefore, Sino-Soviet détente should be expected and the question will then become whether, and to what extent, détente becomes rapprochement.

But since the nuclear question is central to our discussion of Chinese policy options, the fact cannot be ignored that the United States is responsible for the defense of its two proto-nuclear client states, South Korea and Taiwan, and that the degree of Sino-Soviet rapprochement will determine much of the nature of future Washington-Tokyo military ties and of Japan's own nuclear policy. Moreover, a post-Maoist China that settled important differences with the Soviet Union would be in a better position to address the Taiwan question, and thus drive the United States to adopt a tougher stance in defense of the island. Japan might then find its long-term interests served in maintaining an autonomous Taiwan and the stage would be set for the reemergence of a Communist versus non-Communist, Eurasian mainland versus Eurasian periphery division in world politics that would be exceedingly dangerous to all. If either Taiwan or South Korea were, in such a situation, to demonstrate a nuclear capacity, Japan would have little choice but to join them. Thus, too great a movement by Peking back to Moscow and away from Washington would be much to China's strategic disadvantage. So if post-Maoist Chinese decisionmakers are rational, they will play a cooperative game with both the United States and the Soviet Union, moving cautiously to settle some of their arguments with the Russians but not simultaneously upsetting the Americans and their Asian allies.

Which way China moves, and how far, depends chiefly on the character of the successor regime in Peking. If a radical-leftist group grasps the mantle of power after Mao, one could expect a continuation of present policies, with growing freedom of maneuver as Chinese nuclear strength grows. The question concerning Chinese nuclear policy in this atmosphere would be whether such a regime would move too precipitously to acquire an ICBM capability against the United States and a nuclear powered SLBM fleet that would greatly disturb Japan, and whether continued American tergiversations on Taiwan would drive Peking to part with Washington, thus turning Taiwan into a Far Eastern Israel.

If a bureaucratic-pragmatic regime comes to power (or remains in power, since, without Mao and a few radical followers, that is the overall character of the present Party leadership), settlement with the Soviet Union would seem to follow, along with industrial and technological growth rates that would allow for near nuclear superpower status by 1985. But in that situation *there would be no need* for China to go to such lengths, for the policy of such a leadership would be to lower the level of international tensions with both Moscow and Washington (although long-term ideological goals would not necessarily be forgotten). A pragmatic regime might indeed be satisfied with a minimal deterrent posture pointed principally at Moscow and only residually at Washington and its Asian allies. It would, characteristically, be able to amass more nuclear capability than the leftist or military regime alternatives while doing a more credible job at home, but might decide to forego the temptation to acquire a massive nuclear force in favor of a smaller, more reliable one embodying technology nearly the equivalent of its Soviet and American rivals.

A military regime, on the other hand, unduly fearing Soviet intentions, might undertake nuclear programs of such scale and momentum that the United States and its Asian allies would not only draw together (or, were the United States still in a phase of retrenchment from defense commitments in Asia, to prompt one or more of the three American allies to develop nuclear weapons), but would also seek to further nuclear cooperation with Moscow, now as a means of protection against China. This is, however, unlikely, because the probability of military rule in China is relatively low and because Soviet and American force levels and technologies will, even in 1985, be much beyond the Chinese, as long as Moscow and Washington desire it to be that way. A military regime in Peking sworn to catch up strategically with the other two would cause them to run ahead even faster.

If the nuclear policies of China's Northeast Asian neighbors are largely determined by American policy, which in turn is heavily influenced by Chinese attitudes themselves (we exclude, perhaps too hastily, any decisive reversal of the present American course vis-à-vis Peking by any incoming Administration of whatever political coloration), what about the Soviet Union itself, and of *its* Asian nuclear client, India? It seems highly unlikely that the Soviet leadership would change its China policy in the foreseeable future, for two reasons. One is that the internal dynamics of the Soviet Party provide little reason to contemplate leadership change other than marginal in nature. The other is that the Soviet Party rightly regards its strategy toward China as a winning one.

Having provided, perhaps too well, for its own defense against what it perceives to be Chinese excesses along the border, Moscow long ago adopted a policy of waiting—for Mao to die, for more moderate elements to come to power, for the Chinese military-industrial complex to assert its increasing role in Peking (a role Moscow correctly perceives as much less anti-Soviet than Mao), and for bureaucratic-pragmatism to emerge from the impulse to "modernization," turning China into a socio-political-economic entity much like the Soviet Union itself. Moscow thus presumes that, as long as it does not burn all its bridges to Peking, the internal evolution of forces in China will eventually bring a pro-Moscow leadership back into the fold, politically and perhaps militarily, if not ideologically. The Kremlin would be glad to put aside its ideological differences with China on a let's-agree-to-disagree basis if only greater military security and international freedom of movement could be attained at the same time. There is every reason to think that Moscow has judged the situation correctly and that, therefore, time operates in its favor. Only Mao's fast-shortening lifespan stands in the way.

India at present is of virtually no concern to China, since New Delhi has no demonstrated delivery capability. The future is likely to be different, however, since India will most probably attempt to protect itself from the possible withdrawal of the Soviet nuclear shield attendant upon Sino-Soviet rapprochement and in any case is likely to work itself out of its present international isolation and one-sided relationship with Moscow. Hence, India will probably attempt to provide itself with a credible, if still minimal, delivery capability against Chinese cities by late in this decade. Although the Chinese force level at that point will be much larger, well-protected, and sophisticated, and although the Chinese will have had much more experience than India in command and control systems and in thinking about nuclear strategy, the emerging India force will be more than a mere thorn in China's side. Just as China, after deploying a few nuclear warheads, once argued to the Soviet Union, that any attack could risk several Soviet cities, Peking would not henceforth dare to attack India, nuclearly or conventionally. There would also be problems stemming from Indian strategy, since the vast disparity in force levels and sophistication would indicate at least the possibility of an Indian launch-on-warning, counter-city strategy that could, in a crisis, lead to Chinese preemption. So China will have to behave more circumspectly toward India after Indian bombs are revealed to exist, even if the Moscow-New Delhi Friendship Treaty were not renewed or if close Sino-Soviet ties were reestablished.

Conclusions

What generalities concerning Chinese nuclear strategy in the 1976-1985 period emerge from this discussion? We have considered three groupings of factors that seem to us to determine much of the content and direction of Chinese strategy: domestic (political and economic), technological, and international. Although there are variations in detail, it turned out that these factors can be grouped together, generally around the domestic political factor, in a manner outlined in Table VI-1. The set of policies associated with the bureaucratic-pragmatic regime seems on balance to be the one which is most likely to occur, and the military regime and its group of associated policies are the next in line.

It is now possible to consider the kinds of nuclear policies that may be undertaken by the Chinese in terms of the list of variables critical to such a policy and in terms of *departures from* the continuation of present policies, as detailed previously. Perhaps the most important conclusion is that whatever

Table VI-1
Chinese Nuclear Strategy, 1976-1985

Domestic Regime	Economic Policy	Technological Policy	International Policy
Bureaucratic-pragmatic	Balanced growth; high rate	Internal and external technology generation; high rate	Sino-Soviet *détente*; balance between United States and Soviet Union
Radical-leftist	Lower growth; agricultural priority	Internal technology generation; lower rate	No Sino-Soviet *détente*; *détente* with United States; isolation
Military	Unbalanced growth; industry extractive of agriculture; initial high rate, then low	Internal and external technology generation; reasonably high rate	Sino-Soviet *rapprochement*; disenchantment with United States

combination of domestic, technological, and international circumstances occurs, the momentum of the Chinese program, already great, will continue with such force that, by 1985, its size and diversity will be very great indeed. Although the policy variations which the three alternative regimes might follow are significant, they are relatively small when compared with the very hugeness of the force that will then be available to Peking.

The bureaucratic regime would depart from the linear extrapolation of present policies in several respects: the number of warheads would probably be over 2,000; movement to a triad of deterrent systems would be gradual, in order not to jeopardize relations with the United States unduly or frighten Japan into embarking upon a nuclear program of its own; both Soviet and American nuclear forces and cities would be targeted; and such multi-polar deterrent safety devices as hot lines to Moscow and Washington could be installed. The Maoist strategy of national defense would be nearly entirely superseded by one emphasizing conventional defense, including meeting the enemy at and beyond the border and the utilization of both strategic and tactical nuclear weapons; and strategic arms limitations talks could be opened with both of the superpowers.

Policies of a military regime would also lead to more than 2,000 warheads, but its movement to a triad set of systems would be relatively fast, leading to a deterioration of relations with the United States and the possibility of South Korean, Taiwan, or Japanese nuclear armament. In other respects the policies of this type of government would be similar to those of the bureaucratic regime, except that the rate of economic growth is likely to be uneven, with the image of great strength at the beginning of the decade being replaced at its end by one of a tethered giant (due to the decline of living standards in the countryside and the loss of popular support by much of the population). One crucial difference, stemming from a military regime's propensity to settle disputes with the Soviet Union and not the United States, is that strategic arms limitation talks would be opened with Moscow but not with Washington. Depending on the status of Soviet-American arms limitation talks, this could present Peking and Washington with the anomalous situation of negotiating with each other in this realm indirectly.

A radical-leftist regime would depart most clearly from the straight-line projection regarding nuclear development to 1985. Its policy, founded on continued enmity with the Soviet Union and, thus, détente with the United States and Japan, would eschew building a SLBM fleet and perhaps even from a large number of ICBMs. Because of its policy toward the acquisition of military technology, its force level would grow more slowly, only approaching the two thousand warhead mark by the end of the decade ahead. It would probably not have the resources to put into a number of new systems and thus could well forego building a supersonic strategic bomber and a second or third generation family of missiles. Finally, it might not wish to conduct any arms control negotiations at all, since its position would be to mark out as independent a political path as possible, making only necessary and temporary compromises with the United States in order to stave off perceived Soviet threats.

From the point of view of Chinese national interests, it would seem that the set of policies associated with the bureaucratic alternative would benefit China most. China would be militarily as strong as possible; it would have settled the most important of its problems with the Soviet Union and would develop its relations with the United States and Japan while not pushing South Korea, Taiwan, or Japan into nuclear weapons production (although one or more of them might go nuclear anyway); and Peking's influence would be maximized by balancing Moscow and Washington. In short, China will have become a near superpower and its policies would have to be taken into account throughout the globe.

The military regime alternative would be nearly as effective, but Chinese influence would stem from the fear and opposition in non-Communist states that a new Soviet-Chinese combination would engender. China would thus cut herself off from much of the world. Taiwan would probably be lost for good. More importantly, the domestic problems that her drive to military superpower status would produce would fatally weaken both her image as a revolutionary leader whose domestic policies should be admired and imitated and lessen the degree of her popular support at home.

The radical alternative would be able to keep its mantle of revolutionary virtue, but would greatly jeopardize its overall security by not settling the border dispute with Moscow and by falling ever-farther behind the two superpowers in the technological sophistication of its weapons systems. Taiwan would not be recovered, although the possibility of so doing would remain. Since there will be at least two new weapons revolutions in the coming ten years—the change in tactics and force structure stemming from the mass employment of precision guided weapons and the possible replacement of missiles as a whole by directed energy offensive and defensive systems—such a regime could find itself in difficult straits indeed.

The Soviet Union and the United States have quite different interests in which regime emerges. Moscow would heavily favor (indeed, it already does) the bureaucratic regime, would be equally well-disposed toward a military regime, at least in the short run (it could be an economic albatross later), and would be least tolerant of an effective radical regime. American interests are precisely the reverse. However, evaluation of the probabilities of the three alternatives reflects Soviet, and not American, preferences. Thus, to the extent that our analysis bears relation to reality, Moscow has time working in its favor.

The Shanghai Communiqué and Future Sino-American Relations

The two case studies demonstrate important aspects of issue-oriented Chinese policy likely to affect Peking's relations with its Asian neighbors and the two superpowers. For the United States, however, the character of future ties with China will depend upon how the two states approach the resolution of remaining territorial, economic, and diplomatic differences. For that, we need to inspect the recent past of Sino-American history and to consider likely future trends.

The Shanghai Communiqué, signed at the end of the American presidential visit to China in early 1972, still forms the basis of current Sino-American relations and indicates the future direction toward which the two countries envisage their relations moving. Subsequent developments, such as the establishment of liaison offices in each other's capitals, the large increase in Sino-American trade and the exchange of scientific, technical, and other delegations, the several trips by the secretary of state, the decline in the number of American military personnel on Taiwan, and the second presidential visit, all are directly in line with the letter, if sometimes not the spirit, of that document. In order to understand the reasons for this major shift in Washington-Peking relations, the intended meaning of its sometimes enigmatic phrasing, and probable future trends, it is useful to look at that document in some detail, to consider whether the original motivations of the two powers in signing it in the first place are still present (or, alternatively, whether events have worn away the basis of the agreement, turning the framework it set up into a hollow shell), and what might be the next stage in Sino-American relations as a whole.

The core of the document, and the foundation of current Sino-American relations, is to be found in the third and fourth sections of the communiqué, devoted, respectively, to a series of general statements of the principles of international relations and to separate statements on Taiwan. In the third section, the two states agree to govern their mutual relations on the basis of the so-called five principles of peaceful coexistence, since 1954 the declaratory basis of Chinese foreign policy. This gives the United States no difficulty, since the five principles are merely a succinct statement of general principles of international relations long recognized in international law as the basis for peaceful relations among all states, much less those with different socio-political systems. The United States, in fact, in many of its declarations, often refers to the same set of principles as governing its own understanding of the basis of international comity.

More important is the joint expression of five other principles that, taken together, amount to a proto-alliance of the two powers. In all five instances, the Soviet Union was on the mind of the negotiators as the object causing China and America to draw together. Thus, Peking and Washington express their opinion that "progress toward the normalization of (Sino-American) relations is in the interests of all countries," i.e., especially the Soviet Union, which is thereby asked not to be unduly concerned, even though the communiqué represents a confluence of interests of its two greatest rivals.

There is, indeed, definite indication that China and America would, under certain circumstances, line up together against Russian attempts to expand its sphere of influence. First, Peking and Washington agree to oppose "the efforts by any other country or group of countries" (read: the Soviet Union and/or the Soviet Union and India) "to establish . . . hegemony" in the Asia-Pacific region. Second, the two states announce their opposition to interstate "collusion" or attempts by "major countries" (read: the Soviet Union) "to divide up the world into spheres of interest." These two clauses amount to joint support of the principles of the balance of power in the Far East and reflect Chou En-lai's and Henry Kissinger's thinking about the most realistic manner of structuring world politics. Existing spheres of influence can continue to exist, as can alliances, even "collusion" between major and minor powers. But expansion of Soviet influence will be jointly (if still separately) resisted.

Third, in an enigmatic clause, the two parties pledged not to "enter into agreements or understandings with the other directed against other states." The obvious import of this is that while existing alliances directed against the other may be kept—China with the Soviet Union, the United States with Japan, South Korea, and, importantly, Taiwan—neither party will sign further agreements with these states that could be interpreted as hostile to the other. While the way is still open to sign new agreements with third states, by implication China becomes a silent third party to any new American agreement with other Asian states (including the Soviet Union), as does the United States with possible new Chinese agreements with such states (again, including the Soviet Union). The effect is to provide a modicum of stability to future Far Eastern international politics and to give China and America insurance against surprising turns of events. China has American verbal assurances against anti-Peking, Soviet-American "collusion" in such areas as SALT, overall Soviet-American political cooperation, and the European Security Conference; the United States has Chinese verbal assurance, for whatever it is worth, that Peking will not allow post-Maoist Sino-Soviet rapprochement to be directed overtly against Washington. Finally, each party declared its interest in reducing "the danger of international military conflict." While this probably concerns Sino-American relations directly, especially in the Taiwan Straits and in Southeast Asia, it was read, correctly, in Moscow as cautious American support for Peking in the Sino-Soviet border dispute.

It was only agreement on the fourth section of the communiqué, dealing with Taiwan, that made issuance of a joint statement possible, for it was in this area that Sino-American differences are sharpest. Superficially, irreconcilable differences seemed to continue, but close inspection of the communiqué, plus generally held assumptions concerning Chinese military capabilities with regard to Taiwan, lead to the conclusion that the two sides "agreed to disagree" on the issue and not permit it to stand in the way of the development of relations in other areas. China stated that "Taiwan is a province of China," while the United States averred that it "does not challenge" the position of "all Chinese" that "Taiwan is a part of China."

It is true that China specifically excluded the Taiwan question from peaceful resolution under the doctrine of peaceful coexistence between states by declaring that "the liberation of Taiwan is China's internal affair in which no other country has the right to interfere." Moreover, it might seem that the United States had agreed to stand aside upon Chinese use of force against Taipei, since it agreed to "progressively reduce its forces and military installations on Taiwan." But the United States, in the President's State of the World Report for 1972, specifically reaffirmed the American treaty commitment to Taiwan, and in the communiqué stated it would withdraw only "as the tension in the area diminished." Moreover, in commentary surrounding the communiqué it was specifically suggested that the two sides had come to a private understanding that China will not use force to resolve the Taiwan question, a suggestion not countered by either government. The trade-off was the American declaration on Taiwan just mentioned plus the commitment eventually to leave the island in exchange for an unwritten Chinese promise not to use force. But the subsequent posting of a new and well-known ambassador to Taipei, together with the very slow rate of withdrawal of American military personnel from the island, served as concrete indications of the firmness of the interim American commitment to Taiwan.

In addition to putting the Taiwan issue on ice (as well as pressuring the Nationalists to accommodate themselves with the Taiwanese natives), the agreement recognized existing realities. In the American case, reduction of forces in the Taiwan Straits area was an important element in the policy to partially withdraw, militarily, from Asia, and was being put into practice even before the Peking visit. In the Chinese case, the continuation of the 1954 Washington-Taipei defense treaty, together with the innate difficulty of invading the island, made the probability of military success low. In effect, the Communists were trusting to the erosion of time to get the better of the Nationalists, to American opinion (and hence to the North Vietnamese/Vietcong military) to force a general retreat from the Far East, and to the slowness of Japanese remilitarization and awakened interest in Far Eastern security in forestalling that country's involvement in the Taiwan problem.

There may have been a further trade-off. In its attempt to strengthen its northern border, nothing would be more advantageous to Peking than temporarily lessening military tensions in the Taiwan Straits. If Peking were to persuade the United States to convince the Nationalists not to threaten to use the offshore island (where Taiwan had concentrated 40 percent of its forces) as staging areas for an attempted invasion of the mainland, the Communists would be able to transfer large forces to the north. This is, in fact, what seems to have occurred. After the Nixon visit, the Communists began withdrawing men and equipment from the Fukien Straits area and sending them to the Soviet border. They even modified the rate of military procurement, as we noted earlier. Thus, a direct result of the Nixon visit was a major change in the balance of power between the Soviet Union and China.

Underlying Motivations

The United States and China had quite different motivations for deciding to address the range of issues that had separated them for nearly a quarter century. In the American case, two reasons come to mind. The most important factor was that ending the vicious cycle of enmity with the People's Republic of China was considered a laudatory goal in its own right. President Nixon announced even before his Administration began that improvement of relations with Peking would be a principal foreign policy goal. He also accelerated the series of unilateral moves toward China begun during the Kennedy Administration and carried forward in the Johnson era. Nixon, and Henry Kissinger, considered it an anamoly and a danger that the two major powers had not yet found a way of at least engaging in a dialogue over important international topics, and while not convinced that harmonious relations would be restored merely through en- hanced contact, they did conclude that differences were being exacerbated merely because of poor channels of communication.

The second motivation stemmed from the secretary of state's basic approach to world politics and American foreign policy. Convinced that America had seriously overextended itself in the two decades past, but equally convinced that the Soviet Union was an increasingly powerful opponent, Kissinger concluded that a different "mix" of forces and range of involvements was necessary. The revised goal was to maintain American commitments (which were assessed more directly in accord with perceived interests) at a lower level of cost—psychologi- cal, material, and fiscal. Two elements in the new policy were the assumption that a multipolar world was inherently safer than a bipolar (or modified bipolar) one and that, given the vast and continuing increase in Russian power and influence, the United States needed much greater assistance than formerly in countering Soviet forward movement.

On both counts the United States found an incentive to repair its relations with Mainland China. If the balance of power was to be the organizing principle of the emerging world, it followed that China, an important part of any worldwide balance would have to be dealt with directly. This was especially true if American and Chinese interests related to the Soviet Union were to be regarded as parallel. In an emerging five-power world, the American ideal was to keep its close ties with Japan and Europe, and to develop relations with China, thus presenting the Soviet Union with a potential four-to-one lineup of powers against it. More negatively, it would be disastrous for the United States if China and the Soviet Union were to rekindle their friendship in the post-Maoist era. Washington felt it would have to move with speed, as well as skill, in opening a dialogue, and subsequently developing relations, with Peking before Mao and Chou passed from the scene. The United States hoped thereby to prevent Sino-Soviet rapprochement altogether or, failing that, to set strict limits on it.

Chinese motivations were, for the most part, quite different from those of the

Americans. However, two elements were almost mirror images of the corresponding American drives. One was the decision to "help" the United States to exit gracefully from Asia at a time when America was weakened at home and internationally, and the desire to replace Washington's influence with Peking's. While the United States had no intention of leaving the Asian scene entirely, much less of seeing its position of authority replaced by that of its most willful opponent, there were obvious parallels, however temporary, between the American principle of generally lessened commitments in Asia and the Chinese recovery of activism in foreign policy.

It is important to note that while the Chinese made this change in their policy for their own reasons, the timing of the decision—somewhere before the Ninth Congress of the Chinese Communist party in April 1969—was quite close to the first enunciation of the Nixon Doctrine in late 1969. This may have been merely fortuitous, but the break in the vicious cycle was consciously and independently made by both sides. The Chinese felt they had the United States on the run, given American difficulties in Vietnam, and hoped to take advantage of this situation to gain admittance to the United Nations and to isolate Taiwan. But Peking must have realized that there would be no real possibility of repossessing Taiwan without American cooperation, nor would there be much chance of extending Chinese influence in general without attempting to quiet Washington's fears concerning ultimate Chinese intentions. Thus, in an era when "peaceful coexistence" seemed again to sum up Chinese foreign policy and when Peking, perhaps correctly, thought it could greatly expand its influence into new regions, it made sense to achieve a *modus vivendi* with the United States. The series of Chinese policy statements since the Shanghai Communiqué—principally at the Tenth Party Congress and the Fourth National People's Congress, as well as continued Chinese participation in concrete measures to improve Sino-American relations directly, indicate no change in this assessment.

A second element closely reflected American reasoning for opening the door to less distant relations. China felt the need to provide itself with a lengthy period of relative external harmony in order to make up for time lost in economic development during the Cultural Revolution and to repair the domestic political and social structure. The perturbations surrounding the removal of Lin Piao as Mao Tse-tung's successor and the consequent reopening of that question toward the end of Mao's long rule only reinforced Chou En-lai's feeling that improvement of relations with Washington was imperative despite its possibly disfunctional effects at home. There *have* been signs that the new departure in Sino-American relations did influence the domestic situation: Chou himself came under direct and continual attack from the Left and a debate on the merits of dealing with the Americans was precipitated. But Chou persisted— backed throughout by Mao himself—and the result (even after his own death) has been a general lowering of tensions, together with significant economic progress at home, and major advances, in terms of recognition, trade, United

Nations activity, and military security, abroad. Thus, if Mao and Chou felt they were taking a gamble by signing agreements with the Americans, it paid off well.

The most important Chinese motivation, however, stemmed from Peking's apprehensions over the military imbalance with the Soviet Union and the threat of overt Russian military moves against Chinese territory or Chinese nuclear and missile facilities. With as many as a million well-equipped and mechanized Russian troops along or near the border, and with the Chinese temporarily unable to respond in similar numbers and degree of modernization, Mao and his associates felt it necessary to lessen tensions with the United States, which controlled the threats to Chinese security from the east and the south.

Mao could have eased border tensions with the Russians merely by signing a new and equitable border treaty with Moscow, while the border negotiations themselves significantly reduced the Soviet threat. Nonetheless, Mao apparently thought it necessary to take out some insurance in Washington against a sudden Czechoslovakia-like military move by Moscow and to break out of the isolation into which Soviet diplomacy since 1966 had progressively forced Peking. Moreover, Mao evidently considered it possible to maneuver between Moscow and Washington in such a manner that he could choose the proper degree of friendliness or hostility at each moment, while retaining his domestic political base. Finally, it seems to have been decided that China could not afford to engage in a crash armaments program and simultaneously step up agricultural development and basic investment in heavy industry and high technology.

Consequences for the United States

What have been the consequences of the new Sino-American arrangement? For the United States, American policymakers found it more difficult to promote a policy of stringent anti-communism while China continued to take peaceful coexistence as its guiding foreign policy principle and as some progress was made in Sino-American relations. This phase of Chinese foreign policy may continue for some years, if the political line-ups at the Tenth Party Congress and the Fourth National People's Congress persist and if the results of the removal of Teng Hsiao-p'ing do not shake the precarious left-right balance in the leadership. However, because changes in Chinese behavior abroad tend to be dependent upon the character of domestic politics, Chinese foreign policy has not been consistent. Nonetheless, for the foreseeable future (two to four years and possibly longer), relatively harmonious relations with Peking seem to be in store. This depends, to be sure, on whether further progress on the solution of the Taiwan issue will come after the 1976 presidential elections.

While understanding of political necessities in an election year, the Chinese have indicated their displeasure with the pace of change and no doubt will press for full recognition. This implies an end to the American recognition of the Republic of China to the Defense Treaty with the Nationalists, two steps which

Washington has been reluctant to take. Indeed, since the establishment of liaison offices, American motivations for change in the status quo declined measurably: with diplomatic ties with Peking in all but name, and with continued diplomatic presence in Taipei, the Americans felt no need to go much further. But the Chinese soon added pressure, by hinting several times to Washington that Peking's relations with Moscow could be improved any time the Chinese care to do so.

More importantly, it is possible to envisage full diplomatic recognition of Peking without at the same time cutting all ties—diplomatic, trade, and defense—with Taiwan. A provincial consulate could remain on the island. A trade mission could be set up on the Japanese model. And even though Taipei would have no formal defense commitment, it would have an informal one through the Shanghai Communiqué itself, the relevant clauses of which could be reiterated by the United States and made a part of the American declaration of recognition of Peking. In other words, the United States would allow the Defense Treaty with Taiwan to expire in exchange for a Chinese pledge not to use military force to change the status quo, failing which the United States would be free to use its own means, including military, to defend the island.

In the absence of direct conflict with China, the consequences of the "turning inward" of American political interest (prompted by Vietnam, Watergate, and economic recession) will have limited ability to jeopardize the American position abroad. A pleasant concomitant is that the American people can, for the first time, consider the relative merits of communism in China in more or less objective fashion. This presumes, of course, that a more than token level of academic and journalistic exchanges and tourism will develop, and that high levels of trade will continue, thus enabling sizable numbers of American citizens to observe communism in China for what it is.

Finally, of central importance to American foreign policy and to the stability of the international political system is the enhanced maneuverability in the international political system that the emerging tie with Peking has given Washington in its competition throughout the world with the Soviet Union. Russia is immeasurably stronger than it was more than a decade ago during the Cuban missile crisis and is capable, for the first time, of interjecting itself into almost every local dispute as witness the Angolan events of 1975. It is to the latter competition that Washington must devote its principal diplomatic and military resources during the late 1970s and beyond. America can thus only welcome a lessening of tensions with Peking and can only look with favor upon a Chinese disposition toward cooperative, if separately motivated and expressed, behavior toward Moscow.

Consequences for China

For China, the agreement with Washington provided three opportunities. Foremost was the ability to stand up to Moscow better. The Soviet Union now had to enter an unknown American element in its calculations vis-à-vis China, despite ever-lessening American propensities to intervene in distant quarrels. Of nearly equal importance was the time Peking has gained to solve its political problems, especially the succession question, and to move ahead more rapidly in economic development. This could lead directly to higher rates of growth and to an even greater measure of economic independence. A third gain was the enhanced prestige accorded to Peking in most sectors of the West and the developing countries. Despite a somewhat tarnished image among far-left revolutionary groups throughout the world, the new relationship with the United States eased China's entré into such regions as the Middle East, parts of Africa, and Latin America, places where American, Russian, and Nationalist Chinese efforts hitherto have combined to restrict their influence.

These advantages did not come without cost, however, for Peking found its freedom constricted in at least three areas. One was obviously its relations with Taiwan, where the Nationalists obtained a new lease on life. Another concerned China's ability to support, materially and ideologically, violent revolutionary groups in developing countries. The contradiction between national and ideological interests, always present in Chinese policy and detailed above, was even more glaring than in recent years. A final limitation upon Chinese freedom of maneuver was in its attitude toward the United States itself. Depending, to be sure, on the nature and direction of future American policy in the Far East and elsewhere, a China in constant contact with Washington and even cooperating with it in certain endeavors was somewhat more likely to mute its verbal criticism of the United States, at home and abroad, and to gauge its diplomatic, economic, and military moves with more than a little attention to what Washington's reaction was likely to be. As we noted in the first part of this chapter, Peking has had to include American policy initiatives and response in its calculations ever since 1949, but the "American factor" now became even more central to Chinese policy shifts.

Consequences for the Soviet Union

The consequences of the Shanghai Communiqué and subsequent developments for the Soviet Union are clear. In a tripolar world, Moscow feared most an alliance or quasi-alliance of its nuclear rivals, and this is the situation that seems to be emerging. Certainly the Washington-Peking tie carries the threat of a grand anti-Soviet alliance, composed of Western Europe, the United States, China, and Japan; that is, all the powers of consequence in today's—or tomorrow's—world. This might not seem the case at present, when Moscow's activity in South Asia, the Middle East, and Southern Africa is so pronounced. Yet one reason why Soviet diplomats worked so hard was to prevent diplomatic isolation in the future. It is true that Soviet diplomacy was sophisticated and tailored to fit specific regions—witness the variety of approaches made to Japan, Iran, and West Germany, to list three states in three different regions. It is also true that Soviet successes appeared particularly noteworthy when compared to American failings in Southeast and South Asia, to say nothing of American problems in the Middle East. But Moscow has now to look forward to potential Washington-Peking cooperation against Soviet policy in many geographic and substantive areas. While this could change greatly if China were to settle outstanding disputes with the Soviet Union or if the policy of "peaceful coexistence" were superseded by a more stringently anti-American line, Soviet planning has had to presume the existence of some sort of Chinese-American "collusion" that would continue for the foreseeable future.

It should be noted that the linchpin of the emerging anti-Soviet *entente* is the series of alliances emanating from Washington and not the Sino-American proto-alliance. That is, it is Washington, not Peking, that is formally allied with Western Europe and Japan, and it is Washington, as well as Peking, that feels the pressure of increasing Soviet military power and thus is attracted to the notion of a cooperative arrangement against the Russians. This is not to say that the elements of rivalry between the United States and China will disappear, that the United States and the Soviet Union will not continue to hold interests in common, or that the United States will not continue to find the management of its multiple alliance structure difficult. It is to assert, however, that as the international political system moves from its previous loose bipolar form to a multiple balance of power arrangement, the likelihood of a four-to-one combination against the Soviet Union must be regarded as within the realm of possibility. The three major conditions are: sufficient fluidity in the system as a whole (so that a capitalist America and a Communist China can, if they so desire, unite against a "revisionist" Russia); a continuation and a development of ties between the three great centers of Western life—Europe, Japan, and North America; and the emergence of Soviet Russia as the world's strongest military power. These three conditions seem to match both present and foreseeable trends.

If such a new equilibrium comes about, there may be a prolonged era of relative international peace, and the Metternichian-Bismarckian policy that seemed to be the historical model favored by Henry Kissinger may well triumph.

Toward a Balanced Multipolar World?

What dangers stand in the way of the realization of this "grand design," that is, the conscious attempt by the United States, and partially by China and even the Soviet Union, to move beyond the cold war framework to a different (if not particularly new) type of international system? One of these is the death of Mao Tse-tung. Chinese policy toward the United States and the Soviet Union is one of the issues over which the succession in China is being fought. Despite the superficial harmony that emerged from the Fourth National People's Congress, a violent struggle for leadership may still result, with the issue of Chinese foreign policy in balance. Perturbations surrounding the death of Chou En-lai are a portent of such a struggle. Limited rapprochement between China and Russia is likely after Mao's death, given that it is Mao himself who is the chief impediment to partial reconciliation. The important question for American foreign policy is how far Sino-American relations can develop before Mao dies. The longer he lives, and the further they develop, the better it will be for the American efforts to encourage multipolarity.

Another pitfall that could possibly disorganize the new American international effort involves unforeseen directions of American domestic politics. Developments stemming, at least partly, from the new Sino-American relationship give the United States the opportunity to go forward with the quest for solutions to its many internal problems. Will America be able to use the time so gained wisely, and keep the strength necessary to play a central role in the world political game? If so, well and good. But if there is too much "turning inward," to the absolute neglect of the changing character of the international system, or if the United States is unable to deal with its domestic ills, economic and social, in a major way, then Washington could find itself confronting a very hostile world when it again decides to look outward. In this regard, the oil and Angolan crises may have been blessings in disguise, for they forced the American public to pay attention to an important foreign policy issue. It is, to be sure, unlikely that "neo-isolationism" in the United States would adversely affect American foreign policy to the point where the defense budget would be gutted and America would drop out of the nuclear weapons competition with the Soviet Union. But it is open to question whether the United States has the will to play an active, leading role in the international sphere while going through several simultaneous social and economic revolutions at home.

A third danger to a peaceful, balance of power-centered, multipolar international system is the sudden emergence of a crisis, in some region or over some issue, that places the major powers, despite their preferences, in direct opposition to one another. One need only refer to the diplomatic history of the last century to realize that one or more "breakpoints" of this sort is often enough to change the nature and direction of international relations for lengthy periods thereafter.

While such crises are a normal concomitant of any configuration of the international system, and hence to be expected to continue with undiminished frequency, there are two potentially troublesome developments that could spell the end of current efforts to assure a reasonably secure future. One is the outbreak of war between local clients of one or more of the three central nuclear actors, or the undertaking of actions that would upset an otherwise stable regional balance. Obvious cases in point are: the incipient breakup of Yugoslavia after Tito; the renewal of hostilities between Israel and the Arab world; a breakthrough in weapon technology capable of being exploited politically only for a short period; an invasion by North Korea of the South when American ground forces are withdrawn; a Sino-Soviet border war that includes some exchange of nuclear weapons; and the fragmentation of West Pakistan followed by Soviet-supported attempts by India to extend its national boundaries. If China and the Soviet Union, as well as the United States, are really interested in a relaxed international atmosphere in order to make progress at home, they will cooperate in approaching the solution of these problems before they become crises. In fact, one talisman of Soviet and Chinese interest in a peaceful future is whether or not they engage in cooperative crisis-prevention.

The other danger occurs when international alliances and alignments become frozen into mutually antagonistic poles. While the present trend is, fortunately, in the opposite direction, it is not difficult to imagine a reversal over the longer term. The realliance of the Soviet Union and China is one such possibility. Another might be the result of a fundamental change in the character of Japanese politics. Although renewed Japanese militancy is not a very likely prospect at the moment, an assertion of military power by Japan could break up the alliance with Washington, draw the United States and China closer together, and possibly even lead to a Japanese understanding with the Soviet Union. This would obviously result in a dangerous confrontation in the Far East.

More likely, perhaps, given the present direction of Japanese politics, is the legitimate assumption of power by a coalition led by the Japanese Socialist party, which would result in the sundering of Tokyo's alliance with Washington and a rapid consolidation of close ties with Peking. Depending on the nature of that accommodation, this could lead to a Sino-Japanese *entente* against the United States and the Soviet Union. Again the risk of confrontation in the Far East would be heightened. These two scenarios are sufficient to underline the argument that perhaps the center of American Far Eastern policy ought to be maintaining good relations with Tokyo as much as providing a new basis for relations with Peking.

Conclusion: Critical Choices for American China Policy

Critical policy choices arise from consideration of each of the issue areas addressed above.

In regard to the *domestic determinants* of Chinese policy, it should be noted that American policy has always been a factor in Chinese domestic politics and is likely to continue to be so in the future. The choice for America is whether to include within the framework of its own China policy, the estimated effect that a given policy would have upon the nature and direction of Chinese domestic life—political, economic, and social. Indeed, American policymakers must decide whether they know enough about Chinese domestic processes to calculate how a given policy initiative is likely to affect events in that country and, if so, whether it is indeed wise to try to influence developments through American policy.

An example is the question of the Maoist succession in China, a process that is central to all aspects of Chinese foreign policy. One option for the United States would be to do what it could to keep the radical followers of Mao in power on the grounds that they would continue to be anti-Soviet and would build up Chinese nuclear capability more slowly than alternative successor regimes. On the other hand, the United States might favor the bureaucratic pragmatists on the basis that the direction of economic investment and rate of growth in China would create greater interest in satisfying consumer demands, linking Peking economically and technologically to the West, increasing contacts with the non-Soviet world and, in general, moderating the stringent anti-Americanism that Maoist radicalism has at times demonstrated. The trouble is that such a regime, in our estimation, would be most likely to settle many of the outstanding disputes with Moscow and hence heighten the probability of renewing the East-West cold war.

Perhaps the best strategy, in general, is not to attempt to influence Chinese domestic matters through short-run policy variations, on the grounds that insufficient information could lead to a backfire, but to gear long-run policies to the promotion of those societal changes in China, which are capable of producing a more benign attitude toward the United States. This is, of course, easier said than done. The question is twofold, first, how to support a radical-Maoist regime in the short run that, being anti-Soviet, is in the American interest. Second, because such a regime would also depend upon anti-American attitudes to justify its domestic policies, how gradually to convince its leadership of America's good intentions and, then, how to encourage it to adopt policies, at home and abroad, favorable to long-term Sino-American rapprochement.

With regard to *Chinese power and interests*, the critical choice for the United States is whether to foster the growth of a strong China capable of attaining an ever-increasing range of its policy goals or whether to inhibit, to the extent possible, such growth. There are arguments for aiding the Chinese. One is that presumably a strong China will act as a bulwark against Soviet expansion in Asia, thereby assisting the United States in its global quest to limit the reach of Soviet power. The other is that a powerful China would hopefully be a responsible China, finally taking its place in the Rooseveltian scheme of Great Power responsibility for global security and prosperity.

The problem is that growth in Chinese power permits Peking to pursue its interests more directly—and some of those, such as the recovery of Taiwan, at least in the short run are opposed to those of the United States—while in the longer term China's interests are likely to expand in proportion to its capabilities. The worst outcome for the United States would be to assist Chinese growth for anti-Soviet reasons and then one day to discover that Moscow and Peking had made up their differences or that the very magnitude of Chinese power was threatening the balance of power in Asia. Destabilization of that sort would probably drive Japan to provide for its own security through remilitarization and by going nuclear, to say nothing of similar consequences in South Korea, Taiwan, Indonesia, and other Asian states. To forestall such developments, given the probably very large increase in Chinese might over the next decades, the United States would be well advised to maintain its present range of alliance commitments in Asia, in order to give reassurance during the period of visible deployment of Chinese military strength. A stable Asian balance is also in Chinese interests, in the short run, since it aids in minimizing Soviet influence.

The choice must still be faced as to whether America really wishes to see a very powerful China some decades hence, given the likelihood of Sino-Soviet détente and given the probable continuation in office of a Chinese Communist leadership dedicated to the eventual eviction of the United States from Asia and the overturning of capitalist socioeconomic system. Even were China tomorrow to find itself with a non-Communist government, the very fact that it can attain eventual near-superpower status would insure a clash of interests with the United States. The problem is that there is distressingly little room for maneuver in Sino-American relations. China will remain anti-Soviet as long as its internal political balance remains much as it is during Mao's lifetime, and there is little that Washington can do to encourage the continuation of that policy. The United States can "give China its due" in Asia, but there are few areas in which Chinese and American interests would not be opposed, if China were to face outward, and assertively, to Asia rather than inward, and defensively, to Russia.

Our analysis of past Chinese policy *propensities vis-à-vis the United States and the Soviet Union* suggests that Peking has sought to maximize its independence by leaning to the side it perceived to be the weaker, when it was thought necessary, or by being independent of both when possible. That is, Chinese policy has generally followed the tradition of the balance of power. Whether this propensity continues in the future depends, as we noted above, on the character of the successor regime. However, it would seem generally in the American interest to favor Chinese independence of the character demonstrated heretofore, because of the confluence of Sino-American interests with respect to the Soviet Union. One means of promoting that independence within the framework of American interests is to strengthen American power and resolve vis-à-vis Moscow, thus convincing Peking that the continuation of the American tie is worth its while. That itself involves critical choices for the United States, in terms of resource trade-offs and the range of its policy options in the SALT, Soviet-American trade, and in competition for influence in the Middle East and elsewhere. Washington must take care, however, to increase the range and breadth of its policy instruments in relation to Moscow but not, at the same time, to threaten China too. This is particularly true of the nuclear missile field, where the kinds of weapon systems and the mode of their deployment must clearly be directed at counteracting the Soviet threat. For example, arms control agreements with Moscow could be shown to the Chinese prior to initialing and efforts be made to convince the Chinese of the nonthreatening nature of these accords.

The choice is perhaps more general. What can America offer the Chinese for continuation of China's policy of cooperation with Washington to contain globally the Russians? Is the United States really prepared, when the chips are down, to ante up Taiwan upon demand? Is it really prepared, in the coming life-and-death contest with Moscow, to offer Peking more than an equal share of power in Asia, if the price of continued Chinese anti-Sovietism were Chinese domination over extended parts of Asia? These choices may well face America in an era of vastly enhanced Chinese power and correspondingly augmented interests, and at a time when the Peking leadership feel severe pressure, internally and from Moscow, for a general settlement with the Soviet Union. Were the United States to agree to a geographic division of responsibility in the joint quest to contain Soviet power, with China "taking responsibility" for much of Asia and the United States concentrating the bulk of its effort in Europe and the Middle East, Washington would forego its historic interest in maintaining a general Asian balance and the autonomy of island states in the Western Pacific. More importantly, America would shrink from global to regional power status. So there is danger in too close a confluence of Sino-American policy interests in relation to the Soviet Union.

Notes

1. Richard Solomon, *Mao's Revolution and the Chinese Political Culture* (Berkeley: University of California Press, 1970).

2. Richard Solomon, "From Commitment to Cant: The Evolving Functions of Ideology in the Revolutionary Process," in Chalmers Johnson (ed.), *Ideology and Politics in Contemporary China* (Seattle: University of Washington Press, 1973), pp. 47-77.

3. In William E. Griffith (ed.), *The Soviet Empire: Expansion and Détente* (Lexington, Mass.: Lexington Books, D.C. Heath and Company, 1976).

4. Quoted in Harry Gelber, "Nuclear Weapons and Chinese Policy," Adelphi Paper 99, London, The International Institute for Strategic Studies, 1973, p. 19.

5. Robert F. Dernberger, "The Economic Consequences of Defense Expenditure Choices in China," in U.S. Congress, Joint Economic Committee, *China: A Reassessment of the Economy* (Washington: Government Printing Office, July 10, 1975), pp. 467-499.

VII

The United States and China

Michel Oksenberg

Less than a decade ago, United States policy in Asia was predicated, in large measure, upon the need to contain China. Chinese communism was deemed a menace, certainly inimical to the interests of the United States. Similarly, the Chinese viewed the United States as their implacable foe. Subsequently, strong practical considerations have driven the policymakers in Washington and Peking along more parallel courses. Peking reacted principally to the assertion of Soviet power throughout Asia and the Soviet military threat directed at China and secondarily to the economic expansion of Japan. Washington realized that Peking was willing to encourage an acceptable Indochina settlement and that cessation of Sino-American enmity would assist efforts to improve Soviet-American relations. The Indochina War had taught both sides that the other's ambitions and capabilities were, after all, limited. And both sides saw the mutual benefit to be derived from increased commercial and technological contacts. Realism triumphed over ideological passions in both countries.

For the time being, Washington and Peking believe they have limited but similar interests, primarily to prevent the Soviet Union from encroaching on China's sovereignty and from establishing positions of primacy not only around China's periphery but in the Middle East, Africa, and Western Europe. The common interests would appear to extend to five related issues as well: (1) the maintenance of stability on the Korean peninsula over the short run (in part to retain Japan's confidence in its security); (2) the prevention of Taipei either declaring its independence or seeking its security through other means (e.g., by going nuclear); (3) the limitation of Vietnamese influence elsewhere in Southeast

269

Asia; (4) the discouragement of Indian dominance of the South Asian subcontinent and; possibly the flow of certain technologies which permit China a greater measure of security in world affairs.

The United States and China are linked *over the short run* primarily by global, strategic concerns: on the joint desire for stability in Asia. The American military presence in the area, a major facilitating ingredient for the relationship, is no longer seen by Peking to be immediately threatening but is viewed as a useful counterweight to the Soviet Union. And Washington has viewed Peking as a place from which limited leverage over Moscow can be secured.

In spite of common strategic interests, however, Sino-American relations remain severely circumscribed; in many ways, Peking and Washington remain adversaries. Beyond a residue of mutual mistrust, the two nations are, after all, committed to quite different values: the United States to freedom, the dignity of the individual, political equality, and the fostering of personal independence and creativity; the People's Republic to collectivism and the submergence of individual identity to a general will. Differences in ideals yield very different long-run goals for the kinds of nations the two wish to nurture in Asia and for the type of world order each envisions.

More than ideological issues distinguish the two countries, for China is a relatively poor country without a major economic stake in the existing world order. To be sure, the People's Republic is developing economically and militarily, and its growing trade has generated an interest in securing prosperous markets and in obtaining price stability for goods it seeks to import. But in comparison to Japan, Western Europe, or the United States, the People's Republic of China (PRC)—self-sufficient in its energy and mineral resources and with the value of its foreign trade less than 8 percent of GNP—is less dependent upon the stability of the international economy. As a result, in many international forums, Peking at least rhetorically champions the causes of the lesser developed countries. Nor have the Chinese yet to engage in serious, quiet dialogue over such issues as disarmament and arms control.

Most significantly, full diplomatic relations have yet to be established, since the United States recognizes the Republic of China government in Taiwan as the government of China; the Mutual Security Treaty of 1954 further links Taipei and Washington. From Peking's vantage, the American protection of Taiwan is an intervention in an unfinished civil war, as Peking claims the island to be part of China. The two countries have unsettled financial claims against each other which prevent normal commercial exchange. Property of the PRC, such as airplanes or ships, are subject to attachment on American soil by U.S. claimants. The Chinese have yet to achieve Most Favored Nation (MFN) trading status, and the sale of potentially strategic and militarily related goods and technology, falling under the so-called Trading with the Enemy Act, must be licensed by the U.S. government. Much Pentagon contingency planning continues to assume a hostile China, and presumably Peking does not presume a benign America in formulating its plans. No American journalists reside in Peking, and the United States is among the few nations not to have entered into a student exchange program with the Chinese.

In sum, while President Nixon correctly claimed that his February 1972 journey to China opened a new page in Sino-American relations, nonetheless by late 1975 the bulk of the chapter remained to be written. The issuance of the Shanghai Communiqué during President Nixon's trip gave a sense of momentum to the process of improving Sino-American relations. That movement was sustained through the first half of 1973, with the high point reached in the spring of that year, when the leaders of the two countries agreed to establish liaison offices—a diplomatic outpost—in each other's capital. Trade in 1973 and 1974 flourished, reaching a total of nearly $1 billion in 1974.

However, beginning in mid-1973, and particularly by mid-1974, that sense of progress began to fade. The indicators were many. Secretary Kissinger's trips in the Falls of 1973 and 1974 to Peking were not as mutually satisfying as his earlier trips. Trade in 1975 fell off, and increasingly the United States began to assume the role of a residual supplier to China. To be sure, three reasons for the decline in trade were China's general balance-of-payments problems in 1974-75, the severe imbalance in Sino-American trade in the U.S. favor, and the overall reduction in Chinese imports of agriculture products. American sales of wheat and cotton, after all, were important factors in the rapid acceleration of United States-China trade. Yet, by early 1975, signs existed that unlike 1972-73, Peking had come to prefer to purchase non-U.S. goods, when price and technological considerations were roughly equal. Moreover, in the trade realm, the Chinese had not responded to a detailed American proposal to settle the frozen assets question, while the United States has yet to extend MFN status to China.

Another sign of the Sino-American connection having reached a plateau or even deteriorated somewhat was the difficulty both sides have had in sustaining and expanding government facilitated cultural contacts. Such exchanges have become a bellwether of the state of relations. On the American side, the U.S. government had clearly indicated to the Chinese that two organizations particularly have Washington's confidence to facilitate the flow of ideas and people: the Committee on Scholarly Communications with the People's Republic of China and the National Committee on United States-China Relations. The number and quality of exchanges arranged through these barometer organizations was to be less in 1976 than they were in 1974.

The reasons for the loss of momentum were many and complex. The American inability or unwillingness to confront Soviet designs called into question in Peking the long-run utility of an American connection while PRC confidence in being able to handle the Soviet threat on its own may have increased from 1971 to 1975. In addition, from China's perspective, the United States may not have abided by its commitments in the Shanghai Communiqué to weaken its links to Taiwan. In particular, the United States appointed Leonard

Unger as ambassador to Taipei, instead of allowing the post to go unfilled, allowed the Republic of China (ROC) to open several new consulates in the United States, and slowed the pace of reducing its forces on Taiwan. Peking expressed annoyance with all these developments. Further, the U.S. government cannot be said to have expedited the flow of technology to China. To the contrary, the U.S. government refused to license the sale of some goods to the PRC on the grounds that the commodities could be defense related.

But Washington could also note that Peking's commitments to the Shanghai Communiqué have not been uniformly strong. The reduction of the American military presence on Taiwan, for example, depended upon the dimunition of tension in the area, and one could perhaps assert that the Chinese military actions in the South China Sea or its military assistance to North Korea have not contributed to relaxation in the area. Nor did the Chinese always facilitate the officially sponsored cultural exchange program.

To catalog specific actions on either side which contributed to the 1973-75 stall is not analytically helpful, however, for the surface events really flowed from the domestic scenes in both countries and from the weak links between the two countries. In essence, both Peking and Washington had become enmeshed in deeply divisive, domestic political struggles; both capitals were swept by complicated strife over succession. Sino-American relations had not been sufficiently solidified before Watergate and its aftermath overwhelmed Washington, thereby reducing the foreign policy latitude of the incumbent president, while in Peking, Chou En-lai, a staunch advocate of the opening to the United States, lay dying of cancer. Others began to snipe at his initiatives. On the eve of his scheduled 1975 trip, President Ford increasingly felt party pressure to hold firm on the Taiwan issue, while in Peking any advocate of flexibility toward the United States in order to normalize relations risks being labeled a "capitulationist" and losing in the succession sweepstakes.

The 1973-75 pause provided a convenient reminder of the fragility of the relationship. The earlier, 1971-73 euphoria and high hopes yielded to more sober appraisal of Sino-American affairs. What precisely are American interests in improved relations? What underlying obstacles within China impede the development of the relationship? Should and can the United States seek to erode the internally generated constraints? What price, if any, should the United States be prepared to pay in order to advance the relationship? And what gains should America legitimately expect in return? The United States' critical choices vis-à-vis China arise from these questions.

The American Interest in China

The exigencies of the moment have been so powerful that Americans may not yet fully comprehend the long term national interests in improved Sino-Amer-

THE UNITED STATES AND CHINA

ican relations. This chapter contends that the United States would benefit from China's continued political development and economic progress and from more cultural and economic contacts with the PRC. Establishment of full diplomatic relations by itself, without other additional actions, would not establish conditions for significant improvements in Sino-American affairs.

Beyond recognition, the challenge for the United States involves pursuing and balancing these somewhat conflicting tasks: (1) providing Peking the opportunities to play constructive roles in solving supranational problems; (2) developing multilateral arrangements in the weak states around China's periphery—particularly in Korea, Indochina and South Asia—that yield Peking a sense of national security, while reducing its future opportunities for expansionism; (3) fostering an institutionalized and, on balance, equitable bilateral relationship; (4) more generally, creating an atmosphere of trust, understanding and credibility among the leaders of both countries through continual consultations during eras of transitions in leadership of the two countries; and (5) retaining the capacity to respond, if a hostile China should emerge.

Simply recognizing Peking and wishing China well will not enhance the chances of wedding United States and Chinese interests. Rather, the major theme of this chapter is that improvement in Sino-American relations involves a laborious process of flexibly piecing together relationships that hopefully aggregate into a joint commitment to the maintenance of a stable, peaceful, mutually beneficial exchange. And the relationship must flow from an understanding of what the United States hopes to get out of the relationship.

To begin with interests only minimally involved, commercial rewards are not likely to be major. Chinese reluctance to accept direct foreign investment is likely to persist. To be sure, select sectors of the American economy may develop a profitable exporting relationship, particularly those which enjoy a competitive edge in international trade: the agricultural sector, the computer industry, the aerospace industry, and purveyors of petroleum exploration technology. On the import side, China could become a modest supplier of petroleum and petroleum products over a ten- to fifteen-year period; in addition, China has substantial deposits of such nonferrous metals as tungsten, tin, manganese, and molybdenum. Further, the PRC could be an attractive source of labor intensive commodities. But the overall capacity and willingness of China to engage in trade in the years ahead is likely to be limited.

Further, the United States will not face a massive, direct military threat from China in the foreseeable future. Peking gradually will acquire ICBMs that will affect America's national security calculations. The Chinese also are evincing interest in developing a blue-water navy, but that will not materialize by the mid or late 1980s. Militarily, then, barring a massive infusion of capital and technology, China in the main will remain a regional power. Not China's direct threat to the United States but America's credible military presence in the Western Pacific and possibly Indian Ocean will link the interests of the two and provide a basis for conflict, cooperation, or accommodation.

The overriding American concern will be for the government of the People's Republic to remain independent and internally effective—for it to maintain the unity of the people and to provide its people with sufficient food, clothing, shelter, and employment. This interest is valid solely on the humanitarian ground that we wish a quarter of mankind well. Premier Chou En-lai often jokingly reminded American guests that the Chinese government did the world a favor simply by feeding its population. His words contain a grain of truth. For, failure of the Chinese government to meet minimum welfare demands of its populace or to retain its unity would have significant, adverse international consequences. A major new burden would be placed upon already overtaxed aid-dispensing agencies. To put this in proper perspective, alone among the developing countries, the People's Republic from 1960 to 1972 was a net *contributor*, not a recipient of foreign aid and credit and maintained a slight balance in its favor in its foreign trade accounts. From 1956 through 1972, it extended over $2.5 billion in credits and grants, although not all commitments were fulfilled. And while it has been a major world importer of grain, Peking has received none in relief but has purchased all in cash.

A politically disunified China would once again become a focal point of international competition. Peking's effective assertion of control over its territory has removed certain areas from contention among foreign powers, particularly Manchuria, the lower Yangtze, Tibet, and Sinkiang. Can there be any doubt that, for example, the Soviet Union would once again assert its influence in Sinkiang or Manchuria, if a disunified China offered the opportunity? At a time when a significant portion of man is not enmeshed in any effective structure of political authority, the People's Republic commands attention and respect simply for its organizational achievement.

As a result of this organization, however, the aspirations of the entire Chinese populace have been awakened. China's quest for greatness—for wealth and power—has involved a maximum national effort. The mass media penetrate nearly every rural village, and the government now provides near universal opportunity for five years of schooling to rural youths and nine years of schooling to urban youths. Chinese under forty years of age—the bulk of the population—have matured under communism. The vast majority possess little knowledge about and have had little contact with the outside world; their education has been more than tinged by virulent nationalistic appeals. The younger generation of Chinese will eventually guide the nation, controlling its expanding military capacity. Possibly, if this generation becomes frustrated in its efforts to continue China's progress, it could direct its frustration outwardly. While China has not exhibited expansionist tendencies thus far, its leaders recognize that the possibility cannot be excluded in the future. And the current generation of China's leaders have bequeathed unto their successors unrealized or internationally unrecognized territorial claims that point in all directions: along the Amur, over Taiwan, far into the South China Sea, along the Northeast

Frontier Agency and in Ladakh and Sinkiang. Such *irredenta* conceivably could be used by a frustrated Chinese leadership in the future to divert domestic discontent. There is a real time pressure, then, to establish as firm contacts as possible with Chinese of all generations *now* in order to minimize the chances of future irrational hostility.

More than reducing the chances of unpleasant futures is at stake. For unmistakably, the world seems to be entering an era of profound pessimism over man's capacity to surmount the crises of poverty and overpopulation. Particularly crucial, of course, are the fates of the developing countries. In this sense, China has become one source of inspiration—not a totally attractive, pleasant beacon, to be sure, but nonetheless one hope that an impoverished nation, if sufficiently endowed with resources, can galvanize itself to eliminate starvation and disease. China is now poised to advance significantly. If China were to fall behind again, if problems of malnutrition, extensive underemployment, and political disorder again occur in China, then pessimism about man's future is appropriate. With all the discipline and sacrifice of the past twenty-five years, if the Chinese do not achieve a breakthrough, then who can? On the other hand, Chinese success may have a particularly timely effect upon the world's deprived—important because the impoverished must at this juncture retain confidence in themselves and a vision of the possible.

While the Chinese economy has performed well during the past twenty years, continued expansion of the economy at growth rates satisfactory to the Chinese probably requires importation of some select technology and capital equipment. It follows that the U.S. interest is to facilitate the flow of knowledge and the exportation of whole plants to China. For normalization—and with it settlement of the claims issue, the extension of Most Favored Nation status (MFN) and the availability of Export-Import Bank financing to assist Chinese purchases—would marginally yet perhaps significantly increase China's trade potential and slightly hasten its economic growth. Perhaps more important, moves in this direction would enhance China's stake in a stable international economic community.

In short, the American interest is in an increasingly prosperous informed China, capable and willing to contribute to the creation of a stable world order. Another way of defending this view is briefly to portray future Chinas that obviously would be inimical to American interests: (1) a highly nationalistic, expansionist, militant China, seeking hegemony over China's periphery; (2) a weakened China, feeling vulnerable and seeking its security and technology through an exclusive alliance with an American adversary—say, the Soviet Union again or perhaps at some point a Japan that is hostile to the United States; (3) a disintegrating China that would be a major claimant on the world's food supplies and a focal point of international competition, (4) a frustrated China, militarily unable to project its own power beyond its borders and politically unable to play a responsible role in building a new international order and as a result acting as a somewhat irrational, disruptive force, preventing the efforts of others to build a durable peace; and (5) a China turned inward, internally cohesive, self-reliant, and isolated from world affairs. (The last alternative is inimical to U.S. interests primarily because the mutual isolation would breed ignorance and the chance of foreign policy miscalculations.) To some extent, these alternatives are not mutually exclusive, and Chinese foreign policy over the past twenty-five years has occasionally demonstrated tendencies in each of these directions. Yet, it is useful to think of each portrayal as a *possible* and dominant thrust of Chinese policy.

At the present time, none of these five alternatives seems likely. The record of the past twenty-five years shows generally that when the Chinese have had the opportunity, they have acted responsibly and cautiously. To be sure, exceptions exist and public rhetoric does not always coincide with statements made privately or with actual deeds. We have learned perhaps too late that the passing generation of Chinese leaders—Mao Tse-tung, Chou En-lai, Teng Hsiao-p'ing— have been realistic and have sought to create a China broadly convergent with many of our own interests: an increasingly prosperous, unified nation independent of foreign control. Indeed, some scholars have argued that other dimensions of post-1949 Chinese foreign policy which were contrary to U.S. interests—the fostering of revolutionary movements, the resort to force in Quemoy-Matsu and India—were rational reactions to enmity and probes initiated against China. Others suggest, though perhaps not persuasively, that Mao's leaning toward the Soviet Union in 1949 and the Sino-Soviet alliance itself resulted from American hostility toward the Chinese Communist party in 1945-49. And more recently, during the Vietnam War and perhaps again during and in the wake of the Lin Piao affair, Mao apparently clashed with the military professionals over defense posture and strategy, with Mao advocating a stance less threatening to the United States.

The record is pertinent, for it suggests that fundamental, "objective" conflicts of interest have not kept the United States and China apart. Rather, the previous enmity stemmed from misunderstandings, a legacy of distrust, the rigid bipolarity of the fifties, and the limited conflicts in specific instances where the interests of the two were joined—principally Korea, Taiwan, and Indochina.

On the other hand, we cannot assume that the current commitment of both sides to improve their relations will persist. One of the four hostile Chinas conceivably could emerge. The leadership of China is now in transition. And there is no reason to assume the new leadership will continue the broad foreign policy lines of the Mao-Chou era. In fact, Mao and Chou have demonstrated concern that their successors may depart from the path they have charted, either resurrecting the Sino-Soviet alliance or asserting Chinese dominance over peripheral states. This uncertainty creates some inducements for the United States to avail itself of opportunities as they arise.

Let us summarize the argument thus far. Nurturing a relationship with China can be defended on several grounds, but each rationale leads to a somewhat different set of policy emphases. We have already mentioned the parallel global strategic interests of the United States and China vis-à-vis the USSR. This requires tacit military cooperation, but little else. It is by no means clear, for example, that such a relationship would necessitate severance of United States ties with Taiwan, nor indeed a high level of explicit understandings. Actions would count more than words in such a relationship. A second level of interest is to establish, with China, Japan, and the Soviet Union, a more stable relationship in East Asia, particularly on such matters as Taiwan, Korea and control of the seas and continental shelf. Pursuit of these interests requires more explicit levels of understandings and commitments and, paradoxically may require a diminution in Sino-Soviet tensions. It most certainly entails recognition of the People's Republic of China (PRC) but probably involves linking recognition to Peking's willingness to assume a responsible stabilizing role in the area.

Finally the long-term interests noted above—the continued economic and political development of China and the expansion of contacts between the two societies—require a more extensive bilateral relationship. United States diplomatic recognition of China from this perspective perhaps should not become linked to strategic *quid-pro-quo* other than peaceful settlement of the Taiwan issue. Rather recognition should be used as an instrument to enhance trade, to expand government facilitated cultural and scientific exchanges, and to engage in discussions about arms control and disarmament. The emphasis on bilateral affairs, moreover, does not lead to China being treated as an object primarily to be used against the Soviets. Indeed, at some point, an improvement in Sino-Soviet relations could be welcomed, provided it did not imperil Sino-American relations, for the reduction in tension would enable China to devote more resources to its internal economic development.

While the three levels of interests—strategic, regional, and bilateral—can be pursued simultaneously, choices of emphasis and style do exist. Herein lies one major decision of the United States in its China policy. Which of the three objectives is to receive primacy? This chapter argues for attaching priority to the long-term bilateral interests, in no small measure because the other two objectives are temporary and easily reversible. The goal must be the gradual engagement of China and the United States in the maintenance of an international order. If that can be brought about, a major step would have been achieved in bridging the potentially explosive gap between the developed and developing worlds.

The Chinese Puzzle

The idiom of the 1970s introduced by the Shanghai Communiqué was that the United States and the People's Republic seek to "normalize" their relations. This essay eschews the use of that unfortunate term, for it is not clear that "normal" relations are in fact what Washington seeks. After all, what does a "normal" relationship with Peking mean? If it connotes an "average" or "typical" relationship, a "normal" relationship with China is not a totally satisfying one. For many countries consider their Chinese connection a difficult one. Their diplomats live in relative isolation in Peking, with hardly any informal contacts with Chinese. Trade is conducted through highly unusual channels. Cultural exchanges are superficial. Only Japan approaches an extensive relationship with the Chinese, and in order to do so the Japanese discipline themselves in ways many others would reject. For example, the Peking-based newspaper correspondents voluntarily accept the conditions Pcking imposes upon their reportage, and the major Japanese newspapers report China in admittedly biased ways—for the larger national purpose of facilitating trade. Nor can the desultory state of Sino-Indian, Sino-Vietnamese, and Sino-Soviet relations be entirely attributed to the non-Chinese partner. The recurring tensions in Sino-Burmese and Sino-North Korean relations are also partly attributable to Chinese actions. Even when China's claims to Taiwan are acknowledged, the record suggests that it is not easy to live with Peking. Thus, although "objective" factors may not separate the United States and China, the very same political and cultural obstacles which inhibit Chinese relations with other countries are likely to interpose themselves in any American effort to piece together a desirable relationship.

In short, the bilateral relationship with Peking which this essay advocates is really an "abnormal" one, both in the mutual satisfaction and in the meaningfulness of the contacts sought. Nor is this a situation of Communist vintage. Recall the enormous American difficulty of dealing with Chiang Kai-shek or the persistent frustrations of the Westerner power in dealing with the Ch'ing Court. The tragic British, French, Japanese, and American responses until very recently were to try to remake China in their own images, so "normal" relations could arise. And it seems the Russians still harbor that desire. That is, one of the illusory "critical choices" which even well-intended foreigners perceived for over a century was that opportunities existed to intervene in Chinese internal affairs and to restructure the society and culture so that beneficial relations would develop. The modern day version of the time honored game is to advocate measures that would strengthen "moderates," "radicals," "the military," or whatever faction seems most enlightened at the moment.

But the difficulty of dealing with China stems from more than the current factional alignment in Peking and may be traced to certain deeper tendencies. To start with, the People's Republic is but twenty-five years removed from a great rural-based revolution during which peasant armies overwhelmed the urban areas. The cities of China not only were the centers of bureaucratic and commercial power, but with the emergence of the Treaty Port system, they became the focal point of the Western presence in China as well. During the late Ch'ing (1842-1911) and Republican (1911-1949) eras, many Chinese in the

Treaty Ports—particularly among the intellectuals and large entrepreneurs—shifted their gaze from the interior of China to the world beyond. Frequently foreign educated, many of the urban elite took world standards and ideas as their point of reference. Certainly the weakened cultural links between the large urban centers and the rural hinterland was a major factor in the disintegration of China under the impact of the West.

The rural tide which swept over the cities had several consequences. To start with, a significant percentage of the Western-oriented elite fled China, and most who remained behind were subjected to harsh control. The links between the cities and the Western world were severed, and the activities in the urban areas—particularly after the Chinese abandonment of the Stalinist model of development—were more tightly integrated with the countryside. In addition, the cities themselves acquired a rusticated air, while the benefits of modernization spread more rapidly to the countryside than has been typical of other developing societies. Renewal of foreign contacts could jeopardize this pattern of development. At least, many Chinese leaders apparently now fear that the urban areas, where external influences would be felt particularly, could again drift from their rural moorings.

The foreign policy consequences of the nature of the Chinese revolution are reenforced by Chinese concepts of the purpose of the state and of the basic nature of man.[a] Traditional concepts survive in Chinese Marxism. Man is considered perfectable, not born in sin. The task of the state is to nurture the moral potential of the populace. We see the absence of Hobbes—of the state conceived to protect the individual from the avarice of his fellow man. Further, in both traditional and Marxist China, man's obligations are owed to the network of social relations in which he is embedded, but not to the development of his individual identity. The task of the state is to cultivate, through education, this sense of obligation.

The rulers of both traditional and contemporary China, have considered one of their principal tasks to be the creation of a moral order. This aspect of China is not likely to change, simply because the Chinese are not reevaluating the basic philosophical assumptions about man and the state which give rise to their social and political forms of organization. The reluctance to risk Chinese virtues in a corrupt world and the inclination to create barriers between the enlightened and the heathen therefore will also remain.

Nor is this concept of morality likely to encompass an aggressive or expansive missionary effort. For virtue is not disseminated primarily through the dispatch of zealous native missionaries who seek to create new moral communities as in the Western Christian tradition. To be sure, the Chinese send intelligence agents and underground workers abroad. But as to proselytizing an ideology, potential

[a] The following paragraphs draw heavily from, though oversimplify, the writings of Donald Munro. See especially his *The Concept of Man in Early China* (Stanford: Stanford Press, 1969).

converts are more likely to be brought to the virtuous center and then encouraged to return home to spread the word. This is being a missionary by staying at home and encouraging others to imbibe in the virtues of the realm.

Implicit in this view is a conception of hierarchy and mutual obligation. We do not wish to imply that the Middle Kingdom syndrome persists or that individual Chinese are unable to establish good personal relations on equal footing. Nor do we wish to assert that Chinese diplomats are unable to maneuver successfully in the current, rather unstructured international system. Clearly the opposite is the case. Yet, indications exist that as a nation, the Chinese do not feel entirely comfortable with bilateral relations among equals. Although Peking proclaims its policies are based on mutual benefit, the way it structures those relationships creates a strong sense of hierarchy—particularly the way visits by world leaders are made to appear to the Chinese populace as exercises of deference which in turn elicit Chinese magnanimity. Visiting heads of state tend to be accorded the same ritual, obtain the same picture with Chairman Mao, and receive roughly the same coverage in the *People's Daily*. The emphasis upon the equality of ritual underscores the Chinese reluctance to deal with the equality of substance.

Even more revealing in this regard was the Chinese perception of the Sino-Soviet alliance. According to their own descriptions, the Soviets were the "elder brother" and the Chinese the "younger." To be sure, the Chinese conceptualization of the alliance was a good deal more complicated than that homey formulation, but Mao's disaffection with the Soviet Union was related to Moscow's failure to act as a proper "elder brother" should: to allow his strength to be used by other members of the clan; to share his wealth; and to be a model worthy of emulation. Interestingly, the more recent Chinese complaints about the United States may grow out of a somewhat similar perspective. Namely, Washington is not acting as an enlightened leading capitalist power ought to act: unyielding in its opposition to its Soviet opponent. In short, Chinese perceptions of hierarchy and preferences for ritual may lead to different unspoken expectations than their partners have.

Establishing links with China is complicated by yet another consideration. Networks of personal relations based on old ties are terribly important in expediting affairs in the large Chinese bureaucracy. Even today, Chinese governmental bureaucracies hardly consist of impersonal, corporate settings where behavior is regulated through contract. Mutual trust and confidence— human relationships—rather than extensive formal rules and codes order the social system. China is, after all, a society in which the skills of managing interpersonal relations are sufficiently widespread that it survives without any lawyers or psychologists. Relations among officials tend to be diffuse and not just limited to professional concerns. People who work together in the same bureaucracy tend to live together in ministry apartment blocs. Marriage among coworkers is widespread, children of office mates typically attend the same schools, and office workers belong to the same political study groups. Contrast this with the highly mobile, litigous minded, contract-oriented American, who is trained for the corporate world of functionally specific relations, and one senses the problems of knitting the two societies closer together. The problem is then compounded by the official state policy which, out of fear of ideological corruption, deters Chinese foreign affairs specialists from establishing the kinds of diffuse personal relations which prevail in their own society. Paradoxically, then, the Chinese government demands its foreign affairs specialists to develop the skills of operating in the impersonal corporate-legal-contractual world of international transactions. They master these skills marvelously, but thereby become aliens in their own society.

One senses out of all of this—the rural base of the Chinese revolution, the commitment to creating a moral order, the penchant for hierarchical relations entailing mutual obligations, a system based on personal ties—that a distinctly *Chinese* state has been regenerated in East Asia. It is not a recreation of previous empires to be sure, but nonetheless a state drawing heavily for its principles of states craft from the rich Chinese experience in governance. Therein lies the enormity of the challenge to American foreign policy in the years ahead—how to create a framework of interaction for two societies, based on such different assumptions about man and his potential. One suspects both societies will have to make adjustments in values and practice if the process is to move forward.

But paradox is built upon paradox. Americans seemed prepared to accept as fact the self-regeneration of the Chinese state—assuming the Chinese successfully surmount their succession crisis, of course. But the Chinese leaders appear less sanguine about their accomplishments. Admittedly, the Chinese take great pride in their achievements of the past twenty-five years: their economic growth, their emergence with a recognized voice on the world scene and their attainment of greater economic equity and security at home. All this has yielded an enhanced Chinese sense of self-dignity and self-confidence. Yet, one also senses a certain tenuousness in the Chinese leadership's appraisal of their nation's development. They ask themselves, have they in fact established a state that can endure? Does the People's Republic promote the goals for which it was intended? The leaders seem divided over these questions.

To understand the issues involved, one must refer to the trauma of modern Chinese history. Even before the Western gunboats arrived in 1884, the once splendid empire was in decay and ferment. From 1840 on, the nation experienced a century of foreign aggression and civil war. The traditional Chinese order so long thought superior had been tested and found wanting. Throughout the dark years, the same quest consumed China's national leaders: the search for the proper route to a Chinese form of modernity. The goal was to attain self-dignity and to regenerate the Chinese order. Ultimately, the chaos spawned the Chinese Communists, who pledged to redeem the national honor through a social and economic transformation and by eliminating the foreigner's privilege. Their aim was to stand up in the world—to create a wealthy, powerful nation. At the same time, the Communists sought a new, distinctive culture which would reestablish Chinese claims to be an exemplary *moral* and *political* order.

The quest for a Chinese modernity therefore contained both spiritual and economic components: the nurturing of new values and the creation of an industrial state. Tensions exist between the two transformations, and a major issue in Chinese politics has been over their appropriate relationship. In particular, industrialization involves the use of foreign technology and the borrowing of Western ideas. On the other hand, the creation of a new social order that would restore Chinese dignity involves development of a distinctive society that draws upon the nation's long cultural heritage. The dilemma is: how much can be borrowed from abroad before a Chinese essence is lost? Indeed, is it possible to divorce technology from value, or will the very act of borrowing not impede the creation of a sense of pride?

In addition, sharp differences among the leaders apparently exist, as they have for over a hundred years, about the relative weight to be assigned to the cultural and economic transformations. Today, as in the past and for the foreseeable future, four discernible views exist on this issue, each with a different foreign policy corollary. The first assigns primacy to cultural rejuvenation. Proper motivation and organization will enable Chinese to surmount all challenges. But the creation of a new moral order requires keeping nefarious foreign influences at a distance. Foreign ties are to be established reluctantly, with safeguards against their morally corrupting effect. A second view deems both cultural and economic change to be equally important. At some moments, the emphasis may have to be upon one or the other, but in the long run both go hand-in-hand. The concern for industrialization produces an eagerness to borrow selectively from the West. On the other hand, Peking's foreign posture must permit China to sever any economically profitable foreign relation that impinges upon her cultural freedom.

The third position attaches primacy to economic change and somewhat lesser importance to cultivating the new Chinese culture. Rapid industrialization acquires priority, in part, because it provides the guns necessary to protect Chinese morality. Extensive foreign involvement is acceptable in order to control, manipulate, and use foreign powers. An adequate foreign policy, therefore, must focus on exploiting existing international opportunities to China's advantage. The fourth position is not openly expressed in the People's Republic today, but may one day reappear. It concentrates exclusively upon economic growth. Appropriate changes in value will soon follow, although the result may not be distinctively Chinese. And maximum economic growth entails extensive involvement with the West-trade, the importation of foreign technology, openness to foreign investment, sending students abroad, and so on.

In addition to the sheer struggle for positions of advantage, these issues have been at the core of Chinese politics in recent years. During the Cultural

Revolution of 1966-1969, Mao Tse-tung purged his likely successor Liu Shao-ch'i and attacked the Party bureaucracy, because they were overemphasizing economic growth and neglecting ideological indoctrination. But to best Liu, Mao had to depend upon such "cultural firsters" as his wife Chiang Ch'ing and a number of Shanghai based idealogues. By 1971, the pendulum had swung the other way, and from 1971 to 1974 clear primacy was attached to economic development and to expanding Western contacts. Aspects of the Cultural Revolution were condemned as placing excessive emphasis upon value change. But in 1975, "economy firsters" drew fire.

The ambiguity in Mao's views of world trends also provides a basis for leadership disagreements over foreign policy. On the one hand, Mao has stressed United States and Soviet "contention and collaboration," and fears long-term Soviet military pressure. This feature of world affairs has led him to emphasize balance-of-power arrangements to maintain stability. On the other hand, Mao has noted the disarray in Western democracies—which he has long anticipated—and has sensed that there will be an era of increasing turmoil, with a gradual shift in the strategic balance toward the developing countries. Sometimes seemingly eager to accelerate this trend, he has cloaked China in the appropriate garb and sought to project China as a leader of the developing world. Certainly this helps explain Chinese rhetoric in support of Third World positions at such recent international conferences as Bucharest on population, Caracas on law of the sea, New York on natural resources, and Rome on agriculture. The most attractive alternative may be to become a more prosperous participant in a world ordered by the great powers, but the drift of international affairs may make this goal impossible. Hence, an enlightened leadership must cultivate other options—that · is making other kinds of China viable: a revolutionary China in a chaotic world, or a developing China in a world dominated by developing countries.

The Maoist ideological legacy, in sum, is sufficiently ambiguous to lend legitimacy to foreign policy orientations toward the great powers, the developing world, revolutionary movements, or even isolationism. In this sense, Maoism without Mao as ultimate arbiter can promote rather than settle policy disputes.

Here, then, is another reason for the difficulty in establishing firm relations with China: the lack of consensus among the leaders over the appropriate relationship with the West. This may not be attributed merely to Mao's penchant for promoting tensions among his subordinates or to the continual efforts of the competitors for the succession to seize issues in order to clobber rivals. For the lack of consensus antedates the Communist era, and the reasons for it will persist until the trauma of the Western impact recedes from living memory and the search for a distinctive Chinese identity fades.

The Choices Ahead

A yawning gap exists between the long-run American interest in encouraging Chinese leaders to assume a responsible role in world affairs and their own limited willingness and capacity to do so. Further, since the United States has little leverage, part of the task is simply to increase America's capacity to elicit a Chinese response. With these considerations in mind, we can assess the future issues in Sino-American relations and sketch how they might be addressed.

Choices of Posture and Style

Paramount, given the lack of influence, are choices of posture, style, and intent; here is where a relationship based on trust begins. One matter of intent is whether to seek to influence Chinese internal politics. Some Americans, for example, advocate yielding on certain issues during eras in which "moderates" or "economic firsters" appear to be in charge, in order for them to demonstrate to their internal rivals that moderation pays. Another reason for initiating proposals of compromise and accommodations during such eras is that the chances are greater the Chinese will respond. After all, to make proposals which are rejected means further concessions may be necessary the next time around. And frequently side costs have to be paid in other capitals simply by making offers on, for example, the Taiwan issue. Why make sacrifices unless the chances are high that a response will be elicited?

Conversely, others suggest that periods of maximum American flexibility should coincide with periods of ideological fervor, to try to induce the "culture firsters" to commit themselves to an improved Sino-American relationship. But there is perhaps greater advantage in maintaining a constant posture based on calculat ons of the United States interest. For one thing, not enough is known about Chinese politics to play the "radical-moderate" game. In addition, consistency has its virtues. But further, our analysis of the internal constraints to an accommodating Chinese policy toward the United States reveals that the obstacles go far beyond any factional alignment of the moment. As with the alleged Soviet interference in Chinese domestic affairs to date, the efforts are likely to be heavy handed and backfire. An example, in fact, may be Roger Hilsman's December 1963 speech identifying China's younger generation as the group to which Washington looked to resuscitate Sino-American relations. The speech may well have intensified Mao's search for "revisionist" tendencies among them. A corollary is that the United States should seek to avoid, as much as possible, becòming identifed with only a portion of the Chinese leadership or used by one group against others. Means should be devised to achieve contact with a wide spectrum of Chinese institutions, including the cultural and military organizations and regional bureaucracies with which contact thus far has been minimal.

Relatedly, the intent should not be to change China's social system. Rather, the goal is to facilitate China's continued internal development along a course determined by China's leaders. The assumption is that the very processes of technology transfer, trade, and cultural exchange, when undertaken in response to Chinese needs and when directly beneficial to the United States, will gradually elicit *foreign* policies desirable to the United States. It is Peking's task, not ours, to monitor implications of exchange upon their society, just as Washington ought to indicate when the exchanges infringe upon America's values. Efforts such as the Jackson Amendment which seeks to alter China's internal control mechanisms in exchange for United States technology are likely to be counterproductive.

The degree to which American statesmen actually immerse themselves in the China issue is also a matter of prime consideration, given the enormous demands upon their time. More simply, how much time at the top levels is to be devoted to Chinese affairs? Where are the decisions relating to China to be made? How much effort is to be exerted in order to comprehend how the Chinese perceive us? And relatedly, what is the role of the China specialists in government policy making?

Clearly, such questions have to be answered in the light of the people and exigencies of the time. But, the tendencies since the middle of World War II have been to distrust the government Chinese specialist as a pleader for Chinese interests, to be insensitive to Chinese perceptions of the United States, and to allow the secretary of state considerable latitude in determining administrative policy. Recall the major impact John Foster Dulles, Dean Rusk, and Henry Kissinger have had on Sino-American relations, frequently in disregard of the staff papers prepared for them. Further, because all three secretaries humanly were not able to devote sustained blocs of time to the China issue and yet tended to emasculate many of their best State Department foreign service officers, bureaucratic initiative frequently passed to agencies charged with managing the adversary relationship: the Pentagon, Central Intelligence Agency (CIA), or even the Treasury Department. The one exception proves the rule, for Nixon and Kissinger's brilliant efforts of 1969-1973 were in fact a successful secret plot to recapture the China issue from recalcitrant, hostile bureaucracies, but from 1973 on some of the American mismanagement could be attributed to failure to lodge the new relationship in a new, supportive bureaucratic structure. At some point, perhaps, it might be wise to vest greater responsibility for managing the relationship at the desk and secretary levels in the State Department.

As to sensitivity to the Chinese views of the United States, perhaps it is particularly worth recalling the need to establish our credibility in Chinese eyes. Much is said about retaining our credibility in Japan, South Korea, Taiwan, and so on. We agree. But the Shanghai Communiqué and possibly the establishment of the liaison offices created expectations in Peking concerning the United States commitment to establishing full diplomatic relations that must be fulfilled, if we are to elicit Peking's trust. For the Chinese Communists on two earlier occasions sought openings to Washington and placed confidence in American words. The first time occurred in 1944-46, when the United States promised to assist Yenan in its negotiations with the Nationalists, but failed to deliver. The second time was in the mid-1950s, when Peking's serious offers to negotiate over the outstanding issues essentially met with an increase in the American military posture in the Western Pacific.

At the heart of matters of sensitivity and credibility is the issue of the relative importance of China. Why should the president or secretary of state really care what the rulers of China think of them, in comparison say to learning what the British, Russians, Japanese, or mayors of American cities think? From this vantage, it is worth recalling the high price Americans paid in, *inter alia*, Korea and Vietnam because of the unwillingness to listen to Chinese voices, and the great gains of 1970-72 when the president and secretary of state were attentive to Chinese signals. And the long-run interests which the United States has in China would suggest the continued benefits from attaching importance to Peking's evolving perceptions of Washington.

Another choice of posture is in the way China is approached. Actions infused with disdain, arrogance, or crudeness are obviously to be eschewed, given extreme Chinese sensitivity and the national quest for dignity. For instance, Secretary Kissinger's fall 1974 trip directly from Vladivostok—Russian territory which the Chinese believed was seized unfairly—seems too bold an instance of playing upon the Sino-Soviet dispute. It may help explain his chilly reception of that trip. On the other hand, approaches as a supplicant or sycophant, which Peking rulers welcome to reinforce their claims to legitimacy, nonetheless do not apparently earn their genuine respect. Thus, the Chinese may have appreciated Senator Mansfield's absolutely glowing report to the Senate on the wonders of the People's Republic he found during his 1975 trip, but he would have earned greater respect from the Chinese if, upon return, he had supported an expanded Pentagon budget to match growing Soviet strength.

Precisely because the Chinese accept symbolic deference, it becomes easy when they are amenable to project an image of a developing relationship without much substance attached to it. A warm welcome in Peking, a large banquet with many dignitaries present, a handshake with the chairman, talks shrouded in mystery, and a communique with veiled references to hidden understandings can create an aura of impending progress, when the reality may have been more humdrum. Or conversely, since the Chinese are such masters in the art of subtle allusion and stage management, during the ritualistic homages of foreigners to Peking the Chinese can easily create a sense of disenchantment and disillusionment when in fact both sides are abiding by previous commitments. The notion is for the Chinese to adopt an aggrieved posture—the magnanimous but rebuffed host—in order to pressure the guests to make concessions they might not otherwise make.

Chinese diplomatic practice, then, poses several issues of style that are likely to persist for a long time. First, to what extent should the United States configure itself and conform to the Chinese diplomatic institutions and customs?

To a surprising extent, Washington has structured itself to fit into Chinese patterns: the two presidential and nine Kissinger journeys to Peking; maintenance of a discrete and rather personalized relationship to which only a very few government officials are privy; and designation of three American organizations to facilitate semi-governmental exchanges—each with their Chinese counterpart institutions (the National Council for United States-China Trade for liaison with the Chinese Commission for the Promotion of International Trade, the Committee on Scholarly Communications with the PRC for liaison with the Chinese Academy of Sciences, and the National Committee on United States-China Relations with, *inter alia*, the People's Institute for Foreign Affairs). But at what point will it be fair to expect high Chinese officials to visit Washington? The Chinese claim Taiwan's continued presence in Washington precludes this, although that did not halt China's desire to send high officials to Japan before Peking-Tokyo ties were firmed. Nonetheless, would it be appropriate, for example, to have the formal announcement of the establishment of diplomatic relations come during a Chinese visit to the United States?

Obviously, these decisions must be made in the context of the times, but at some point, it seems, the Chinese should begin partially to conform to American rituals, in order to symbolize the genuine equity of the relationship. Indeed, Americans may soon weary of seeing their officials always going the other way, and a president might conclude he could secure domestic political advantage by hosting top Chinese leaders.

Second, to what extent should the public image of the relationship coincide with the reality? The temptation may be great both for domestic political purposes and for use vis--vis third parties (such as the USSR) to yield to the Chinese penchant for creating false images of progress and ignoring the real problems of substance. In addition, an aura of good feeling may assist in producing the reality. Yet, both the century long history of Sino-American relations and the record of post-1949 Sino-Indian and Sino-Soviet relations reveal the risk in papering over differences. For when the depth of the differences is discovered, disillusion, anger, and a sense of betrayal arise. From late 1973 to mid-1975, for example, the Nixon and Ford administrations may have erroneously decided—with Chinese complicity—to downplay the Taiwan issue as a continuing stumbling block in expanding bilateral contacts, although the evidence was at hand that the issue continued to disturb Peking. When the problem began to surface again, the reaction was chagrin—as if the Chinese were reintroducing an issue they previously had set aside.

Bilateral Issues

Diplomatic Recognition and the Taiwan Issue. Recognition of the People's Republic of China is no longer a matter of "if," but of "when" and "how." The timing obviously is not just an American choice. In fact, in view of the instability of leadership in Peking, if the United States were to knock on the door in 1976-77 the Chinese might not answer. This would be particularly true if the United States attached conditions to recognition that entailed significant Chinese concessions. The contestants for power might be reluctant to argue the case for yielding out of fear of accusations of being "soft on imperialism" or "selling out Taiwan." So, the timing of the actual establishment of full diplomatic relations is inescapably linked to the American expectations of Peking.

Assuming Washington will seek guarantees or understandings that Peking intends to settle the Taiwan problem peacefully, then two possible times for commencing the discussions suggest themselves. One is early in 1977, when the American political scene has settled but hopefully while Mao is still around to affect the negotiations. The second alternative is to wait until the Peking leadership has sorted itself out. The arguments for the latter course is that informal or implicit understandings secured from the current leadership may not be honored by a different group. But the arguments for an early effort to upgrade the liaison offices to embassy status seem stronger. For one thing, we have earlier argued for a posture in which we calculate American interests and assume the Chinese can do the same; that is, we should not make inferences about Peking's internal affairs but should act on our policies at the earliest moment. But to Americans who are swayed by their assessment of the Chinese domestic scene, we should note that years may pass before a stable leadership emerges. Further, if a Chinese sacrifice on Taiwan is to be secured, Mao's imprimatur would legitimate the transaction. His successors may feel much more restrained. Mao has been one of the most vociferous advocates of improving relations with the United States. Particularly in the light of Mao's deep personal antipathy for the USSR and his fears that his successors may surrender a measure of Chinese autonomy to improve their relations with the Soviets, the chairman may wish to commit his successors to a more institutionalized relationship with the United States.

But what are the terms to be? The Chinese have set three: severance of diplomatic relations with Taipei; abrogation of the defense treaty; and withdrawal of all U.S. military forces from Taiwan. At least publically, the American government has yet to set forth its terms, although allusions to the formula by which Tokyo recognized Peking suggest some of the pieces of the puzzle. These include Peking's understanding that the United States would do the following: (1) retain a semigovernmental office in Taiwan; (2) maintain its extensive commercial and cultural ties with the island; (3) continue its sale of defensive weapons; and (4) as in the Shanghai Communiqué, note that the Chinese on both sides assert there is but one China but reserve its opinion on whether Taiwan is an inalienable part of China. Since many Americans believe that the United States is giving a great deal more than it receives by transferring its ambassador from Taipei to Peking, they wish to add yet other conditions to the establishment of relations. These include settlement of the claims issue, expansion of the facilitated exchange programs, exchange of journalists, and/or a Chinese commitment to promote stability in Korea.

How many of these conditions could or should be built into the agreement, however, also would depend upon the balance struck in the one other major issue involved—Washington's effort both to guarantee that Peking will forego an attempt to recover Taiwan through violence and to retain the capacity to deter the PRC should it seek a military solution. Since it claims Taiwan as part of its territory, Peking has thus far been unwilling to renounce the use of force. A wide range of possible formulas exists to bridge the gap: (1) an explicit, open Chinese statement asserting the right but disclaiming the intent to use force; (2) a private Chinese statement renouncing the use of force; (3) Chinese assurance, in response to a specific American request for it, that Peking would not challenge unilateral American statements of a continued American interest in a peaceful settlement of the issue (i.e., a tacit Peking acceptance of continued American involvement in the protection of Taiwan); or (4) no Chinese response to an American statement during the negotiations that the United States will unilaterally declare its interest in a peaceful settlement (i.e., the United States would interpret and trust Chinese quiescence as acceptance of the American stance).

Any one of these formulas, however, leaves the United States in the awkward position of claiming a security interest in the fate of an entity—Taiwan—which it does not recognize. One of the limitations of such an assertion is whether the Congress would understand and accept the subtlety involved, for congressional support would be essential to sustain such a commitment. Opponents of recognition of Peking point to the likely inability of Congress to support a settlement ambiguous in international law; they also note the general loss of credibility the United States would incur by abrogating the defense treaty. Such people say that unless explicit, no-invasion pledges are secured from Peking, our recognition is tantamount to "abandoning Taiwan." In response, our view is that Congress will have little choice but to support an ambiguous commitment to an entity of Taiwan, if presented with a choice of either that alternative or no support at all. As to the credibility and abandonment argument, all countries *including* Taiwan now expects the United States to recognize Peking. They recognize the issue is not formal recognition but the military connections the United States is willing to sustain subsequently.

On the other hand, some Americans argue that the United States should simply terminate its relations with Taiwan and not retain military links to the island. In our view, this position neglects the considerable, tangible U.S. interest in the island. Not the least significant elements are American investment in Taiwan ($375 million), trade ($3.7 billion total in 1974), and Ex-Im Bank loans and guaranteed ($1.9 billion). Further, rash American moves might lead Taipei to develop nuclear weapons and/or to declare itself the government solely of Taiwan—an act that would unravel the Shanghai Communiqué and create consternation in Peking. But matters of principle are also involved. Under the American aegis, sixteen million Chinese on the island have created a prosperous economy and developed a Chinese culture somewhat distinct from that on the mainland. Any forced reunification, unlikely though that may be, would be traumatic, and the United States simply has the obligation, as a historical legacy, to enable these people peacefully to plan their relationship with the People's Republic at a pace they help set. Another fundamental reason for retaining an American involvement in Taiwan flows from the basic premises of this chapter. If the art of developing a long-term relationship with Peking is to create situations around China's periphery that link Chinese and American interests, Taiwan is one place where that can be done over the long run, and it would be foolish to forego the leverage and opportunity at this early stage.

The question then is whether Peking can realistically be expected to accept as a basis of recognition the Japanese formula plus an acknowledged American interest in the peaceful resolution of the Taiwan problem. Is it worth seeking that solution? Our opinion is "Yes," even if Peking acquiesces to continued U.S. interest at the weaker end of the scale. For China would seem to have little interest in pressing for reunification at the present time. First of all, the island is politically, economically and militarily viable at the present time; Taiwan probably could not be taken by force except at very high cost. Secondly, as previously noted, Taipei enjoys some options of its own—to develop nuclear weapons or to declare itself independent—both of which Peking would wish to discourage. In a way, then, a continued American commitment to Taiwan promotes stability while Peking pursues a long-term strategy of reunification. Peking is unlikely to press for the rapid recovery of Taiwan at this point because of the countermoves that might generate in Taipei, Tokyo, and Washington. But the United States should be prepared to accept a weak Chinese pledge on this issue only in exchange for adequate arrangements on the other matters of bilateral concern—trade, cultural exchanges, and so on. The logic of the situation, at least, suggests Peking would be receptive to American overtures.

Military Posture. A complex American military posture will be called for in the years ahead. On the one hand, China will not pose a major, direct threat and should not be treated as an implacable foe in intelligence gathering efforts, in acquisition and deployment of weapons, or in war gaming. On the other hand, our credible military posture does yield leverage, and we must recognize the possibility that an expansionist China could emerge in the future. This undoubtedly calls for a continued military presence in the Western Pacific—a posture currently deemed useful by the Chinese vis-à-vis the Soviet Union and Japan. More specifically, the development of naval facilities on Diego Garcia, retention of military facilities in the Philippines, maintenance of bases in Thailand (should the Thai government permit it), and continued fulfillment of our treaty obligations in Northeast Asia would enable the United States to balance the expanding Soviet presence in the region.

Another aspect of the military relationship is a dangerous American ignorance about China's precise national security concerns and defense posture, and perhaps a Chinese misunderstanding of our own deterrence strategy. The American intelligence community offers estimates about China's hardware, but is unsure of such matters as China's command and control system to prevent nuclear accidents. Over the long run, it is important to engage the Chinese in serious discussions about these matters—hopefully leading to such proposals as "no first strike" pledges and the creation of nuclear free zones in areas of mutual interest. One choice that may arise is the context in which these discussions ought to take place: bilateral, regional, or global [e.g., inclusion of China in the Strategic Arms Limitation Talks (SALT)]—a decision that can only be evaluated when the opportunity arises. However, bilateral discussions would seem to be the most promising initial forum, particularly if the stress were on security concerns and defense postures rather than arms control. The latter subject has not struck responsive chords to date.

A related issue is the American posture on sale of defense related equipment to China.[1] Peking is clearly interested in the purchase of weapons and defense technology, having ordered in 1975 $200 million worth of jet engines from Rolls Royce to be installed in Chinese manufactured air frames. And reports persisted throughout 1974 and 1975 they were shopping for helicopters as well. One can think of other equipment the Chinese might appreciate, such as over-the-horizon radar, high resolution cameras for Chinese satellites, or improved antitank missiles. Reasons exist for not denying the Chinese such technology: they may one day be turned against us; their acquisition would threaten our Taiwan and South Korean allies; the Russians would get nervous and SALT would be jeopardized.

On the other hand, enhancing Chinese military capability perhaps would further reduce the chances of a Sino-Soviet war or of Soviet intervention in Chinese politics in the post-Mao succession. For Soviet leverage would be reduced, and that seems to the United States interest. In addition, again given the premises of this chapter, military relations at a suballiance level would significantly expand the range of bureaucratic contacts the United States would have in China. Particularly given the extensive Soviet contacts of the 1950s, with the middle and upper echelon professional officers in China, which many Chinese soldiers apparently recall with some fondness, it might be useful to develop some Western links with the People's Liberation Army (PLA). Again, a range of alternatives present themselves: (1) not discouraging allies from selling weapons; (2) exchanging intelligence information; (3) selling technology which the Chinese pledge to use for economic development purposes, but which could be defense related (e.g., certain types of computers); (4) selling limited, specific equipment that is strictly defense and intelligence related; or (5) selling major categories of weapons. If suitable progress is made in developing other facets of the relationship and Chinese weapons development lags seriously, Washington may very well confront significant choices in this realm in the not-too-distant future. And our belief is that the opportunity should not be dismissed lightly.

Trade. A number of issues arise in the economic realm: the degree to which the United States should expedite the flow of technology, the extension of Most Favored Nation trading status to Peking, the settling of the claims issue, the granting of Ex-Im Bank Credit should the Chinese so desire, and the ultimate conclusion with China of various long-term agreements, as we have with other countries, to restrain their exports of various textiles to the United States. Again in keeping with our underlying argument, it would seem in the United States interest to facilitate the flow of technology and to expand trade as rapidly as possible. The United States is likely to enjoy a surplus with China, although to be sure the sums involved will not be significant in terms of overall trade. The larger point, however, is that trade would marginally hasten China's economic growth and would involve the Chinese more extensively in the international economic order.

Cultural Exchange. This will be a most difficult area in which to achieve genuine reciprocity. Yet, over the long run, an equitable relationship in this area is essential. The tendency in Chinese foreign policy—and Japan is the major case in point—has been to retain total control over cultural exchange. Peking has sought and probably will continue to seek to manipulate public opinion about China in other countries for China's advantage. We are not speaking here of subversion, the training of revolutionaries, or even the spread of Marxist-Leninist-Maoist doctrine. Rather, we refer to Peking's penchant for deliberately creating misleading images of China. Peking does this through monitoring what public opinion makers say about China and denying visas to those who displease them. It pressures newspapers not to publish articles deemed hostile. And Peking prevents in-depth research about Chinese society by qualified outsiders while its citizens enjoy such privileges elsewhere. In a sense, Peking's Madison Avenue concern with image management frequently promotes misunderstanding, rather than understanding of China and seeks to play upon emotion, rather than reason.

To appreciate the long-run danger of public ignorance about China requires historical perspective. As Harold Isaacs insightfully noted in his *Scratches on Our Mind*, the Sino-American relationship has been a love-hate affair for over a century. Periods of American emotional attraction to China, during which undue expectations were aroused, repeatedly were then dashed by the hard realities of China, the United States, and world events. The ensuing period became filled with recrimination and disenchantment. Once again, instead of understanding, many Americans are exhibiting an emotional warmth and good feeling toward the Chinese which Peking does much to nurture. We seem to be experiencing one more round in the "love-hate" relationship, although some signs point to an early disenchantment and cynicism following the 1972 euphoria. The only way to break out of this cycle is for the public to acquire adequate perspective upon ourselves and China.

To build a sophisticated China policy upon enlightened public support will require broad based contact—American journalists in Peking, numerous American language students participating in China's established language programs which Americans are not now eligible to attend, meaningful long-term exchanges rather than the current "Cook's tours" and so on. And within the United States, the federal government and foundations must continue their support of the educational programs on China in universities and colleges which they threaten to curtail. The choices in the cultural sphere, then, are the relative weight the U.S. government ought to attach to the cultural dimension of the relationship and the degree of equity it ought to seek. As a small example, Washington long ago in its official publications ceased referring to "Peiping," as Nationalists still call China's capital, and to "Red China," "Communist China," or "Mainland China." Sensitive to Chinese feelings, U.S. publications now refer to "Peking" and the "People's Republic of China." Would it be appropriate to expect no less from Peking and indicate to them our hurt at the continued appellation, "American imperialists" and the continued description of our allies as "running dogs"?

More significantly, should not the government indicate to the Chinese that one bellwether indicator of the state of relations is the level and quality of exchanges through the three designated United States facilitating organizations? Should Congress allow the initiative of designating which of their members visit the PRC to pass to Peking—as now seems to be happening? Or should the Congress establish a regularized exchange program, modeled after the innovative legislative exchange with Japan? Again given our core argument, we suggest that the U.S. government has paid insufficient attention to this dimension of the relationship and must think more systematically about the exchanges which are most relevant to the American interest.

Multilateral Issues

Korea. The Korean peninsula remains one of the world's most dangerous trouble spots. Both North and South are enhancing their military capabilities and neither side is tightly controlled by its allies. China recognizes its short-term interest in continued stability in Korea, for a military confrontation there would present the Soviets with yet another opportunity to extend its influence and would create major national security concerns in Japan. On the other hand,

China must compete with the Soviet Union for influence over Kim Il-sung; Peking cannot afford, as in Vietnam, to allow the North to drift into the Soviet orbit. To an extent, therefore, Kim is able to play off the Soviet Union and China. American resolve in the South, one can argue, would make China more willing to exercise constraint on Kim. For, the Chinese would then realize the chances are low that Kim would actually emerge as a successful unifier of the peninsula; therefore, the need to back him would be less.

In sum, American policy in South Korea cannot be divorced from Sino-American relations. It is one of the places where a firm American posture can link the two in the maintenance of peace. But this requires continued United States willingness to supply weapons to the South and of only a phased withdrawal of forces as the South Koreans develop their non-nuclear capacity to thwart Northern ambitions.

Soviet Union. Sino-Soviet and Soviet-American relations affect almost every aspect of Sino-American affairs. One of the key questions posed earlier in this essay was the degree to which America's posture toward China should primarily be configured in terms of its impact on the other links in the triangular relationship. While arguments can be offered for doing so, our approach would be over the long run to avoid such temptations. To be sure, the American interest in an independent and unified China should lead us in no uncertain terms to stress the high costs of any Soviet intervention in China upon Soviet-American relations. At the same time, one major argument for expanding bilateral relations with Peking now is that it reduces the chances of a future improvement in Sino-Soviet relations that would be aimed against the United States. But, it can also be argued that an improvement in Sino-Soviet relations *after* the United States has consolidated its Peking connection would be in the American interest. The possible benefits might include enhancing the probability of Chinese cooperation in maintenance of Korean stability, facilitating progress at SALT (since a constraining factor upon the Russians is their strategic concern over China), and reducing the Chinese military expenditures—thereby freeing scarce resources for economic development. At some point, then, manipulation of the dispute as Washington has done to date may reach the point of diminishing returns.

Japan. Thus far, the rapid development of Sino-Japanese relations has come at no cost to the Japanese-American alliance. To the contrary, the opposite has occurred and, as China has increased its contacts with Japan, it has increasingly perceived the value of firm Tokyo-Washington ties. For one thing, the Security Treaty does discourage Japan from going nuclear. But further, as China's foreign trade has increased with Japan, Peking has acquired a stake in Japan's continued prosperity. And this in turn depends on Japanese-American trade. Here is one of the clearest instances of the policy recommendations of this chapter at work: of

China developing a commitment to a more stable international system through its participation in it. The United States should simply encourage the trend while ensuring its relations with Japan remain effective.

Supranational Relations

The United States now participates with the People's Republic in numerous international organizations, ranging from the United Nations and its affiliated agencies to international scientific organizations to, in the near future no doubt, the International Olympic Committee. In the distant future, perhaps China will participate in such international financial organizations as the International Monetary Fund, and the World Bank and in multilater.1 disarmament negotiations.

China's role in these organizations thus far has been with a few exceptions, quiet and workmanlike. Its positions generally have not coincided with America's views, but Peking's basic anti-Soviet stance has led it to positions occasionally parallel to those of the United States, such as on Bangladesh. Most disappointing, from the viewpoint of rhetoric, has been the Chinese stance on birth control, the food crisis, and the oil crisis. In each instance, its posture is to appeal to the developing world by attributing these problems to the developed world. Yet, a discrepancy exists between word and deed. China has not yet joined the Organization of Petroleum Exporting Countries (OPEC), and it thus far has refused to cooperate with the tin exporting countries in their efforts to raise the world market price by constricting their exports. In fact, Peking may end up not participating in any of the potential cartels of resource exporting countries, since this would entail the surrender of its autonomy over the management of its resources, something China is reluctant to do. And further, Peking probably has come to realize, through its substantial trade deficits in 1975-76, that the disruption of the world market system is not in its immediate interest.

Undoubtedly a future task will be to secure China's positive contribution to the functioning of organizations attacking the global problems of man: hunger, disease, shortage of raw materials. It is too early to speak meaningfully about the dimensions of that task—for example, how difficult it will be to secure Chinese assistance in global reporting of food production. To date, the PRC has not supplied data to the Economic and Social Commission for Asia and the Pacific (ESCAP) in Bangkok. On the other hand, China is participating in the World Health Organization (WHO)—an area in which its domestic accomplishments are significant—and has expressed interest in global pollution problems. Yet, Chinese involvement in these affairs is still too fresh to pinpoint its future patterns of behavior and the issues they will pose for the United States.

Conclusion

The United States has a major interest in significantly improving its relations with China, though it is by no means certain the Chinese feel the same way. For American leaders believe they have greater interest in securing orderly change in the world than the Chinese do. The Chinese remain more committed to the creation of a world of highly independent nation states, while Washington sees a world of increasing interdependence. With the minimal influence Washington has in Peking, efforts to enlarge the areas of cooperation will require a highly coordinated, patient, flexible, and realistic national effort.

Sino-American relations are likely to pass through three stages, if the effort yields results. The first era in the late 1970s could witness the establishment of full diplomatic relations, the settling of the Taiwan issue, and the creation of a framework in which more extensive ties could be nourished. The second era, probably through the 1980s, would see the United States continuing to try to piece together a more satisfactory relationship and grappling with the problems posed by a more extensive bilateral relationship. The payoffs from the Sino-Soviet dispute conceivably would recede in this era. And then, hopefully a third era could begin, in which the Chinese and Americans could cooperate with others in creating a more just international order.

The time frame may be too long for the gravity of the global problems pressing upon us. But to achieve progress even within that time frame will require the utmost understanding, dedication and discipline of the Congress, the executive branch, and the American people in dealing with China.

Note

1. See Michael Pillsbury, "U.S.-Chinese Military Ties?" *Foreign Policy*, No. 20 (Fall 1975): 50-64.

Index

About the Authors

DONALD C. HELLMANN, Professor of Political Science and Asian Studies at the University of Washington (Seattle), is a specialist on Japanese politics and Asian international relations and has wide experience as a consultant on public policy with the government and private research organizations.

CHALMERS A. JOHNSON, Professor of Political Science at the University of California at Berkeley, is the author of five books on East Asia and a leading international authority on the politics of China and Japan.

GARY SAXONHOUSE, Associate Professor of Economics and Director of the Research Seminar on Japanese Economic and Social Organization at the University of Michigan, has published widely in the field of Japanese economic history, econometrics, and international trade.

HUGH PATRICK, Professor of Far Eastern Economics and the Director of the Economic Growth Center at Yale University, is a leading scholar on the Japanese economy with broad experience as a consultant on public policy.

DWIGHT PERKINS, Professor of Economics at Harvard University, is a leading scholar on the Chinese economy and a frequent consultant to government and research groups in Asia and the United States.

THOMAS ROBINSON, Associate Professor at the Institute for Comparative and Foreign Area Studies and in the department of Political Science at the University of Washington, specializes in Chinese and Soviet politics and foreign policy, international and strategic relations, and Sino-Soviet relations. He has written numerous works on these subjects including his forthcoming books *Lin Piao: A Chinese Military Politician* and *Chinese Foreign Policy*.

MICHEL OKSENBERG, Associate Professor of Political Science at the University of Michigan, is one of the foremost students of the politics of Modern China with extensive experience as a policy advisor.

DATE DUE

DISPLAY			
GAYLORD			PRINTED IN U.S.A.